THE
BILL JAMES
GOLD MINE
2009

THE
BILL JAMES
GOLD MINE
2009

by Bill James

ACTA SPORTS

The Bill James Gold Mine 2009
by Bill James

Edited by John Dewan and Gregory F. Augustine Pierce
Cover Design by Tom A. Wright
Text Design and Typesetting by Patricia A. Lynch
Cover Photo by Samara Pearlstein

Published by ACTA Sports, a division of ACTA Publications
5559 W. Howard Street, Skokie, IL 60077
800-397-2282 www.actasports.com info@actasports.com

Printed in the United States of America by Hess Print Solutions

ISBN: 978-0-87946-369-4
ISSN: 1940-7998
Year: 12 11 10 09
Printing: 5 4 3 2 First Printing

CONTENTS

'Knowledgements

by Bill James

This book has been put together by a large assemblage of saints, geniuses, prodigies, artists, philosophers, philanthropists, stalwarts, veterans, innovators, researchers, potentates, podiatrists, patricians, poodles, mastiffs, masochists, felons, whiners, geeks and escaped lunatics.

It starts with articles that I have written, many of which have been published over the course of the previous year on Bill James Online. Greg Pierce then undertakes the difficult task of sifting through all of my long-winded crap and trying to find stuff that might actually be worth putting on paper, so that's thank-you number one, Greg Pierce.

We build this into a book by surrounding these articles with charts and "nuggets"—a nugget being a small fact which is interesting but which, in our judgment, virtually nobody will know. General John Dewan is in command of this process…did I forget to include military commanders on my list? Sorry about that. Anyway, John runs the process of pulling the book together, so that's thank-you number two, John Dewan.

I'm joking; there isn't a hunted criminal among the lot of them.

Charles Fiore is General Dewan's right-hand man in that process, the guy who rallies the troops and keeps track of the orders. At this point I am going to get in serious trouble trying to rank our contributors, so I'd better drop that, but Charles' role is huge, and vital.

The book is designed by Patricia Lynch, and, having worked with 50 book designers over the years, I can tell you without question that Patricia Lynch is the best. It's a hard job, because this book is pulled together from hundreds of little pieces. The designer has to somehow unify those hundreds of little pieces, but at the same time allow each one to do its own work. It's tough. Thank you, Pat.

Among the people who find the nuggets: Dave Studenmund, Mat Olkin, Mike Webber. Rob Burckhard. Steve Goodfriend. Ben Jedlovec. Nancy Pelosi. You may recognize these names from their many other accomplishments, or perhaps if you have been spending too much time hanging around the post office. I'm joking; there isn't a hunted criminal among the lot of them. They had the thankless task of submitting to John and myself literally thousands of possible nuggets, 80 or 90% of which we rejected, often for reasons so arbitrary and obscure that Mother Theresa would at times have attacked me with a machete and a socket wrench.

Jason Dewan was central to this process, backing up assignments and helping find data. John Vrecsics coordinated the stat checking process at BIS; thank you, sir. Our data comes from BIS, which is Baseball Info Solutions, in Coplay, Pennsylvania. Steve Moyer is President of BIS, and Damon Lichtenwalner is his aide de camp. (I don't know exactly what an aide de camp does, but then I don't know precisely what all of Damon's duties are, either, so I figure it evens out.) Your contributions are appreciated; your data is fantastic.

Pat Quinn works with us in all of our projects, as does Tony Pellegrino. (What do you get if you cross a pelican with a rhinoceros?) Jim Swavely. Todd Radcliffe. Dan Casey. Jeff Spoljaric. Matt Lorenzo. Austin Diamond.Annemarie Stella. Thanks to them. And to Andrew Yankech, Donna Ryding, Mary Eggert, Tom Wright, Brendan Gaughan of ACTA Publications.

There is an article included here from Roel Torres; thank you, Roel. There is a section in Bill James Online in which we answer letters from readers, and a certain number of readers' letters have also been included in this book, so thank you to those readers.

I'm sure I've forgotten somebody. My thanks to all, and my apologies to anyone who was overlooked.

Intro to Sabermetrics

by Bill James

I was asked last June to speak to a Risk Management Seminar organized by someone who has some connection with the Red Sox. I thought about how I would explain sabermetrics to a group of intelligent people who didn't really get what we are doing, and this is what I came up with.

Sabermetrics is descended from traditional sportswriting. Sportswriting consists of two types of things—reporting and analysis. Sabermetrics came from that part of sportswriting which consists of analysis, argument, evaluation, opinion and bullshit. I can tell you very precisely when and how we parted ways with traditional analysis.

Sportswriters discuss a range of questions which are much the same from generation to generation. Who is the Most Valuable Player? Who should go into the Hall of Fame? Who will win the pennant? What factors are important in winning the pennant? If Tampa Bay won the pennant, why did they win it? If Seattle finished last, why did they finish last? How has baseball changed over the last few years? Who is the best third baseman in baseball today? Who is better, Mike Lowell or Eric Chavez?

The questions that sabermetricians deal with in our work are the same as the questions that are discussed by sports columnists and by radio talk show hosts every day. To the best of my knowledge, there is no difference whatsoever in the underlying issues that we discuss. The difference between us is very simple. Sportswriters always or almost always begin their analysis with a position on the issue. Sabermetricians always begin our analysis with the question itself.

If you find a sportswriter debating who should be the National League's Most Valuable Player this season, his article will probably begin by asserting a position on the issue, and then will argue for that position. If you find 100 articles by sportswriters debating issues of this type, in all likelihood all 100 articles will do this.

What sabermetricians do is simply begin by asking "Who is the National League's Most Valuable Player this season?" rather than to begin by stating that "Albert Pujols is the National League's Most Valuable Player this season, and let me tell you why." That is the entire dif-

The things that we do not know are inexhaustible.

ference between sabermetrics and traditional sportswriting. It isn't the use of statistics. It isn't the use of formulas. It is merely the habit of beginning with a question, rather than beginning with an answer.

From this very small difference, profound changes arise. A person who begins by asserting a position on an issue naturally focuses on what he knows. "What facts do I know," he asks himself, "that will help me to explain why Mike Lowell is better than Eric Chavez?"

The person who begins with the question itself…who is better, Mike Lowell or Eric Chavez…the person who begins with the question itself naturally focuses not on what he *does* know, but on what he does *not* know. I misstated that just a little bit. The person who begins with the question itself naturally focuses first on what he *needs* to know. As soon as he begins to think through what he needs to know, however, it will become apparent that he does not know many of the things that he needs to know to really answer the question.

Every large general question in baseball can be broken down into smaller and more specific questions, which can be broken down into yet smaller and yet more specific questions, which can be broken down into yet smaller and yet more specific questions. Eventually you reach the level at which the questions have small and definite answers, even though you may not know what those answers are. The question of who is better, Mike Lowell or Eric Chavez, for example, leads to the question "What are the elements of a third baseman's job?" Well, there is hitting, fielding, baserunning, and off-the-field contributions…if you want to count those.

The question of who is a better fielder breaks down into 20 other questions. Who is quicker? Who is more reliable? Who makes more mistakes? Who has a better arm? Who is better at anticipating the play, and position-

Sabermetrics came from that part of sportswriting which consists of analysis, argument, evaluation, opinion and bullshit.

ing himself correctly? Who is better at going to his left, or to his right? Who is better at applying the tag if he needs to make a tag on a runner?

At that level, the questions that sabermetricians ask ourselves are actually very much like the questions that scouts ask. Scouts try to answer them by their expert judgment. We are not experts, and so we try to find ways to answer them that do not rely on our judgment. In that way, sabermetrics forms a kind of transition between journalism, from which it descended, and scouting. In any case, the question of who is better at applying the tag if he needs to make a tag play leads to the question, "How many times a year does a third baseman have to make a tag play?" That is a question that has an actual answer. I don't know what the answer is, but there is an answer to that question. In a few years, somebody will have that answer.

The question of who is better, Mike Lowell or Eric Chavez, contains within it probably several hundred smaller questions. The person who begins by asking that question naturally realizes that he does not know the answers to most of those smaller questions. He then proceeds inevitably to ask, "How can I find the best answer to those questions?"

When a person begins with the larger question itself, he inevitably winds up confronting his own ignorance and trying to find ways to fill in the gaps in his knowledge. The person who begins with a position on the issue never sees his own ignorance, and, in fact, deliberately avoids seeing his own ignorance. The person who begins with a position on the issue and argues for that position naturally tries to *hide* his ignorance of the other smaller issues, since the things that he doesn't know are a weakness in his argument. The person who begins with the question itself, on the other hand, inevitably winds up reveling in his own ignorance, celebrating his ignorance, and sharing it freely with the world at large.

The person who begins with a position on the issue, by this process, becomes a borrower from the Bank of Knowledge. He borrows from the things that others know, and uses them to construct an argument.

The person who begins with the issue itself, on the other hand, eventually becomes a contributor to the Bank of Knowledge. Forced to confront his own ignorance, he is forced to find ways to figure out the information that he is missing—ways to count things that haven't been counted, or ways to estimate the parameters of things that are unknown. Through this process, he winds up contributing

things that were not known before.

This is essentially what sabermetricians do: We try to construct knowledge to fill in some of the spaces in our massive ignorance. We are not people who know things. We are people who are honest enough to admit that we *don't* understand things, and frankly, we don't believe that you understand them, either.

Because we have been involved in the effort to figure out the things that we don't understand for a long time now, we have developed an inventory of a few hundred standard methods that can be used to analyze a new question. What sabermetricians do for the teams that employ us is to try to draw from that inventory tools that can be used to study whatever it is that the teams need to study. Suppose that a team is considering trading for a new pitcher, for example. The General Manager might ask, "What do you think is the chance that this pitcher will retain value over the life of his contract?" This is the "risk management" that I am supposedly discussing here. There are several ways to approach that problem. One is to look for similar pitchers. If you can identify 25 other very similar pitchers over the last twenty years, you can study their health records as they moved forward. You can do a characteristics analysis. There are observable characteristics of durable pitchers, such as a high strikeout rate and a record of moderate but consistent workloads, and you can compare the pitcher you are studying to the characteristics of healthy pitchers.

The first rule of sabermetrics is: We are not experts. We are not people who "know" things about baseball players. We are people who know how to study things about baseball players. When our General Manager asks me a question about a player or about the game in general, he is not asking me for what I know. He is asking me to study the issue.

And the second rule is: We are never certain. The talk show hosts are 100% certain. The sports columnists are

The difference between knowledge and BS is that knowledge moves forward, whereas BS moves in circles.

100% certain. We are just doing the best we can. Our methods are always flawed, and our answers are usually tentative and muddled.

But the difference between knowledge and BS is that knowledge moves forward, whereas BS moves in circles. When I develop a new method to analyze a baseball question, someone will point out the flaws in that method, and then someone else will suggest an entirely different method to approach the problem, and then someone else will point out the flaws in that entirely different method, and then someone else will figure out a way to combine the best features of both methods into one method that is better than either one. We wind up with methods that get better over time.

And also, we wind up with lots of numbers, which is why people perceive us as statisticians. Go back to the number of tag plays made at third base. It's a significant piece of information that doesn't exist. It's very difficult to take a throw from right field—a long throw—and apply the tag to a fast-moving target which is taking evasive action. It's not an easy thing to do, and if the third baseman makes an extra play in that situation, that has the same value as his hitting a triple. Eventually, somebody will find some way to measure this, and the product of this will be stated as a number, which, since we are dealing with baseball, will be called a statistic.

But sabermetricians are no more statisticians than we are historians, or scouts, or accountants, or computer programmers. I suspect that everything we do is much the same as what many of you do. We look to the past, and we try to organize the things we have seen so that they make some sense. We ask ourselves "How many of those were there?" and "How many of those other things were there?" and "How many of them ended well?" and "How many of them ended badly?"—just as I would imagine most of you do.

Often people wonder if we will run out of things to study, and what I always say is that there will never be a shortage of ignorance. I have realized recently that some people take this wrong, and that when I say that there will never be a shortage of ignorance they think that I am referring to some other group of people, some "ignorant" group of people, when in reality what I am talking about is myself and my own ignorance. I will never understand baseball; I will never understand 1% of what I need to understand. My view of our work is that we are attacking a mountain range of ignorance with a spoon and a used toothbrush. The things that we do not know are inexhaustible.

I will never understand baseball; I will never understand 1% of what I need to understand.

Arizona Diamondbacks

Arizona Diamondbacks – 2008
Team Overview

Description		Ranking
Won-Lost Record	82-80	
Place	2nd of 5 in National League West	
Runs Scored	720	19th in the majors
Runs Allowed	706	9th in the majors
Home Runs	159	16th in the majors
Home Runs Allowed	147	5th in the majors
Batting Average	.251	27th in the majors
Batting Average Allowed	.256	9th in the majors
Walks Drawn	587	7th in the majors
Walks Given	451	3rd in the majors
OPS For	.742	19th in the majors
OPS Against	.716	6th in the majors
Stolen Bases	58	24th in the majors
Stolen Bases Allowed	87	12th in the majors

Key Players

Pos	Player	G	AB	R	H	2B	3B	HR	RBI	SB	CS	BB	SO	Avg	OBP	Slg	OPS	WS
C	Chris Snyder	115	334	47	79	22	1	16	64	0	0	56	101	.237	.348	.452	.800	15
1B	Chad Tracy	88	273	25	73	16	0	8	39	0	0	16	49	.267	.308	.414	.722	4
2B	Orlando Hudson	107	407	54	124	29	3	8	41	4	1	40	62	.305	.367	.450	.817	17
3B	Mark Reynolds	152	539	87	129	28	3	28	97	11	2	64	204	.239	.320	.458	.779	17
SS	Stephen Drew	152	611	91	178	44	11	21	67	3	3	41	109	.291	.333	.502	.836	21
LF	Conor Jackson	144	540	87	162	31	6	12	75	10	2	59	61	.300	.376	.446	.823	17
CF	Chris Young	160	625	85	155	42	7	22	85	14	5	62	165	.248	.315	.443	.758	17
RF	Justin Upton	108	356	52	89	19	6	15	42	1	4	54	121	.250	.353	.463	.816	8

Key Pitchers

Pos	Player	G	GS	W	L	Sv	IP	H	R	ER	SO	BB	BR/9	ERA	WS
SP	Brandon Webb	34	34	22	7	0	226.2	206	95	83	183	65	11.24	3.30	21
SP	Dan Haren	33	33	16	8	0	216.0	204	86	80	206	40	10.42	3.33	19
SP	Randy Johnson	30	30	11	10	0	184.0	184	92	80	173	44	11.45	3.91	12
SP	Doug Davis	26	26	6	8	0	146.0	160	76	70	112	64	14.05	4.32	7
SP	Micah Owings	22	18	6	9	0	104.2	104	73	69	87	41	13.50	5.93	2
CL	Brandon Lyon	61	0	3	5	26	59.1	75	34	31	44	13	13.35	4.70	6
RP	Tony Pena	72	0	3	2	3	72.2	80	38	35	52	17	12.39	4.33	6
RP	Chad Qualls	77	0	4	8	9	73.2	61	29	23	71	18	10.02	2.81	11

Picking Up Your Defense

Brandon Webb led the majors in runners reaching base on errors, 17. Only one of them scored. Kevin Slowey, who got a ton of flyballs instead of a ton of groundballs, allowed only one runner to reach on an error all year.

Brandon Webb – 2008
Runs Allowed Analysis

Reached by Single:	157	Scored:	44	28%
Reached by Double:	33	Scored:	12	36%
Reached by Triple:	3	Scored:	2	67%
Reached by Homer:	13			
Reached by Walk:	65	Scored:	17	26%
Reached by HBP:	12	Scored:	4	33%
Reached by Error:	17	Scored:	1	6%
Reached by FC - All Safe:	3	Scored:	1	33%
Reached by FC - Out:	17	Scored:	1	6%
Reached by Other:	1	Scored:	0	0%
Total On Base	321	Scored:	95	30%
Stolen Bases Allowed:	24	Scored:	8	33%
Caught Stealing:	10	Scored:	0	0%
Steal Attempts:	34	Scored:	8	24%
Intentional Walks:	5	Scored:	2	40%

Kevin Slowey – 2008
Runs Allowed Analysis

Reached by Single:	98	Scored:	21	21%
Reached by Double:	38	Scored:	19	50%
Reached by Triple:	3	Scored:	1	33%
Reached by Homer:	22			
Reached by Walk:	24	Scored:	8	33%
Reached by HBP:	4	Scored:	2	50%
Reached by Error:	1	Scored:	1	100%
Reached by FC - Out:	6	Scored:	0	0%
Total On Base	196	Scored:	74	38%
Stolen Bases Allowed:	4	Scored:	3	75%
Caught Stealing:	4	Scored:	0	0%
Steal Attempts:	8	Scored:	3	38%
Intentional Walks:	1	Scored:	0	0%

Max Scherzer posted a creditable 3.41 ERA in 7 starts, but the Diamondbacks lost all seven of them.

Arizona Diamondbacks – 2008
Performance by Starting Pitcher

Games Started By	GS	RS	RA	Won	Lost
Webb, Brandon	34	153	126	24	10
Haren, Dan	33	168	129	20	13
Johnson, Randy	30	113	126	14	16
Davis, Doug	26	120	131	11	15
Owings, Micah	18	76	89	7	11
Petit, Yusmeiro	8	40	36	3	5
Scherzer, Max	7	16	35	0	7
Gonzalez, Edgar	6	34	34	3	3
Team Totals	162	720	706	82	80

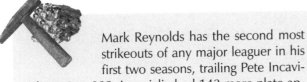

Mark Reynolds has the second most strikeouts of any major leaguer in his first two seasons, trailing Pete Incaviglia 353 to 333. Incaviglia had 142 more plate appearances, so Inky's strikeout rate was 1 per 3.31 plate appearances, while Reynolds was 1 per 3.08 plate appearances. Benji Gil is the only player with more strikeouts per plate appearances in his first two seasons (minimum 150 total games played) than Reynolds (1 per 3.077 to 1 per 3.084).

D'back reliever Juan Cruz had a 2.61 ERA in 2008 despite throwing 19.2 pitches per inning. Every other major league pitcher who averaged more than 19 pitches an inning had an ERA over 4.00.

Mark Reynolds – 2008
Pitch Analysis

Overall		
Pitches Seen	2598	
Taken	1391	54%
Swung At	1207	46%
Pitches Taken		
Taken for a Strike	390	28%
Called a Ball	1001	72%
Pitches Taken by Pitch Location		
In Strike Zone	390	28%
High	202	15%
Low	374	27%
Inside	126	9%
Outside	286	21%
Swung At		
Missed	455	38%
Fouled Off	410	34%
Put in Play	342	28%
Swung At by Pitch Location		
In Strike Zone	878	74%
High	53	4%
Low	124	10%
Inside	41	3%
Outside	86	7%

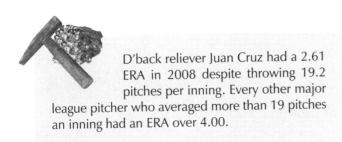

Orlando Hudson started 105 of the Diamondbacks' first 117 games of the season at second base. He had won three straight Gold Gloves coming into the 2008 season, but his fielding declined sharply in 2008, according to the *Fielding Bible* data.

Orlando Hudson – 2008
Second Base Plus/Minus Data

SECOND BASE														
			GROUND DP				PLAYS				PLUS/MINUS			
							Expected Outs		Outs Made					
Year	Team	Inn	GIDP	GIDP Opps	Pct	Rank	GB	Air	GB	Air	To His Right	Straight On	To His Left	GB	Air	Total	Rank
2006	Ari	1349.0	195	101	.518	15	419	118	427	123	-3	-11	+23	+8	+5	+13	5
2007	Ari	1183.1	166	89	.536	13	312	101	323	110	-8	-5	+25	+11	+9	+20	3
2008	Ari	904.2	106	53	.500	17	248	101	241	104	-11	0	+4	-7	+3	-4	21

Randy Johnson's weakness in 2008: groundballs. Batters who hit the ball on the ground hit .313 against the Unit, while hitting .207 against Brandon Webb and .246 against Dan Haren.

Stephen Drew increased his batting average from .238 in 2007 to .291 in 2008, and his extra-base hits rose from 44 to 76.

There were two big changes from 2007 to 2008 that fueled this change.

1. In 2008 the rate of balls that Drew hit that were line drives climbed from 16% to 23%, resulting in 35 more line-drive hits than the year before.

2. He also hit nine more home runs on flyballs in 2008, which helped raise his batting average on flyballs from .182 to .250, and his slugging percentage on flyballs from .460 to .660.

Stephen Drew– 2007
Hitting Analysis

Batting Right-Handed								1B	-	2B	-	3B	-	HR
Total on Ground Balls	170	Outs	130	Hits	40	Average	.235	Hit Type 39	-	1	-	0	-	0
Total on Line Drives	74	Outs	22	Hits	52	Average	.712	Hit Type 39	-	10	-	3	-	0
Total on Fly Balls	205	Outs	169	Hits	36	Average	.182	Hit Type 6	-	17	-	1	-	12
All Balls in Play	456	Outs	327	Hits	129	Average	.291	Hit Type 85	-	28	-	4	-	12

Stephen Drew– 2008
Hitting Analysis

Batting Right-Handed								1B	-	2B	-	3B	-	HR
Total on Ground Balls	177	Outs	139	Hits	38	Average	.215	Hit Type 36	-	2	-	0	-	0
Total on Line Drives	115	Outs	28	Hits	87	Average	.777	Hit Type 53	-	28	-	6	-	0
Total on Fly Balls	216	Outs	163	Hits	53	Average	.250	Hit Type 13	-	14	-	5	-	21
All Balls in Play	512	Outs	334	Hits	178	Average	.355	Hit Type 102	-	44	-	11	-	21

Jon Rauch was 0-6 with a 6.56 ERA for the Diamondbacks, a far cry from his 4-2, 2.98 record (with 17 saves) for the Nationals in the first half of the year. It's hard to spot statistical differences in his performance between his two teams, but one difference does stand out: Batters swung at 34% of his pitches outside the strike zone when Rauch was with the Nationals. But with the Diamondbacks, batters swung at only 19% of those pitches.

The Brothers Upton

Justin and B.J. Upton are two of the most promising young players in baseball. But they did show their youth defensively in the outfield. They were both in the top five in Defensive Misplays plus Errors among outfielders in Major League Baseball last year. Justin was especially troubled as he managed being in the top five despite playing only 101 games in the outfield. The others all had at least 133 games.

Most Outfield Defensive Misplays Plus Errors – 2008

Brad Hawpe, Col	42
B.J. Upton, TB	41
Carlos Gomez, Min	40
Lastings Milledge, Was	39
Justin Upton, Ari	38
Aaron Rowand, SF	38

Adam Dunn and Jack Cust are both left-handed hitting, right-handed throwing left fielders. But that's where the similarity begins. Check out their relative skill assessments (using percentile rankings among left fielders):

	Dunn	Cust
Plate Discipline:	96%	98%
Hitting for Power:	91%	83%
Running:	67%	39%
Fielding:	7%	20%
Hitting for Average:	7%	9%

Last year, Dunn and Cust both achieved something pretty rare: they hit over 30 home runs and reached base more often by a walk or HBP than by a hit. I should say, this used to be a rare achievement before the last decade, when Mark McGwire, Barry Bonds and Jason Giambi did it several times each. But if you skip those players (for reasons I won't go into here), you find only three other players who hit over 30 homers and walked more often than hit in a major league season:

Batter	Year	HR	Hits	BB & HBP
Mickey Tettleton	1995	32	102	114
Jack Clark	1987	35	120	136
Jimmy Wynn	1969	33	133	151

Adam Dunn and Jack Cust are not only extremely similar, they are extremely, uniquely similar.

Atlanta Braves

Description		Ranking
Won-Lost Record	70-90	
Place		4th of 5 in National League East
Runs Scored	753	15th in the majors
Runs Allowed	778	20th in the majors
Home Runs	130	20th in the majors
Home Runs Allowed	156	7th in the majors
Batting Average	.270	8th in the majors
Batting Average Allowed	.263	15th in the majors
Walks Drawn	618	5th in the majors
Walks Given	586	20th in the majors
OPS For	.753	15th in the majors
OPS Against	.758	19th in the majors
Stolen Bases	58	24th in the majors
Stolen Bases Allowed	113	20th in the majors

Key Players

Pos	Player	G	AB	R	H	2B	3B	HR	RBI	SB	CS	BB	SO	Avg	OBP	Slg	OPS	WS
C	Brian McCann	145	509	68	153	42	1	23	87	5	0	57	64	.301	.373	.523	.896	18
1B	Mark Teixeira	103	381	63	108	27	0	20	78	0	0	65	70	.283	.390	.512	.902	14
2B	Kelly Johnson	150	547	86	157	39	6	12	69	11	6	52	113	.287	.349	.446	.795	19
3B	Chipper Jones	128	439	82	160	24	1	22	75	4	0	90	61	.364	.470	.574	1.044	23
SS	Yunel Escobar	136	514	71	148	24	2	10	60	2	5	59	62	.288	.366	.401	.766	13
LF	Gregor Blanco	144	430	52	108	14	4	1	38	13	5	74	99	.251	.366	.309	.676	11
CF	Mark Kotsay	88	318	39	92	17	3	6	37	2	3	25	34	.289	.340	.418	.758	7
RF	Jeff Francoeur	155	599	70	143	33	3	11	71	0	1	39	111	.239	.294	.359	.653	5

Key Pitchers

Pos	Player	G	GS	W	L	Sv	IP	H	R	ER	SO	BB	BR/9	ERA	WS
SP	Jair Jurrjens	31	31	13	10	0	188.1	188	87	77	139	70	12.52	3.68	11
SP	Jorge Campillo	39	25	8	7	0	158.2	158	74	69	107	38	11.17	3.91	9
SP	Tim Hudson	23	22	11	7	0	142.0	125	53	50	85	40	10.58	3.17	10
SP	Jo-Jo Reyes	23	22	3	11	0	113.0	134	77	73	78	52	15.05	5.81	0
SP	Charlie Morton	16	15	4	8	0	74.2	80	56	51	48	41	14.83	6.15	0
CL	Mike Gonzalez	36	0	0	3	14	33.2	26	21	16	44	14	10.96	4.28	3
RP	Will Ohman	83	0	4	1	1	58.2	51	27	24	53	22	11.35	3.68	5
RP	Blaine Boyer	76	0	2	6	1	72.0	73	51	47	67	25	12.50	5.88	1

A Chipper When He Bats Right-Handed

Hitters as a whole pull about 59 percent of the balls they put into play. Left-handed batters hit about 59% to the right of second base and righties hit about 59% to the left of second base. Turns out, it's about 70% on groundballs and short liners, while its less than 50% (around 48) on balls hit in the air. Chipper Jones has a different way to approach this. When he bats left-handed he pulls the ball 66 percent of the time, but batting right-handed he tends to go the opposite way with a pull-percentage of only 52 percent.

Chipper Jones – 2008
Hitting Analysis

Batting Right-Handed								1B		2B		3B		HR
Total Hit to Left	43	Outs	27	Hits	16	Average	.381	Hit Type	12	-	2	-	0	-	2
Total Hit to Center	57	Outs	35	Hits	22	Average	.386	Hit Type	14	-	5	-	0	-	3
Total Hit to Right	40	Outs	17	Hits	23	Average	.590	Hit Type	20	-	2	-	1	-	0
All Balls in Play	140	Outs	79	Hits	61	Average	.442	Hit Type	46	-	9	-	1	-	5

Chipper Jones – 2008
Hitting Analysis

Batting Left-Handed								1B		2B		3B		HR
Total Hit to Left	55	Outs	34	Hits	21	Average	.382	Hit Type	13	-	5	-	0	-	3
Total Hit to Center	82	Outs	49	Hits	33	Average	.413	Hit Type	20	-	4	-	0	-	9
Total Hit to Right	105	Outs	60	Hits	45	Average	.429	Hit Type	34	-	6	-	0	-	5
All Balls in Play	242	Outs	143	Hits	99	Average	.413	Hit Type	67	-	15	-	0	-	17

Chipper Jones hit twelve home runs to center field last year; only Ryan Howard hit more. It was also more than Jones hit to left and right fields combined. (Jones also hit one line drive home run to right.) Only B.J. Upton, among all qualified major league batters, managed to hit more home runs to center than right and left combined.

Chipper Jones – 2008
Hitting Analysis

Total								1B		2B		3B		HR
Fly Balls to Left	41	Outs	34	Hits	7	Average	.175	Hit Type	1	-	1	-	0	-	5
Fly Balls to Center	54	Outs	37	Hits	17	Average	.321	Hit Type	2	-	3	-	0	-	12
Fly Balls to Right	31	Outs	19	Hits	12	Average	.400	Hit Type	4	-	4	-	0	-	4
All Balls in Play	382	Outs	222	Hits	160	Average	.423	Hit Type	113	-	24	-	1	-	22

Buddy Carlyle was a pure reliever in 2008 after primarily starting in 2007, and he threw his cut fastball a lot more while pretty much ditching the curve. The changes seemed to work: His groundball rate rose from 32% to 44% and his ERA dove from 5.21 to 3.59.

	IP	FB	Curve	Cutter
2007	107	69%	14%	6%
2008	63	71%	2%	18%

Over the last seven years, John Smoltz is 21-12 against sub-.500 teams, 29-19 against .500-and-better teams.

Tom Glavine is 44-26 against sub-.500 teams, but just 37-45 against teams with winning records.

John Smoltz
Career Records Against Quality of Opposition

Opponent	G	IP	W	L	SO	BB	ERA
.600 teams	11	22.1	1	1	17	7	3.63
.500 - .599 teams	161	498.2	28	18	458	125	3.01
.400 - .499 teams	129	372.1	20	11	356	72	3.09
sub .400 teams	15	28.1	1	1	25	4	1.59

Tom Glavine
Career Records Against Quality of Opposition

Opponent	G	IP	W	L	SO	BB	ERA
.600 teams	13	74.0	3	8	32	30	6.32
.500 - .599 teams	101	615.0	34	37	285	226	4.27
.400 - .499 teams	93	568.1	41	25	342	174	3.26
sub .400 teams	6	36.0	3	1	21	8	1.50

Jeff Francoeur has now played three full years in the majors, and during that time only two players have made more outs than he has: Jose Reyes and Jimmy Rollins.

Jeff Bennett tied San Diego's Cla Meredith for the highest groundball rate in the National League last year, at 66.8%.

When Kelly Johnson's plate appearances lasted three pitches or less, he batted almost 200 points higher than when they were longer than three pitches.

Kelly Johnson – 2008
Short and Long AB

	AB	H	HR	RBI	Avg	OBP	Slg	OPS
One and done	74	31	3	16	.419	.427	.627	1.053
Short	279	107	8	47	.384	.386	.569	.955
Long	268	50	4	22	.187	.321	.310	.631
7 Up	43	8	1	6	.186	.352	.279	.631

Gregor Blanco had the worst batting average on flyballs in the majors last year (.078). The good news is that he stayed away from flies and hit almost twice as many groundballs; the bad news is that he batted only .225 (about average) on groundballs.

Gregor Blanco – 2008
Hitting Analysis

Batting Left-Handed								1B		2B		3B		HR
Total on Ground Balls	151	Outs	117	Hits	34	Average	.225	Hit Type	32	–	2	–	0	–	0
Total on Line Drives	73	Outs	20	Hits	53	Average	.726	Hit Type	39	–	11	–	3	–	0
Total on Fly Balls	80	Outs	74	Hits	6	Average	.078	Hit Type	3	–	1	–	1	–	1
All Balls in Play	340	Outs	232	Hits	108	Average	.326	Hit Type	89	–	14	–	4	–	1

58.2% of Yunel Escobar's batted balls were groundballs. Only Derek Jeter had a higher percentage (58.3%).

Yunel Escobar – 2008
Hitting Analysis

Batting Right-Handed								1B		2B		3B		HR
Total on Ground Balls	259	Outs	189	Hits	70	Average	.270	Hit Type	65	–	5	–	0	–	0
Total on Line Drives	76	Outs	20	Hits	56	Average	.747	Hit Type	42	–	12	–	2	–	0
Total on Fly Balls	110	Outs	90	Hits	20	Average	.183	Hit Type	3	–	7	–	0	–	10
All Balls in Play	460	Outs	312	Hits	148	Average	.328	Hit Type	112	–	24	–	2	–	10

Tough League

Braves rookie Charlie Morton didn't put up pretty numbers (4-8 with a 6.15 ERA), but he didn't get any favors from the schedule maker, either. Twelve of his 15 starts came against teams that finished with a winning record, including five starts against teams that ultimately made the playoffs.

Charlie Morton
Career Records Against Quality of Opposition

Opponent	G	IP	W	L	SO	BB	ERA
.600 teams	2	8.1	1	1	7	5	7.56
.500 - .599 teams	11	50.0	2	6	28	27	6.66
.400 - .499 teams	2	11.0	0	1	9	6	4.91
sub .400 teams	1	5.1	1	0	4	3	1.69

The 96 Families of Hitters

by Bill James

Those of you who have read my stuff over the years know that I have long been looking for some way to classify hitters into "families." I've tried a couple of other things to do this, but I have another idea here, and I think maybe this is it.

Each player has a unique, but not totally unique, ratio of doubles to triples to homers. The most common extra base hit ratio is what I call a 6-1-3 ratio—about twice as many doubles as homers, and about three times as many homers as triples. 30 doubles, 5 triples, 15 homers. Amos Otis, for example, had 374 doubles in his career, 193 home runs—about a 2-1 ratio—and had 66 triples. That's a 6-1-3 ratio (374-66-193). Jay Bell had a 6-1-3 ratio (394-67-195), and Roy White (300-51-160), and Kirby Puckett (414-57-207). It's a common ratio.

Over the last couple of years I have gotten into the habit, without really thinking it through, of categorizing players by this ratio. I look at Paul Konerko and say, "Oh, that's a 5-0-5 pattern", or whatever. It occurred to me recently that perhaps I could make this into a formal categorization process.

But first, the obligatory "Why are we doing this?" paragraphs.

Whenever you can identify players who have two things or three things or four things in common, it is extremely likely that they will also have other things in common. If you identify the most-similar player to a player born in California, very often you will find another player born in California. If you identify the most-similar player to a 6-foot-5-inch left-handed pitcher, very often you will find another 6-foot-5-inch lefty. If you identify the most similar hitter to someone from the 1960s, very often you find someone else from the 1960s.

Thus, if you can identify "families" of hitters, it is possible that you can learn things that you didn't know by generalizing about the characteristics of the family. If half the members of a family ground into a lot of double plays and you have no GIDP data about the other half, it is likely that they also will have grounded into a good many double plays. If you observe that some members

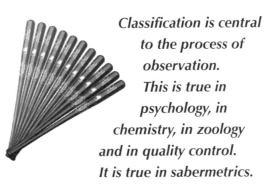

Classification is central to the process of observation.
This is true in psychology, in chemistry, in zoology and in quality control.
It is true in sabermetrics.

of a family age well, you might be able to predict that other members of the family, still in mid-career, will also age well. If you find that some members of a family have difficulty making the jump from A ball to AA, you might anticipate that other members of the family might have the same problem. If you notice that some members of a family are prone to a particular type of injury, you might want to do preventive training for other members of the family. If one member of a family is arrested after being caught with a 14-year-old in his room, you might not wish to generalize from that, or even bring it up at the family reunion.

Classification is central to the process of observation. This is true in psychology, in chemistry, in zoology and in quality control. It is true in sabermetrics. For years I have looked for some way to classify hitters. Now I think that I have it.

OK, let's move on. The first thing we have to do is to figure, for each ten extra base hits that each player has, how many are doubles, how many are triples, how many are home runs—rounded off to the nearest integer, of course. Well, sometimes you can't round it off to the nearest integer and get ten. Sometimes you get eleven, and sometimes you get nine. Harmon Killebrew had 33% doubles, 3% triples, and 64.6% home runs. If you round that off you get 3-0-6, whereas for Hal McRae you get 7-1-3, and for Joe Rudi, 6-1-4.

We don't want some players rounding off to nine or eleven, because we're trying to put hitters into groups with similar hitters, and these nines and elevens tend to take players out of the groups. The next thing we have to do, then, is to round the numbers off so that they add up to ten. I would explain how we do this if I had any reason to believe that you would have trouble figuring it out on your own.

What if a player has 140 doubles, 30 triples, 30 homers? That comes out to 7-1.5-1.5. How do you break the tie?

In case of ties I assigned the overage to the lower category—that is, to triples rather than homers, and to doubles rather than triples or homers. This player would be classified a 7-2-1.

OK, we've got everybody's extra base hits now grouped into a "ten-pattern". In theory there are 55 possible ten-patterns. However, of those 55 possible ten-patterns, there are only 26 which have actually occurred among players with 1000 or more plate appearances. The 26 which have actually occurred are:

9-1-0
9-0-1
8-2-0
8-1-1
8-0-2
7-3-0
7-2-1
7-1-2
7-0-3
6-4-0
6-3-1
6-2-2
6-1-3
6-0-4
5-4-1
5-3-2
5-2-3
5-1-4
5-0-5
4-5-1
4-4-2
4-2-4
4-1-5
4-0-6
3-1-6
3-0-7

The only player in history who was 4-5-1 was Joe Visner (1885-1891), while the only two players who were 4-4-2 were Lew Whistler (1890-1893) and Jeff Stone (1983-1990). All of them did it in careers that barely cleared the 1000-plate appearance mark. These are not ratios that a player would likely sustain over a longer career.

OK, so we can sort players into those 26 categories, and, generally speaking, we can observe that some players within those categories do look very much alike. There is an obvious problem. Alex Rodriguez is 4-0-6, and so is Russell Branyan. Can one really say that Russell Branyan and Alex Rodriguez are members of the same family of hitters?

Of course not. Stan Musial and Craig Paquette are both 5-1-4s. We have to do something to recognize quality of contribution distinctions. After experimenting with different ways to slice the loaf, I decided that the most obvious one worked the best: On base plus slugging (OPS).

Players with an OPS over .900 I marked "A".
Players with an OPS of .8334 to .8999 I marked "B".
Players with an OPS of .7667 to .8333 I marked "C".
Players with an OPS of .7000 to .7666 I marked "D".
Players with an OPS of .6334 to .6999 I marked "E".
Players with an OPS of .5667 to .6333 I marked "F".
Players with an OPS below .5666 I marked "G".

Although many of the "Fs" and "Gs" disappeared later in the process, since there were rarely enough of them to form families.

Anyway, with his very high OPS Alex Rodriguez was now classified as 406 A, while Russell Branyan was classified as 406 C. This would have given us, in theory, 182 "families" of players—26 times 7—except that about 40% of those were empty sets.

The goal of the system is to put hitters into groups with similar hitters. The only two players in history who have a ten-pattern of 3-0-7 are Mark McGwire and Harmon Killebrew. McGwire, however, has an OPS over .900, which makes him 307 A, and Killebrew has an OPS just below .900, which makes him 307 B.

Obviously Killebrew and McGwire are similar hitters and belong in the same family, but that only makes a family of two. Our goal in this particular exercise is not to celebrate the uniqueness of Mark McGwire, but to place him in a group with those hitters to whom he is most similar. There are other hitters who are fairly similar—Sammy Sosa, Hank Sauer, Rocky Colavito, Frank Howard, etc.—so why don't we put him where they are? Those guys are in group 406 B, so I moved Killebrew and McGwire to group 406 B.

The rule I made up in my head was that each player should be in a family of at least ten players; no groups of less than ten. In practice, I had many, many players who were in groups of eight and nine, and only a manageable number in groups of seven or less, so I adjusted the rule to families of at least eight.

In a few cases these "forced classifications" were debatable. There are only six players in history who have a "natural code" of 406 A, so I tried to group the 406 As with the 406 Bs, and, since there were more 406 Bs than 406 As, I called them all 406 B. But this put Alex Rodriguez (naturally a 406 A) in the same family of hitters with Harmon Killebrew (naturally a 307 B), which...A-Rod and Killer are both great hitters, but not really that similar. I wound up moving two of the 406 As (A-Rod and Ken Griffey Jr.) into group 415 A, a group which also includes Mel Ott, Willie Mays, Hank Aaron, Babe Ruth and Barry Bonds, and moved the other four 406 As (Jim Thome, Adam Dunn, Ryan Howard and Mike Piazza) into group 406 B, with Killebrew, McGwire and Rocky Colavito.

It's not a perfect process, and if you can find some better way to make those hard borderline sorts, well, that's what separates knowledge from BS; knowledge is something you can build on. Anyway, my next problem was large, sloppy groups. Large families become ragged and ill-defined. The largest family remaining at this point was 613 D, a group which included 173 players ranging from Khalil Greene to Don Mueller. Don Mueller was a 1950s outfielder who never struck out and would typically hit around .300 with less than ten homers a year. How does he wind up in a group with Khalil Greene?

He doesn't belong with him, of course, and I decided to break up the large families into groups of 80 or less... actually 81 or less, since the one family which had 81 seems fairly cohesive, and I didn't see that I needed to split it up. I decided to further divide the too-large families by the ratio of base hits to secondary bases, secondary bases being defined as extra bases on hits, plus walks, plus stolen bases. I divided 613 D into three groups— 613 D1, which contains Khalil Greene along with players like Gary Redus, Oddibe McDowell, Lee Mazzilli, Lloyd Moseby, Tony Phillips, Tommy Harper, Vince DiMaggio, Ken Henderson and Devon White, 613 D2, which contains players like Emil Brown, Ed Charles, Gabe Kapler, Jose Cardenal and Claudell Washington, and 613 D3, which contains guys who hit .300 sometimes like Don Mueller, Jimmie Piersall, Bobby Avila, Cleon Jones and Vic Power. 613 D1 has an average batting average of .254 but with a good many strikeouts and walks and a few homers, while 613 D3 has an average batting average of .274 with few walks, fewer strikeouts, fewer stolen bases and slightly fewer home runs.

Of course, smaller groups also tend to become ragged sometimes; that is, smaller families of players sometimes contain players that one would not tend to think of as similar. One more problem. As I was writing up the system, explaining who goes where, I became aware that the exceptionally high-walk players, like Ed Yost, Gene Tenace and Mickey Tettleton, stuck out like sore thumbs in this system as I had established it. They just didn't fit; their exceptional high-walk totals caused them to be classified, given the idiosyncrasies of this system, with players whose batting averages were 50 points higher and who also had more power. I had to create two special groups, ending with a "W" code, to put some of the high-walk players into families together.

In a perfect categorization system,
   a) players who were very similar would always be in the same family, and
   b) players who were not similar would never be in the same family.

This isn't a perfect system, and it doesn't meet either of those criteria perfectly. Because it relies on drawing lines between groups of players, and because those lines have to be arbitrarily determined, it does sometimes separate players who seem very similar. Because it doesn't look at every facet of the player's skills, it sometimes puts together players who seem very dissimilar. It isn't a perfect system. But I have been wanting to have a way to classify hitters into families for a long time, and this is the best thing I've come up with.

I wound up with 96 families of hitters, which include all non-pitchers in history with 1000 or more plate appearances.

The 96 Families

In a separate article on www.billjamesonline.com (Appendix to 96 Families), I have listed all players in history and the family they are in—in fact, I listed them twice, once by the family and once alphabetically. But here I wanted to offer a few more general observations about the families of hitters.

The system is intended to be sort of intuitive. Who would be in family 811 C, for example?

Well, let's see...811 means singles hitters, obviously, since the home run number is very low—eight doubles for each homer. That means five homers a season or less. C indicates hitters who have an OPS around .800, and .800 is a high OPS for a singles hitter, so 811 C would be high-average singles hitters.

Freddy Sanchez a year ago was 811 C—the only contemporary player who was 811 C. Billy Herman was 811 C, and Lou Boudreau, Joe Sewell. Wade Boggs is in group 811 C; Boggs has a natural code of 811 B, but is the only player in history who would be 811 B, so the family 811 C were his nearest relatives. No one in history is or would naturally be 811 A. Singles hitters don't have an OPS over .900. So Freddy Sanchez was classed in a family with Billy Herman, Lou Boudreau, Joe Sewell, Wade Boggs and a handful of other guys; it's a small family, eight players. But then in 2008 Freddy had a poor year, and he shifted into class 712 D, in with guys like Tony Fernandez and Red Schoendienst. He's less special than he was a year ago.

721 C are the same type of guys as 811 C, only they run well enough to hit a few more triples (Rod Carew, Frankie Frisch, Lyman Bostock, Ben Chapman), and 721 B are the similar hitters only with even higher averages or a bit more power (Paul Waner, Nap Lajoie, Pete Browning, Heinie Manush). Tris Speaker and Ed Delahanty, who would naturally be classified 721 A, are included in 721 B because they would otherwise be a family of two.

The chart below summarizes the 96 families. The players listed here are generally the best players in the family, or the most recognizable names, and they tend to be a little better than the center of the group. Each group represents a range of ability; these players represent the top end of the range. I was trying to use the most recognizable names to characterize the skills of the group, and the most recognizable are more recognizable because they were better.

For a lot of the families, a player might be a regular if

he was an infielder or a catcher, but a part-time player if he was an outfielder. Thus, group 514 D2 includes Gary Gaetti, Pedro Feliz, Bill Freehan, Earl Battey and Benito Santiago—regulars and even minor stars—but also includes many guys who were about the same as hitters, but weren't true regulars because they were outfielders (Rip Repulski, Jerry Martin, Glenn Braggs, Pedro Munoz, Matt Mieske, Carmelo Castillo), I'm just pointing this out to remind you that it is a classification of hitters, not players. More understanding of the 96 families can be garnered from studying the rosters in the companion article, "Appendix to 96 Families," at www.billjamesonline.com.

I'll make notes below about the eighteen families that had an average OPS over .800. The categories are the code of the family (Family), the number of players in the family (#), the number of players in the family who are in the Hall of Fame (Hall), the average batting average for the players in the family (B Avg), the average on-base percentage of the family members (OBP), and the average Slugging Percentage (Slg). And I'll give a few examples of the most prominent players who are in each of the 96 families. Appendix A contains the .800-or-higher-OPS players in the top eighteen families and their lifetime hitting stats.

Family	#	Hall	B Avg	OBP	Slg	Leading Players
415 A	14	10	.300	.402	.566	Hank Aaron, Willie Mays, Frank Robinson, Babe Ruth

The only players in this family who are not in the Hall of Fame are Barry Bonds, A-Rod, Ken Griffey Jr. and Dick Allen. The family consists primarily of 50s, 60s and 70s outfielders, but also includes Mel Ott, Jimmie Foxx, and Mike Schmidt.

Family	#	Hall	B Avg	OBP	Slg	Leading Players
514 A	13	7	.318	.404	.557	Stan Musial, Lou Gehrig, Joe DiMaggio, Larry Walker

This group is dominated by 1930s superstars, including Hack Wilson and Hank Greenberg. Larry Walker and Brian Giles have joined the group in recent years.

Family	#	Hall	B Avg	OBP	Slg	Leading Players
505 A	19	1	.300	.397	.559	Ted Williams, Gary Sheffield, Frank Thomas

The reason these players aren't in the Hall of Fame is that they are almost all active or recently retired. Bagwell, Chipper, Vladimir, Juan Gone and Jim Edmonds are in this group, as is Manny Ramirez. Although we all know that Manny is truly one of a kind.

Family	#	Hall	B Avg	OBP	Slg	Leading Players
406 B	17	2	.271	.368	.517	Sammy Sosa, Willie McCovey, Harmon Killebrew

The "0" in the triples column, plus more homers than doubles, usually indicates a slower player. These are the slugging first basemen and corner outfielders—Colavito, Hank Sauer, Jay Buhner, Jim Gentile, Ryan Howard.

Family	#	Hall	B Avg	OBP	Slg	Leading Players
721 B	8	6	.338	.401	.477	Tris Speaker, Nap Lajoie, Paul Waner, Ed Delahanty

This group begins with Cap Anson and ends with Paul Waner.

Family	#	Hall	B Avg	OBP	Slg	Leading Players
631 B	14	10	.335	.412	.464	Ty Cobb, Honus Wagner, Eddie Collins, Jesse Burkett

The last player in this group was Earle Combs, retired 1935. The non-Hall of Famers in the family are Joe Jackson, Tip O'Neill, Dave Orr and John McGraw, who of course is in the Hall of Fame as a manager and was a great player as well.

Family	#	Hall	B Avg	OBP	Slg	Leading Players
523 B	21	9	.311	.385	.489	Roberto Clemente, Rogers Hornsby, Al Simmons

Curtis Granderson is in this group as of now, which, if he stays there, would make him the first player in the family since Clemente. But that grouping could change as Granderson ages and slows down, leading to fewer triples.

Curtis Granderson is in the 523 B group as of now, which, if he stays there, would make him the first player in the family since Clemente. But that grouping could change as Granderson ages and slows down, leading to fewer triples.

Family	#	Hall	B Avg	OBP		Leading Players
604 B	22	1	.295	.374	.497	Carl Yastrzemski, Jeff Kent, Will Clark

Many young players in this family now—David Wright, Garrett Atkins, Miguel Cabrera, Victor Martinez. Also many active veterans.

Family	#	Hall	B Avg	OBP		Leading Players
712 B	8	2	.322	.392	.474	Tony Gwynn, Mickey Cochrane, Riggs Stephenson

Surprisingly, despite the high average, this group has mostly players who were short-term regulars—Dale Alexander, Earl Webb, Ike Boone, Babe Phelps. It is not a cohesive family, and I wonder whether I should have broken it up and assigned the players elsewhere.

Family	#	Hall	B Avg	OBP		Leading Players
613 B	24	7	.306	.379	.485	George Brett, Luis Gonzalez, Joe Medwick, Derek Jeter

Bernie Williams, Minnie Minoso, Babe Herman, Bobby Abreu, Nomar Garciaparra, Jackie Robinson, Robinson Cano, Hanley Ramirez all here.

Family	#	Hall	B Avg	OBP		Leading Players
415 B	10	3	.273	.364	.499	Reggie Jackson, Eddie Mathews, Willie Stargell

Modern slugging outfielders, mostly…Eric Davis and his BFF Daryl Strawberry both here.

Family	#	Hall	B Avg	OBP		Leading Players
514 B	31	2	.286	.370	.492	Al Kaline, Billy Williams, Dwight Evans, Moises Alou

Brad Hawpe, J. D. Drew, Jason Bay and Carlos Beltran in this family.

Family	#	Hall	B Avg	OBP		Leading Players
622 B	19	9	.317	.392	.469	Charlie Gehringer, George Sisler, Enos Slaughter

1920s Hall of Famers. Enos Slaughter is the only member of this group to have played since Charlie Gehringer retired.

Family	#	Hall	B Avg	OBP		Leading Players
505 B	25	2	.277	.362	.493	Eddie Murray, Fred McGriff, Orlando Cepeda, Aramis

Pat Burrell and Ryan Klesko here too.

Family	#	Hall	B Avg	OBP		Leading Players
703 C	16	0	.287	.362	.444	Craig Biggio, John Olerud, Don Mattingly, Sean Casey
415 C	36	2	.263	.340	.463	Ernie Banks, Yogi Berra, Willie Horton

In this case the superstars (Banks and Berra) are very atypical of the group. The core of this family is .280 hitters with 30 homers a year—Joe Adock, Roy Sievers, the 1950s Frank Thomas, John Mayberry, Jim Lemon, Jesse Barfield, Bob Allison, Wally Post, Dick Stuart, Jim Ray Hart, Tony Conigliaro, Nate Colbert, Bob Cerv.

Family	#	Hall	B Avg	OBP		Leading Players
514 C1	51	1	.264	.351	.449	Dave Winfield, Chili Davis, Ron Santo, Joe Carter

Short essay. It is odd to see Ron Santo, with a good on-base percentage (.362), listed here with Joe Carter, who would swing at anything. They are otherwise similar—.270, 30 homers, 110 RBI; that's Carter or Santo. I have tried before to group players into families based on strikeout and walk frequencies, but that doesn't work either; it leads to unlike hitters being grouped together because they have similar strikeout/walk ratios. If you sort players on BOTH the extra base hit ratio and the strikeout/walk ratio, you wind up with a lot of families of three players. There just doesn't seem to be a perfect way to do it.

Family	#	Hall	B Avg	OBP		Leading Players
406 C	10	0	.247	.330	.470	Boog Powell, Dave Kingman, Cecil Fielder

Leon Wagner, Gus Zernial, Gorman Thomas, Ron Kittle in this group.

Family	#	Hall	B Avg	OBP		Leading Players
505 C	47	2	.262	.340	.459	Don Baylor, Gary Carter, Johnny Bench, Jermaine Dye
604 C	61	2	.274	.346	.451	Cal Ripken, Steve Garvey, Paul O'Neill, Ernie Lombardi
622 C	45	4	.295	.362	.435	Zack Wheat, Tim Raines, Kenny Lofton, Ichiro Suzuki
613 C2	48	4	.292	.351	.445	Paul Molitor, Robin Yount, Vada Pinson, Al Oliver
532 C	9	0	.295	.352	.442	Harry Stovey, Buck Freeman, Carl Crawford

Family	#	Hall	B Avg	OPB	Slg	Leading Players
811 C	8	4	.306	.376	.418	Wade Boggs, Billy Herman, Joe Sewell, Lou Boudreau
721 C	42	7	.303	.373	.421	Rod Carew, Frankie Frisch, Richie Ashburn
631 C	28	5	.301	.372	.421	Willie Keeler, Pie Traynor, Edd Rousch, Jake Beckley
514 C2	52	3	.277	.341	.451	Harold Baines, Andre Dawson, Tony Perez, Carlton Fisk
613 C1	48	2	.275	.358	.435	Rickey Henderson, Roberto Alomar, Joe Morgan
523 C	11	0	.277	.356	.436	Andy Van Slyke, Wally Moon, Bob Skinner
712 C	33	1	.294	.370	.422	Pete Rose, Mark Grace, Keith Hernandez, George Kell
514 W	19	0	.245	.358	.429	Dick McAuliffe, Darren Daulton, Brad Wilkerson
541 D	21	2	.282	.349	.396	Sam Crawford, Buck Ewing, Lance Johnson
604 D	69	0	.256	.323	.416	Tim Wallach, Larry Parrish, Bret Boone, Terry Steinbach
613 D1	55	0	.255	.341	.398	Tony Phillips, Jay Bell, Toby Harrah, Devon White
820 D	8	0	.294	.358	.378	Charlie Jamieson, Johnny Pesky, Bucky Harris
703 D	37	0	.270	.335	.401	Gregg Jefferies, Carlos Baerga, Wil Cordero
532 D	14	0	.276	.334	.402	Owen Wilson, Casey Stengel, Deion Sanders
514 D2	41	0	.261	.315	.420	Gary Gaetti, Benito Santiago, Juan Encarnacion
514 D1	40	0	.248	.333	.402	Ruben Sierra, Sal Bando, Davey Lopes
730 D	17	2	.293	.358	.376	Sam Rice, Hughie Jennings, Juan Pierre
622 D	71	2	.275	.341	.392	Lou Brock, Pee Wee Reese, Mickey Rivers, Ralph Garr
613 D2	58	0	.265	.329	.403	Alan Trammell, Marquis Grissom, Joe Rudi
712 D2	61	1	.282	.336	.397	Bill Buckner, Red Schoendienst, Tony Fernandez
631 D1	43	2	.274	.356	.376	Harry Hooper, Brett Butler, Bid McPhee
631 D2	46	1	.290	.345	.387	Lloyd Waner, Willie Wilson, Hal Chase, Manny Mota
721 D1	62	6	.279	.357	.373	Max Carey, Phil Rizzuto, Willie Randolph, Junior Gilliam
523 D	24	0	.263	.330	.399	Willie Davis, Jim Fregosi, Juan Samuel
406 D	12	0	.229	.312	.417	Rob Deer, Steve Balboni, Dave Duncan
613 D3	58	1	.274	.326	.403	Brooks Robinson, Buddy Bell, Carney Lansford
505 D	43	0	.243	.315	.413	Graig Nettles, Lance Parrish, Tony Batista, Joe Crede
721 D2	62	2	.289	.341	.385	Nellie Fox, Jimmie Collins, Willie McGee, Matty Alou
712 D1	62	0	.267	.342	.383	Jimmie Dykes, Edgar Renteria, Orlando Cabrera
811 D	33	1	.286	.350	.375	Dick Bartell, Rick Ferrell, Billy Goodman, Johnny Ray
415 D	34	0	.240	.311	.409	Tony Armas, Joe Pepitone, Woodie Held
721 W	14	0	.253	.381	.328	Eddie Yost, Eddie Stanky, Max Bishop
640 E	9	0	.279	.344	.364	Harry Bay, John Coleman, Tim O'Rourke
802 E	18	0	.263	.330	.352	Ken Reitz, Dave Magadan, Rich Dauer, Brent Mayne
613 E1	59	0	.241	.312	.361	Paul Blair, Jim Sundberg, John Roseboro, Alan Ashby
910 E	9	0	.273	.339	.334	Muddy Ruel, Johnny Bassler, Pinky May
721 E2	57	2	.265	.322	.351	Luis Aparicio, Bobby Wallace, Billy Jurges
721 E1	53	1	.259	.335	.337	Roger Peckinpaugh, Johnny Evers, Harold Reynolds
514 E	48	0	.239	.299	.373	Clete Boyer, Jim Spencer, Steve Yeager, Craig Paquette
712 E1	53	0	.248	.325	.347	Royce Clayton, Brad Ausmus, Chris Speier
622 E	67	0	.259	.312	.359	Bert Campaneris, Tony Taylor, Bill Virdon, Neifi Perez
613 E2	59	1	.254	.304	.366	Bill Mazeroski, Frank White, Leo Cardenas, Angel Berroa

Family	#	Hall	B Avg	OPB	Slg	Leading Players
703 E	34	0	.246	.305	.364	Terry Kennedy, Dan Wilson, Rick Dempsey, Pat Borders
721 E3	57	0	.273	.317	.351	Garry Templeton, Bill Russell, Dave Cash
631 E	81	2	.263	.320	.347	Maury Wills, Joe Tinker, Monte Ward, Omar Moreno
811 E	77	1	.266	.325	.342	Omar Vizquel, Ozzie Smith, Dick Groat
712 E3	54	0	.263	.310	.356	Tony Pena, Enos Cabell, Manny Trillo, Tony Kubek
712 E2	54	0	.255	.314	.352	Dave Concepcion, Steve Sax, Bob Boone
604 E	22	0	.236	.298	.368	Bo Diaz, Joe Oliver, Dave Valle
730 E	47	1	.266	.327	.337	Rabbit Maranville, Eddie Foster, Shano Collins
541 E	19	0	.257	.320	.344	Harry Lord, John Hummel, Greasy Neale
523 E	20	0	.238	.300	.357	Roy Smalley Sr., Jake Wood, Larry Stahl
820 E	49	1	.263	.327	.329	Milt Stock, Sparky Adams, Luke Sewell (Ray Schalk)
532 E	11	0	.238	.300	.340	Tom Brown, Fred Pfeffer, Dick Johnston
901 E	8	0	.260	.315	.324	Jody Reed, Marty Barrett, Mike Redmond
730 F	39	0	.249	.306	.305	Larry Bowa, Bud Harrelson, Kid Gleason
721 F1	49	0	.238	.305	.305	Freddie Patek, Julio Cruz, Jose Uribe
721 F2	49	0	.248	.291	.315	Don Kessinger, Ozzie Guillen, Alfredo Griffin
820 F	49	0	.248	.301	.304	George Stovall, Tommy Thevenow, Frank Taveras
811 F	49	0	.244	.297	.307	Tim Foli, Mark Belanger, Horace Clarke
712 F	61	0	.234	.292	.312	Ed Brinkman, Bucky Dent, Dick Schofield Sr.
802 F	12	0	.237	.296	.307	Bob Swift, Glenn Hoffman, Johnny Oates
613 F	36	0	.225	.280	.322	Aurelio Rodriguez, Bobby Knoop, Phil Roof
703 F	14	0	.222	.280	.319	Buck Martinez, Matt Walbeck, Bob Melvin
631 F	59	0	.237	.289	.309	Tommy Corocoran, Bones Ely, Wid Conroy
622 F	19	0	.229	.288	.309	George Strickland, Dave Nelson, Herm Winningham
541 F	22	0	.228	.272	.304	Pop Corkhill, Bill Kuehne, Billy Maloney
640 F	14	0	.234	.277	.293	Roger Metzger, Rodney Scott, Sadie Houck
910 F	21	0	.239	.284	.284	Skeeter Newsome, Felix Fermin, John Peters
721 G	22	0	.220	.261	.278	Doug Flynn, Dal Maxvill, Al Weis
811 G	18	0	.220	.265	.269	Hal Lanier, Tim Cullen, Jeff Torborg
730 G	15	0	.220	.261	.271	George McBride, Joe Gerhardt, Bill Bergen
820 G	30	0	.221	.263	.263	Lee Tannehill, Bill Killefer, Charley O'Leary

Post Script: After finishing this article, three ways occurred to me that I could have done this better. First, I should have added to the definition of a "family" that a family of players should have been defined by *as many shared characteristics as can be identified for a suitable group.* Second, consistent with that change, I should have changed the parameters of a family from eight to eighty players to eight to twenty players—thus adding additional identifying patterns to the larger groups to break them down into tighter "families". In other words, take the 49 players in 811 F and break them down into three groups based on strikeout/walk ratios and/or speed, thus making more compact, more unified families. Third, I should have "named" the families after their most prominent players, as I have done informally before, rather than allowing the families to be defined by codes. If I had identified group 703 F as the "Buck Martinez/Bob Melvin" family, for example, the average fan would have been much more able to relate to that, more able to understand what I was doing. But maybe I should leave that up to you. You pick your two favorite players in each family and name the family after them. You'll remember them that way and it will be more fun than if I named them for you.

On the next few pages, all the hitters in the major leagues who had a lifetime OPS of .800 or higher is listed with their other "family" members. You can "name" each of these for yourself, if you like. For example:

Family 413A	Group Name	*Mays*	–	*Mantle*
Family 514A	Group Name	*DiMaggio*	–	*Greenberg*
Family 505A	Group Name	*Ramirez*	–	*Ortiz*

Family 415 A   Group Name _____ – _____

Player	Years	G	AB	R	H	2B	3B	HR	RBI	BB	SO	Avg	OBP	Slg	Gp
Hank Aaron	23	3298	12364	2174	3771	624	98	755	2297	1402	1383	.305	.374	.555	415 A
Barry Bonds	22	2986	9847	2227	2935	601	77	762	1996	2558	1539	.298	.444	.607	415 A
Willie Mays	22	2992	10881	2062	3283	523	140	660	1903	1463	1526	.302	.384	.557	415 A
Frank Robinson	21	2808	10006	1829	2943	528	72	586	1812	1420	1532	.294	.389	.537	415 A
Mel Ott	22	2730	9456	1859	2876	488	72	511	1860	1708	896	.304	.414	.533	415 A
Ken Griffey Jr.	20	2521	9316	1612	2680	503	38	611	1772	1240	1682	.288	.373	.547	415 A
Babe Ruth	22	2503	8399	2174	2873	506	136	714	2210	2062	1330	.342	.474	.690	415 A
Mike Schmidt	18	2404	8352	1506	2234	408	59	548	1595	1507	1883	.267	.380	.527	415 A
Mickey Mantle	18	2401	8102	1677	2415	344	72	536	1509	1733	1710	.298	.421	.557	415 A
Jimmie Foxx	20	2317	8134	1751	2646	458	125	534	1921	1452	1311	.325	.428	.609	415 A
Alex Rodriguez	15	2042	7860	1605	2404	428	26	553	1606	980	1641	.306	.389	.578	415 A
Duke Snider	18	2143	7161	1259	2116	358	85	407	1333	971	1237	.295	.380	.540	415 A
Dick Allen	15	1749	6332	1099	1848	320	79	351	1119	894	1556	.292	.378	.534	415 A
Ralph Kiner	10	1472	5205	971	1451	216	39	369	1015	1011	749	.279	.398	.548	415 A

Family 514 A   Group Name _____ – _____

Player	Years	G	AB	R	H	2B	3B	HR	RBI	BB	SO	Avg	OBP	Slg	Gp
Stan Musial	22	3026	10972	1949	3630	725	177	475	1951	1599	696	.331	.417	.559	514 A
Lou Gehrig	17	2164	8001	1888	2721	535	162	493	1995	1508	790	.340	.447	.632	514 A
Larry Walker	17	1988	6907	1355	2160	471	62	383	1311	913	1231	.313	.400	.565	514 A
Joe DiMaggio	13	1736	6821	1390	2214	389	131	361	1537	790	369	.325	.398	.579	514 A
Brian Giles	14	1786	6302	1103	1854	401	54	285	1055	1157	804	.294	.404	.511	514 A
Johnny Mize	15	1884	6443	1118	2011	367	83	359	1337	856	524	.312	.397	.562	514 A
Chuck Klein	17	1753	6486	1168	2076	398	74	300	1201	601	521	.320	.379	.543	514 A
Hank Greenberg	13	1394	5193	1051	1628	379	71	331	1276	852	844	.313	.412	.605	514 A
Hack Wilson	12	1348	4760	884	1461	266	67	244	1063	674	713	.307	.395	.545	514 A
Ken Williams	14	1397	4860	860	1552	285	77	196	913	566	287	.319	.393	.531	514 A
Charlie Keller	13	1170	3790	725	1085	166	72	189	760	784	499	.286	.410	.518	514 A
Lefty O'Doul	11	970	3264	624	1140	175	41	113	542	333	122	.349	.413	.532	514 A
Matt Holliday	5	698	2656	479	848	188	23	128	483	251	505	.319	.386	.552	514 A

Family 505 A   Group Name _____ – _____

Player	Years	G	AB	R	H	2B	3B	HR	RBI	BB	SO	Avg	OBP	Slg	Gp
Gary Sheffield	21	2476	8949	1592	2615	454	25	499	1633	1435	112	.292	.394	.516	505 A
Frank Thomas	19	2322	8199	1494	2468	495	12	521	1704	1866	1667	.301	.419	.555	505 A
Ted Williams	19	2292	7706	1798	2654	525	71	521	1839	2021	709	.344	.482	.634	505 A
Jeff Bagwell	15	2150	7797	1517	2314	488	32	449	1529	1401	1558	.297	.408	.540	505 A
Manny Ramirez	16	2103	7610	1444	2392	507	18	527	1725	1212	1667	.314	.411	.593	505 A
Chipper Jones	15	2023	7337	1378	2277	449	35	408	1374	1242	1142	.310	.408	.548	505 A
Carlos Delgado	16	2009	7189	1226	2010	476	17	469	1489	1097	1725	.280	.383	.546	505 A
Jim Edmonds	16	1925	6612	1207	1881	414	25	382	1176	974	1659	.284	.377	.528	505 A
Jason Giambi	14	1850	6332	1116	1812	362	9	396	1279	1205	1308	.286	.408	.534	505 A
Vladimir Guerrero	13	1750	6617	1126	2136	404	43	392	1268	666	813	.323	.389	.575	505 A
Juan Gonzalez	17	1689	6556	1061	1936	388	25	434	1404	457	1273	.295	.343	.561	505 A
Albert Belle	12	1539	5853	974	1726	389	21	381	1239	683	961	.295	.369	.564	505 A
Mo Vaughn	12	1512	5532	861	1620	270	10	328	1064	725	1429	.293	.383	.523	505 A
Lance Berkman	10	1371	4802	896	1449	328	24	288	961	883	953	.302	.413	.560	505 A
David Ortiz	12	1301	4631	812	1329	345	13	289	969	721	973	.287	.382	.554	505 A
Albert Pujols	8	1239	4578	947	1531	342	13	319	977	696	506	.334	.425	.624	505 A
Mark Teixeira	6	904	3414	566	989	223	13	203	676	442	694	.290	.378	.541	505 A
Travis Hafner	7	729	2518	432	711	172	10	147	504	406	611	.282	.391	.534	505 A
Prince Fielder	4	513	1789	279	498	104	5	114	312	235	397	.278	.370	.533	505 A

Family 406 B   Group Name _____ – _____

Player	Years	G	AB	R	H	2B	3B	HR	RBI	BB	SO	Avg	OBP	Slg	Gp
Sammy Sosa	18	2354	8813	1475	2408	379	45	609	1667	929	2306	.273	.344	.534	406 B
Harmon Killebrew	22	2435	8147	1283	2086	290	24	573	1584	1559	1699	.256	.376	.509	406 B
Willie McCovey	22	2588	8197	1229	2211	353	46	521	1555	1345	1550	.270	.374	.515	406 B
Jim Thome	17	2011	6841	1338	1925	369	24	507	1398	1459	2043	.281	.409	.565	406 B
Jose Canseco	17	1887	7057	1186	1877	340	14	462	1407	906	1942	.266	.353	.515	406 B
Norm Cash	17	2089	6705	1046	1820	241	41	377	1103	1043	1091	.271	.374	.488	406 B
Mike Piazza	16	1912	6911	1048	2127	344	8	427	1335	759	1113	.308	.377	.545	406 B
Mark McGwire	16	1874	6187	1167	1626	252	6	583	1414	1317	1596	.263	.394	.588	406 B
Rocky Colavito	14	1841	6503	971	1730	283	21	374	1159	951	880	.266	.359	.489	406 B
Frank Howard	16	1895	6488	864	1774	245	35	382	1119	782	1460	.273	.352	.499	406 B
Jay Buhner	15	1472	5013	798	1273	233	19	310	965	792	1406	.254	.359	.494	406 B
Hank Sauer	15	1399	4796	709	1278	200	19	288	876	561	714	.266	.347	.496	406 B
Roy Campanella	10	1215	4205	627	1161	178	18	242	856	533	501	.276	.360	.500	406 B
Bob Horner	10	1020	3777	560	1047	169	8	218	685	369	512	.277	.340	.499	406 B
Jim Gentile	9	936	2922	434	759	113	6	179	549	475	663	.260	.368	.486	406 B
Chris Hoiles	10	894	2820	415	739	122	2	151	449	435	616	.262	.366	.467	406 B
Ryan Howard	5	572	2071	360	578	99	7	177	499	331	692	.279	.380	.590	406 B

Family 721 B   **Group Name** _____ – _____

Player	Years	G	AB	R	H	2B	3B	HR	RBI	BB	SO	Avg	OBP	Slg	Gp
Tris Speaker	22	2789	10195	1882	3514	792	222	117	1537	1381	220	.345	.428	.500	721 B
Paul Waner	20	2549	9459	1626	3152	603	190	113	1309	1091	376	.333	.404	.473	721 B
Nap Lajoie	21	2480	9589	1504	3242	657	163	82	1599	516	85	.338	.380	.466	721 B
Cap Anson	22	2276	9101	1719	2995	528	124	97	1879	952	294	.329	.395	.446	721 B
Ed Delahanty	16	1835	7505	1599	2597	522	185	101	1464	741	244	.346	.412	.505	721 B
Heinie Manush	17	2009	7653	1287	2524	491	160	110	1173	506	345	.330	.377	.479	721 B
Pete Browning	13	1183	4820	954	1646	295	85	46	353	466	167	.341	.403	.467	721 B
Jake Stenzel	9	766	3024	662	1024	190	71	32	533	299	71	.339	.408	.480	721 B

Family 631 B   **Group Name** _____ – _____

Player	Years	G	AB	R	H	2B	3B	HR	RBI	BB	SO	Avg	OBP	Slg	Gp
Ty Cobb	24	3034	11434	2245	4189	725	296	117	1933	1249	357	.366	.433	.512	631 B
Eddie Collins	25	2826	9948	1821	3312	438	186	47	1300	1503	286	.333	.424	.429	631 B
Honus Wagner	21	2792	10430	1736	3415	640	252	101	1732	963	327	.327	.391	.466	631 B
Jesse Burkett	16	2067	8421	1720	2850	321	182	75	952	1029	230	.338	.415	.447	631 B
Joe Kelley	17	1842	7006	1421	2220	358	194	65	1194	911	163	.317	.402	.451	631 B
Dan Brouthers	19	1673	6711	1523	2296	460	205	106	1296	840	238	.342	.423	.519	631 B
Billy Hamilton	14	1591	6268	1690	2158	242	94	40	736	1187	218	.344	.455	.432	631 B
Earle Combs	12	1455	5748	1186	1866	309	154	58	628	670	278	.325	.397	.462	631 B
Elmer Flick	13	1482	5593	947	1750	267	164	48	756	597	0	.313	.389	.445	631 B
Joe Jackson	13	1330	4981	873	1774	307	168	54	785	519	158	.356	.423	.518	631 B
Ross Youngs	10	1211	4627	812	1491	236	93	42	592	550	390	.322	.399	.441	631 B
John McGraw	16	1099	3924	1024	1309	121	70	13	462	836	74	.334	.465	.410	631 B
Tip O'Neill	10	1054	4255	880	1386	222	92	52	558	421	146	.326	.392	.458	631 B
Dave Orr	8	791	3289	536	1126	198	108	37	270	98	50	.342	.366	.502	631 B

Family 406 C   **Group Name** _____ – _____

Player	Years	G	AB	R	H	2B	3B	HR	RBI	BB	SO	Avg	OBP	Slg	GP
Boog Powell	17	2042	6681	889	1776	270	11	339	1187	1001	1226	.266	.361	.462	406 C
Greg Vaughn	15	1731	6103	1017	1475	284	23	355	1072	865	1513	.242	.337	.470	406 C
Cecil Fielder	13	1470	5157	744	1313	200	7	319	1008	693	1316	.255	.345	.482	406 C
Gus Zernial	11	1234	4131	572	1093	159	22	237	776	383	755	.265	.329	.486	406 C
Russ Branyan	11	766	2000	283	460	96	7	133	320	281	797	.230	.328	.485	406 C

Family 523 B   Group Name _____ – _____

Player	Years	G	AB	R	H	2B	3B	HR	RBI	BB	SO	Avg	OBP	Slg	Gp
Roberto Clemente	18	2433	9454	1416	3000	440	166	240	1305	621	1230	.317	.359	.475	523 B
Goose Goslin	18	2287	8656	1483	2735	500	173	248	1609	949	585	.316	.387	.500	523 B
Al Simmons	20	2215	8761	1507	2927	539	149	307	1827	615	737	.334	.380	.535	523 B
Rogers Hornsby	23	2259	8173	1579	2930	541	169	301	1584	1038	679	.358	.434	.577	523 B
Roger Connor	18	1997	7794	1620	2467	441	233	138	1322	1002	449	.317	.397	.486	523 B
Jim Bottomley	16	1991	7471	1177	2313	465	151	219	1422	664	591	.310	.369	.500	523 B
Tony Lazzeri	14	1740	6297	986	1840	334	115	178	1191	870	864	.292	.380	.467	523 B
Earl Averill	13	1669	6359	1224	2020	401	128	238	1165	775	518	.318	.395	.533	523 B
Mike Tiernan	13	1476	5906	1313	1834	256	162	106	851	747	318	.311	.392	.463	523 B
Sam Thompson	15	1407	5984	1256	1979	340	160	127	1299	450	226	.331	.384	.505	523 B
Jack Fournier	15	1530	5208	821	1631	252	113	136	859	587	408	.313	.392	.483	523 B
Jeff Heath	14	1383	4937	777	1447	279	102	194	887	593	670	.293	.370	.509	523 B
Gavvy Cravath	11	1221	3951	575	1134	232	83	119	719	560	514	.287	.379	.478	523 B
Mike Donlin	12	1049	3854	669	1282	176	97	51	543	312	39	.333	.386	.468	523 B
Ripper Collins	9	1084	3784	615	1121	205	65	135	659	356	373	.296	.360	.492	523 B
Bill Joyce	8	904	3304	820	970	152	106	70	607	718	280	.294	.435	.467	523 B
George Harper	11	1073	3398	505	1030	158	43	91	528	389	208	.303	.380	.455	523 B
Bill Lange	7	811	3195	689	1055	133	80	39	578	350	86	.330	.401	.459	523 B
Del Bissonette	5	604	2291	359	699	117	50	66	391	233	269	.305	.371	.486	523 B
Dick Wakefield	9	638	2132	334	625	102	29	56	315	360	270	.293	.396	.447	523 B
Curtis Granderson	4	373	1395	232	390	76	36	50	162	131	366	.280	.343	.493	523 B

Family 604 B   Group Name _____ – _____

Player	Years	G	AB	R	H	2B	3B	HR	RBI	BB	SO	Avg	OBP	Slg	Gp
Carl Yastrzemski	23	3308	11988	1816	3419	646	59	452	1844	1845	1393	.285	.379	.462	604 B
Jeff Kent	18	2298	8498	1320	2461	560	47	377	1518	801	1522	.290	.356	.500	604 B
Edgar Martinez	18	2055	7213	1219	2247	515	15	309	1261	1283	1202	.312	.418	.516	604 B
Will Clark	15	1976	7173	1186	2176	440	47	284	1205	937	1190	.303	.384	.497	604 B
Shawn Green	15	1951	7082	1129	2003	445	35	328	1070	744	1315	.283	.355	.494	604 B
Todd Helton	12	1661	5962	1143	1957	471	31	310	1116	1041	810	.328	.428	.574	604 B
Dante Bichette	14	1704	6381	934	1906	401	27	274	1141	355	1078	.299	.336	.499	604 B
Magglio Ordonez	12	1541	5861	933	1830	375	18	268	1095	537	708	.312	.371	.520	604 B
Cliff Floyd	16	1611	5303	824	1477	340	23	233	865	600	1057	.279	.359	.483	604 B
Jorge Posada	14	1483	4982	762	1379	317	9	221	883	790	1177	.277	.380	.477	604 B
Mike Sweeney	14	1324	4795	713	1434	305	5	199	849	491	561	.299	.368	.489	604 B
Geoff Jenkins	11	1349	4700	688	1293	303	22	221	733	418	1186	.275	.344	.490	604 B
Miguel Cabrera	6	880	3310	534	1022	219	12	175	650	378	718	.309	.381	.541	604 B
Hideki Matsui	6	774	2892	474	852	175	10	112	507	352	410	.295	.371	.478	604 B
David Wright	5	703	2650	464	819	183	10	130	489	340	499	.309	.389	.533	604 B
Victor Martinez	7	722	2658	357	793	170	1	88	451	296	356	.298	.370	.462	604 B
Garrett Atkins	6	647	2434	357	725	150	6	89	431	238	361	.298	.360	.474	604 B
Nick Johnson	7	637	2082	338	560	141	3	81	317	388	439	.269	.396	.456	604 B
Brian McCann	4	473	1635	200	486	121	1	70	295	151	218	.297	.358	.501	604 B
Bill Salkeld	6	356	850	111	232	39	2	31	132	182	101	.273	.402	.433	604 B

Family 712 B Group Name _____ – _____

Player	Years	G	AB	R	H	2B	3B	HR	RBI	BB	SO	Avg	OBP	Slg	Gp
Tony Gwynn	20	2440	9288	1383	3141	543	85	135	1138	790	434	.338	.388	.459	712 B
Mickey Cochrane	13	1482	5169	1041	1652	333	64	119	832	857	217	.320	.419	.478	712 B
Riggs Stephenson	14	1310	4508	714	1515	321	54	63	773	494	247	.336	.407	.473	712 B
Dale Alexander	5	662	2450	369	811	164	30	61	459	248	197	.331	.394	.497	712 B
Earl Webb	7	650	2161	326	661	155	25	56	333	260	202	.306	.381	.478	712 B
Joe Mauer	5	561	2059	325	653	128	14	44	301	292	233	.317	.399	.457	712 B
Babe Phelps	11	726	2117	239	657	143	19	54	345	160	157	.310	.362	.472	712 B
Ike Boone	8	356	1159	176	370	78	11	26	192	139	67	.319	.393	.473	712 B

Family 613 B Group Name _____ – _____

Player	Years	G	AB	R	H	2B	3B	HR	RBI	BB	SO	Avg	OBP	Slg	Gp
George Brett	21	2707	10349	1583	3154	665	137	317	1595	1096	908	.305	.369	.487	613 B
Luis Gonzalez	19	2591	9157	1412	2591	596	68	354	1439	1155	1218	.283	.367	.479	613 B
Bernie Williams	16	2076	7869	1366	2336	449	55	287	1257	1069	1212	.297	.381	.477	613 B
Derek Jeter	14	1985	8025	1467	2535	411	57	206	1002	813	1376	.316	.387	.458	613 B
Joe Medwick	17	1984	7635	1198	2471	540	113	205	1383	437	551	.324	.362	.505	613 B
Kirby Puckett	12	1783	7244	1071	2304	414	57	207	1085	450	965	.318	.360	.477	613 B
Bobby Abreu	13	1799	6490	1174	1946	454	53	241	1084	1160	1405	.300	.405	.498	613 B
Minnie Minoso	17	1835	6579	1136	1963	336	83	186	1023	814	584	.298	.389	.459	613 B
Gabby Hartnett	20	1990	6432	867	1912	396	64	236	1179	703	697	.297	.370	.489	613 B
Bill Dickey	17	1789	6300	930	1969	343	72	202	1209	678	289	.313	.382	.486	613 B
Babe Herman	13	1552	5603	882	1818	399	110	181	997	520	553	.324	.383	.532	613 B
Nomar Garciaparra	13	1369	5426	910	1702	362	52	226	920	395	526	.314	.363	.525	613 B
Jackie Robinson	10	1382	4877	947	1518	273	54	137	734	740	291	.311	.409	.474	613 B
Chick Hafey	13	1283	4625	777	1466	341	67	164	833	372	477	.317	.372	.526	613 B
Roy Cullenbine	10	1181	3879	627	1072	209	32	110	599	852	399	.276	.408	.432	613 B
John Kruk	10	1200	3897	582	1170	199	34	100	592	649	701	.300	.397	.446	613 B
Rusty Greer	9	1027	3829	643	1166	258	25	119	614	519	555	.305	.387	.478	613 B
Zeke Bonura	7	917	3582	600	1099	232	29	119	704	404	180	.307	.380	.487	613 B
Don Hurst	7	905	3275	510	976	190	28	115	610	391	210	.298	.375	.478	613 B
Robinson Cano	4	573	2218	303	671	151	15	62	309	99	272	.303	.335	.468	613 B
Grady Sizemore	4	525	2061	378	583	130	29	78	259	245	474	.283	.369	.488	613 B
Hanley Ramirez	4	467	1863	369	574	128	21	79	207	200	347	.308	.379	.527	613 B
Phil Weintraub	7	444	1382	215	407	67	19	32	207	232	182	.295	.398	.440	613 B
Hack Miller	6	349	1200	164	387	65	11	38	205	64	103	.322	.361	.490	613 B

Family 415 B   Group Name _____ – _____

Player	Years	G	AB	R	H	2B	3B	HR	RBI	BB	SO	Avg	OBP	Slg	Gp
Reggie Jackson	21	2820	9864	1551	2584	463	49	563	1702	1375	2597	.262	.356	.490	415 B
Eddie Mathews	17	2391	8537	1509	2315	354	72	512	1453	1444	1487	.271	.376	.509	415 B
Jim Rice	16	2089	8225	1249	2452	373	79	382	1451	670	1423	.298	.352	.502	415 B
Willie Stargell	21	2360	7927	1195	2232	423	55	475	1540	937	1936	.282	.360	.529	415 B
Gil Hodges	18	2071	7030	1105	1921	295	48	370	1274	943	1137	.273	.359	.487	415 B
Darryl Strawberry	17	1583	5418	898	1401	256	38	335	1000	816	1352	.259	.357	.505	415 B
Larry Doby	13	1533	5348	960	1515	243	52	253	970	871	1011	.283	.386	.490	415 B
Eric Davis	17	1626	5321	938	1430	239	26	282	934	740	1398	.269	.359	.482	415 B
Al Rosen	10	1044	3725	603	1063	165	20	192	717	587	385	.285	.384	.495	415 B
Carlos Pena	8	794	2665	404	669	128	18	163	466	408	810	.251	.355	.496	415 B

Family 514 B   Group Name _____ – _____

Player	Years	G	AB	R	H	2B	3B	HR	RBI	BB	SO	Avg	OBP	Slg	Gp
Al Kaline	22	2834	10116	1622	3007	498	75	399	1583	1277	1020	.297	.376	.480	514 B
Billy Williams	18	2488	9350	1410	2711	434	88	426	1475	1045	1046	.290	.361	.492	514 B
Dwight Evans	20	2606	8996	1470	2446	483	73	385	1384	1391	1697	.272	.370	.470	514 B
Ellis Burks	18	2000	7232	1253	2107	402	63	352	1206	793	1340	.291	.363	.510	514 B
Bob Johnson	13	1863	6920	1239	2051	396	95	288	1283	1075	851	.296	.393	.506	514 B
Reggie Smith	17	1987	7033	1123	2020	363	57	314	1092	890	1030	.287	.366	.489	514 B
Fred Lynn	17	1969	6925	1063	1960	388	43	306	1111	857	1116	.283	.360	.484	514 B
Moises Alou	16	1927	6988	1105	2117	419	39	332	1278	735	890	.303	.369	.517	514 B
Cy Williams	19	2002	6780	1024	1981	306	74	251	1005	690	721	.292	.365	.470	514 B
Vic Wertz	17	1862	6099	867	1692	289	42	266	1178	828	842	.277	.364	.469	514 B
Rudy York	13	1603	5891	876	1621	291	52	277	1152	791	867	.275	.362	.483	514 B
Ray Lankford	14	1701	5747	968	1561	356	54	238	874	828	1550	.272	.364	.477	514 B
Ryan Klesko	16	1736	5611	874	1564	343	33	278	987	817	1077	.279	.370	.500	514 B
Carlos Beltran	11	1481	5719	1035	1605	318	63	263	987	683	1043	.281	.357	.496	514 B
Dolph Camilli	12	1490	5353	936	1482	261	86	239	950	947	961	.277	.388	.492	514 B
Pedro Guerrero	15	1536	5392	730	1618	267	29	215	898	609	862	.300	.370	.480	514 B
Sid Gordon	13	1475	4992	735	1415	220	43	202	805	731	356	.283	.377	.466	514 B
Hal Trosky	11	1347	5161	835	1561	331	58	228	1012	545	440	.302	.371	.522	514 B
Wally Berger	11	1350	5163	809	1550	299	59	242	898	435	693	.300	.359	.522	514 B
Derrek Lee	11	1385	4825	762	1357	303	23	238	738	621	1150	.281	.367	.502	514 B
Tommy Henrich	11	1284	4603	901	1297	269	73	183	795	712	383	.282	.382	.491	514 B
Alfonso Soriano	10	1205	4934	797	1391	309	23	270	705	298	1069	.282	.329	.518	514 B
J.D. Drew	11	1209	3995	768	1134	213	41	192	637	687	865	.284	.392	.502	514 B
Bob Nieman	12	1113	3452	455	1018	180	32	125	544	435	512	.295	.373	.474	514 B
Richard Hidalgo	9	987	3459	531	929	214	19	171	560	358	737	.269	.345	.490	514 B
George Selkirk	9	846	2790	503	810	131	41	108	576	486	319	.290	.400	.483	514 B
Jason Bay	6	771	2782	476	785	164	20	149	491	397	734	.282	.375	.516	514 B
Chase Utley	6	735	2739	490	817	189	22	130	492	272	496	.298	.375	.526	514 B
Monte Irvin	8	764	2499	366	731	97	31	99	443	351	220	.293	.383	.475	514 B
Joe Hauser	6	629	2044	351	580	103	28	80	356	250	228	.284	.367	.479	514 B
Brad Hawpe	5	583	1913	266	540	103	18	88	341	285	498	.282	.375	.493	514 B

Family 622 B   **Group Name** _____ – _____

Player	Years	G	AB	R	H	2B	3B	HR	RBI	BB	SO	Avg	OBP	Slg	Gp
Charlie Gehringer	19	2323	8860	1774	2839	574	146	184	1427	1185	372	.320	.404	.480	622 B
Enos Slaughter	19	2380	7946	1247	2383	413	148	169	1304	1018	538	.300	.382	.453	622 B
George Sisler	15	2055	8267	1284	2812	425	164	102	1175	472	327	.340	.379	.468	622 B
Harry Heilmann	17	2148	7787	1291	2660	542	151	183	1539	856	550	.342	.410	.520	622 B
Joe Cronin	20	2124	7579	1233	2285	515	118	170	1424	1059	700	.301	.390	.468	622 B
Kiki Cuyler	18	1879	7161	1305	2299	394	157	128	1065	676	752	.321	.386	.474	622 B
Hugh Duffy	17	1737	7042	1552	2282	325	119	106	1302	662	211	.324	.384	.449	622 B
Arky Vaughan	14	1817	6622	1173	2103	356	128	96	926	937	276	.318	.406	.453	622 B
Bill Terry	14	1721	6428	1120	2193	373	112	154	1078	537	449	.341	.393	.506	622 B
Bob Meusel	11	1407	5475	826	1693	368	95	156	1067	375	619	.309	.356	.497	622 B
George Grantham	13	1444	4989	912	1508	292	93	105	712	717	526	.302	.392	.461	622 B
John Stone	11	1199	4491	739	1391	268	105	77	707	463	352	.310	.376	.468	622 B
Denny Lyons	13	1121	4294	932	1333	244	69	62	569	621	212	.310	.407	.443	622 B
Benny Kauff	8	859	3094	521	961	169	57	49	454	367	313	.311	.389	.450	622 B
Joe Harris	10	970	3035	461	963	201	64	47	517	413	188	.317	.404	.472	622 B
Eddie Morgan	7	771	2810	512	879	186	45	52	473	385	252	.313	.398	.467	622 B
Ray Blades	10	767	2415	467	726	133	51	50	340	331	310	.301	.395	.460	622 B
Ray Grimes	6	433	1537	269	505	101	25	27	263	204	133	.329	.413	.480	622 B
Jimmy Bannon	4	366	1433	292	459	76	24	19	253	152	101	.320	.390	.447	622 B

Family 415 C   **Group Name** _____ – _____

Player	Years	G	AB	R	H	2B	3B	HR	RBI	BB	SO	Avg	OBP	Slg	GP
Ernie Banks	19	2528	9421	1305	2583	407	90	512	1636	763	1236	.274	.330	.500	415 C
Dale Murphy	18	2180	7960	1197	2111	350	39	398	1266	986	1748	.265	.346	.469	415 C
Yogi Berra	19	2120	7555	1175	2150	321	49	358	1430	704	414	.285	.348	.482	415 C
Bobby Bonds	14	1849	7043	1258	1886	302	66	332	1024	914	1757	.268	.353	.471	415 C
George Foster	18	1977	7023	986	1925	307	47	348	1239	666	1419	.274	.338	.480	415 C
Roy Sievers	17	1887	6387	945	1703	292	42	318	1147	841	920	.267	.345	.475	415 C
Ron Gant	16	1832	6449	1080	1651	302	50	321	1008	770	1411	.256	.336	.468	415 C
Joe Adcock	17	1959	6606	823	1832	295	35	336	1122	594	1059	.277	.337	.485	415 C
Bob Allison	13	1541	5032	811	1281	216	53	256	796	795	1033	.255	.358	.471	415 C
Roger Marris	12	1463	5101	826	1325	195	42	275	851	652	733	.260	.345	.476	415 C
Jesse Barfield	12	1428	4759	715	1219	216	30	241	716	551	1234	.256	.335	.466	415 C
Oscar Gamble	17	1584	4502	656	1195	188	31	200	666	610	546	.265	.356	.454	415 C
Wally Post	15	1204	4007	594	1064	194	28	210	699	331	813	.266	.323	.485	415 C
Dick Stuart	10	1112	3997	506	1055	157	30	228	743	301	957	.264	.316	.489	415 C
Jim Ray Hart	12	1125	3783	518	1052	148	29	170	578	380	573	.278	.345	.467	415 C
Charlie Maxwell	12	1133	3245	478	856	110	26	148	532	484	545	.264	.360	.451	415 C
Tony Conigliaro	8	876	3221	464	849	139	23	166	516	287	629	.264	.327	.476	415 C
Hank Thompson	9	933	3003	492	801	104	34	129	482	493	337	.267	.372	.453	415 C
Bob Cerv	12	829	2261	320	624	96	26	105	374	212	392	.276	.340	.481	415 C
Luke Easter	6	491	1725	256	472	54	12	93	340	174	293	.274	.350	.481	415 C

Family 505 B Group Name _____ – _____

Player	Years	G	AB	R	H	2B	3B	HR	RBI	BB	SO	Avg	OBP	Slg	Gp
Eddie Murray	21	3026	11336	1627	3255	560	35	504	1917	1333	1516	.287	.359	.476	505 B
Rafael Palmeiro	20	2831	10472	1663	3020	585	38	569	1835	1353	1348	.288	.371	.515	505 B
Fred McGriff	19	2460	8757	1349	2490	441	24	493	1550	1305	1882	.284	.377	.509	505 B
Andres Galarraga	19	2257	8096	1195	2333	444	32	399	1425	583	2003	.288	.347	.499	505 B
Orlando Cepeda	17	2124	7927	1131	2351	417	27	379	1365	588	1169	.297	.350	.499	505 B
Jack Clark	18	1994	6847	1118	1826	332	39	340	1180	1262	1441	.267	.379	.476	505 B
Andruw Jones	13	1836	6617	1066	1716	338	35	371	1131	744	1470	.259	.339	.489	505 B
Greg Luzinski	15	1821	6505	880	1795	344	24	307	1128	845	1495	.276	.363	.478	505 B
Kent Hrbek	14	1747	6192	903	1749	312	18	293	1086	838	798	.282	.367	.481	505 B
Tim Salmon	14	1672	5934	986	1674	339	24	299	1016	970	1360	.282	.385	.498	505 B
David Justice	14	1610	5625	929	1571	280	24	305	1017	903	999	.279	.378	.500	505 B
Ted Kluszewski	15	1718	5929	848	1766	290	29	279	1028	492	365	.298	.353	.498	505 B
Scott Rolen	12	1505	5498	954	1558	380	32	261	1012	718	1097	.283	.372	.507	505 B
Paul Konerko	12	1548	5548	807	1539	279	6	298	957	603	895	.277	.352	.491	505 B
Danny Tartabull	14	1406	5011	756	1366	289	22	262	925	768	1362	.273	.368	.496	505 B
Troy Glaus	11	1395	4969	835	1271	273	10	304	877	788	1269	.256	.360	.498	505 B
Carlos Lee	9	1365	5197	813	1498	313	12	253	901	423	716	.288	.342	.499	505 B
Matt Stairs	16	1662	4937	737	1313	284	13	254	864	674	1037	.266	.358	.483	505 B
Richie Sexson	12	1367	4928	748	1286	260	17	306	943	588	1313	.261	.344	.507	505 B
Aramis Ramirez	11	1328	4957	686	1406	303	16	249	881	396	756	.284	.341	.502	505 B
Pat Burrell	9	1306	4535	655	1166	253	14	251	827	785	1273	.257	.367	.485	505 B
Kevin Mitchell	13	1223	4134	630	1173	224	25	234	760	491	719	.284	.360	.520	505 B
John Jaha	10	826	2775	470	730	126	5	141	490	430	686	.263	.369	.465	505 B
Justin Morneau	6	732	2681	393	754	159	12	133	523	274	447	.281	.348	.498	505 B
Kal Daniels	7	727	2338	391	666	125	8	104	360	365	493	.285	.382	.479	505 B
Morgan Ensberg	8	731	2204	340	579	102	10	110	347	332	436	.263	.362	.468	505 B
Erubiel Durazo	7	624	1948	333	547	108	6	94	330	307	428	.281	.381	.487	505 B

Family 703 C Group Name _____ – _____

Player	Years	G	AB	R	H	2B	3B	HR	RBI	BB	SO	Avg	OBP	Slg	Gp
John Olerud	17	2234	7592	1139	2239	500	13	255	1230	1275	1016	.295	.398	.465	703 C
Don Mattingly	14	1785	7003	1007	2153	442	20	222	1099	588	444	.307	.358	.471	703 C
Jose Vidro	12	1418	5113	720	1524	341	12	128	654	478	556	.298	.359	.445	703 C
Sean Casey	12	1405	5066	690	1531	322	12	130	735	477	577	.302	.367	.447	703 C
David Segui	15	1456	4847	683	1412	284	16	139	684	524	687	.291	.359	.443	703 C
John Valentin	11	1105	3917	614	1093	281	17	124	558	463	524	.279	.360	.454	703 C
Lyle Overbay	8	852	2932	391	824	215	7	86	393	370	589	.281	.362	.447	703 C
Kevin Youkilis	5	553	1922	325	555	138	8	66	314	277	397	.289	.385	.472	703 C
Ryan Zimmerman	4	445	1753	240	494	124	9	58	258	156	328	.282	.341	.462	703 C
Ryan Church	5	437	1316	180	358	90	6	47	202	139	336	.272	.347	.457	703 C

Family 415 C1   **Group Name** _____ _ _____

Player	Years	G	AB	R	H	2B	3B	HR	RBI	BB	SO	Avg	OBP	Slg	Gp
Dave Winfield	22	2973	11003	1669	3110	540	88	465	1833	1216	1686	.283	.353	.475	514 C1
Chili Davis	19	2436	8673	1240	2380	424	30	350	1372	1194	1698	.274	.360	.451	514 C1
Ron Santo	15	2243	8143	1138	2254	365	67	342	1331	1108	1343	.277	.362	.464	514 C1
Ken Singleton	15	2082	7189	985	2029	317	25	246	1065	1263	1246	.282	.388	.436	514 C1
Bobby Bonilla	16	2113	7213	1084	2010	408	61	287	1173	912	1204	.279	.358	.472	514 C1
Gary Matthews	16	2033	7147	1083	2011	319	51	234	978	940	1125	.281	.364	.439	514 C1
Bobby Murcer	17	1908	6730	972	1862	285	45	252	1043	862	841	.277	.357	.445	514 C1
Rick Monday	19	1986	6136	950	1619	248	64	241	775	924	1513	.264	.361	.443	514 C1
Reggie Sanders	17	1777	6241	1037	1666	341	60	305	983	674	1614	.267	.343	.487	514 C1
Kirk Gibson	17	1635	5798	985	1553	260	54	255	870	718	1285	.268	.352	.463	514 C1
Joe Gordon	11	1566	5707	914	1530	264	52	253	975	759	702	.268	.357	.466	514 C1
Bill Nicholson	16	1677	5546	837	1484	272	60	235	948	800	828	.268	.365	.465	514 C1
Raul Mondesi	13	1525	5814	909	1589	319	49	271	860	475	1130	.273	.331	.485	514 C1
Jackie Jensen	11	1438	5236	810	1463	259	45	199	929	750	546	.279	.369	.460	514 C1
Earl Torgeson	15	1668	4969	848	1318	215	46	149	740	980	653	.265	.385	.417	514 C1
Bobby Higginson	11	1362	4910	736	1336	270	33	187	709	649	796	.272	.358	.455	514 C1
Carl Everett	14	1405	4809	707	1304	258	26	202	792	442	1021	.271	.341	.462	514 C1
Sixto Lezcano	12	1291	4134	560	1122	184	34	148	591	576	768	.271	.360	.440	514 C1
Leon Durham	10	1067	3587	522	992	192	40	147	530	444	679	.277	.356	.475	514 C1
Dale Long	10	1013	3020	384	805	135	33	132	467	353	460	.267	.341	.464	514 C1
Stan Lopata	13	853	2601	375	661	116	25	116	397	393	497	.254	.351	.452	514 C1
Craig A. Wilson	7	698	2010	303	527	100	14	99	292	198	643	.262	.353	.474	514 C1
Otto Velez	11	637	1802	244	452	87	11	78	272	336	414	.251	.369	.441	514 C1
Dan Uggla	3	459	1774	315	465	112	11	90	270	193	461	.262	.341	.490	514 C1
Dick Kokos	5	475	1558	239	410	82	9	59	223	242	252	.263	.365	.441	514 C1
Don Lenhardt	5	481	1481	192	401	64	9	61	239	214	235	.271	.365	.450	514 C1
Josh Willingham	5	416	1422	196	378	82	11	63	219	174	326	.266	.361	.472	514 C1
Jayson Werth	6	460	1394	229	367	66	12	57	222	188	424	.263	.355	.451	514 C1
Jon Nunnally	6	364	885	162	218	47	12	42	125	146	239	.246	.354	.469	514 C1

Baltimore Orioles

Baltimore Orioles – 2008
Team Overview

Description		Ranking
Won-Lost Record	68-93	
Place	5th of 5 in American League East	
Runs Scored	782	10th in the majors
Runs Allowed	869	27th in the majors
Home Runs	172	12th in the majors
Home Runs Allowed	184	19th in the majors
Batting Average	.267	11th in the majors
Batting Average Allowed	.277	27th in the majors
Walks Drawn	533	19th in the majors
Walks Given	687	28th in the majors
OPS For	.762	11th in the majors
OPS Against	.796	27th in the majors
Stolen Bases	81	16th in the majors
Stolen Bases Allowed	130	23rd in the majors

Key Players

Pos	Player	G	AB	R	H	2B	3B	HR	RBI	SB	CS	BB	SO	Avg	OBP	Slg	OPS	WS
C	Ramon Hernandez	133	463	49	119	22	1	15	65	0	0	32	62	.257	.308	.406	.714	11
1B	Kevin Millar	145	531	73	124	25	0	20	72	0	1	71	93	.234	.323	.394	.717	10
2B	Brian Roberts	155	611	107	181	51	8	9	57	40	10	82	104	.296	.378	.450	.828	20
3B	Melvin Mora	135	513	77	146	29	2	23	104	3	7	37	70	.285	.342	.483	.826	17
SS	Juan Castro	54	151	15	31	6	0	2	16	0	0	10	26	.205	.256	.285	.541	2
LF	Luke Scott	148	475	67	122	29	2	23	65	2	2	53	102	.257	.336	.472	.807	11
CF	Adam Jones	132	477	61	129	21	7	9	57	10	3	23	108	.270	.311	.400	.711	9
RF	Nick Markakis	157	595	106	182	48	1	20	87	10	7	99	113	.306	.406	.491	.897	23
DH	Aubrey Huff	154	598	96	182	48	2	32	108	4	0	53	89	.304	.360	.552	.912	21

Key Pitchers

Pos	Player	G	GS	W	L	Sv	IP	H	R	ER	SO	BB	BR/9	ERA	WS
SP	Daniel Cabrera	30	30	8	10	0	180.2	199	109	105	95	90	15.35	5.25	6
SP	Jeremy Guthrie	30	30	10	12	0	190.2	176	82	77	120	58	11.38	3.63	13
SP	Garrett Olson	26	26	9	10	0	132.2	168	100	98	83	62	16.15	6.65	1
SP	Brian Burres	31	22	7	10	0	129.2	165	90	87	63	50	15.34	6.04	2
SP	Radhames Liz	17	17	6	6	0	84.1	99	67	63	57	51	16.33	6.72	0
CL	George Sherrill	57	0	3	5	31	53.1	47	28	28	58	33	13.67	4.73	7
RP	Jamie Walker	59	0	1	3	0	38.0	53	31	29	24	11	15.39	6.87	0
RP	Jim Johnson	54	0	2	4	1	68.2	54	18	17	38	28	11.14	2.23	8

Baltimore batters hit .267 overall, but they hit .287 with runners in scoring position, the second-highest average in the majors. They were led by Melvin Mora, who hit .360 in 150 at-bats with runners in scoring position, but three other players also hit above .300 in those situations. The list of all Oriole batters with at least 100 at-bats with runners in scoring positon is:

Batter	At-bats	BA
Melvin Mora	150	.360
Aubrey Huff	153	.320
Ramon Hernandez	114	.316
Nick Markakis	151	.311
Brian Roberts	106	.274
Kevin Millar	145	.269
Adam Jones	120	.258
Luke Scott	100	.240

Less Is Mora

Melvin Mora singled in the most runs in baseball last year (41). He did it with only 92 singles; Ichiro Suzuki had nearly twice as many singles (180) but drove in only 17 runs with them.

Melvin Mora – 2008
RBI Analysis

Hits		RBI Hits		RBI Total		Drove In	
Home Runs:	23			RBI on Home Runs:	37	Freddie Bynum	3
Triples:	2	RBI Triples:	1	RBI on Triples:	1	Juan Castro	4
Doubles:	29	RBI Doubles:	14	RBI on Doubles:	19	Alex Cintron	1
Singles:	92	RBI Singles:	34	RBI on Singles:	41	Brandon Fahey	1
		Other RBI: Walks	0	Sacrifice Flies:	6	Ramon Hernandez	4
		Other RBI: Ground Outs	0			Luis Hernandez	3
				Total Other:	0	Aubrey Huff	7
						Adam Jones	7
				Total RBI:	104	Nick Markakis	20
						Lou Montanez	1
						Garrett Olson	1
						Jay Payton	2
						Brian Roberts	27
						His Own Bad Self	23
						Total	104

18 of Melvin Mora's 23 home runs in 2008 came in at bats that ended with 3 pitches. When the at bat ran longer than 3 pitches his batting average dropped 110 points.

Melvin Mora – 2008
Short and Long AB

	AB	H	HR	RBI	Avg	OBP	Slg	OPS
One and done	52	18	3	18	.346	.370	.593	.963
Short	263	89	18	68	.338	.363	.597	.960
Long	250	57	5	36	.228	.330	.351	.680
7 Up	44	9	1	10	.205	.255	.318	.574

Pitching in the American League East, Jeremy Guthrie has had plenty of opportunities to pitch against top-notch teams. In fact, he has pitched nearly twice as many games against foes with records above .500 as below—and has pitched very well against good teams.

Jeremy Guthrie
Career Records Against Quality of Opposition

Opponent	G	IP	W	L	SO	BB	ERA
.600 teams	3	15.0	2	0	9	4	3.60
.500 - .599 teams	44	229.1	7	12	158	66	3.96
.400 - .499 teams	22	110.2	7	3	77	38	4.23
sub .400 teams	9	48.0	1	2	23	20	2.81

Look but Don't Touch

Nick Markakis increased his walks in 2008 from 61 to 99, primarily because he learned to lay off the high fastball. In 2007 he chased 74 pitches up out of the strike zone. In 2008 he cut that to 43.

In 2007 he chased the high pitch more often than 75% of major league hitters; in 2008, less often than 75%.

Nick Markakis – 2007
Pitch Analysis

Pitches Taken by Pitch Location		
In Strike Zone	506	34%
High	167	11%
Low	335	23%
Inside	125	8%
Outside	339	23%
Swung At by Pitch Location		
In Strike Zone	888	75%
High	74	6%
Low	101	9%
Inside	57	5%
Outside	59	5%

Nick Markakis – 2008
Pitch Analysis

Pitches Taken by Pitch Location		
In Strike Zone	477	31%
High	224	14%
Low	335	21%
Inside	136	9%
Outside	391	25%
Swung At by Pitch Location		
In Strike Zone	848	78%
High	43	4%
Low	78	7%
Inside	49	5%
Outside	68	6%

Cabrera

In the eight games that he won in 2008, Daniel Cabrera walked only eight men. You may look at the chart below and say "well, yeah, sure," but believe me, these are very unusual numbers. Most pitchers walk about the same number of batters per start when they "win" the game as they do when they lose—more walks per inning when they lose, but fewer innings, thus about the same number of walks per game in wins as in losses.

Cabrera was 8-10. Comparing Cabrera to pitchers with similar records and also with control troubles...

Brandon Backe (9-14) walked 2.7 batters per start in his wins, 2.4 in his other games. Garrett Olson (9-10) was at 2.2 and 2.5. Jonathan Sanchez (9-12) walked 2.3 batters per start in his wins, 2.7 in his other games. Radhames Liz (6-6) was at 3.0 and 3.0, and Tom Gorzelanny (6-9) walked 3.8 batters per start in wins, 3.1 in other games.

Cabrera was at 1.0 walks per start in wins, 3.7 in other games.

Daniel Cabrera – 2008
Decision Analysis

Group	G	IP	W	L	Pct	H	R	SO	BB	ERA
Wins	8	59.0	8	0	1.000	48	15	29	8	2.29
Losses	10	53.2	0	10	.000	75	44	36	32	6.88
No Decisions	12	67.1	0	0	—	76	50	30	50	6.55

The Index of Self-Destructive Acts is
Wild Pitches, plus
Hit Batsmen, plus
Balks, plus
Errors
Per 9 innings.

The highest Index of Self-Destructive acts in the major leagues in 2008, among pitchers pitching 100 innings, was by Daniel Cabrera—18 hit batsmen, 15 wild pitches, 2 balks and 1 error. 1.80 Self-Destructive Acts per 9 innings.

The lowest ISDA was 0.16, by Cole Hamels:

1. Cole Hamels	0.16	1. Daniel Cabrera	1.80
2. Derek Lowe	0.21	2. Vicente Padilla	1.79
3. Joel Pineiro	0.24	3. Jorge de la Rosa	1.52
4. Aaron Harang	0.24	4. Fausto Carmona	1.49
5. Jeff Francis	0.25	5. Micah Owings	1.46

San Francisco reliever Wild Bill Sadler, however, threw 8 Wild Pitches and hit 8 batters with pitches in just 44 innings on the mound, giving him an index of more than 3.00 Self-Destructive acts per 9 innings.

One of the reasons Aubrey Huff had a fine year was that he avoided groundballs more often than in any previous year we've tracked. It matters: His slugging percentage on groundballs was .280; on fly balls, it was .813.

Year	GB%
2002	45%
2003	47%
2004	45%
2005	47%
2006	45%
2007	46%
2008	41%

Jim Johnson pitched 68.2 innings last year without giving up a home run, the highest inning total of any pitcher with no home runs allowed. Overall, his slugging percentage allowed (.235) was bettered by just two other pitchers who pitched at least 50 innings (Mariano Rivera and Grant Balfour).

Jim Johnson
Record of Opposing Batters

Season	AB	R	H	2B	3B	HR	RBI	BB	SO	SB	CS	GIDP	Avg	OBP	Slg	OPS
2006	16	8	9	3	0	1	8	3	0	1	0	0	.563	.619	.938	1.557
2007	8	2	3	0	0	0	2	2	1	0	0	0	.375	.455	.375	.830
2008	247	18	54	4	0	0	17	28	38	3	2	14	.219	.305	.235	.539

The Long and Short of It

One of the profiles we present on Bill James Online is batter performance in short at-bats vs. long at-bats, and also (at the extremes) in one-pitch at-bats versus at-bats lasting seven or more pitches.

At a glance, it looks like hitters do better in short at-bats. The major league batting average in short at-bats (meaning 3 pitches or less) is .301; in long at-bats it is .223, since the great majority of strikeouts occur in longer at-bats. The OPS of hitters in a short at-bat is .784; in a long at-bat it is .700.

This is a profoundly misleading statistic, for a host of reasons.

1) There is a sorting bias. If a hitter swings early in the count and makes contact, that makes it a short at-bat. If he swings early in the count but misses, that makes it more likely to be a long at-bat. Thus, when the hitter "succeeds" at a very low level—when he puts the ball in play—that routes the at-bat toward the "early" division. When he fails totally—when he swings and misses—that routes the at-bat toward the "late" division. This biases the data.

2) The batting average is lower in a long at-bat—but the on-base percentage, which is a much more important statistic—is higher. The on-base percentage in short at-bats is .317; in long at-bats it is .352. Walks also occur only in longer at-bats.

3) OPS, for this particular split, just doesn't work. OPS relies on the "good-enough-for-government-work" assumption that one point of on-base percentage is as valuable as one point of slugging percentage. So long as both the on-base percentage and the slugging percentage are within normal ranges, that's usually good enough.

But on a more careful analysis:

a) One point of on-base percentage is worth significantly more than one point of slugging percentage, and

b) The proper relationship between the two isn't their total, but their product: on-base TIMES slugging percentage.

The split also doesn't reflect the effect, if there is one, of long at-bats grinding down the pitcher and setting up future hitters. That's another debate, but the long at-bat/short at-bat split also doesn't reflect the fact that, if the hitter makes a habit of swinging early in the count, the pitcher will exploit this by getting the hitter to chase outside the zone. The split makes it appear that the batter does best in short at-bats, but... that's really NOT the case most of the time.

Boston Red Sox

Boston Red Sox – 2008
Team Overview

Description		Ranking
Won-Lost Record	95-67	
Place	2nd of 5 in American League East	
Runs Scored	845	3rd in the majors
Runs Allowed	694	7th in the majors
Home Runs	173	11th in the majors
Home Runs Allowed	147	5th in the majors
Batting Average	.280	3rd in the majors
Batting Average Allowed	.250	4th in the majors
Walks Drawn	646	1st in the majors
Walks Given	548	15th in the majors
OPS For	.805	2nd in the majors
OPS Against	.713	4th in the majors
Stolen Bases	120	7th in the majors
Stolen Bases Allowed	96	15th in the majors

Key Players

Pos	Player	G	AB	R	H	2B	3B	HR	RBI	SB	CS	BB	SO	Avg	OBP	Slg	OPS	WS
C	Jason Varitek	131	423	37	93	20	0	13	43	0	1	52	122	.220	.313	.359	.672	8
1B	Kevin Youkilis	145	538	91	168	43	4	29	115	3	5	62	108	.312	.390	.569	.958	27
2B	Dustin Pedroia	157	653	118	213	54	2	17	83	20	1	50	52	.326	.376	.493	.869	26
3B	Mike Lowell	113	419	58	115	27	0	17	73	2	2	38	61	.274	.338	.461	.798	12
SS	Julio Lugo	82	261	27	70	13	0	1	22	12	4	34	51	.268	.355	.330	.685	2
LF	Manny Ramirez	100	365	66	109	22	1	20	68	1	0	52	86	.299	.398	.529	.926	14
CF	Coco Crisp	118	361	55	102	18	3	7	41	20	7	35	59	.283	.344	.407	.751	11
RF	J.D. Drew	109	368	79	103	23	4	19	64	4	1	79	80	.280	.408	.519	.927	16
DH	David Ortiz	109	416	74	110	30	1	23	89	1	0	70	74	.264	.369	.507	.877	15

Key Pitchers

Pos	Player	G	GS	W	L	Sv	IP	H	R	ER	SO	BB	BR/9	ERA	WS
SP	Daisuke Matsuzaka	29	29	18	3	0	167.2	128	58	54	154	94	12.29	2.90	16
SP	Jon Lester	33	33	16	6	0	210.1	202	78	75	152	66	11.90	3.21	18
SP	Tim Wakefield	30	30	10	11	0	181.0	154	89	83	117	60	11.29	4.13	10
SP	Josh Beckett	27	27	12	10	0	174.0	173	80	78	172	34	11.15	4.03	11
SP	Clay Buchholz	16	15	2	9	0	76.0	93	63	57	72	41	16.11	6.75	0
CL	Jonathan Papelbon	67	0	5	4	41	69.1	58	24	18	77	8	8.57	2.34	15
RP	Javier Lopez	70	0	2	0	0	59.1	53	18	16	38	27	12.44	2.43	6
RP	Manny Delcarmen	73	0	1	2	2	74.1	55	28	27	72	28	10.41	3.27	7

Maybe He Can Room
with Buchholz

Ramon Ramirez' fastball averaged 92.5 miles per hour last year, but he threw it less than half the time. He also liked to throw his changeup and slider—in fact, he threw his changeup to left-handed batters more often than he threw the fastball.

Only two other relievers (John Grabow of Pittsburgh and Edwar Ramirez of the Yankees) threw a change more often than Ramirez.

Ramon Ramirez – 2008
Pitch Type Analysis

Overall		
Total Pitches	1128	
Fastball	527	47%
Changeup	362	32%
Slider	204	18%
Split Finger	4	0%
Not Charted	31	3%

	Vs. RHB		Vs. LHB	
Total Pitches	593		535	
Outs Recorded	124		91	
Fastball	296	50%	231	43%
Changeup	106	18%	256	48%
Slider	176	30%	28	5%
Split Finger	0	0%	4	1%
Not Charted	15	3%	16	3%

Separated at Birth?

Who do you like better: Jon Lester or Cole Hamels?

OK, how did you decide?

Cole Hamels was born December 27, 1983.

Jon Lester was born eleven days later, on January 7, 1984.

Both men were born on the West Coast.

Both men are pitchers, and both are left-handed pitchers.

Hamels is listed as 6-3, 190 pounds; Lester is listed at 6-2, 190.

Both players were drafted out of high school in 2002, and both players signed out of high school. (On draft day Hamels was listed at 6-3, 175 pounds and Lester at 6-4, 200. So apparently Hamels has grown a little and Lester has shrunk to get to the same size.)

Cole Hamels made his major league debut on May 12, 2006. Jon Lester made his major league debut four weeks later.

Through three seasons in the majors, both men have had winning records every season, Hamels going 38-23 (.623) and Lester going 27-8 (.771).

Both men had ERAs over 4.00 in 2006 and ERAs just over 3.00 in 2008.

Both men pitched 200 innings for the first time in 2008.

Both men had career-best ERAs, although both had lower winning percentages in 2008 than they had entering the season.

Both men have been World Series heroes. Hamels pitched 6 good innings in the final game of the 2008 World Series, although he wasn't credited with the win. Lester pitched 5 2/3 shutout innings in the final game of the 2007 series, winning the game.

Although it may be a little bit subjective, both Hamels and Lester have picture-perfect deliveries which enable them to throw hard with a fluid, easy motion.

Who do you want?

I'd take Lester. Hamels is great; Hamels is sensational. Lester throws a little bit harder (92.1 average fastball velocity, vs. 90.4 for Hamels). Hamels' strikeout rate is a little bit higher, because of his outstanding changeup, but Lester gets many more groundballs. Hamels in 2008 gave up 28 homers and induced 15 double plays. Lester gave up half as many homers (14) and induced almost twice as many double plays (27).

I'm prejudiced, obviously. I was in the park when Jon Lester threw his no-hitter. I'd still take Lester. Two more evenly matched players, you'd be hard pressed to find.

Don't Carry Nothin'
but the Righteous and Holy

If those who are waiting to get into heaven are said to be in purgatory, could those who are waiting to get into the Hall of Fame perhaps be in Utica?

Jim Rice, who won his MVP Award in 1978, will go into the Hall of Fame this summer with Joe Gordon, who won his in 1942. These lag times are not unusual; 31 years is actually a fairly short interval between MVP and UBP (Ugly Brass Plaque).

Most players who win MVP Awards will eventually be in the Hall of Fame.

Dealing with the BBWAA MVP Awards beginning in 1931, the first 16 players who won the Award are all in the Hall of Fame today, although some of them were elected only after decades in Utica. The first MVP who is not in the Hall of Fame (yet) is Bucky Walters in 1939.

In the 1930s, then, 17 out of 18, or 94%.

1930s	17	18	94%
1940s	13	20	65%
1950s	14	20	70%
1960s	12	20	60%
1970s	8	21	38%
1980s	9	20	45%
1990s	3	20	15%

There are 21 in the 1970s because there was a tie in the voting. If we assume that…well, let me back up a minute. One can't *assume* that the Hall of Fame will be as kind to the stars of the 1970s and 80s as it was to the stars of the 1950s and 60s; it may not be. To this point, the 1950s and 60s have not caught up with the 1920s and 30s.

However, it does seem quite obvious that there are many players from the 1970s and 1980s who will, eventually, be in the Hall of Fame—thus, that these percentages will flatten out over time. 1971 NL MVP Joe Torre is an obvious Hall of Famer. 1972 AL MVP Dick Allen is probably going in sometime, as is 1985 AL MVP Don Mattingly, and 1986 MVP Roger Clemens. 1973 NL MVP Pete Rose may eventually stumble down the right pathway.

Beyond those, there are many MVPs of the 1970s and 1980s who are…well, not what you or I might think of as a Hall of Famer, but still as well qualified as Joe Gordon, Travis Jackson, Phil Rizzuto, Bobby Doerr, Chick Hafey, Ted Lyons and dozens of others who have already gotten the plaque. Among these: Vida Blue (1971 American League), Steve Garvey (1974 National League), Fred Lynn (1975 American League), Thurman Munson (1976 American League) Dave Parker (1978 National League), Keith Hernandez (1979 National League), Dale Murphy (1982 and 1983 National League) and Andre Dawson (1987 National League). I would predict that at least sixty percent of the 1970s and 1980s MVPs will eventually be enshrined.

Throwback

The only major league players in 2008 who had more doubles than strikeouts were Dustin Pedroia and Mike Sweeney. Pedroia won an MVP Award; Sweeney won a minor league contract with the Mariners.

In the 1920s 40% of all major league regulars had more doubles than strikeouts. In the 1930s this dropped to 28%; in the 1940s, to 18%. In the 1950s it dropped to 10%. In the 1960s it dropped to 1%—actually, 1.35%.

Since then the percentage has bobbed up and down, but we're back at 1%. Pedroia was the first player to win an MVP Award with more doubles than strikeouts since Don Mattingly in 1985.

There were two American League players in 2008 who had an on-base percentage of .400 and a slugging percentage of .500 in 400 or more at-bats. They were both right fielders. Can you name them?

Yeldarb notlim and werd d. j.

Read it backwards.

Plaxico Burress Award

Daisuke Matsuzaka in 2008 walked 63 batters in games that he won. No other major league pitcher was close to that number:

	Wins	Walks In Wins
1. Daisuke Matsuzaka	18	63
2. Edinson Volquez	17	50
3. Tim Lincecum	18	47
4. A. J. Burnett	18	46
5. Brandon Webb	22	37

It's a Closer Thing

There were 426 major league pitchers who worked 30 or more innings in 2008.
61 of those—one-seventh—struck out more than one batter an inning.
29 of the 426 walked less than two batters per nine innings.
Four pitchers did both—Mariano Rivera, Jonathan Papelbon, Trevor Hoffman and Billy Wagner:

Name	Team	G	IP	SO	BB	W	L	Sv	ERA
Papelbon, Jonathan	Red Sox	67	69.1	77	8	5	4	41	2.34
Wagner, Billy	Mets	45	47.0	52	10	0	1	27	2.30
Rivera, Mariano	Yankees	64	70.2	77	6	6	5	39	1.40
Hoffman, Trevor	Padres	48	45.1	46	9	3	6	30	3.77

Lopez

In his three years in the Boston bullpen, hitters facing Javier Lopez have posted an OPS of .702, .695 and .699.

Major league hitters with OPS in that range last year included Marco Scutaro (.697), Yuniesky Betancourt (.691), Mark Ellis (.694), Jamey Carroll (.700), and David Eckstein (.692).

Pawtucket Plus

At Pawtucket last year Red Sox farmhand Chris Carter hit .300 with an .871 OPS. The Red Sox don't really have a seat for him, but…what does that translate to at a major league level?

If you want to know what a Red Sox farm hand will hit in the major leagues, just take what he hits at Pawtucket and add a few points to the OPS. Going back ten years or more, it is hard to find a real exception to that rule, among players who have gotten a reasonable number of major league at-bats.

Trot Nixon hit .284 with an .843 OPS at Pawtucket (1997-1998). In his first 8 seasons in the majors he hit .280 with an OPS of .863.

David Eckstein hit .246 with a .665 OPS at Pawtucket (2000). In his major league career he has hit .284 with an OPS of .712.

Wilton Veras at Pawtucket (2000-2002) hit .232 with an OPS of .579; in the majors he hit .262 with an OPS of .637.

Kevin Youkilis hit .260 at Pawtucket with an .809 OPS (2003-2005). In the majors he has hit .289 with an OPS of .857.

Kelly Shoppach hit .243 at Pawtucket with an OPS of .820 (2004-2005). So far in the majors he has hit .252 with an OPS of .793.

Dustin Pedroia hit .289 at Pawtucket with an OPS of .786 (2005-2006); so far in the majors he is at .313 and .828.

Willie Harris at Pawtucket in 2006 hit just .208 with an OPS of .686. In the majors (626 games over a long period of years) he has hit .248 with an OPS of .667.

David Murphy at Pawtucket hit .273 with a .780 OPS (2006-2007); so far in the majors (174 games) he has hit .286 with an .814 OPS.

Freddy Sanchez hit .310 at Pawtucket with an .824 OPS (2002-2003). In his first 477 major league games (mostly with Pittsburgh) he hit .310 with a .782 OPS.

Jacoby Ellsbury hit .298 with a .740 OPS at Pawtucket (2007) and has so far hit .293 in the majors, with a .756 OPS.

Exceptions? Well, Jed Lowrie hit .282 with a .824 OPS at Pawtucket (2007-2008), and has so far hit only .258 (.739) in the majors, but that's just 260 at-bats. Brandon Moss, now with Pittsburgh, has similar data in a similar number of at-bats, but. . .he'll go off this year.

Adam Hyzdu spent generations at Pawtucket waiting for his chance and "failed" his major league trials, but Adam Hyzdu's major league RBI rate (61 RBI in 407 plate appearances) was better than Eddie Murray's or Reggie Jackson's, so I cling to the illusion that Hyzdu might have been OK in the majors, given a better look. Nomar Garciaparra hit .343 at Pawtucket, but that was just 43 games, and in his first four years in the majors he hit .357 and .372. Basically, there is a long line of players ready to argue that what a player does in Pawtucket, he can do in the major leagues.

Okajima

There were no stolen bases against Hideki Okajima in 2008; he was third in the majors in innings pitched with no stolen bases allowed, behind Josh Rupe of Texas and Geoff Geary of Houston. Otherwise, the batting line against Okajima in 2008 was extremely similar to his first American season in 2007:

Season	AB	R	H	2B	3B	HR	RBI	BB	SO	SB	CS	GIDP	Avg	OBP	Slg	OPS
2007	248	17	50	6	1	6	15	17	63	5	0	6	.202	.255	.306	.561
2008	231	18	49	9	0	6	29	23	60	0	1	1	.212	.283	.329	.612

Papi

In 2006 David Ortiz hit .330 with 16 homers in 109 at-bats against the league's best pitchers, the pitchers with ERAs under 3.50. Over the last two years, however, premier pitchers have almost totally stymied him:

David Ortiz – 2007
Batting Performance by Quality of Opposing Pitcher

	AB	H	HR	RBI	Avg	OPS
Pitcher with ERA <= 3.50	109	21	5	17	.193	.631
Pitcher with ERA 3.51 to 4.25	176	58	9	34	.330	1.037
Pitcher with ERA 4.26 to 5.25	107	42	4	21	.393	1.148
Pitcher with ERA over 5.25	157	61	17	45	.389	1.330

David Ortiz – 2008
Batting Performance by Quality of Opposing Pitcher

	AB	H	HR	RBI	Avg	OPS
Pitcher with ERA <= 3.50	110	20	4	16	.182	.657
Pitcher with ERA 3.51 to 4.25	117	30	5	17	.256	.798
Pitcher with ERA 4.26 to 5.25	101	31	7	22	.307	1.030
Pitcher with ERA over 5.25	88	29	7	34	.330	1.076

Gems

by Bill James

This is the kind of thing I love to do. I love to pick up a word or an expression that is in common usage in baseball, give it an operational definition, and then explore the concept in ways that can't be examined without an operational definition.

That's what we did with "manufactured runs", for example. That's what we did with the "batter's temperature", or the "pitcher's temperature". It is taking a term that is in everyday use, and giving it a functional definition.

"He pitched a gem, but has nothing to show for it."

If a pitcher pitched a very good game his previous outing, what does the announcer say: "He pitched a *gem* his last time out." Or if a pitcher pitches well but doesn't get a win, what does the ESPN reporter say? "He pitched a gem for the Brewers, but has nothing to show for it."

This subject arose because the Red Sox in late April, 2008, had four straight outstanding starts—a game in which Clay Buchholz took a one-hitter into the bottom of the eighth, only to lose on a two-run home run (Game Score: 75), a career-high thirteen strikeouts by Josh Beckett, four hits, two runs, one earned run, also a loss (Game Score: 75), a one-hitter through eight innings for Jon Lester, bullpen got the win (Game Score: 82), and seven innings of two-hit shutout ball by Daisuke Matsuzaka, the bullpen again getting the win (Game Score: 75).

This four-game run of pitching gems didn't prove anything about how good the Red Sox pitching was going to be last year, because you have times every year when things go one way or the other, but I couldn't remember any team having four games in a row of that quality in many years. In 2003, for example, the Red Sox had only five Game Scores all year of 75 or higher—all of those by Pedro Martinez. So then I started thinking about gems, and how to define gems and how to talk about gems, and I came back up with this concept of the gem: A gem is something *beyond* a quality start; it's a *sterling* quality start. It's a diamond, or an emerald. It's a game you brag about, a box score you keep.

I started by defining a gem as a game with a Game Score of 75 or higher, since that was what the Red Sox

had done, but that turns out to be far too high.

Why is it too high? It's too high because it's out of line with the way the term is used in everyday language. No announcer would hesitate to describe any of the following games as gems:

IP	H	R	ER	BB	SO
7	3	0	0	1	4
7	3	0	0	3	6
7	4	0	0	1	5
8	4	1	1	1	3
7	2	1	1	1	4
7	3	1	1	2	7
7	6	1	1	0	10
7	4	0	0	3	5
7	4	0	0	2	4
7	6	1	1	1	10
7	4	1	1	1	6
7	3	0	0	3	2
8	5	3	2	0	8
7	3	2	2	1	7
8	6	2	2	1	8
7	5	1	1	3	8
7	4	1	1	4	7
8⅔	8	2	2	0	8
7	5	2	1	1	8
6	2	1	1	3	7
8	6	2	2	2	8
7	5	1	1	1	5
7	3	1	1	1	1
7	4	1	1	3	4
8	7	2	2	2	8
6	4	1	1	2	8
6	3	2	2	3	10
6	4	0	0	2	3
7	6	2	2	2	10
8	5	3	3	2	7
6⅔	3	1	1	4	5

But none of these is a Game Score of 75 or higher. I decided that a better definition of a gem is any start by a pitcher
  a) with a Game Score of 65 or higher, or
  b) with six or more innings of shutout baseball.

In the chart above, the bottom five of those starts have Game Scores of 65. That's as low as we can reasonably go in defining a gem without making up a definition that no longer comports with common usage.

By our definition, an average pitcher, in the rotation all year, will throw about six gems. 19% of all starts are classed as gems; it works out to 19% almost every year since 2002. Let's say a rotation pitcher makes 31, 32 starts a year; 19% of that is six gems a year. Let's take Oliver Perez of the Mets in 2007, to pick a pitcher and a year at random. He had 29 starts:

- On April 6 at Atlanta, Perez limited the Braves to five hits, one run over seven innings.
- On May 13 against the Brewers in Shea Stadium he pitched his best game of the year—a one-hit shutout into the ninth, departed after a solo homer with one out in the ninth.
- On May 23, again at Atlanta, he pitched seven innings of shutout baseball.
- On June 15, facing the Yankees at Yankee Stadium, he pitched seven-and-a-third innings of shutout baseball, out-dueling Roger Clemens.
- On July 20 at Dodger Stadium he pitched seven-and-a-third, limiting the Dodgers to one run and striking out eight.
- On August 24, facing the Dodgers again back in Shea Stadium, he pitched seven innings of three-hit, shutout baseball.
- On September 22, facing the Marlins in Miami, he pitched eight innings, striking out eight, walking no one, giving up six hits and two runs, one of those un-earned.

Seven gems, and Perez won all of them. He was 7-0 with a 0.69 ERA in those starts. He had other good games, other wins, other well-pitched losses, but those were the highlights of his season…the gems that year. About one game a month, Perez dominated. That year, he had seven as an individual; the Florida Marlins had eight as a team. Dontrelle Willis had one—his next-to-last start of the season.

If 19% of all starts are gems, that also means that there are five or six pitching gems each day in the major leagues—30 teams, a full schedule is 30 starts, 19% of that is a little short of six. Less on Monday and Thursday. 48% of major league starts are Quality Starts. About 40% of Quality Starts are Gems.

Of course, some pitchers pitch more gems than others. CC Sabathia lead Major League Baseball with 18 (9 for the Brewers and 9 for the Indians), but that was split over two leagues. The league leaders in 2008 were Tim Lincecum of the San Francisco Giants, who pitched 16 gems, and Cliff Lee of Cleveland Indians, who pitched 13. These are the league leaders since 2002 (and my thanks to Damon Lichtenwalner and Pat Quinn, who generated this data). Pitchers who also won the Cy Young Award marked with an asterisk:

2008 MLB	CC Sabathia, 18
2008 AL	Cliff Lee, 13*
2008 NL	Tim Lincecum, 16*
2007 AL	Josh Beckett, 13
2007 NL	Jake Peavy, 18*
2006 AL	Johan Santana, 18*
2006 NL	Four pitchers with 14
2005 AL	Johan Santana, 19
2005 NL	Roger Clemens, 18
2004 AL	Johan Santana, 20*
2004 NL	Randy Johnson, 18
2003 AL	Pedro Martinez, 17
2003 NL	Jason Schmidt, 16
2002 AL	Derek Lowe and Pedro Martinez, 16 each
2002 NL	Randy Johnson, 22*

The 2002 data is interesting in this way. The American League leaders, Lowe and Martinez, were teammates, giving Boston two #1 starting pitchers that year, for which reason they had 51 gems—which, astonishingly, did not lead the American League. The A's, with Mulder, Zito and Hudson, had 52. In the NL, meanwhile, Randy Johnson's 22 were closely followed by teammate Curt Schilling's 19—giving Arizona a total of 56 gems, the highest total in

A gem is something beyond a quality start; it's a sterling quality start. It's a diamond, or an emerald. It's a game you brag about, a box score you keep.

the majors since 2002. Other than the Red Sox, A's and Snakes in 2002, only one team since 2002 has had as many as 51 gems—but the major league "gem percentage" was not terribly high that season; it was 19.8%. It was just a season in which a few teams had most of the best pitchers.

The data above suggests that the pitcher who throws the most gems often wins the Cy Young Award, although we don't know for sure how often. What the record is, again, I don't know. Doc Gooden in '85 threw 25 gems. Koufax threw 30 in '63, 30 in '65, and 31 in '66.

Talking about these exceptional performances is the normal thing to do here, but we are, in a sense, losing sight of our real focus. This is not another way to spot the greatest pitchers—we have lots of those—but rather, a way to acknowledge the better games. Only a few pitchers throw 12, 15, 20 gems a year, and even fewer pitchers have thrown more, but the normal rule is that a pitcher throws a game like this about once a month.

The great **Mike Mussina** threw 9 gems in 2002, 10 in 2003, 6 in 2004, 7 in 2005, 9 in 2006, 2 in 2007, and 7 in 2008.

Bob Gibson had 482 career starts, almost half of which—238—were gems. He pitched 27 gems in 1968—27 in 34 starts. His career record in his gems was 191-37. In 1968 he threw 15 consecutive gems, losing the first three and then winning the next 12, including his scoreless-inning streak.

Don Sutton had 756 career starts, of which 272 were gems, or 36%. He was 223-49 in gems, and threw 21 gems in '72, 21 again in '73.

Ferguson Jenkins had 228 gems in 594 career starts, or 38%. He was 189-26 in his gems, and had a career-high 22 gems in 1974.

Bert Blyleven had 237 gems in 685 career starts, or 35%. He was 180-28 in his gems, and had a career-high 21 gems in 1973. Blyleven had 57 gems in his career in which he was not credited with a win, as opposed to 47 for Gibson, 49 for Sutton, and 39 for Ferguson Jenkins.

It is certain that the percentage of gems would have been higher in the 1960s or the 1970s than it is now—in the 1960s because of the very low run totals, and in the 1970s because of the high numbers of complete games. I would be surprised if it was *much* higher. Game Scores are pretty tightly anchored to 50, so that it would be very hard to imagine that as much as 25% of starts would be gems. It's 19% now; it might have been 21-22% in the 1960s, but I'm guessing.

When a pitcher throws a gem, what is his winning percentage? Does the team that has the most gems over the season usually win the pennant? What is the record for consecutive gems by a pitching staff? If a pitcher who has been struggling throws a gem, does it indicate that he has turned a corner? How many gems are there in a Hall of Fame career?

I don't know the answers to any of these questions, and I can't tell you, based on a theory and a couple of days of research, whether the gem counts will be useful to us or won't. I just thought I'd put it out there, and see whether anybody liked it. If you've got any feedback, meet me at BillJamesOnline.com and we'll talk about it some more.

This is not another way to spot the greatest pitchers—we have lots of those—but rather, a way to acknowledge the better games.

Chicago Cubs

Chicago Cubs – 2008
Team Overview

Description		Ranking
Won-Lost Record	97-64	
Place	1st of 6 in National League Central	
Runs Scored	855	2nd in the majors
Runs Allowed	671	3rd in the majors
Home Runs	184	8th in the majors
Home Runs Allowed	160	9th in the majors
Batting Average	.278	5th in the majors
Batting Average Allowed	.242	1st in the majors
Walks Drawn	636	2nd in the majors
Walks Given	548	15th in the majors
OPS For	.797	3rd in the majors
OPS Against	.711	3rd in the majors
Stolen Bases	87	14th in the majors
Stolen Bases Allowed	87	12th in the majors

Key Players

Pos	Player	G	AB	R	H	2B	3B	HR	RBI	SB	CS	BB	SO	Avg	OBP	Slg	OPS	WS
C	Geovany Soto	141	494	66	141	35	2	23	86	0	1	62	121	.285	.364	.504	.868	21
1B	Derrek Lee	155	625	93	181	41	3	20	90	8	2	71	119	.291	.361	.462	.823	17
2B	Mark DeRosa	149	505	103	144	30	3	21	87	6	0	69	106	.285	.376	.481	.857	23
3B	Aramis Ramirez	149	554	97	160	44	1	27	111	2	2	74	94	.289	.380	.518	.898	25
SS	Ryan Theriot	149	580	85	178	19	4	1	38	22	13	73	58	.307	.387	.359	.745	16
LF	Alfonso Soriano	109	453	76	127	27	0	29	75	19	3	43	103	.280	.344	.532	.876	16
CF	Jim Edmonds	85	250	47	64	17	2	19	49	0	1	45	58	.256	.369	.568	.937	10
RF	Kosuke Fukudome	150	501	79	129	25	3	10	58	12	4	81	104	.257	.359	.379	.738	15

Key Pitchers

Pos	Player	G	GS	W	L	Sv	IP	H	R	ER	SO	BB	BR/9	ERA	WS
SP	Ryan Dempster	33	33	17	6	0	206.2	174	75	68	187	76	11.19	2.96	18
SP	Ted Lilly	34	34	17	9	0	204.2	187	96	93	184	64	11.35	4.09	12
SP	Carlos Zambrano	30	30	14	6	0	188.2	172	85	82	130	72	11.93	3.91	16
SP	Jason Marquis	29	28	11	9	0	167.0	172	87	84	91	70	13.47	4.53	8
SP	Rich Harden	12	12	5	1	0	71.0	39	17	14	89	30	9.00	1.77	8
CL	Kerry Wood	65	0	5	4	34	66.1	54	24	24	84	18	10.72	3.26	12
RP	Bob Howry	72	0	7	5	1	70.2	90	44	42	59	13	13.37	5.35	3
RP	Carlos Marmol	82	0	2	4	7	87.1	40	30	26	114	41	8.97	2.68	12

The Cubs led the league in runs scored by a wide margin—56 more runs than the second-place team—and a key factor was the depth of their attack. They led the league in RBIs from the first, seventh, eighth and ninth lineup positions, and they led in runs scored from the sixth and seventh positions.

Chicago Cubs – 2008
Runs and RBI by Batting Order

Pos	Players	Runs	RBI
1	Soriano (105 G), Johnson (18 G)	117	**100**
2	Theriot (104 G), Fukudome (19 G)	101	48
3	Lee (154 G)	104	105
4	Ramirez (146 G)	108	124
5	Fukudome (59 G), Soto (34 G), Edmonds (33 G)	99	83
6	DeRosa (70 G), Soto (47 G), Edmonds (21 G)	**101**	94
7	DeRosa (44 G), Soto (41 G), Fukudome (19 G)	**91**	107
8	Cedeno (29 G), Johnson (28 G), Blanco (27 G)	83	**83**
9	Lilly (33 G), Dempster (31 G), Zambrano (29 G)	51	**67**
	Total	855	811

Carlos Marmol is your classic fastball/slider pitcher. In fact, he is apparently perfectly torn between his two favorite pitches. He only threw one more slider than fastball last year—just one out of 1,509—and it didn't matter whether the batter was a righty or lefty. Carlos dealt his pitches with equanimity.

Marmol gained confidence in his slider in 2007 and it made a difference. His 2006 ERA of 6.08 dropped big time as he 1) moved to the bullpen, and 2) began throwing the slider half the time.

	Slider %	ERA
2006	7%	6.08
2007	50%	1.43
2008	47%	2.68

Carlos Marmol – 2008
Pitch Type Analysis

Overall		
Total Pitches	1509	
Fastball	705	47%
Curveball	52	3%
Changeup	1	0%
Slider	706	47%
Not Charted	45	3%

	Vs. RHB		Vs. LHB	
Total Pitches	828		681	
Outs Recorded	153		109	
Fastball	390	47%	315	46%
Curveball	33	4%	19	3%
Changeup	0	0%	1	0%
Slider	389	47%	317	47%
Not Charted	16	2%	29	4%

Don't Mess with Mister In-Between

Kosuke Fukudome's inaugural major league season didn't go as well as hoped, but Fukudome handled good pitching when given a chance. He batted .281, with a .781 OPS, against pitchers with a 3.50 ERA or lower.

Kosuke Fukudome – 2008
Batting Performance by Quality of Opposing Pitcher

	AB	H	HR	RBI	Avg	OPS
Pitcher with ERA <= 3.50	128	36	3	14	.281	.781
Pitcher with ERA 3.51 to 4.25	151	35	4	16	.232	.679
Pitcher with ERA 4.26 to 5.25	130	31	1	12	.238	.690
Pitcher with ERA over 5.25	92	27	2	16	.293	.840

Over the last five years, Rich Harden has only allowed a .614 OPS to opposing batters. That's the best mark in that timeframe for all pitchers with 50 or more starts.

Rich Harden – 2003-2008
Record of Opposing Batters

Season	AB	R	H	2B	3B	HR	RBI	BB	SO	SB	CS	GIDP	Avg	OBP	Slg	OPS
2003	278	38	72	12	1	5	33	40	67	9	2	11	.259	.351	.363	.714
2004	708	90	171	32	4	16	77	81	167	11	6	18	.242	.320	.366	.685
2005	463	42	93	20	1	7	32	43	121	4	4	10	.201	.271	.294	.564
2006	162	22	31	5	0	5	17	26	49	2	3	3	.191	.304	.315	.618
2007	89	7	18	3	0	3	6	11	27	1	1	5	.202	.290	.337	.627
2008	526	38	96	18	2	11	37	61	181	7	7	2	.183	.270	.287	.557

Alfonso Soriano – 2007
Pitch Analysis

Alfonso Soriano is more likely to swing the bat than not. That's not a big deal—30 full-time major leaguers had a swing percentage greater than 50% last year. But of all batters with more swings than pitches taken, Soriano missed most often (27%).

Overall		
Pitches Seen	1842	
Taken	867	47%
Swung At	975	53%
Swung At		
Missed	266	27%
Fouled Off	355	36%
Put in Play	354	36%

Alfonso Soriano led off for the Cubs in 105 games last year, but scored on a teammate's home run only once. He scored on his own home run 29 times.

Ryan Dempster's conversion from mildly successful closer to wildly successful starter was a little different than the script you might have expected. As a reliever in 2007, Dempster threw only 45% fastballs. That's a low percentage, particularly for a reliever who often has to warm up quickly and rely on one or two pitches. He threw 20% changeups and 32% sliders.

As a starting pitcher last year, Dempster relied on his fastball more often, using it 55% of the time and cutting down on both the changeup and slider. The starting role seemed to help Dempster, but throwing his fastball more often was the real difference in 2008.

Ryan Dempster – 2007
Pitch Type Analysis

Overall		
Total Pitches	1030	
Fastball	461	45%
Changeup	207	20%
Slider	333	32%
Pitchout	13	1%
Not Charted	16	2%

	Vs. RHB		Vs. LHB	
Total Pitches	511		519	
Outs Recorded	111		89	
Fastball	216	42%	245	47%
Changeup	44	9%	163	31%
Slider	242	47%	91	18%
Pitchout	1	0%	12	2%
Not Charted	8	2%	8	2%

Ryan Dempster – 2008
Pitch Type Analysis

Overall		
Total Pitches	3341	
Fastball	1845	55%
Curveball	1	0%
Changeup	550	16%
Slider	905	27%
Pitchout	1	0%
Not Charted	39	1%

	Vs. RHB		Vs. LHB	
Total Pitches	1739		1602	
Outs Recorded	336		284	
Fastball	940	54%	905	56%
Curveball	1	0%	0	0%
Changeup	105	6%	445	28%
Slider	674	39%	231	14%
Pitchout	1	0%	0	0%
Not Charted	18	1%	21	1%

Since his great 2005 season, when he batted .335 with 46 home runs, Derrek Lee's hitting performance has steadily eroded. In the four years since, he has hit more groundballs and less flyballs, and his batting average on both types of batted balls has declined. All of these trends seemed to accelerate in 2008.

Season	GB%	BA/GB	FB%	BA/FB
2005	38.6%	.300	39.4%	.305
2006	41.3%	.281	38.4%	.306
2007	41.2%	.282	38.2%	.281
2008	44.9%	.237	33.7%	.257

The Cubs threw more sliders than any other team last year. 23% of their pitches were sliders; the second-highest total was 19%, posted by the Tigers. Nobody threw the slider more often than Mike Wuertz (at least, no one with at least 10 innings pitched) and Carlos Marmol added his own slider emphasis. Ryan Dempster and Ted Lilly led the starters.

The leading slider-happy Cub pitchers (minimum of 40 innings pitched) were:

Name	Slider %	IP
Mike Wuertz	60%	44.2
Carlos Marmol	47%	87.1
Jon Lieber	39%	46.2
Ryan Dempster	27%	206.2
Ted Lilly	23%	204.2
Kerry Wood	23%	66.1
Bob Howry	22%	70.2
Jason Marquis	16%	167.0
Sean Gallagher	15%	58.2
Carlos Zambrano	13%	188.2
Sean Marshall	12%	65.1
Rich Harden	3%	71.0

Chicago White Sox

Chicago White Sox – 2008
Team Overview

Description		Ranking
Won-Lost Record	89-74	
Place	1st of 5 in American League Central	
Runs Scored	811	6th in the majors
Runs Allowed	729	13th in the majors
Home Runs	235	1st in the majors
Home Runs Allowed	156	7th in the majors
Batting Average	.263	18th in the majors
Batting Average Allowed	.261	13th in the majors
Walks Drawn	540	16th in the majors
Walks Given	460	5th in the majors
OPS For	.780	6th in the majors
OPS Against	.731	10th in the majors
Stolen Bases	67	22nd in the majors
Stolen Bases Allowed	139	24th in the majors

Key Players

Pos	Player	G	AB	R	H	2B	3B	HR	RBI	SB	CS	BB	SO	Avg	OBP	Slg	OPS	WS
C	A.J. Pierzynski	134	534	66	150	31	1	13	60	1	0	19	71	.281	.312	.416	.728	8
1B	Paul Konerko	122	438	59	105	19	1	22	62	2	0	65	80	.240	.344	.438	.783	10
2B	Alexei Ramirez	136	480	65	139	22	2	21	77	13	9	18	61	.290	.317	.475	.792	18
3B	Joe Crede	97	335	41	83	18	1	17	55	0	3	30	45	.248	.314	.460	.773	10
SS	Orlando Cabrera	161	661	93	186	33	1	8	57	19	6	56	71	.281	.334	.371	.705	19
LF	Carlos Quentin	130	480	96	138	26	1	36	100	7	3	66	80	.288	.394	.571	.965	23
CF	Nick Swisher	153	497	86	109	21	1	24	69	3	3	82	135	.219	.332	.410	.743	12
RF	Jermaine Dye	154	590	96	172	41	2	34	96	3	2	44	104	.292	.344	.541	.885	17
DH	Jim Thome	149	503	93	123	28	0	34	90	1	0	91	147	.245	.362	.503	.865	17

Key Pitchers

Pos	Player	G	GS	W	L	Sv	IP	H	R	ER	SO	BB	BR/9	ERA	WS
SP	Gavin Floyd	33	33	17	8	0	206.1	190	107	88	145	70	11.73	3.84	15
SP	Mark Buehrle	34	34	15	12	0	218.2	240	106	92	140	52	12.22	3.79	16
SP	John Danks	33	33	12	9	0	195.0	182	74	72	159	57	11.22	3.32	17
SP	Javier Vazquez	33	33	12	16	0	208.1	214	113	108	200	61	12.14	4.67	11
SP	Jose Contreras	20	20	7	6	0	121.0	130	64	61	70	35	12.50	4.54	7
CL	Bobby Jenks	57	0	3	1	30	61.2	51	18	18	38	17	10.07	2.63	13
RP	Matt Thornton	74	0	5	3	1	67.1	48	20	20	77	19	9.22	2.67	10
RP	Octavio Dotel	72	0	4	4	1	67.0	52	34	28	92	29	11.55	3.76	6

The White Sox were 9-31 (a .225 winning percentage) in games in which they hit no home runs—the third-worst record in the majors in homerless games. Only the Nationals (18-63, .222) and Padres (15-52, .225) were worse. But fortunately for the Sox, they didn't have a lot of homerless games.

Chicago White Sox – 2008
Record by Home Runs

Home Runs	W	-	L
0 homers	9	-	31
1 homer	32	-	22
2 homers	22	-	15
3 or more homers	26	-	6

The White Sox led the majors in home runs by a comfortable margin, with 235. New Comiskey is a notorious home run park, and the White Sox played to their park's strength by leading the majors in proportion of flyballs hit at 41%.

12.7% of Chicago's flyballs resulted in home runs, the highest figure in the American League.

The White Sox were 54-28 in their home park, but 35-46 on the road.

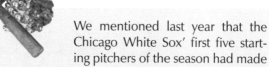

We mentioned last year that the Chicago White Sox' first five starting pitchers of the season had made 150 starts three straight years, and then they did it again in 2008. No other team has had even one season of 150 starts out of their first five pitchers in the past three years. There is credit to be spread around here, but however you split it up between Ozzie, pitching coach Don Cooper, the training staff, and Mark Buehrle, it is an impressive streak.

Chicago White Sox – 2008
Starts Made by First Five Starting Pitchers

Pitcher	2005	2006	2007	2008
Buehrle, M	33	32	30	34
Garcia, F	33	33		
Contreras, J	32	30	30	20
Garland, J	32	32	32	
Hernandez, O	22			
Vazquez, J		32	32	33
Danks, J			26	33
Floyd, G				33
Total	153	159	150	153

American League – 2008

Team	Apr	May	June	July	Aug	Sept	Total
Los Angeles	29	21	21	20	22	22	135
Baltimore	25	21	16	15	13	4	94
Boston	27	26	17	23	22	19	134
Chicago	26	29	27	23	24	24	153
Cleveland	26	21	16	13	12	10	98
Detroit	25	22	19	17	15	12	110
Kansas City	25	22	17	16	16	15	111
Minnesota	24	23	22	20	18	16	123
New York	28	21	14	11	13	12	99
Oakland	22	22	20	14	7	5	90
Seattle	26	28	22	19	17	8	120
Tampa Bay	25	23	21	20	22	20	131
Texas	26	14	13	14	11	9	87
Toronto	27	29	25	19	20	19	139

Play Deep

Carlos Quentin hit 46 flyballs to left. Half of them left the yard.

Carlos Quentin – 2008
Hitting Analysis

Batting Right-Handed								1B	2B	3B	HR
Ground Balls to Left	99	Outs	82	Hits	17	Average	.172	Hit Type	12 -	5 -	0 -	0
Ground Balls to Center	54	Outs	32	Hits	22	Average	.407	Hit Type	22 -	0 -	0 -	0
Ground Balls to Right	14	Outs	12	Hits	2	Average	.143	Hit Type	2 -	0 -	0 -	0
Line Drives to Left	34	Outs	11	Hits	23	Average	.676	Hit Type	17 -	5 -	0 -	1
Line Drives to Center	16	Outs	0	Hits	16	Average	1.000	Hit Type	13 -	3 -	0 -	0
Line Drives to Right	12	Outs	2	Hits	10	Average	.833	Hit Type	7 -	3 -	0 -	0
Fly Balls to Left	46	Outs	21	Hits	25	Average	.543	Hit Type	0 -	2 -	0 -	23
Fly Balls to Center	61	Outs	46	Hits	15	Average	.246	Hit Type	1 -	5 -	1 -	8
Fly Balls to Right	67	Outs	59	Hits	8	Average	.125	Hit Type	1 -	3 -	0 -	4
Total on Ground Balls	167	Outs	126	Hits	41	Average	.246	Hit Type	36 -	5 -	0 -	0
Total on Line Drives	62	Outs	13	Hits	49	Average	.790	Hit Type	37 -	11 -	0 -	1
Total on Fly Balls	174	Outs	126	Hits	48	Average	.281	Hit Type	2 -	10 -	1 -	35
Total Hit to Left	179	Outs	114	Hits	65	Average	.363	Hit Type	29 -	12 -	0 -	24
Total Hit to Center	131	Outs	78	Hits	53	Average	.405	Hit Type	36 -	8 -	1 -	8
Total Hit to Right	93	Outs	73	Hits	20	Average	.222	Hit Type	10 -	6 -	0 -	4
All Balls in Play	403	Outs	265	Hits	138	Average	.345	Hit Type	75 -	26 -	1 -	36

In addition to the White Sox' success at keeping their starting pitchers healthy, they also had the highest percentage of games started by Opening Day lineup starters of any team in the majors. The White Sox' nine Opening Day starters started 1,155 games during the season, and all nine started at least 92 games.

Chicago White Sox – 2008

Pos	Player	Starts
C	Pierzynski	127
1B	Konerko	121
2B	Uribe	92
3B	Crede	95
SS	Cabrera	160
LF	Swisher	143
CF	Ramirez	125
RF	Dye	153
DH	Thome	139
Total		1155

John Danks came into his own in 2008, and one of the reasons was the addition of a cut fastball to his repertoire. It pretty much replaced his curveball, which he threw 17% of the time in 2007 but just 6% of the time in 2008.

John Danks – 2008
Pitch Type Analysis

Overall		
Total Pitches	3144	
Fastball	1629	52%
Curveball	193	6%
Changeup	626	20%
Slider	142	5%
Cut Fastball	509	16%
Not Charted	45	1%

John Danks – 2007
Pitch Type Analysis

Overall		
Total Pitches	2407	
Fastball	1429	59%
Curveball	407	17%
Changeup	492	20%
Slider	13	1%
Not Charted	66	3%

Phat Pitches

When batters swung at a Bobby Jenks pitch in 2005, they missed more than one time in four. In 2008, they missed less than one time in six:

Year	Contact Rate
2005	74.5%
2006	77.8%
2007	79.1%
2008	84.5%

Now that Greg Maddux has finally retired, Gavin Floyd can take over as the easiest pitcher to run on in the major leagues.

There were 37 bases stolen against Floyd in 2008—nine more than any other major league pitcher:

1. Gavin Floyd   37 for 42
2. Jair Jurrjens   28 for 31
3. Daniel Cabrera   27 for 31
4. Tim Wakefield   27 for 37

Every hitter who has a bad year feels, at times, like he is hitting line drives right at people. The hitter who really was hitting line drives at people last year was Paul Konerko.

The major league batting average on line drives last year was .701. Paul Konerko's average on line drives, over the last seven years, is .702. But last year Konerko hit "just" .551 on line drives—the lowest average of any major league hitter hitting 50 or more line drives.

Know When to Walk Away
Know When to Run

by Bill James

What is the value of a stolen base, to each major league team?

Not all major league teams are the same, of course; there are some teams that, with a man on first and one out, should just sit back and play for a big inning, and there are some teams who might be better off trying to steal. Since we now have data on how often each major league team scores given each base/out situation (the "24 States Analysis" in the Statistics section of Bill James Online), I thought I would look at the question of whether those teams which *should* steal bases most often, actually *do* steal bases most often.

On the two ends of the spectrum last season: the Detroit Tigers and the Chicago White Sox. The Tigers scored 1.09 runs per inning when they had a man on first and none out, and 1.22 runs per inning when they had a man on second and none out, so they apparently gained only .13 runs by a stolen base in that situation. They apparently gained even less by stealing second with one out, increasing their expected runs from .58 to .68, and gained virtually nothing by stealing with two out, increasing from .24 to .29. Overall, and assuming the three situations are equal, the Tigers appeared to gain only .091 runs by stealing second base, increasing the average of the three from .638 to .729.

The White Sox, on the other hand, appeared to have huge gains from getting the runner to second, increasing their expected runs from .80 to 1.38 with no one out, .62 to .80 with one out, and .23 to .36 with two out. One out, two out, or three out, the White Sox apparently gained far more from a stolen base than would the Tigers. Overall, again assuming the three are equal, the White Sox increased their expected runs, by stealing second, from .549 to .846, a gain of .297. The White Sox' apparent gain on a stolen base attempt was more than three times larger than the Tigers'.

I thought I would look at the question of whether those teams which should steal bases most often, actually do steal bases most often.

Then we look at the *cost* of a stolen base attempt, should the runner be thrown out. The Tigers, losing the base runner, go from
1.09 to .30 with no one out,
.58 to .12 with one out, and
.24 to zero with two out.

That's an average loss of .498 runs. The Tigers, then, have an average gain of .091 runs when they steal a base, but an average loss of almost half a run when they are caught stealing. For a stolen base attempt to pay off, then, the Tigers would need to be successful 85% of the time.

The White Sox, on the other hand, go down when the runner is caught stealing from
.80 to .34 with no one out,
.62 to .12 with one out, and
.23 to zero with two out.

An average loss of .397 runs. The White Sox, then, have a gain of .297 runs against a loss of .397 runs. The White Sox, then, could apparently profit by a stolen base attempt if the attempt was successful just 57.2% of the time.

The Real Question

The question I was trying to get to was: Do those teams which *should* run most often, by this method, *actually* run most often?

No. Not at all; the method simply does not work. It does not predict actual stolen base attempts, at all, at least with the 2008 data.

There are obvious flaws in the method. The biggest problem is that we are assuming that these measured outcomes are real numbers, that, because the Tigers *did* score 1.091 runs per inning when they had a man on first and none out, that they could *expect* to score 1.091 runs

The four teams which should have been most willing to risk a base runner in a stolen base attempt finished 25th, 27th, 28th and 30th in the majors last year in the number of stolen base attempts.

per inning when they had a man on first and none out. In reality, the season is not long enough to provide reliable data for each of the "24 States". The Tigers had 351 situations in which they had a runner on first and none out, and only 103 situations in which they had a runner on second and none out. To get a stable measurement of the actual relationship between the two, you'd have to have at least 2,000 game situations in each group.

That's the biggest problem, but there are others. I assumed that the three out situations were of equal importance, which is not *exactly* true, although it is fairly close, and I assumed that there were no other stolen base situations, which of course is not exactly true. By assuming this, we're implicitly assuming that the manager knows on opening day what his team's performance will be by the end of the season.

Still, I would have guessed, going into this study, that there would be *some* relationship between how often teams *should* attempt to steal, measured in this way, and how often they *do* attempt to steal. There is none…well, there's an inverse relationship, but there is no positive relationship. By this method, the four teams which should have been most willing to risk a base runner in a stolen base attempt were the White Sox, the Braves, the Dia-

mondbacks and the Padres, in that order. In fact, those four teams finished 25th, 27th, 28th and 30th in the majors last year in the number of stolen base attempts.

Conclusions

What do we take from this, other than the fact that our method doesn't work? What I take from it is this: the number of stolen bases you have tends to vary with how much speed you *have*, rather than with how much speed you *need*. The Padres, for example, could have benefited from stolen base attempts at a 62% rate, which is very low. But your base stealers are usually your shortstop and your outfielders. For the Padres, that was Khalil Greene, Brian Giles, Jody Gerut and Chase Headley—none of whom can run. The Padres had a major-league low 53 stolen base attempts.

Which is not necessarily a bad thing. They could have generated *some* runs by stealing bases—a few. A dozen, a couple of dozen. They missed the playoffs by approximately 250 runs. If Chase Headley develops into a hitter with a .400 on-base percentage, which he may do, that's a lot more significant for them than stealing a few bases.

What I take from it is this: the number of stolen bases you have tends to vary with how much speed you have, rather than with how much speed you need.

Wipeout

by Bill James

Last season, as was reported in the Gold Mine, the Cincinnati Reds won 24 games that were started by Aaron Harang—the most wins in the major leagues behind any one pitcher. Not all of those wins were credited to Harang, but his "individual" won-lost record was a handsome 16-6.

So the next year, Harang goes 6-17…almost a mirror reversal. He didn't pitch all that badly last season, although his ERA went up from 3.73 to 4.78 (NL average was 4.29). Still, whereas the previous year he was always in the right stadium at the right time, last year he was consistently on the wrong mound after batting practice. I got to thinking about historic wipeouts by pitchers, and how you would score them.

Suppose you multiply Harang's Wins last year (16) by his Losses this year (17); that's 272. Multiply his Losses last year (6) by his Wins this year (6); that's 36. His Wipeout Score is 36 to 272, or –236; we'll call it 236, since the minus sign is a constant. That was the highest in the majors since 2000.

And, as you know, twentieth century baseball records no longer exist, since they were all wiped out by the Millennium Bug. No, since Wipeout Scores are based on Wins and Losses and the biggest Won and Lost numbers all belong to the ancients, all of the biggest Wipeout Scores belong to 19th century pitchers. These are the biggest by decade:

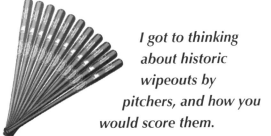

I got to thinking about historic wipeouts by pitchers, and how you would score them.

- **Will White** in 1879 was 43-31. In 1880 he was 18-42—a Wipeout Score of 298.
- **Charlie Buffinton** in 1885 dropped from 48-16 to 22-27—a Wipeout Score of 944, the largest of all time.
- **Silver King** in 1891 dropped from 30-22 to 14-29; there's a league change involved, but I don't want to get into it. Wipeout Score of 562.
- **Long Tom Hughes** was 20-7 with the World Champion Red Sox in 1903. Jumping to the Highlanders that winter, he dropped to 9-24 in 1904—a Wipeout Score of 417.

- **Jack Quinn**, 26-14 in 1914, dropped to 9-22 in 1915, a Wipeout Score of 446. He was out of the majors in twenty years.
- **Joe Oeschger** was a 20-game winner in 1921 (20-14), the year after he engaged in the famous 26-inning duel with Leon Cadore. But the year after that he was 6-21, a Wipeout Score of 336. He never won more than 5 games again.
- **Lefty Gomez** in 1934 dropped from 26-5 to 12-15 (Wipeout Score of 330).
- **Bobo Newsom** in 1941 dropped from 21-5 to 12-20 (Wipeout Score of 360). There is no truth to the rumor that Bobo had reported seeing a lemur after the 1940 World Series.
- **Bob Friend** in 1958 went 22-14; in 1959 he dropped to 8-19. He probably pitched as well in 1959 as he had in 1958, but his Wipeout Score (306) was still the highest of the decade.
- **Dick Ellsworth** followed a stellar 22-10 campaign with the Cubs in 1963 with a 14-18 stinker in 1964 (Wipeout Score of 256). His teammate that second season, Larry Jackson, picked up the slack, going 24-11—but then won the wipeout trophy for the entire sixties with a 14-21 mark in '65 (Wipeout Score of 350). The Cubs two "wipeout aces" in '65 were Jackson (14-21) and Ellsworth (14-15).
- I have written about this season numerous times before, so won't again, but **Steve Carlton** underwent a severe personality transplant after falling from 27-10 in 1972—a year in which he was certainly one of the greatest pitchers who ever lived—to 13-20 in 1973. His Wipeout Score (410) is the highest in the majors since 1920.

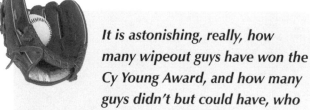

It is astonishing, really, how many wipeout guys have won the Cy Young Award, and how many guys didn't but could have, who have just totally wet the bed (thank you, Kobe) the next season.

- **Frank Viola** was Cy Young in 1988, going 24-7; the next year he was 13-17, a Wipeout Score of 317.
- **Bob Welch** in 1990 was 27-6, although anybody who was paying close attention knew that he wasn't really *that* good. The next year he was 12-13—a Wipeout Score of 279.
- **Jamie Moyer**, 21-7 in 2003, was 7-13 in 2004—the biggest Wipeout Score (224) of our new century. Until Aaron Harang.

A not-very-interesting list, but I had to run it. To be eligible for the list a pitcher has to have a losing record the second year, a winning record the first.

It is astonishing, really, how many wipeout guys have won the Cy Young Award, and how many guys didn't but could have, who have just totally wet the bed (thank you, Kobe) the next season. The 1962 Reds had Bob Purkey (23-5) and Joey Jay (21-14). The next year they went 6-10 and 7-18—and yet the '63 Reds, remarkably, won 86 games and hung in the pennant race into September. Bob Turley, Vern Law, Denny McLain, Pete Vuckovich, Mike McCormick and Mark Davis all did terrible pratfalls after a Cy Young season—Randy Johnson, too, but in Randy's case it was after a long string of Cy Young seasons. That's more like Warren Spahn in '64 or Juan Marichal in '72 than an actual wipeout. Even a Hall of Fame run has to run out of gas sometime.

Johnny Antonelli wiped out three times. After being perhaps the best pitcher in baseball in 1954 (21-7, 2.29 ERA) he was under .500 in 1955 (14-16). After recovering to go 20-13 in 1956 he dropped 18 games in 1957 (12-18). After going 19-10 in 1959, he dropped to 6-7 in 1960—effectively ending his career. A similar career was Bret Saberhagen, who wiped out twice after Cy Young Awards, following a 20-6 season (1985) with 7-12, and 23-6 (1989) with 5-9. Between those two he did one of the greatest mid-season wipeouts of all time. At the All-Star break in '87 he was 15-3 with a 2.49 ERA. The second half he was 3-7 with a 4.61 ERA.

The little lefthander Bobby Shantz won the American League MVP Award with the Philadelphia A's in 1952, going 24-7. The next year he was 5-9. The bigger lefthander

Vida Blue won the American League MVP with the same franchise in 1971 (two stops later), going an almost-identical 24-8. The next season, after a nasty salary battle, he was an almost-identical 6-10.

Jim Lonborg, Cy Young winner and World Series hero with a 22-9 mark in 1967, wiped out literally that winter—skiing accident—and finished 6-10 in '68, the same as Vida Blue in '72.

Don Newcombe, winner of the first Cy Young Award after going 27-7 in 1956, got rocked in the World Series (ERA of 21.21), started drinking heavily that winter, and was 11-12 in '57.

Sammy Ellis in 1965 went 22-10, perhaps pitching more innings than he was really prepared by training and experience to pitch. The next year he was 12-19, and he never had another winning season. A very similar season was by Ron Bryant in 1973—24-12, although he pitched no shutouts, walked 115, struck out only 143 and had an unimpressive 3.53 ERA. The next year things caught up with him, and he finished an ugly 3-15. He never won a *game* after that season. Ellis at least won some more games; Bryant never tasted victory again.

The same year Steve Carlton went from 27-10 to 13-20, Stan Bahnsen also followed a 20-win season with a 20-loss season, although he had to pitch a billion innings to do it, 21-16 to 18-21. Back in the old days, when pitchers would win 20 games with some regularity, a good many pitchers followed 20-win seasons with 20-loss seasons, among them:

- Roscoe Miller in 1902 (23-13 to 7-20),
- Togie Pittinger in 1903 (27-16 to 18-22),
- Long Tom Hughes in 1904 (listed above),
- Al Orth in 1907 (27-17 to 14-21),
- Russ Ford in 1912 (22-11 to 13-21),
- Howie Camnitz in 1913 (22-12 to 9-20),
- Rube Marquard in 1914 (23-10 to 12-22),
- Jack Quinn in 1915 (listed above),
- Eppa Rixey in 1917 (22-10 to 16-21),
- Hooks Dauss in 1920 (21-9 to 13-21),
- Joe Oeschger in 1922 (listed above),
- Bobo Newsom in 1941 (listed above),
- Murry Dickson in 1952 (20-16 to 14-21),
- Mel Stottlemyre in 1966 (20-9 to 12-20),
- Larry Jackson in 1965 (listed above)
- Luis Tiant in 1969 (21-9, 9-20),
- Steve Carlton in 1973 (listed above),
- Stan Bahnsen in 1973 (listed above),
- Wilbur Wood in 1975 (20-19 to 16-20),
- Jerry Koosman (21-10 in 1976, 8-20 in 1977).

And I probably missed some…I was kind of looking for these scatter-shot. Alex Kellner, 20-12 as a rookie in 1949, was 8-20 in 1950. Eight-and-twenty appears to be the favorite record for good pitchers having lousy years.

Noodles Hahn in 1900 dropped from 23-8 to 16-

20—in part because the consolidation of the National League, with four teams dropping out and the best players concentrated on just eight teams, was a lot tougher in 1900 than it was in 1899.

George McConnell, 25-10 in the Federal League in 1915, pitched in the same park in 1916, but with a different team in a different league, and with much different results: 4-12 with the Cubs.

Steve Gromek went 19-9 in 1945—dropped to 5-15 in 1946, when Ted Williams and friends returned from military service.

You see, the thing is that we're always looking for cause and effect, so we always wind up *seeing* cause and effect, whether it is there or not. Steve Gromek goes 19-9 during World War II, then goes 5-15 after the war is over, so it's easy for us to say that he was never really very good, it was just the war years, all the good players were toting firearms. It's easy for us to say that Noodles Hahn dropped off because the league consolidated its talent and George McConnell dropped off because he was facing better hitters and Bobo Newsom dropped off because he saw a lemur, but the reality is that the same sorts of things happen every year, whether there is a war ending or not. The human mind is damned to see cause and effect in everything that happens. This is why we can never understand the world.

Chief Bender, 17-3 with the American League champion Philadelphia A's in 1914, jumped to the Federal League in 1915 and was 4-16—a whopping 650-point drop in winning percentage, while going from the "strong" league to the startup league.

Art Houtteman, just 22 years old when he went 19-12 in 1950, missed 1951 due to military obligations—and lost 20 games when he returned in 1952 (our old friend, 8-20).

Jim Merritt, after going 20-12 in 1970, was 1-11 in 1971, leading the Reds in a plunge from 102 wins to sub-.500.

Wayne Garland signed a ten-year contract with the Indians after he went 20-7 in 1976. He went 13-19 in '77, and never won more than six games again.

Kevin Tapani, 19-9 with the Cubs in 1998, was 6-12 in '99.

Jose Lima, 21-10 in 1999, celebrated the new millenium with a 7-16 log.

Omar (You Beautiful) Daal dropped that same season from 16-9 to 4-19.

These are not historic wipeouts, but they're recent, and I figure Aaron Harang might relate to them. And I thought perhaps he could use the company.

The human mind is damned to see cause and effect in everything that happens. This is why we can never understand the world.

Cincinnati Reds

Cincinnati Reds – 2008
Team Overview

Description		Ranking
Won-Lost Record	74-88	
Place	5th of 6 in National League Central	
Runs Scored	704	22nd in the majors
Runs Allowed	800	22nd in the majors
Home Runs	187	7th in the majors
Home Runs Allowed	201	22nd in the majors
Batting Average	.247	29th in the majors
Batting Average Allowed	.275	24th in the majors
Walks Drawn	560	13th in the majors
Walks Given	557	16th in the majors
OPS For	.729	23rd in the majors
OPS Against	.796	26th in the majors
Stolen Bases	85	15th in the majors
Stolen Bases Allowed	95	14th in the majors

Key Players

Pos	Player	G	AB	R	H	2B	3B	HR	RBI	SB	CS	BB	SO	Avg	OBP	Slg	OPS	WS
C	Paul Bako	99	299	30	65	11	2	6	35	0	2	34	90	.217	.299	.328	.626	7
1B	Joey Votto	151	526	69	156	32	3	24	84	7	5	59	102	.297	.368	.506	.874	19
2B	Brandon Phillips	141	559	80	146	24	7	21	78	23	10	39	93	.261	.312	.442	.754	19
3B	Edwin Encarnacion	146	506	75	127	29	1	26	68	1	0	61	102	.251	.340	.466	.807	14
SS	Jeff Keppinger	121	459	45	122	24	2	3	43	3	1	30	24	.266	.310	.346	.657	10
LF	Adam Dunn	114	373	58	87	14	0	32	74	1	1	80	120	.233	.373	.528	.901	15
CF	Corey Patterson	135	366	46	75	17	2	10	34	14	9	16	57	.205	.238	.344	.582	2
RF	Ken Griffey Jr.	102	359	51	88	20	1	15	53	0	1	61	64	.245	.355	.432	.787	11

Key Pitchers

Pos	Player	G	GS	W	L	Sv	IP	H	R	ER	SO	BB	BR/9	ERA	WS
SP	Edinson Volquez	33	32	17	6	0	196.0	167	82	70	206	93	12.58	3.21	16
SP	Bronson Arroyo	34	34	15	11	0	200.0	219	116	106	163	68	13.19	4.77	10
SP	Johnny Cueto	31	31	9	14	0	174.0	178	101	93	158	68	13.45	4.81	6
SP	Aaron Harang	30	29	6	17	0	184.1	205	104	98	153	50	12.55	4.78	6
SP	Josh Fogg	22	14	2	7	0	78.1	97	69	66	45	27	14.94	7.58	0
CL	Francisco Cordero	72	0	5	4	34	70.1	61	28	26	78	38	13.05	3.33	11
RP	Jeremy Affeldt	74	0	1	1	0	78.1	78	36	29	80	25	12.18	3.33	6
RP	David Weathers	72	0	4	6	0	69.1	76	27	25	46	30	14.15	3.25	6

The Cincinnati Reds in 2008 were 11-65 (.145 percentage) when their starting pitcher posted a Game Score under 50. Nobody wins regularly without a good performance by the starter—but the Reds were the worst.

Cincinnati Reds – 2008
Performance by Quality of Start

Game Score	#	ERA	W -	L
80 and above	1	2.00	1 -	0
70 to 79	15	1.07	14 -	1
60 to 69	29	2.69	19 -	10
50 to 59	41	2.83	29 -	12
40 to 49	25	5.53	6 -	19
30 to 39	22	6.86	4 -	18
20 to 29	18	7.11	1 -	17
Below 20	11	10.34	0 -	11

Slow Starters

The Cincinnati Reds in 2008 were 28 games under .500 by the end of the second inning—ahead 44 times, behind 72 times.

The Atlanta Braves, on the other hand, were over .500 after two innings—ahead 56 times, behind 54.

By the end of the game the Reds were up to 74-88, while the Braves were down to 72-90.

Cincinnati Reds – 2008
Innings Ahead Behind Tied

Inning	1	2	3	4	5	6	7	8	9	Extra	Final
Ahead	35	44	44	48	51	57	59	63	65	9	74
Behind	48	72	77	81	85	83	83	84	80	8	88
Tied	79	46	41	33	26	22	20	15	17	14	—

Atlanta Braves – 2008
Innings Ahead Behind Tied

Inning	1	2	3	4	5	6	7	8	9	Extra	Final
Ahead	36	56	64	65	66	73	69	68	69	3	72
Behind	42	54	71	74	80	73	75	79	80	10	90
Tied	84	52	27	23	16	16	18	15	13	17	—

Edwin Encarnacion was the most extreme pull hitter in the majors last year. Nearly 54% of his batted balls were pulled to left field and he managed to nudge only two line drives to the opposite field. It's an extreme approach, but it generally worked. He batted 260 points higher on pulled balls than on balls to the opposite field.

Edwin Encarnacion – 2008
Hitting Analysis

Batting Right-Handed								1B		2B		3B		HR
Ground Balls to Left	96	Outs	71	Hits	25	Average	.260	Hit Type	19 -	6	- 0	-	0
Ground Balls to Center	36	Outs	28	Hits	8	Average	.222	Hit Type	8 -	0	- 0	-	0
Ground Balls to Right	9	Outs	7	Hits	2	Average	.222	Hit Type	2 -	0	- 0	-	0
Line Drives to Left	42	Outs	10	Hits	32	Average	.762	Hit Type	15 -	16	- 0	-	1
Line Drives to Center	21	Outs	7	Hits	14	Average	.700	Hit Type	13 -	1	- 0	-	0
Line Drives to Right	2	Outs	1	Hits	1	Average	.500	Hit Type	1 -	0	- 0	-	0
Fly Balls to Left	81	Outs	54	Hits	27	Average	.342	Hit Type	2 -	3	- 0	-	22
Fly Balls to Center	62	Outs	50	Hits	12	Average	.200	Hit Type	6 -	2	- 1	-	3
Fly Balls to Right	60	Outs	54	Hits	6	Average	.100	Hit Type	5 -	1	- 0	-	0
Total on Ground Balls	141	Outs	106	Hits	35	Average	.248	Hit Type	29 -	6	- 0	-	0
Total on Line Drives	65	Outs	18	Hits	47	Average	.734	Hit Type	29 -	17	- 0	-	1
Total on Fly Balls	203	Outs	158	Hits	45	Average	.226	Hit Type	13 -	6	- 1	-	25
Total Hit to Left	219	Outs	135	Hits	84	Average	.387	Hit Type	36 -	25	- 0	-	23
Total Hit to Center	119	Outs	85	Hits	34	Average	.293	Hit Type	27 -	3	- 1	-	3
Total Hit to Right	71	Outs	62	Hits	9	Average	.127	Hit Type	8 -	1	- 0	-	0
All Balls in Play	409	Outs	282	Hits	127	Average	.314	Hit Type	71 -	29	- 1	-	26

Edinson Volquez – 2008
Pitch Type Analysis

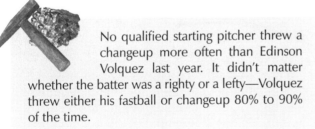

No qualified starting pitcher threw a changeup more often than Edinson Volquez last year. It didn't matter whether the batter was a righty or a lefty—Volquez threw either his fastball or changeup 80% to 90% of the time.

Overall		
Total Pitches	3386	
Fastball	1849	55%
Curveball	304	9%
Changeup	1065	31%
Slider	120	4%
Pitchout	6	0%
Not Charted	42	1%

	Vs. RHB		Vs. LHB	
Total Pitches	1682		1704	
Outs Recorded	293		295	
Fastball	916	54%	933	55%
Curveball	130	8%	174	10%
Changeup	510	30%	555	33%
Slider	98	6%	22	1%
Pitchout	4	0%	2	0%
Not Charted	24	1%	18	1%

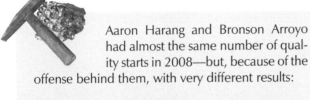

Aaron Harang and Bronson Arroyo had almost the same number of quality starts in 2008—but, because of the offense behind them, with very different results:

	Won-Lost	
Harang	4 - 8	No Decision—5
Arroyo	14 - 1	No Decision—3

Adam Dunn scored more runs on his home runs (40) than on hits by his team-mates (39). Dunn and Mike Napoli were the only major leaguers to accomplish this feat (minimum of 20 runs scored) in 2008.

Adam Dunn – 2008
Runs Scored Analysis

Reached on		Runs Scored After	
Home Runs	40		40
Doubles	23	Scored after Double	6
Singles	59	Scored after Single	14
Walk/HBP	129	Scored after Walk/HBP	17
Reached on Error	2	Scored after ROE	1
Reached on Forceout	8	Vultured Runs	1
		Total Runs Scored	79
Brought in by		**Driven in by**	
Single	10	Himself	40
Double	8	Joey Votto	11
Triple	2	Mark Reynolds	7
His own home run	40	Edwin Encarnacion	6
Other home run	8	Miguel Montero	2
Sac Fly	6	Paul Bako	2
Walk, Error, or Other	5	Scott Hatteberg	2
		Tony Clark	1
		Aaron Harang	1
		Andy Phillips	1
		Brandon Phillips	1
		Chris Burke	1
		Chris Snyder	1
		Corey Patterson	1
		Jamie D'Antona	1
		Jeff Keppinger	1

Hopper Redux

Jerry Hairston led off 106 innings in 2008, batting leadoff in 44 games. In those 106 innings the Reds scored 82 runs, which is basically 7 runs a game. The only major league player with a higher average was the Rangers' David Murphy.

Jerry Hairston – 2008
Performance as Leadoff Man

Innings Led Off:	106		
Team Scored:	82	Runs	.77 per inning
Reached Base Leading Off:	45		
Team Scored:	58	Runs	1.29 per inning
Did Not Reach:	61		
Team Scored:	24	Runs	.39 per inning
Other Innings for Team:	1351		
Team Scored:	622	Runs	.46 per inning

Pesky Wabbits

Norris Hopper as a fourth outfielder for the Reds in 2007 had a remarkable year, hitting .329 with a .371 on base percentage and 14 stolen bases. Last year Hopper was hurt, and his place was taken by Jerry Hairston—who had a similar but even better season, hitting .326 with a .384 on base percentage and 15 stolen bases. They were basically the same player except that Hairston can also play the infield and hit for more power.

The thing is, neither Hopper nor Hare-ston is really that good—or, at least, nobody believes they are. Hopper is a knockaround guy who is 30, is never expected to be a regular; Hairston is 33 and is never going to be a regular. But the Reds really got some great mileage out of them:

Player, Year	G	AB	R	H	2B	3B	HR	RBI	BB	SO	SB	Avg	OBA	Slg
Hopper, 2007	121	307	51	101	14	2	0	14	20	33	14	.329	.371	.388
Hairston, 2008	80	261	47	85	20	2	6	36	23	36	15	.326	.384	.487

After batting .206 and .189 the last two years, Jerry Hairston batted .326 for the Reds last year in 261 at-bats. Two things stand out:

- 27.5% of the pitches he hit were line drives (in 2006, it was 17%; in 2007, it was 14%). Hairston led the majors with that figure.
- He hit .329 on groundballs (compared to .214 in 2006 and .217 in 2007). The major league leader was Rickie Weeks at .345.

Micah Owings in college was an outstanding pitcher, and also an outstanding Designated Hitter. When he was drafted the decision was made to put him on the mound, which was predictable because major league teams need a whole lot more pitchers than they do DHs.

But I'm thinking, from his professional standpoint, he might want to reconsider this. Owings hit over .300 again last year (17 for 56) with three doubles and a homer. His major league career average is now .319 (37 for 116) with a .552 slugging percentage. And you know, this pitching thing really isn't going all that well for him, is it? He's 14-17 with an ERA of 4.97.

George Brett had a brother, Ken Brett, who was always a better hitter, growing up, than George was. One time in the majors he homered in four straight starts. He was a pretty good pitcher when he was 100% healthy, which wasn't very often, and when he got to be about 30 they asked him, if he had it to do over again, would he maybe be an outfielder, rather than a pitcher?

"Absolutely", Brett replied. "It's too late now, but I know now that's what I should have done."

Cleveland Indians

Cleveland Indians – 2008
Team Overview

Description		Ranking
Won-Lost Record	81-81	
Place	3rd of 5 in American League Central	
Runs Scored	805	7th in the majors
Runs Allowed	761	17th in the majors
Home Runs	171	13th in the majors
Home Runs Allowed	170	14th in the majors
Batting Average	.262	19th in the majors
Batting Average Allowed	.273	21st in the majors
Walks Drawn	560	13th in the majors
Walks Given	444	2nd in the majors
OPS For	.763	9th in the majors
OPS Against	.754	17th in the majors
Stolen Bases	77	19th in the majors
Stolen Bases Allowed	67	4th in the majors

Key Players

Pos	Player	G	AB	R	H	2B	3B	HR	RBI	SB	CS	BB	SO	Avg	OBP	Slg	OPS	WS
C	Kelly Shoppach	112	352	67	92	27	0	21	55	0	0	36	133	.261	.348	.517	.865	14
1B	Ryan Garko	141	495	61	135	21	1	14	90	0	0	45	86	.273	.346	.404	.750	15
2B	Asdrubal Cabrera	114	352	48	91	20	0	6	47	4	4	46	77	.259	.346	.366	.713	12
3B	Casey Blake	94	325	46	94	24	0	11	58	2	0	33	68	.289	.365	.465	.830	14
SS	Jhonny Peralta	154	605	104	167	42	4	23	89	3	1	48	126	.276	.331	.473	.804	19
LF	Ben Francisco	121	447	65	119	32	0	15	54	4	3	40	86	.266	.332	.438	.770	9
CF	Grady Sizemore	157	634	101	170	39	5	33	90	38	5	98	130	.268	.374	.502	.876	26
RF	Franklin Gutierrez	134	399	54	99	26	2	8	41	9	3	27	87	.248	.307	.383	.691	5
DH	David Dellucci	113	336	41	80	19	2	11	47	3	2	24	76	.238	.307	.405	.711	5

Key Pitchers

Pos	Player	G	GS	W	L	Sv	IP	H	R	ER	SO	BB	BR/9	ERA	WS
SP	Cliff Lee	31	31	22	3	0	223.1	214	68	63	170	34	10.20	2.54	24
SP	Fausto Carmona	22	22	8	7	0	120.2	126	80	73	58	70	15.29	5.44	3
SP	Paul Byrd	22	22	7	10	0	131.0	146	70	66	56	24	12.02	4.53	6
SP	Jeremy Sowers	22	22	4	9	0	121.0	141	84	75	64	39	13.61	5.58	2
SP	CC Sabathia	18	18	6	8	0	122.1	117	54	52	123	34	11.33	3.83	8
CL	Jensen Lewis	51	0	0	4	13	66.0	68	29	28	52	27	13.64	3.82	6
RP	Rafael Perez	73	0	4	4	2	76.1	67	32	30	86	23	10.85	3.54	8
RP	Rafael Betancourt	69	0	3	4	4	71.0	76	41	40	64	25	12.80	5.07	3

By most accounts, the Cleveland bullpen was the league's worst last year. Their totals of 31 Saves and 51 Holds were both low figures in the AL and their bullpen ERA (5.13) was only slightly better than the worst in the majors (5.15, the Rangers).

In looking at relievers with at least 15 relief appearances, only two of them, Rafael Perez and Lewis Jensen, had ERA's under 4.50.

Cleveland Indians – 2008

Player	Pos	T	Rel G	Clean	BS Win	Saves	Opps	Holds	Sv/Hold Pct	OPS	ERA
						Relief Results					
Borowski,Joe	CL	R	18	12	1	6	10	0	.60	.978	7.56
Perez,Rafael	SU	L	73	45	1	2	7	25	.84	.649	3.54
Betancourt,Rafael	LM	R	69	40	1	4	8	12	.80	.789	5.07
Lewis,Jensen	LM	R	51	29	0	13	14	4	.94	.771	3.82
Rincon,Juan	LM	R	47	21	0	0	0	3	1.00	.831	5.86
Mujica,Edward	LM	R	33	20	1	0	2	1	.33	.849	6.75
Kobayashi,Masa	UR	R	57	33	0	6	9	2	.73	.757	4.53
Donnelly,Brendan	UR	R	15	10	0	0	0	4	1.00	.941	8.56

(Table includes only pitchers with at least 15 relief games.)

CL—Closer
SU—Set Up Reliever
LM—Long Man
UR—Utility Reliever

Another indictment of the Cleveland bullpen: The Indians were leading their opponents 83 times in the fifth inning of their games, which was the best fifth-inning record in the American League last year and third best in the majors. They finished 81-81—no other team finished the season with less total wins than fifth-inning leads.

Cleveland Indians – 2008
Innings Ahead Behind Tied

Inning	1	2	3	4	5	6	7	8	9	Extra	Final
Ahead	45	64	66	75	83	82	76	77	76	5	81
Behind	32	43	53	55	62	63	65	68	72	9	81
Tied	85	55	43	32	17	17	21	17	14	8	—

Which batting order position is mostly likely to lead their team in RBI?

4th – 14.5 teams were led in RBI by their clean-up hitter
3rd – 10
5th – 4.5 (tie in Florida)
6th – 1 – Cleveland with 106 RBI, filled most frequently by Garko, Shoppach, and Blake

Asdrubal Cabrera reached base leading off an inning 27 times in 2008, and the Indians scored 43 runs in those innings—the highest production rate in the majors in that situation.

Asdrubal Cabrera – 2008
Performance as Leadoff Man

Innings Led Off:	82		
Team Scored:	63	Runs	.77 per inning
Reached Base Leading Off:	27		
Team Scored:	43	Runs	1.59 per inning
Did Not Reach:	55		
Team Scored:	20	Runs	.36 per inning
Other Innings for Team:	1357		
Team Scored:	742	Runs	.55 per inning

A "Houdini" is credited to any pitcher who:

a) finds himself in a bases-loaded, no-out jam,
b) gets out of it

Six times last year, Indians opponents performed a Houdini. Cleveland had the bases loaded with no outs and failed to score a run. That level of failed promise led the majors—the Rockies and the Giants each did it five times. To add insult to injury, Casey Fossum pulled it off against the Indians twice in the same month.

Player	Date	Inning	Team
Ryan Rowland-Smith	30-Apr	Bot 8	Sea
Joe Blanton	14-May	Bot 5	Oak
Casey Fossum	9-Jul	Top 5	Det
Casey Fossum	30-Jul	Bot 12	Det
Darren Oliver	16-Aug	Bot 7	LAA
Dennys Reyes	15-Sep	Bot 8	Min

There were 41 players who had five hits in a game in 2008, but only one who did it twice. Jhonny Peralta had three doubles, a single and a homer against the White Sox on June 30, and two doubles, two singles and a bomb against Tampa Bay on August 6.
And the Indians lost both games.

Jhonny Peralta – 2008
Games with X Hits

	G	AB	R	H	2B	3B	HR	RBI	Avg
0 Hits	48	173	10	0	0	0	0	6	.000
1 Hits	58	229	37	58	9	1	10	38	.253
2 Hits	39	160	40	78	24	2	8	35	.488
3 Hits	7	33	12	21	4	1	3	5	.636
5 Hits	2	10	5	10	5	0	2	5	1.000

Grady Sizemore had another great year, but he's also developed a weakness: groundballs. Sizemore has become extremely pull-conscious with his grounders, and it appears that defenses have wised up. His batting average on pulled grounders dropped to .172 last year, perhaps because defenses beginning to shift in that direction.

Year	GB% to Left	BA on GBs to Right
2005	19%	.203
2006	8%	.224
2007	8%	.202
2008	5%	.172

At the age of 29, Cliff Lee had a season unlike anything he had done before at the major league level. To put it in perspective, batters posted an OPS of only .633 against Lee last year, compared to a career OPS allowed of .761 before 2008. That .130 decrease is about the same amount that Andruw Jones' performance plummeted in 2007; after accruing a career OPS of .850 through 2006, Jones' OPS in 2007 was .724.

Cliff Lee – 2002-2008
Record of Opposing Batters

Season	AB	R	H	2B	3B	HR	RBI	BB	SO	SB	CS	GIDP	Avg	OBP	Slg	OPS
2002	35	2	6	1	0	0	1	8	6	2	1	0	.171	.326	.200	.526
2003	186	28	41	5	1	7	24	20	44	4	2	7	.220	.301	.371	.672
2004	702	113	188	43	4	30	103	81	161	9	5	10	.268	.350	.469	.819
2005	774	91	194	46	3	22	84	52	143	7	4	10	.251	.295	.403	.698
2006	807	114	224	47	1	29	101	58	129	7	2	14	.278	.330	.446	.776
2007	395	73	112	28	1	17	66	36	66	4	1	7	.284	.352	.489	.841
2008	847	68	214	33	6	12	66	34	170	3	0	27	.253	.285	.348	.633

There were six major league players last year who had more than 638 at bats. These six players averaged 663 at bats, and 74 strikeouts.

Kelly Shoppach has 638 major league at bats, and he has struck out 241 times. Shoppach strikes out, then, with a frequency that would normally preclude his being an effective major league hitter—and yet he has been. Why?

Great results on his flyballs. A very high percentage of his flyballs have been home runs—21% in 2008—

and, of those which aren't home runs, an unusual percentage so far have fallen in for doubles. Shoppach hit .436 last year on his flyballs (41 for 95)—the highest average of any major league player hitting more than 30 flies.

Is this ultimately sustainable? Well, Shoppach is a good defensive catcher. He had a .517 slugging percentage last year. He doesn't have to have a .517 slugging percentage every year to keep his job. If he hits .240 with a .450 slugging, he's probably going to keep his job.

Franklin Gutierrez led all major league right fielders in defensive plus/minus ratings for the second straight season. He accomplished this despite playing just 53% of the Indians' innings in right field in 2008, and 40% in 2007.

Franklin Gutierrez – 2008
Leaderboard, Right Field

Player	+/-
Franklin Gutierrez	+29
Brian Giles	+22
Randy Winn	+16
Alex Rios	+16
Ichiro Suzuki	+13
Denard Span	+12
Nick Markakis	+11
Elijah Dukes	+11
Endy Chavez	+11
David Murphy	+11

Franklin Gutierrez
Right Field Plus/Minus Data

			THROWING					PLAYS		PLUS/MINUS		
Year	Team	Inn	Opps To Advance	Extra Bases	Kills	Pct	Rank	Expected Outs	Outs Made	Total	Enhanced	Rank
2006	Cle	212	33	18	1	.545		47	50	+3	+6	0
2007	Cle	578.2	63	36	1	.571	28	128	136	+8	+20	1
2008	Cle	763.2	91	35	3	.385	8	208	224	+16	+29	1

Anthony Reyes was a breath of fresh air for a beleaguered Cleveland pitching staff at the end of last year, but Indian fans shouldn't get too excited. Although he posted an outstanding ERA (1.83) in just 34 innings, his strikeout rate was very low (more than two strikeouts a game lower than in limited St. Louis time) and his walk rate was over one walk a game higher.

If those rates are any indication of how he'll perform in the American League next year, his ERA will be much, much higher.

	STL	CLE
IP	14.7	34.3
ERA	4.91	1.83
K/G	6.4	4.1
BB/G	1.9	3.3

Gold Glove Sluggers

by Bill James

I got a question recently about whether the tendency of the Gold Glove voters to award the Gold Glove to guys who are big names because they are big hitters has gotten worse in recent years. I suppose the first thing I should say in response to this is that the Gold Glove voting system has never been a good one.

I generally defend the Gold Glove voting, because

a) I have always thought it was useful to have an actual record of the subjective judgments of the time, even when those subjective judgments are whacko, and

b) some people overstate how bad the voting is.

The Gold Glove selections aren't systematically bad, but they are spotty. It is an extremely bad voting system that leads frequently to poor selections, and leads sometimes to absolutely ridiculous voting selections. It always has:

The Gold Glove selections aren't systematically bad, but they are spotty.

- In 1958, an American League Gold Glove in the outfield went to Norm Siebern, who was with the Yankees and hit .300, but who was not a good outfielder. Siebern embarrassed the then-new award by making a costly mistake in the outfield in the third game of the '58 World Series, then making two costly mistakes in the fourth game, quickly becoming notorious for his defense. He spent almost all of the rest of his career as a first baseman.

- From 1962 to 1977, Jim Kaat won a Gold Glove every year whether he deserved it or not. Kaat was a wonderful fielder, a big guy who was nonetheless extremely quick and quite graceful—but *some* of his Gold Glove selections are absurd. In 1965 he led American League pitchers in errors, with 6, fielding .929 (which actually was up a point from 1964, when he had fielded .928)—but won the Gold Glove anyway. In 1969 he led all major league pitchers in errors with 8, fielding .826 (!), but won the Gold Glove anyway. In 1972 he missed over half the season with an injury, fielded .923—and won the Gold Glove anyway. In 1977 he fielded .897—but won the Gold Glove anyway.

- In 1975 Joe Rudi won a Gold Glove in the outfield although he had played only 44 games in the outfield, having played first base most of the year (91 games at first.)

- In 1999 Rafael Palmeiro won the Gold Glove at first base although he had been a DH most of the season, playing just 28 games at first.

These kinds of Gold Glove selections are beyond defense; they are simply and obviously wrong. Usually the poor selections—like those this year of Michael Young of the Rangers and Nate McLouth of the Pirates—are less definitively wrong.

Until the last few years our ways of measuring defense were (1) not very reliable and (2) not widely circulated. John Dewan and his *Fielding Bible* and other new research on defense have changed all that for good. It may be that the Gold Glove awards are no worse than ever, but that they *appear* worse because the public knows much more now, and is less accepting of awards being given to less-qualified players.

The essential problem with the Gold Glove vote is that it is an "unconstrained plurality" with few parameters. An unconstrained plurality is always at risk of delivering an irrational result, because in certain circumstances it allows fifteen or twenty percent of the voters to determine the outcome. The Gold Glove voting system is founded on two principles:

1) If we get the right people to vote, the system will work.

2) The right people to vote on this award are the coaches and managers.

Both of these principles are nonsense. Coaches and managers *don't* necessarily know who is a good fielder and who isn't. Some do and some don't, but it isn't essential to their job to know that. And many of them don't take the vote seriously, in the sense that they don't do anything to prepare for the vote. Most importantly, the idea that if you get the right people to vote, the system will work is childish nonsense, ignorant of history.

That's not to say that the Gold Glove system always fails. It gets a reasonable result 80, 85% of the time. The problem is that the system *can* fail horribly, so it does sometimes. There's no second tier to the vote; there's no preliminary screening or meaningful eligibility criteria, no review. It's just…we vote, we announce the winners. Even if it's Nate McLouth or Rafael Palmeiro.

Anyway, the question before the house is whether the tendency to select the best hitters as the Gold Glove winners has gotten worse over time. The answer is that it has not. The Gold Glove winners have always been generally very good hitters; in fact, there has never been a year in which the Gold Glove winners were not, in general, above-average hitters.

I studied the issue in this way. First, I took from each season the players with the most plate appearances, up to a number equivalent to ten times the number of teams in the majors—that is, 160 players from 1957-1960, 180 in 1961, 200 from 1962-1968, 240 from 1969-1976, 260 from 1977-1992, 280 from 1993-1997, and 300 from 1998 to the present. It works out loosely to "everybody with 250 or more plate appearances". The most plate appearances by any player excluded from the study was 276, by Johnny Edwards in 1973, and the fewest plate appearances by any player who was included in the study, other than the 1981 and 1994 strike-shortened seasons, was 230, by several different players (there are several different years in which the cutoff ends at 230; in the strike years the cutoff goes as low as 164).

Anyway, we have ten players per team per season…not ten players from each and every team, but ten on average in every year. The regulars. I then sorted these players by OPS, and coded the top 10% as a "10" Offensive Performance Group, the next 10% as "9", the next 10% as "8", etc. I then looked at the scores of the Gold Glove winners (ignoring the pitchers, of course.)

That may sound easy, but remember: I'm not a programmer. It took me about ten hours. Anyway, the one season in which the Gold Glove winners were the best hitters, relative to norms, was…well, actually, there were two seasons: 1967 and 1984. These are the Gold Glove Teams for those two seasons:

Pos	Player	YEAR	HR	RBI	Avg	OPS	Perf Gp
AL C	Bill Freehan	1967	20	74	.282	.835	10
AL 1B	George Scott	1967	19	82	.303	.839	10
AL 2B	Bobby Knoop	1967	9	38	.245	.657	4
AL 3B	Brooks Robinson	1967	22	77	.269	.763	8
AL SS	Jim Fregosi	1967	9	56	.290	.744	8
AL OF	Carl Yastrzemski	1967	44	121	.326	1.040	10
AL OF	Paul Blair	1967	11	64	.293	.799	9
AL OF	Al Kaline	1967	25	78	.308	.952	10
NL C	Randy Hundley	1967	14	60	.267	.725	7
NL 1B	Wes Parker	1967	5	31	.247	.704	6
NL 2B	Bill Mazeroski	1967	9	77	.261	.644	4
NL 3B	Ron Santo	1967	31	98	.300	.906	10
NL SS	Gene Alley	1967	6	55	.287	.728	7
NL OF	Willie Mays	1967	22	70	.263	.787	9
NL OF	Curt Flood	1967	5	50	.335	.793	9
NL OF	Roberto Clemente	1967	23	110	.357	.954	10

Pos	Player	YEAR	HR	RBI	Avg	OPS	Perf Gp
AL C	Lance Parrish	1984	33	98	.237	.730	6
AL 1B	Eddie Murray	1984	29	110	.306	.918	10
AL 2B	Lou Whitaker	1984	13	56	.289	.764	7
AL 3B	Buddy Bell	1984	11	83	.315	.840	9
AL SS	Alan Trammell	1984	14	69	.314	.851	9
AL OF	Dave Winfield	1984	19	100	.340	.908	10
AL OF	Dwayne Murphy	1984	33	88	.256	.814	9
AL OF	Dwight Evans	1984	32	104	.295	.920	10
NL C	Tony Pena	1984	15	78	.286	.758	7
NL 1B	Keith Hernandez	1984	15	94	.311	.859	10
NL 2B	Ryne Sandberg	1984	19	84	.314	.887	10
NL 3B	Mike Schmidt	1984	36	106	.277	.919	10
NL SS	Ozzie Smith	1984	1	44	.257	.684	4
NL OF	Dale Murphy	1984	36	100	.290	.919	10
NL OF	Bob Dernier	1984	3	32	.278	.718	5
NL OF	Andre Dawson	1984	17	86	.248	.710	5

The average Offensive Performance Group for every major league season, by this method, is 5.500; it cannot go higher or lower. But the average Offensive Performance Group of the Gold Glove teams in these two seasons was 8.19. The average was high in 1967 because

   a) good-hitting catchers won the Gold Glove in both leagues,

   b) a very good-hitting shortstop won the Gold Glove in the American League, and

   c) the NL's Gold Glove shortstop also had a good year with the bat.

This left the second basemen, Knoop and Mazeroski, as the only below-average hitters on the team. The NL's Gold Glove first baseman, Wes Parker, was a famous good-field, no-hit player, but his .704 OPS for 1967 was 40 points above the major league average. In a year in which only 16 major league regulars hit .300—one per team—six of the sixteen won Gold Gloves.

In 1967, nine Gold Glove winners where in the top 20% of all hitters; in 1984, ten were. Three Gold Glove winners of 1984 were below-average hitters—Bob Dernier, Andre Dawson and Ozzie Smith—but none of them were much below average. .300 hitters and power hitters dominate both teams.

It may be that the Gold Glove awards are no worse than ever, but that they appear worse because the public knows much more now, and is less accepting of awards being given to less-qualified players.

The weakest-hitting Gold Glove teams of all time were in 1962 and 1964. The teams above had an average Offensive Performance Group" of 8.19; in 1962 that average was 6.06, and in 1964 it was 6.13:

Pos	Player	YEAR	HR	RBI	Avg	OPS	Perf Gp
AL C	Earl Battey	1962	11	57	.280	.741	5
AL 1B	Vic Power	1962	16	63	.290	.737	5
AL 2B	Bobby Richardson	1962	8	59	.302	.743	6
AL 3B	Brooks Robinson	1962	23	86	.303	.828	8
AL SS	Luis Aparicio	1962	7	40	.241	.614	1
AL OF	Mickey Mantle	1962	30	89	.321	1.091	10
AL OF	Jim Landis	1962	15	61	.228	.711	4
AL OF	Al Kaline	1962	29	94	.304	.969	10
NL C	Del Crandall	1962	8	45	.297	.765	6
NL 1B	Bill White	1962	20	102	.324	.868	9
NL 2B	Ken Hubbs	1962	5	49	.260	.646	2
NL 3B	Jim Davenport	1962	14	58	.297	.813	8
NL SS	Maury Wills	1962	6	48	.299	.720	4
NL OF	Bill Virdon	1962	6	47	.247	.631	1
NL OF	Willie Mays	1962	49	141	.304	.999	10
NL OF	Roberto Clemente	1962	10	74	.312	.805	8

Pos	Player	YEAR	HR	RBI	Avg	OPS	Perf Gp
AL C	Elston Howard	1964	15	84	.313	.825	9
AL 1B	Vic Power	1964	3	17	.239	.570	1
AL 2B	Bobby Richardson	1964	4	50	.237	.626	2
AL 3B	Brooks Robinson	1964	28	118	.317	.889	10
AL SS	Luis Aparicio	1964	10	37	.266	.688	4
AL OF	Vic Davalillo	1964	6	51	.270	.663	4
AL OF	Jim Landis	1964	1	18	.208	.577	1
AL OF	Al Kaline	1964	17	68	.293	.851	9
NL C	Johnny Edwards	1964	7	55	.281	.721	6
NL 1B	Bill White	1964	21	102	.303	.829	9
NL 2B	Bill Mazeroski	1964	10	64	.268	.681	4
NL 3B	Ron Santo	1964	30	114	.313	.962	10
NL SS	Ruben Amaro	1964	4	34	.264	.648	3
NL OF	Willie Mays	1964	47	111	.296	.990	10
NL OF	Curt Flood	1964	5	46	.311	.734	6
NL OF	Roberto Clemente	1964	12	87	.339	.872	10

In 1962 (which was a hitter's year), only three high-impact hitters won Gold Gloves, those being the Hall of Fame outfielders Mantle, Mays and Kaline, while two guys won Gold Gloves who hit in the .240s with little power and few walks (Virdon and Aparicio.) In 1964, although four high-impact hitters won Gold Gloves, they were joined by an outfielder who hit .208 (Jim Landis), a first baseman who drove in only 17 runs (Vic Power), and five more below-average hitters.

But, in fact, the differences between the 1964 team—one of the weakest-hitting of all time—and the 1967 team—one of the strongest—are not that great, nor are these years separated in time by a margin large enough for us to describe them as coming from different eras with different attitudes about who should win the Gold Glove, the Oscar, the Emmy, or the hand of the maiden. Even the weakest-hitting Gold Glove team, the 1962 team, had a performance group average of 6.06, as opposed to a league average of 5.50. Even in 1962, half of the Gold Glove winners hit .290 or better. These disparate votes, really, are just something that happened. Vic Power in '64 wound up with a Gold Glove in '64 because he was a brilliant defensive first baseman, and even though he was on the way out by '64, no one else had stepped forward to claim that position, so some of the voters went back to Power. It doesn't really say anything about the era or the beliefs of Gold Glove voters; it is just something that happened.

The average Offensive Performance Group of all 52 Gold Glove teams is summarized in the chart below:

YEAR	Average	YEAR	Average	YEAR	Average
1957	7.75	1974	7.56	1991	7.88
1958	6.75	1975	6.31	1992	7.06
1959	7.75	1976	7.25	1993	7.56
1960	7.38	1977	6.63	1994	7.25
1961	6.44	1978	6.81	1995	6.75
1962	6.06	1979	7.19	1996	7.69
1963	6.50	1980	6.88	1997	7.88
1964	6.13	1981	7.00	1998	7.31
1965	7.63	1982	7.69	1999	7.69
1966	7.19	1983	7.44	2000	7.25
1967	8.19	1984	8.19	2001	7.31
1968	7.00	1985	7.29	2002	7.06
1969	6.69	1986	7.13	2003	7.06
1970	6.44	1987	7.06	2004	6.63
1971	6.31	1988	6.81	2005	6.94
1972	6.38	1989	6.31	2006	7.00
1973	6.44	1990	7.00	2007	7.47
				2008	7.19

In 1962 (which was a hitter's year), only three high-impact hitters won Gold Gloves, those being the Hall of Fame outfielders Mantle, Mays and Kaline, while two guys won Gold Gloves who hit in the .240s with little power and few walks (Virdon and Aparicio.)

These are the 2008 Gold Glove teams:

Pos	Player	YEAR	HR	RBI	Avg	OPS	Perf Gp
AL C	Mauer,Joe	2008	9	85	.328	.864	8
AL 1B	Pena,Carlos	2008	31	102	.247	.871	9
AL 2B	Pedroia,Dustin	2008	17	83	.326	.869	9
AL 3B	Beltre,Adrian	2008	25	77	.266	.784	6
AL SS	Young,Michael	2008	12	82	.284	.741	4
AL OF	Hunter,Torii	2008	21	78	.278	.810	7
AL OF	Sizemore,Grady	2008	33	90	.268	.876	9
AL OF	Suzuki,Ichiro	2008	6	42	.310	.747	5
NL C	Molina,Yadier	2008	7	56	.304	.740	4
NL 1B	Gonzalez,Adrian	2008	36	119	.279	.871	9
NL 2B	Phillips,Brandon	2008	21	78	.261	.754	5
NL 3B	Wright,David	2008	33	124	.302	.924	10
NL SS	Rollins,Jimmy	2008	11	59	.277	.786	6
NL OF	Beltran,Carlos	2008	27	112	.284	.876	9
NL OF	Victorino,Shane	2008	14	58	.293	.799	7
NL OF	McLouth,Nate	2008	26	94	.276	.853	8

Only one true top-level hitter—David Wright—won a Gold Glove in 2008. Numerous other top-level hitters could and perhaps should have won—Kevin Youkilis (10), Albert Pujols (10), Alex Rodriguez (10), Mark Teixeira (10), J. D. Drew (10), Chase Utley (10), Josh Hamilton (10), Nick Markakis (10), Matt Holliday (10). Evan Longoria (9). I personally would have voted for Youkilis over Pena, Pujols over Gonzalez, Markakis over Ichiro, and Matt Holliday over Nate McLouth—but they didn't win.

People say that Michael Young won the AL Shortstop Award with his bat, but look at who didn't win: Aviles (8), Peralta (7), and Jeter (6). And, if the voters are just going for the best hitters, what about Chase Utley? Utley is clearly the best-hitting second baseman in the NL, and he is an outstanding defensive player as well—but he didn't win. The vote went to a much weaker hitter.

We could do a trend-line analysis of this data in different ways. If you take a ten-year moving average, the lowpoint of that line would be 1978, and the highpoint would be 2000. From 1969 to 1978 more weak hitters won Gold Gloves than in any other ten-year period. From 1991 to 2000, fewer weak hitters won Gold Gloves than in any other period. In other words, the tendency to give Gold Gloves to good hitters was stronger in the 1990s than in any other time period. Since 2000 this ten-year average has trended downward:

End Year	Ten-Year Moving Average
2000	7.43
2001	7.38
2002	7.38
2003	7.33
2004	7.26
2005	7.28
2006	7.21
2007	7.17
2008	7.16

The overall average for the 52-year-history of the award is 7.09. Both the 2008 figure (7.19) and the ten-year moving average (7.16) are very near the historic norms.

I do believe that the numbers have trended downward since 2000 in part because of the Rafael Palmeiro fiasco in 1999. I think that that woke people up a little bit, and got them to take their votes a little bit more seriously. However, in general, there is little evidence of an actual change in how voters are influenced by hitting stats in selecting Gold Glove winners. It has always been a valuable and flawed process in which big hitters do well; it is still a valuable and flawed process in which big hitters do well.

The question before the house is whether the tendency to select the best hitters as the Gold Glove winners has gotten worse over time. The answer is that it has not.

Colorado Rockies

Colorado Rockies – 2008
Team Overview

Description		Ranking
Won-Lost Record	74-88	
Place	3rd of 5 in National League West	
Runs Scored	747	17th in the majors
Runs Allowed	822	24th in the majors
Home Runs	160	15th in the majors
Home Runs Allowed	148	6th in the majors
Batting Average	.263	16th in the majors
Batting Average Allowed	.276	25th in the majors
Walks Drawn	570	12th in the majors
Walks Given	562	18th in the majors
OPS For	.751	16th in the majors
OPS Against	.775	22nd in the majors
Stolen Bases	141	2nd in the majors
Stolen Bases Allowed	86	11th in the majors

Key Players

Pos	Player	G	AB	R	H	2B	3B	HR	RBI	SB	CS	BB	SO	Avg	OBP	Slg	OPS	WS
C	Chris Iannetta	104	333	50	80	22	2	18	65	0	0	56	92	.264	.390	.505	.895	17
1B	Todd Helton	83	299	39	79	16	0	7	29	0	0	61	50	.264	.391	.388	.779	8
2B	Clint Barmes	107	393	47	114	25	6	11	44	13	4	17	69	.290	.322	.468	.790	12
3B	Garrett Atkins	155	611	86	175	32	3	21	99	1	1	40	100	.286	.328	.452	.780	13
SS	Troy Tulowitzki	101	377	48	99	24	2	8	46	1	6	38	56	.263	.332	.401	.732	9
LF	Matt Holliday	139	539	107	173	38	2	25	88	28	2	74	104	.321	.409	.538	.947	21
CF	Willy Taveras	133	479	64	120	15	2	1	26	68	7	36	79	.251	.308	.296	.604	6
RF	Brad Hawpe	138	488	69	138	24	3	25	85	2	2	76	134	.283	.381	.498	.879	16

Key Pitchers

Pos	Player	G	GS	W	L	Sv	IP	H	R	ER	SO	BB	BR/9	ERA	WS
SP	Aaron Cook	32	32	16	9	0	211.1	236	102	93	96	48	12.26	3.96	15
SP	Ubaldo Jimenez	34	34	12	12	0	198.2	182	97	88	172	103	13.36	3.99	11
SP	Jorge de la Rosa	28	23	10	8	0	130.0	128	77	71	128	62	13.64	4.92	5
SP	Jeff Francis	24	24	4	10	0	143.2	164	84	80	94	49	13.53	5.01	5
SP	Greg Reynolds	14	13	2	8	0	62.0	83	58	56	22	26	16.40	8.13	0
CL	Brian Fuentes	67	0	1	5	30	62.2	47	22	19	82	22	10.05	2.73	12
RP	Taylor Buchholz	63	0	6	6	1	66.1	45	23	16	56	18	8.82	2.17	9
RP	Manny Corpas	76	0	3	4	4	79.2	93	41	40	50	23	13.33	4.52	6

The Rockies were unable to recover when they got a bad outing from their starting pitcher. When the Rockies starter posted a Game Score less than 40, the team was 5 – 48. That .094 winning percentage was the worst in the majors.

Colorado Rockies – 2008
Performance by Quality of Start

Game Score	#	ERA	W -	L
80 and above	2	0.00	2 -	0
70 to 79	14	0.84	12 -	2
60 to 69	20	1.89	16 -	4
50 to 59	37	2.70	26 -	11
40 to 49	36	5.34	13 -	23
30 to 39	21	6.10	3 -	18
20 to 29	17	8.81	1 -	16
Below 20	15	11.19	1 -	14

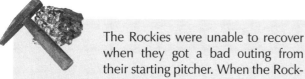

Get On Your Knees and Pray

The Rockies pray that they don't get fooled again. At least not as often as they did in 2008. They fell for the Houdini trick (opposing pitcher single handedly gets out of a bases loaded, no out jam without a run scoring) more than all but one other National League team. The opposition magician left the Rockies gasping six times, tying them with the Giants.

That First Guy Was a Killer

When Livan Hernandez retired the first batter in an inning, the opposition averaged only 2.66 runs per nine innings (just around the major league average). But when the first runner reached, Hernandez gave up more runs than any other pitcher in the majors: 13.1 per nine innings.

Livan Hernandez – 2008
Inning Analysis

Innings Pitched	180.0
Runs Allowed	129
Innings Started	188
Runs in Those Innings	132
Shutout Innings	124
One-Run Innings	27
Two-Run Innings	19
Three-Run Innings	9
Four-Run Innings	7
Five-Run Innings	1
Seven-Run Innings	1
Got First Man Out	122
Runs Scored in Those Innings	36
Runs/9 Innings	2.66
First Man Reached	66
Runs Scored in Those Innings	96
Runs/9 Innings	13.09
1-2-3 Innings	65
10-pitch Innings (or less)	44
Long Innings (20 or more pitches)	35
Failed to Finish Inning	12

Garrett Atkins

Over the last two years, Colorado third baseman Garrett Atkins has undergone a quite remarkable degeneration in his strikeout to walk ratio. In 2006, at the age of 26, Atkins' strikeout/walk ratio was better than even—79 walks, 76 strikeouts. In 2008 he walked only 40 times and struck out 100 times.

You can measure the degeneration in a player's strikeout/walk ratio in this way. Step 1, multiply his walks in the first year (79) by his strikeouts in the second year (100...7900). Step 2, multiply his walks in the second year (40) by his strikeouts in the first year (76...3040). Step 3, divide the second figure by the first (3040/7900 = .38). Step 4, subtract from 1.00 (1.00 - .38 = .62). Atkins has undergone a 62% deterioration in his strikeout/walk ratio over a period of two years, when he should be in his prime.

This is not the worst degeneration in strikeout/walk ratio between ages 26 and 28 in baseball history, but it's high on the list. Among other players with comparable big steps backward in those years: Joe Cunningham (72%), Carlos Baerga (67%), Deron Johnson (61%), Cookie Rojas (59%), Willie Aikens (55%), Chili Davis (46%), Cleon Jones (43%), Edgar Renteria (42%), and John Mayberry (41%).

It could be that, with the aging of Todd Helton, Atkins has felt more of the pressure of being the Rockies' RBI guy, and has tried to expand his strike zone, Joe Carter-like, to drive in runs. In 2006 Garrett hit .319 with the bases empty, and .341 with runners in scoring position. In 2008 he hit .322 with the bases empty, but .225 with runners in scoring position.

Above-average pitchers stopped Willy Taveras cold last year. In 2007, when he batted .320 overall, he batted .347 against pitchers with an ERA of 3.50 or less.

Willy Taveras – 2008
Batting Performance by Quality of Opposing Pitcher

	AB	H	HR	RBI	Avg	OPS
Pitcher with ERA <= 3.50	117	24	0	3	.205	.547
Pitcher with ERA 3.51 to 4.25	147	32	1	6	.218	.515
Pitcher with ERA 4.26 to 5.25	120	35	0	8	.292	.653
Pitcher with ERA over 5.25	95	29	0	9	.305	.750

Aaron Cook had 305 groundball outs in 2008, second-most in the major leagues (Brandon Webb had 319). Cook's totals were:

Batters Faced	886
Reached Base	326
Retired	560

Retired by:

Strikeout	96
Ground Out	305
Line Out	15
Fly Out	106
Pop Out	38
Other	0

Todd Helton and the Cooperstown Express

Is Todd Helton a Hall of Famer?

It's a disorienting question, because

1) Helton's batting numbers are fantastic, but

2) The context is extremely unusual.

Helton's peak years were in the middle of a historic offensive boom, and he was playing in a park where curve balls wouldn't curve and checked-swing bloopers have been known to rocket off the wall. In 2001 and 2003, the Colorado Rockies scored more runs than the 1961 Yankees—and didn't come close to playing .500 baseball either year.

Helton created a lot of runs, yes, but he created a lot of runs in a time and place in which it took an enormous number of runs to win. The Todd Helton Hall of Fame case is reminiscent of the 1970s debate about Chuck Klein, finally elected to the Hall of Fame in 1980, after all the sportswriters who had covered him were dead and buried. Klein had phenomenal numbers, but he played in a hitters' haven at the peak of the 1920s-1930s offensive boom, and most of the old guys who had seen him play didn't think of him as an outstanding player. Actually, some of Klein's numbers look a lot like Helton's. Klein in 1930 hit .386 with 59 doubles and 40 homers. Helton in 2000 hit .372 with 59 doubles and 42 homers. Also, Helton's period of dominance—like Klein's—was relatively short. Helton was a dominant player from 2000 to 2005; Klein, from 1929 to 1933.

OK, so his numbers are great, but there's a lot of air in them, and, if you let the air out, how good is he?

There is a logical pathway to answer that question:

1) Figure how many runs he created,

2) Figure out how many runs it took to win a ballgame in the time and place where he played, and

3) Divide (1) by (2).

How many **wins** is he responsible for, as a player? This is what greatness is about, for a baseball player—winning ballgames. I call them Win Shares and Loss Shares.

These are Todd Helton's Win Shares and Loss Shares, year by year since he came to the majors in 1997:

1997	2-3	.470
1998	16-11	.591
1999	15-13	.553
2000	24-3	.885
2001	24-5	.835
2002	22-6	.800
2003	27-2	.939
2004	25-1	.969
2005	21-5	.825
2006	18-10	.647
2007	23-6	.787
2008	10-7	.584
Total	228-70	.766

I credit Helton with 228 Win Shares—228 thirds of a win, since there are three shares in each win—and I hold him responsible for 70 Loss Shares.

Is that a Hall of Fame number? It could be. My standard...and I'm not married to this; I'm just trying it out...but my standard is that a Hall of Fame player should have 300 Career Win

Shares or be 100 "shares" over .500, one or the other. Helton does not have 300 Win Shares and probably will not get there, but he is +158.

If a player has both 300 Win Shares and is +100, in my mind that's a Hall of Famer; if he has neither, in my mind he is not a Hall of Famer. If he meets one standard but not the other, that puts him in a gray area—but +158 is a genuinely impressive number.

Let's compare Helton to some similar players who are in the Hall of Fame, and some who aren't. I drew up a list of comparable players. Alphabetically: Dick Allen, Albert Belle, Dolph Camilli, Will Clark, Hank Greenberg, Babe Herman, Frank Howard, Indian Bob Johnson, Ralph Kiner, Chuck Klein, Ted Kluszewski, Edgar Martinez, Johnny Mize and Bill Terry. Greenberg, Kiner, Klein, Mize and Terry are in the Hall of Fame; the others are not.

These players (1) were all tremendous hitters, but (2) all had relatively short careers, for outstanding hitters, and (3) all had limited defensive value. Not insulting their defense; some of them were good fielders and some weren't, but Joe DiMaggio and Roy Campanella were defensive superstars as well as great hitters who had short careers. You can't argue that Todd Helton should be in the Hall of Fame because he was a better hitter than Roy Campanella.

There's another player who has the same characteristics, and who actually belongs in the group. That's Mark McGwire. I left him out because I figured that, if I included him, it becomes a Mark McGwire debate, and we've all heard that debate before; I don't want to be dragged off course by that one.

This chart compares Helton's Win Shares and Loss Shares to these other Hall of Famers and Hall of Fame candidates. The first two numbers on each line are the player's batting Win Shares and Loss Shares, the Winning Percentage as a hitter, then the fielding Win Shares and Loss Shares, the Winning Percentage as a fielder, then the total Win Shares and Loss Shares and Winning Percentage. I'll list the players in declining order of overall Winning Percentage, and I'll mark the Hall of Famers with an asterisk:

Name	Batting	%	Fielding	%	Overall	%
* Johnny Mize	242-11	.955	47-55	.460	289-66	.813
* Hank Greenberg	188-21	.900	42-35	.539	228-56	.802
Edgar Martinez	259-36	.878	11-37	.270	270-73	.787
Dick Allen	235-29	.889	37-52	.418	272-81	.771
Todd Helton	190-48	.799	38-22	.636	228-70	.766
Will Clark	240-52	.823	39-48	.448	279-100	.737
* Bill Terry	201-50	.800	54-49	.525	255-99	.720
* Ralph Kiner	183-34	.842	24-50	.322	207-84	.711
Babe Herman	180-45	.800	39-53	.427	219-98	.691
Dolph Camilli	171-49	.776	40-48	.457	211-97	.685
Albert Belle	183-65	.737	22-40	.351	205-106	.660
Frank Howard	209-66	.759	25-56	.308	234-123	.655
Bob Johnson	214-65	.767	32-65	.329	228-130	.637
* Chuck Klein	185-71	.723	30-67	.309	215-138	.610
Ted Kluszewski	161-80	.667	31-46	.401	192-126	.603

Here are my conclusions:

1) Helton has been, adjusted for context, a much better player than Chuck Klein, and also clearly better than Ralph Kiner.

2) Klein's selection to the Hall of Fame was probably a mistake—not that I'm in any position to complain, since I myself did not have a clear picture of his accomplishments until many years after his selection. But it appears to me, at this late date, that the oldtimers who saw him play were basically right about him.

3) Helton, as best I am able to evaluate this by statistical analysis, appears to be the best defensive player in the group. To get an accurate line on a first baseman's defense, by the stats, is very difficult, and we should not have a lot of confidence that we've got it right. However, we do things, to evaluate first basemen, like looking at the number of errors charged to the team's third basemen and shortstops (figuring that a good defensive first baseman should save his team throwing errors) and estimating the number of 3-6-3 and 3-6-1 double plays that the team has had. I take the subject seriously and I do the best I can with it, and my conclusion is that Todd Helton is the best first baseman and the best defensive player in this group.

4) Both Mize and Greenberg are no-questions-asked Hall of Famers, and really, they should be viewed as players who cleared the 300-Win standard. Both players missed three prime seasons due to World War II, without which it is very likely that they would have been over 300 Wins.

5) It will be surprising to most of you, and it is surprising to me, that Mize ranks ahead of Greenberg. However, it is my opinion that this conclusion stands up on examination.

Greenberg has bigger numbers, meaning that Greenberg created more runs. If you just look at them in the Encyclopedia, it appears that Greenberg is a little bit better. Greenberg in 1937 created about 163 runs (and drove in 183). Those are fantastic numbers, but Greenberg was playing in a league that averaged 5.23 runs per team per game—and in by far the best hitter's park in that league, with a park factor of 120 (meaning that the park increased offense in that season by about 20%.)

Mize in 1939 created "only" 147 runs, but that was playing in a league that averaged 4.44 runs per team per game, and in a park that, while it was still very good for a hitter, was nowhere near as hitter-friendly as Tiger Stadium. Mize's season, in context, is clearly better than Greenberg's—and, in fact, all of Mize's best seasons are clearly better than any of Greenberg's. I am surprised to learn this.

6) Ted Kluszewski, Bob Johnson and Albert Belle were not Hall of Fame players, but they were substantially as good as Chuck Klein. They were very good.

7) Frank Howard, Dolph Camilli and Babe Herman met what we might consider sort of minimum standards for a possible Hall of Famer, and Ralph Kiner was a hair better than they were. They shouldn't be at the head of the line.

8) Todd Helton is not a bad Hall of Fame candidate. There's a lot of guys who have plaques who weren't the player that Helton has been. However, there are at least a couple of players who probably should go in before him.

9) In this group of players, Helton was the best defensive player and Edgar Martinez the worst—but Martinez was still a greater player than Helton.

Superficially, Martinez batting numbers may not be as good as Helton's—but you put Edgar Martinez in Coors' Field in his prime seasons, and you've got a .400 hitter. Todd Helton's batting averages at home, from 1998 to 2007, were .354, .385, .391, .384, .378, .391, .368, .353, .338 and .333. Helton always hit better at home than he did on the road, literally every year of his career, and many times the advantages were huge:

.354 vs. .273
.385 vs. .252
.384 vs. .286
.378 vs. .281
.353 vs. .287
.338 vs. .266

His career batting average is .362 at home, .294 on the road. Martinez' career batting averages were .311 at home, .312 on the road—with most of the home runs on the road.

For the sake of clarity, we don't evaluate hitters by what their batting average is at home, or what it is on the road; that's just an explanation. We evaluate hitters by three questions: How many runs did he create, how many outs did he make, and, in the time and place where he played, how many runs did it take to win a ballgame?

Todd Helton has been a great hitter—but Edgar Martinez was much better. Todd Helton was a great hitter on the level of Bill Terry. Edgar Martinez was a great hitter on the level of Hank Greenberg.

Will Clark, as well, might go into the Hall of Fame ahead of Helton, and, depending on how you feel about his off-field issues, Dick Allen. I've always felt that Will Clark was a Hall of Famer. Helton is +158, which is great. Clark was +179. I always thought Clark was an outstanding fielder, too, but our system fails to document that.

But getting into Edgar Martinez and Will Clark and (shudder) Dick Allen...that's dragging us off-topic, as if we had included Mark McSteroids. The question on the table was "Is Todd Helton deserving of serious Hall of Fame consideration?"

And the answer is "Yes".

Foul Play

In our mind's eye, the hitter who constantly fouls off pitches is the slap-hitting "bat control specialist" who chokes up on the bat, and finally dumps a little hit just beyond the outstretched reach of an infielder. The mind can play tricks on you. Todd Helton is no slap hitter yet he has fouled off the highest percentage of pitches he's swung at since 2002 in all of baseball. Here's the top-ten list of the players fouling off the highest percentage of pitches:

2002- 2008
(minimum 4000 pitches seen)

Name	Fouled Off %
Todd Helton	47%
Orlando Palmeiro	45%
Brian Roberts	44%
So Taguchi	44%
Cory Sullivan	44%
Kevin Millar	44%
Grady Sizemore	43%
Johnny Damon	43%
Kevin Youkilis	43%
Nick Punto	43%

Jason Grilli threw his slider nearly twice as often in 2008 as he had in 2007. He threw it to lefthanded hitters 29% of the time in 2008, compared to only 7% the year before.

Jason Grilli – 2007
Pitch Type Analysis

Overall		
Total Pitches	1376	
Fastball	935	68%
Curveball	58	4%
Changeup	80	6%
Slider	281	20%
Cut Fastball	1	0%
Pitchout	7	1%
Not Charted	14	1%

	Vs. RHB		Vs. LHB	
Total Pitches	861		515	
Outs Recorded	163		76	
Fastball	547	64%	388	75%
Curveball	45	5%	13	3%
Changeup	12	1%	68	13%
Slider	244	28%	37	7%
Cut Fastball	1	0%	0	0%
Pitchout	3	0%	4	1%
Not Charted	9	1%	5	1%

Jason Grilli – 2008
Pitch Type Analysis

Overall		
Total Pitches	1300	
Fastball	739	57%
Curveball	11	1%
Changeup	38	3%
Slider	479	37%
Pitchout	3	0%
Not Charted	30	2%

	Vs. RHB		Vs. LHB	
Total Pitches	673		627	
Outs Recorded	133		92	
Fastball	357	53%	382	61%
Curveball	7	1%	4	1%
Changeup	1	0%	37	6%
Slider	300	45%	179	29%
Pitchout	2	0%	1	0%
Not Charted	6	1%	24	4%

Detroit Tigers

Detroit Tigers – 2008
Team Overview

Description		Ranking
Won-Lost Record	74-88	
Place	5th of 5 in American League Central	
Runs Scored	821	5th in the majors
Runs Allowed	857	26th in the majors
Home Runs	200	4th in the majors
Home Runs Allowed	172	15th in the majors
Batting Average	.271	7th in the majors
Batting Average Allowed	.274	22nd in the majors
Walks Drawn	572	11th in the majors
Walks Given	644	25th in the majors
OPS For	.784	4th in the majors
OPS Against	.791	25th in the majors
Stolen Bases	63	23rd in the majors
Stolen Bases Allowed	69	5th in the majors

Key Players

Pos	Player	G	AB	R	H	2B	3B	HR	RBI	SB	CS	BB	SO	Avg	OBP	Slg	OPS	WS
C	Ivan Rodriguez	82	302	33	89	16	3	5	32	6	1	19	52	.295	.338	.417	.756	10
1B	Miguel Cabrera	160	616	85	180	36	2	37	127	1	0	56	126	.292	.349	.537	.887	20
2B	Placido Polanco	141	580	90	178	34	3	8	58	7	1	35	43	.307	.350	.417	.768	15
3B	Carlos Guillen	113	420	68	120	29	2	10	54	9	3	60	67	.286	.376	.436	.811	13
SS	Edgar Renteria	138	503	69	136	22	2	10	55	6	3	37	64	.270	.317	.382	.699	11
LF	Marcus Thames	103	316	50	76	12	0	25	56	0	3	24	95	.241	.292	.516	.808	7
CF	Curtis Granderson	141	553	112	155	26	13	22	66	12	4	71	111	.280	.365	.494	.858	20
RF	Magglio Ordonez	146	561	72	178	32	2	21	103	1	5	53	76	.317	.376	.494	.869	16
DH	Gary Sheffield	114	418	52	94	16	0	19	57	9	2	58	83	.225	.326	.400	.725	5

Key Pitchers

Pos	Player	G	GS	W	L	Sv	IP	H	R	ER	SO	BB	BR/9	ERA	WS
SP	Armando Galarraga	30	28	13	7	0	178.2	152	83	74	126	61	11.03	3.73	13
SP	Justin Verlander	33	33	11	17	0	201.0	195	119	108	163	87	13.25	4.84	8
SP	Kenny Rogers	30	30	9	13	0	173.2	212	118	110	82	71	15.13	5.70	4
SP	Nate Robertson	32	28	7	11	0	168.2	218	124	119	108	62	15.05	6.35	1
SP	Zach Miner	45	13	8	5	0	118.0	118	60	56	62	46	12.97	4.27	8
CL	Todd Jones	45	0	4	1	18	41.2	50	30	23	14	18	15.55	4.97	3
RP	Aquilino Lopez	48	0	4	1	0	78.2	86	33	31	61	22	12.58	3.55	6
RP	Bobby Seay	60	0	1	2	0	56.1	59	28	28	58	25	13.74	4.47	3

Power Addicts

The Detroit Tigers' record in games in which they failed to hit at least two home runs was 36-67.

Detroit Tigers – 2008
Record by Home Runs

Home Runs	W	-	L
0 homers	13	-	38
1 homer	23	-	29
2 homers	24	-	15
3 or more homers	14	-	6

Choosy

Curtis Granderson had the fewest one-pitch at-bats (17) of any player who qualified for the batting title.

Curtis Granderson – 2008
Short and Long AB

	AB	H	HR	RBI	Avg	OBP	Slg	OPS
One and done	17	5	1	2	.294	.294	.529	.824
Short	231	72	9	27	.312	.318	.513	.831
Long	322	83	13	39	.258	.393	.478	.872
7 Up	43	9	3	5	.209	.433	.465	.898

After exhibiting one of the worst "platoon splits" in the majors in 2007, Curtis Granderson significantly improved his batting average against left-handers last year.

	2007	2008
RHP	.337	.288
LHP	.160	.259

Justin Verlander is 25-7 in his career against losing teams but 21-27 against winning teams.

Justin Verlander
Career Records Against Quality of Opposition

Opponent	G	IP	W	L	SO	BB	ERA
.600 teams	1	5.2	0	1	3	4	9.53
.500 - .599 teams	53	326.2	21	26	254	118	4.90
.400 - .499 teams	34	211.1	18	6	177	76	3.15
sub .400 teams	9	56.1	7	1	43	21	2.56

Aquilino Lopez in 2008 was charged with allowing only 33 runs (31 earned runs), but gave up a whopping 54 RBI. What that means is, Lopez was giving up a whole lot of runs—21, to be exact—that went on somebody else's record. The 21 RBI minus runs was easily the highest total in the majors; a couple of guys had 15.

On the other end, Justin Verlander was charged with 119 runs allowed, but gave up "only" 96 RBI, meaning that there were 23 runs there that either weren't driven in or were driven in on somebody else's watch. This, again, was the largest number of "Runs Minus RBI allowed" in the majors...in fact, these are the major league leaders:

1. Justin Verlander, Detroit   23
2. Nate Robertson, Detroit   20
3. Garret Olson, Baltimore   19
4. Kenny Rogers, Detroit   18

And Armando Galarraga, the Tigers other starter, isn't far off the list, either.

Verlander didn't have a good year, and I'm not trying to make it sound like he did. Among the 142 major league pitchers who pitched 100 or more innings in '08, Verlander ranked 103rd in ERA. But the Tiger bullpen really wasn't helping him, either, and if we figured that one-half of the responsibility for the run scored goes to the pitcher who is on the mound when the run actually scores, Verlander would move from 103rd on the ERA list to 91st.

There's Just Too Much Confusion
And I Can't Get No Relief

Thirteen relief pitchers registered a "Hold" for the Tigers in 2008, more than any other team, and thirteen pitchers also had a save opportunity for them. The only one with an ERA better than 3.50 was Joel (Zoom Zoom) Zumaya, who (a) was hurt most of the year, and (b) had an ERA of 3.47.

Player	Saves	Save Opps	Holds	Relief ERA
Jones,Todd	18	21	0	4.97
Rodney,Fernando	13	19	5	4.91
Farnsworth,Kyle	0	3	3	6.75
Zumaya,Joel	1	5	5	3.47
Rapada,Clay	0	0	2	4.22
Seay,Bobby	0	1	13	4.47
Lopez,Aquilino	0	1	4	3.55
Glover,Gary	0	1	3	4.43
Miner,Zach	0	3	6	4.23
Fossum,Casey	0	1	6	5.66
Dolsi,Freddy	2	3	7	3.97
Cruceta,Francisco	0	2	1	5.40
Beltran,Francis	0	0	2	4.85
Galarraga,Armando	0	1	0	12.00

As bad as the Tigers' season was, how bad would it have been if it wasn't for Armando Galarraga?

Detroit Tigers – 2008
Performance by Starting Pitcher

Games Started By	GS	RS	RA	Won	Lost
Verlander, Justin	33	140	179	13	20
Rogers, Kenny	30	133	163	12	18
Robertson, Nate	28	145	168	11	17
Galarraga, Armando	28	155	118	18	10
Team Totals	162	821	857	74	88

Tiger rookie pitcher Armando Galarraga threw his slider more frequently than any pitcher in the majors last season, among those who qualified for the ERA title. Galarraga threw his slider 38% of the time, Randy Johnson was the second most frequent nickel curve user at 35%. Only 10 pitchers used a slider more than 25% of the time.

Armando and Nate and Rany

Our friend Rany Jazayerli likes a "Three true outcomes" analysis, based on strikeouts, walks and home runs. Those three outcomes, he argues...I hope he doesn't mind my paraphrasing...those three outcomes are true tests of a what a batter or a pitcher can do. Singles, doubles, runs scored, RBI. ...those things involve large elements of luck. Strikeouts, walks, and home runs; either you do it or you don't.

Armando Galarraga and Nate Robertson, teammates with the 2008 Tigers, are a stress test for the theory. Based on a "three true outcomes" analysis, there is little difference between them. They faced almost the same number of hitters (761 vs. 746, Robertson ahead). They gave up almost the same number of walks (62 vs. 61), almost the same number of home runs (26 vs. 28), and were separated by only 18 in strikeouts (108 vs. 126, Galarraga ahead.)

Problem was, everything went right for Galarraga, and everything and his brother went wrong for Robertson. Galarraga gave up 90 singles; Robertson gave up 134. Galarraga gave up 28 doubles; Robertson gave up 53. Galarraga had a winning record and a 3.73 ERA. Robertson had a losing record and an ERA higher than the Michigan unemployment rate.

Can all of that possibly be just luck? Well, yeah... it can. I don't know whether it was or not. But it is certainly true that the three true outcomes are much more reliable predictors of future performance than are the generalized collection categories like Wins, Losses and ERA.

Trammell

by Bill James

I received a note from a Detroit Tigers fan who is very disappointed in the lack of Hall of Fame support given to Alan Trammell. This is especially true considering a contemporary, Ozzie Smith, who was very close with Trammell in Win Shares, went in on the first ballot.

Among still-active players, Omar Vizquel, who I feel was significantly inferior as a player to Trammell, projects in last year's *Gold Mine* at 80% likelihood of going into the Hall of Fame. This lead to two questions from the Trammell supporter: 1) Do I think Alan's support will improve over time? 2) If he had won the MVP he deserved in 1987, would that have significantly changed the perception of him?

Let's do an inventory of the issues involved there:

1) Was Alan Trammell as good (or substantially as good) as Ozzie Smith?
2) If so, why did Ozzie do better in Hall of Fame voting?
3) Was Trammell, in fact, substantially better than Omar Vizquel?
4) If so, why I am saying that Vizquel is a likely Hall of Famer?
5) Did Trammell actually deserve the MVP Award in 1987?
6) If Trammell had won the Award, would that have made a big difference in MVP voting?
7) Will Trammell's support improve over time?
8) (The big one) is Trammell in fact a player of Hall of Fame stature?

Win Shares and Loss Shares, which are the successor to Win Shares, are a way of attempting to state each player's contribution to his team as a won-lost record.

This is why I can't listen to talk radio, by the way. People say things, and, in seemingly simple and straightforward assertions, there are a dozen issues that could be analyzed. The host will focus on one of those assertions to debate, making 25 more debatable statements in the process, and the next caller will focus on one of those, making sixteen more and throwing in some ridiculous crap about Prince Fielder having the greatest hot streak in National League history. You can go from Alan Trammell to Jackie Robinson's college football career to blood doping in greyhound races in three phone calls. I am always trying to outline in my mind the debate that is going on and focus on the issues capable of resolution, and I just can't keep up. I feel like Stan Laurel with Ollie pulling up the carpet on him. I get head over heels confused, and I get frustrated because I can't keep up, so I just turn it off. I write because it gives me an opportunity to organize the debate in my head.

Anyway, I have been meaning to introduce the concept of Win Shares and Loss Shares, so let's take the opportunity to do that. Win Shares and Loss Shares, which are the successor to Win Shares, are a way of attempting to state each player's contribution to his team as a won-lost record. Let's take on the issues above one by one:

1) Was Alan Trammell substantially as good as Ozzie Smith?

According to the Win Shares/Loss Shares method, he was. We credit Ozzie with a career record of 325-231 (325 Win Shares, 231 Loss Shares), a .585 percentage. We have Trammell at 282-176, a .616 percentage. By any kind of Value over Replacement Level analysis, those are comparable career records. Using Win Shares/Loss Shares, I have Ozzie as a .486 player offensively, but .880 defensively, compared to Trammell below:

	Batting	Fielding	Total
Ozzie	203-218 (.486)	123-17 (.880)	325-231 (.585)
Trammell	214-142 (.601)	68-34 (.667)	282-176 (.616)

2) If so, why did Ozzie do better in Hall of Fame voting?

I'll offer two explanations. One is that extreme excellence in one area is easy to explain to people. Ozzie, beyond question, was a brilliant defensive shortstop—perhaps the best ever. People get that. Trammell was a less brilliant defender but a better hitter, roughly the same overall, but that's harder to explain to people.

The other answer is that either
a) many people overvalue defense, or
b) the Win Shares system undervalues defense.

Many people think playing defense is a shortstop's job, period. I think they're exaggerating the value of shortstop defense, but it's difficult to prove the issue one way or the other.

3) Was Alan Trammell, in fact, substantially better than Omar Vizquel?

According to Win Shares/Loss Shares he was, yes. Let's add Vizquel to the Ozzie/Trammell comparison above:

	Batting	Fielding	Total
Ozzie	203-218 (.486)	123-17 (.880)	325-231 (.585)
Trammell	214-142 (.601)	68-34 (.667)	282-176 (.616)
Vizquel	180-241 (.427)	77-33 (.704)	257-273 (.485)

Our system sees Vizquel as
a) a good defensive shortstop—a little better than Trammell, but
b) not in Ozzie's class as a defensive player, and
c) weaker than Ozzie with the bat.

If we assume that Value Over Replacement Level begins at .400, we would have Ozzie at +103, Trammell at +99, Vizquel at +45. If we assume that the replacement level is .333, we would have Ozzie at +140, Trammell at +129, Vizquel at +80. Trammell is close to Ozzie and far better than Vizquel.

Looking at both players in their peak seasons, Vizquel's peak was from 1995-1999, when we credit him with a won-lost contribution of 83-70. Trammell's peak was from 1983-1987, when we credit him with a won-lost contribution of 112-40.

4) If so, why am I saying that Vizquel is a likely Hall of Famer?

It's a perception of a perception. It is my belief that Vizquel is widely perceived as a defensive genius on a par with Ozzie, and as a player who has had a career much like Ozzie's. I could be wrong, and I hope I am, but it is my belief that Omar is married to Ozzie in the minds of many sportswriters, and that this is likely to work in his favor when he becomes eligible for the Hall of Fame.

5) Did Alan Trammell actually deserve the MVP Award in 1987?

I think so. I thought that he did at the time, and, twenty years later with better methods of analysis and more data available, this is still what I think. This is a Win Shares/Loss Shares comparison of Trammell and George Bell, 1987:

	Batting	Fielding	Total
Bell	20- 5 (.787)	4- 3 (.604)	24- 8 (.749)
Trammell	23- 0 (.985)	4- 2 (.654)	27- 2 (.915)

I kind of think that, with the Hall of Fame ballot as crowded as it is likely to be over the next twenty years, there will be little room for players to gather strength in the voting as many players historically have done.

6) If he had won the Award, would that have made a big difference in MVP voting?

Perhaps it would have, but there are a bunch of shortstops with MVP Awards and marginal Hall of Fame credentials who didn't exactly catch fire in Hall of Fame voting. Dick Groat, NL MVP in 1960 (and runner-up in 1963) had a long career with many accomplishments, but never got above 2% (7 votes) in Hall of Fame balloting. Maury Wills won the MVP Award in '62 and was constantly referred to by the late, great Jim Murray as an obvious Hall of Famer, but never got above 41% in the voting. Roger Peckinpaugh had a good career with an MVP Award in 1924, but never got above 1%. Phil Rizzuto had a good career with an MVP Award in 1950, but never got above 38% in the actual voting, although he was elected by the Council of Elders in 1994.

One can make an argument that it was the MVP Award that legitimized the push for Rizzuto in the early 1990s, and ultimately got him enshrined. That could be. One can certainly argue that Lou Boudreau's MVP season in 1948 made him a Hall of Famer. But there are any number of similar players in the Hall without MVP Awards—Luis Aparicio, Pee Wee Reese and Travis Jackson—and there are any number of other players who got the benefit of organized bandwagons like Rizzuto—Enos Slaughter, Bill Mazeroski and Richie Ashburn—although they never won the MVP.

I think the evidence is that the MVP Award is a factor in how players are perceived post-career, but it's a very small factor, rather than a very large one. Probably the best test case for this will be Barry Larkin. Larkin's career is a good deal like Trammell's, but, for whatever reason, he did win the Award one year. He'll be on the ballot for next year's Hall of Fame vote, and we'll see what kind of a difference that makes. Although I think, in all candor, that Larkin's credentials are a little better than Trammell's.

7) Will Trammell's support improve over time?

History would suggest that it may, but honestly, I am skeptical about the relevance of this history. I kind of think that, with the ballot as crowded as it is likely to be over the next twenty years, there will be little room for players to gather strength in the voting as many players historically have done. Some players will do this, certainly, but I think that, because of the larger number of players with longer careers, more players will be crowded out and blocked off. I honestly don't know the answer to your question, but I wouldn't be optimistic.

8) (The $64,000 question) is Trammell in fact a player of Hall of Fame stature?

The standard I am developing…not entirely sure whether I am going to stick with this…but the standard that seems to be evolving for me is that a Hall of Fame player should meet, at a minimum, one of these two standards: 300 Win Shares, or 100 more Win Shares than Loss Shares. Trammell misses 300 Win Shares but is +106 in wins over losses, thus he is, in my view, at least minimally qualified for the Hall of Fame. On the other hand, this standard isn't meaningful at this point to anybody except me. For example, Buddy Bell is both over 300 and +100, and yet no one seems to think of him as a Hall of Fame player.

Trammell was certainly a better player than some shortstops now in the Hall of Fame, including Rizzuto, Sewell, Tinker and Travis Jackson. If you want to argue for him, I'm certainly not arguing against him, but on the other hand, I don't know that we want to carry forward that "Dave Bancroft Line", as Stan Grosshandler used to call it, where the Hall of Fame ceases to be golden and becomes a little more brass. I'll stay out of it. I'll argue for Ron Santo, Minnie Minoso and now Bert Blyleven, but otherwise I'm going to stay out of it.

Trammell was certainly a better player than some shortstops now in the Hall of Fame, including Rizzuto, Sewell, Tinker and Travis Jackson.

Florida Marlins

Florida Marlins – 2008
Team Overview

Description		Ranking
Won-Lost Record	84-77	
Place		3rd of 5 in National League East
Runs Scored	770	13th in the majors
Runs Allowed	767	19th in the majors
Home Runs	208	3rd in the majors
Home Runs Allowed	161	10th in the majors
Batting Average	.254	24th in the majors
Batting Average Allowed	.258	11th in the majors
Walks Drawn	543	15th in the majors
Walks Given	586	20th in the majors
OPS For	.759	13th in the majors
OPS Against	.740	13th in the majors
Stolen Bases	76	20th in the majors
Stolen Bases Allowed	110	19th in the majors

Key Players

Pos	Player	G	AB	R	H	2B	3B	HR	RBI	SB	CS	BB	SO	Avg	OBP	Slg	OPS	WS
C	Matt Treanor	65	206	18	49	7	0	2	23	1	0	18	53	.238	.306	.301	.607	5
1B	Mike Jacobs	141	477	67	118	27	2	32	93	1	0	36	119	.247	.299	.514	.812	14
2B	Dan Uggla	146	531	97	138	37	1	32	92	5	5	77	171	.260	.360	.514	.874	24
3B	Jorge Cantu	155	628	92	174	41	0	29	95	6	2	40	111	.277	.327	.481	.808	19
SS	Hanley Ramirez	153	589	125	177	34	4	33	67	35	12	92	122	.301	.400	.540	.940	32
LF	Josh Willingham	102	351	54	89	21	5	15	51	3	2	48	82	.254	.364	.470	.834	13
CF	Cody Ross	145	461	59	120	29	5	22	73	6	1	33	116	.260	.316	.488	.804	16
RF	Jeremy Hermida	142	502	74	125	22	3	17	61	6	1	48	138	.249	.323	.406	.729	13

Key Pitchers

Pos	Player	G	GS	W	L	Sv	IP	H	R	ER	SO	BB	BR/9	ERA	WS
SP	Ricky Nolasco	34	32	15	8	0	212.1	192	88	83	186	42	10.17	3.52	14
SP	Scott Olsen	33	33	8	11	0	201.2	195	106	94	113	69	11.92	4.20	8
SP	Josh Johnson	14	14	7	1	0	87.1	91	36	35	77	27	12.26	3.61	6
SP	Mark Hendrickson	36	19	7	8	0	133.2	148	87	81	81	48	13.53	5.45	3
SP	Andrew Miller	29	20	6	10	0	107.1	120	78	70	89	56	15.09	5.87	0
CL	Kevin Gregg	72	0	7	8	29	68.2	51	30	26	58	37	12.06	3.41	11
RP	Matt Lindstrom	66	0	3	3	5	57.1	57	21	20	43	26	13.19	3.14	6
RP	Renyel Pinto	67	0	2	5	0	64.2	52	33	32	56	39	13.22	4.45	3

The Marlins were the first team in major league history to have each of its regular infielders hit at least 25 home runs, and they came within one Jorge Cantu homer of making it 30 each. Cantu gave it his best shot, hitting seven home runs in the first fourteen games of September to reach 29, but didn't hit that one extra homer in his last eight games.

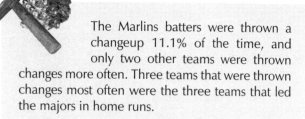

The Marlins batters were thrown a changeup 11.1% of the time, and only two other teams were thrown changes more often. Three teams that were thrown changes most often were the three teams that led the majors in home runs.

Team	Changeups	Home Runs
White Sox	11.6% (1st)	235 (1st)
Phillies	11.3% (2nd)	214 (2nd)
Marlins	11.1% (3rd)	208 (3rd)

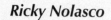

Ricky Nolasco

As a rookie in 2006, Rickie Nolasco went 11-11, but had a 4.82 ERA and struck out only 99 hitters. In 2007 he missed most of the season with an injury, and then last year he struck out 186 and cut his ERA to 3.52. What happened?

New slider.

Nolasco in 2006 threw no sliders. Last year he threw the slider 16% of the time. In 2006 he got 22% swings-and-misses on pitches outside the strike zone. Last year it was 29%.

You Ain't Scoring Anyway

Ricky Nolasco demonstrated pinpoint control with only 42 walks in 212.1 innings in 2008. But even when he did walk a guy, only 4 of the 42 came around to score, the lowest percentage in the majors.

Ricky Nolasco – 2008
Runs Allowed Analysis

Reached by Single:	115	Scored:	29	25%
Reached by Double:	44	Scored:	17	39%
Reached by Triple:	5	Scored:	4	80%
Reached by Homer:	28			
Reached by Walk:	42	Scored:	4	10%
Reached by HBP:	6	Scored:	3	50%
Reached by Error:	10	Scored:	2	20%
Reached by FC - Out:	19	Scored:	1	5%
Total On Base	269	Scored:	88	33%
Stolen Bases Allowed:	7	Scored:	2	29%
Caught Stealing:	5	Scored:	0	0%
Steal Attempts:	12	Scored:	2	17%
Intentional Walks:	6	Scored:	0	0%

Dan Uggla in 2008 batted .524 with the bases loaded, driving in 25 runs in 23 situations.

Matt Lindstrom's career ERA against losing teams (5.09) is more than three times higher than it is against winning teams (1.64).

Matt Lindstrom
Career Records Against Quality of Opposition

Opponent	G	IP	W	L	SO	BB	ERA
.600 teams	5	5.1	0	0	2	0	0.00
.500 - .599 teams	74	66.0	4	3	60	22	1.77
.400 - .499 teams	54	49.0	2	4	41	24	5.51
sub .400 teams	4	4.0	0	0	2	1	0.00

RBI Lost

How often does a leadoff man come up with no one on base? 67% of the time. Or conversely, 33% of the time with a least one man on base. Overall, MLB hitters come up with at least one man on base about 45% of the time. Here's the breakdown by lineup position:

Batting Order Slot	Percentage of time at least one man on base
1	33%
2	43
3	48
4	50
5	48
6	46
7	46
8	46
9	45

How many runs would Hanley Ramirez have driven in last year if he hadn't been hitting leadoff?

About 112. The number of runs a player can be expected to drive in can be estimated by dividing his total bases by four, and adding his home runs. The majority of major league regulars last year were within 10% of the RBI estimated by that formula, and more than 80% were within 20%.

Hanley was the majors #1 "RBI under achiever", by far, driving in 67 against an expectation of 112.5 (-45.5). No other major league player was off his estimate, high or low, by more than 31 runs.

Ramirez had over 400 at bats with the bases empty.

When Hanley Ramirez hit the first pitch, he batted .481 with a .975 slugging percentage.

Hanley Ramirez – 2008
Short and Long AB

	AB	H	HR	RBI	Avg	OBP	Slg	OPS
One and done	79	38	11	20	.481	.494	.975	1.469
Short	260	100	22	40	.385	.394	.728	1.122
Long	329	77	11	27	.234	.407	.386	.793
7 Up	53	13	1	3	.245	.444	.352	.796

I'm Not Joshing

The Marlins were 11-3 in Josh Johnson's starts last season, good for a .786 winning percentage. The only pitchers with more starts and a higher team winning percentage in 2008 were Chien-Ming Wang (12-3) and Dasuke Matsuzaka (23-6).

Florida Marlins – 2008
Performance by Starting Pitcher

Games Started By	GS	RS	RA	Won	Lost
Olsen, Scott	33	157	164	15	18
Nolasco, Ricky	32	154	116	21	11
Miller, Andrew	20	91	114	7	13
Hendrickson, Mark	19	96	101	10	9
Johnson, Josh	14	78	48	11	3
Volstad, Chris	14	50	54	8	6
Sanchez, Anibal	10	53	54	4	6
Badenhop, Burke	8	34	46	2	6
Tucker, Ryan	6	35	44	3	3
VandenHurk, Rick	4	17	22	2	2
de la Cruz, Frankie	1	5	4	1	0
Team Totals	161	770	767	84	77

Alfredo Amezaga played four different positions last year and was above average at all four of them, according to our Plus/Minus Fielding System.

Position	Innings	+/-
Center Field	457.1	+12
Shortstop	125.1	+2
Second Base	73.0	+3
Third Base	25.2	+2

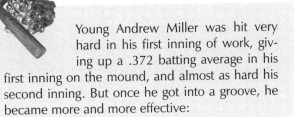

Young Andrew Miller was hit very hard in his first inning of work, giving up a .372 batting average in his first inning on the mound, and almost as hard his second inning. But once he got into a groove, he became more and more effective:

Inning	G	PA	BA
1st	20	104	.372
2nd	20	91	.321
3rd	19	85	.282
4th	18	75	.250
5th	15	58	.255
6th	10	32	.207
7th	9	33	.185
8th	5	14	.333

Let's Call It Even and Quit

Luis Gonzalez, a Florida outfielder in 2008, is unsigned as of mid-February. If he never plays again, Gonzalez will finish his career with 2,591 games played, and 2,591 hits. While most players, of course, average about one hit per game, there is no other player since 1900 with EXACTLY one hit per game in a career longer than 60 games. These are the longest careers—all 19th-century guys except Gonzalez:

Luis Gonzalez	2591 games	2591 hits
Duke Farrell	1583 games	1583 hits
Candy Nelson	624 games	624 hits
Doc Kennedy	160 games	160 hits
Abner Powell	78 games	78 hits

Houston Astros

Houston Astros – 2008
Team Overview

Description		Ranking
Won-Lost Record	86-75	
Place	3rd of 6 in National League Central	
Runs Scored	712	21st in the majors
Runs Allowed	743	14th in the majors
Home Runs	167	14th in the majors
Home Runs Allowed	197	21st in the majors
Batting Average	.263	17th in the majors
Batting Average Allowed	.264	17th in the majors
Walks Drawn	449	26th in the majors
Walks Given	492	9th in the majors
OPS For	.737	20th in the majors
OPS Against	.768	21st in the majors
Stolen Bases	114	9th in the majors
Stolen Bases Allowed	47	1st in the majors

Key Players

Pos	Player	G	AB	R	H	2B	3B	HR	RBI	SB	CS	BB	SO	Avg	OBP	Slg	OPS	WS
C	Brad Ausmus	81	216	15	47	8	0	3	24	0	2	25	41	.218	.303	.296	.600	8
1B	Lance Berkman	159	554	114	173	46	4	29	106	18	4	99	108	.312	.420	.567	.986	36
2B	Kaz Matsui	96	375	58	110	26	3	6	33	20	5	37	53	.293	.354	.427	.781	12
3B	Ty Wigginton	111	386	50	110	22	1	23	58	4	6	32	69	.285	.350	.526	.876	14
SS	Miguel Tejada	158	632	92	179	38	3	13	66	7	7	24	72	.283	.314	.415	.729	14
LF	Carlos Lee	115	436	61	137	27	0	28	100	4	1	37	49	.314	.368	.569	.937	22
CF	Michael Bourn	138	467	57	107	10	4	5	29	41	10	37	111	.229	.288	.300	.588	7
RF	Hunter Pence	157	595	78	160	34	4	25	83	11	10	40	124	.269	.318	.466	.783	19

Key Pitchers

Pos	Player	G	GS	W	L	Sv	IP	H	R	ER	SO	BB	BR/9	ERA	WS
SP	Roy Oswalt	32	32	17	10	0	208.2	199	89	82	165	47	11.04	3.54	16
SP	Brian Moehler	31	26	11	8	0	150.0	166	79	76	82	36	12.36	4.56	7
SP	Wandy Rodriguez	25	25	9	7	0	137.1	136	65	54	131	44	12.12	3.54	9
SP	Brandon Backe	31	31	9	14	0	166.2	202	114	112	127	77	15.28	6.05	2
SP	Shawn Chacon	15	15	2	3	0	85.2	88	52	48	53	41	13.76	5.04	2
CL	Jose Valverde	74	0	6	3	44	72.0	62	28	27	83	23	10.88	3.38	14
RP	Doug Brocail	72	0	7	5	2	68.2	63	30	30	64	21	11.40	3.93	7
RP	Wesley Wright	71	0	4	3	1	55.2	45	34	31	57	34	13.42	5.01	3

The Astros fell behind in the first inning more than any other team in the majors. They increased the percentage of the games they led in every inning.

Houston Astros – 2008
Innings Ahead, Behind, or Tied

Inning	1	2	3	4	5	6	7	8	9	Extra	Final
Ahead	40	51	59	65	68	70	71	78	80	5	86
Behind	56	66	71	74	76	75	70	72	72	3	75
Tied	65	44	31	22	17	16	20	11	8	11	—

Houston Astros – 2008
Percentage of Time Leading Games

Inning	1	2	3	4	5	6	7	8	9	Extra	Final
%	.417	.436	.454	.468	.472	.483	.504	.520	.526	.625	.534

Berkman Minus Bagwell and Biggio

The Astros had the majors' best OPS from the cleanup spot, but the NL's worst OPS from both the #3 spot and the leadoff spot.

They also scored only 712 runs in 2008, 22 below the National League average. Part of the problem was their lead-off hitters, who posted an on-base percentage of .290. That ranked 29th in the majors.

Houston Astros – 2008
Productivity by Batting Order Position

Pos	Players	Avg	OBP	Slg	OPS
1	Bourn (70 G), Matsui (40 G), Erstad (26 G)	.237	.290	.335	.625
2	Matsui (54 G), Loretta (29 G), Bourn (19 G)	.300	.356	.430	.786
3	Tejada (102 G), Berkman (53 G)	.277	.339	.417	.756
4	Berkman (103 G), Lee (54 G)	.338	.416	.611	1.027
5	Lee (60 G), Blum (42 G), Tejada (36 G)	.261	.310	.485	.795
6	Pence (83 G), Blum (34 G), Wigginton (29 G)	.281	.328	.485	.813
7	Wigginton (48 G), Pence (23 G), Bourn (20 G)	.273	.331	.402	.733
8	Ausmus (59 G), Quintero (48 G), Towles (45 G)	.208	.285	.301	.586
9	Oswalt (30 G), Backe (28 G), Moehler (25 G)	.173	.228	.244	.473
	Total	.263	.323	.415	.737

In the opening weeks of the 2008 season, Lance Berkman was the hottest hitter in the major leagues. Hitting .299 through April 29, he drove in 2 runs with a single on April 30. In his next game, May 2, he hit a home run, and, in the following game, two singles and another RBI.

Then he got *really* hot; on May 4 he was 4-for-5 with two doubles, a tater and 4 RBI. The next game he was 5-for-5, two more doubles and scored 4 runs. Then he was 2-for-3 with a homer, 2-for-3 without a homer, 3-for-4 with a double and a homer, 2-for-3 with another double, 1-for-4 with an RBI, and 3-for-4 with a double and another homer.

It's hard to say when the hot streak ends. As of May 18, with his consecutive-game hitting streak still intact, he had four straight two-hit games, homering in two of them. In a 17-game stretch he hit .545 (36 for 66) with 8 homers and 21 RBI.

We take each player's "temperature" after each game; yeah, it's a silly task, but somebody has to do it. On May 9 and May 10, Berkman's temperature was 123°. Only two other players in 2008 had comparable hot streaks—Alfonso Soriano, beginning just a few days later, and Melvin Mora in August.

Lance Berkman – 2008
Hot and Cold Summary

Season Ending Temperature	62°
High Point of the Season	123° on May 10 and May 9
Low Point of the Season	53° on September 18
Days Over 100°	14
Days Under 50°	0
Average Daily Temperature	78.9°

Lance Berkman nearly doubled his doubles total last year, raising his total from 24 to 46. As a righthanded hitter, he hit exactly as many doubles as the year before (6), but from the left side he went from 18 to 40. Batting lefty, he hit 129 flyballs in both seasons; 21 of them went for doubles in 2008, compared to only six the year before.

Lance Berkman – 2008
Hitting Analysis

Total									1B		2B		3B		HR
Fly Balls to Left	65	Outs	40	Hits	25	Average	.397	Hit Type	2	–	9	–	0	–	14
Fly Balls to Center	62	Outs	48	Hits	14	Average	.233	Hit Type	0	–	7	–	1	–	6
Fly Balls to Right	48	Outs	31	Hits	17	Average	.354	Hit Type	3	–	6	–	0	–	8
All Balls in Play	451	Outs	278	Hits	173	Average	.388	Hit Type	94	–	46	–	4	–	29
Batting Right-Handed									**1B**		**2B**		**3B**		**HR**
Fly Balls to Left	13	Outs	8	Hits	5	Average	.385	Hit Type	0	–	0	–	0	–	5
Fly Balls to Center	12	Outs	11	Hits	1	Average	.091	Hit Type	0	–	0	–	0	–	1
Fly Balls to Right	21	Outs	18	Hits	3	Average	.143	Hit Type	2	–	1	–	0	–	0
All Balls in Play	129	Outs	86	Hits	43	Average	.339	Hit Type	30	–	6	–	0	–	7
Batting Left-Handed									**1B**		**2B**		**3B**		**HR**
Fly Balls to Left	52	Outs	32	Hits	20	Average	.400	Hit Type	2	–	9	–	0	–	9
Fly Balls to Center	50	Outs	37	Hits	13	Average	.265	Hit Type	0		7		1		5
Fly Balls to Right	27	Outs	13	Hits	14	Average	.519	Hit Type	1	–	5	–	0	–	8
All Balls in Play	322	Outs	192	Hits	130	Average	.408	Hit Type	64	–	40	–	4	–	22

Lance Berkman's improvement as a baserunner last year extended beyond his surprising 18-for-22 performance as a basestealer. He also scored from second 16 times, after having done it only six times the year before, and was thrown out on the bases five fewer times.

Lance Berkman – 2002-2008
Baserunning Analysis

Year	1st to 3rd Adv	1st to 3rd Opp	2nd to Home Adv	2nd to Home Opp	1st to Home Adv	1st to Home Opp	DP Opp	GIDP	Bases Taken	BR Outs	BR Gain	SB Gain	Net Gain
2002	13	35	15	27	3	6	153	10	19	3	+9	0	+9
2003	5	30	15	25	4	11	123	10	21	3	+1	-1	0
2004	3	25	9	23	1	6	121	10	17	5	-10	-5	-15
2005	1	19	3	16	2	6	117	18	7	8	-36	+2	-34
2006	8	19	9	13	1	8	153	11	12	5	+1	-1	0
2007	8	34	6	16	3	5	132	11	16	7	-9	+1	-8
2008	6	28	16	24	3	7	120	13	25	2	+16	+10	+26
Totals	44	190	73	144	17	49	919	83	117	33	-29	+6	-23
		23%		51%		35%		9%					

Brandon Backe had the highest slugging percentage allowed among all qualifying (162 innings) major league pitchers last year. For comparison's sake, David Wright batted .302 with a .390 OBP and a .534 slugging percentage.

Brandon Backe – 2002-2008
Record of Opposing Batters

Season	AB	R	H	2B	3B	HR	RBI	BB	SO	SB	CS	GIDP	Avg	OBP	Slg	OPS
2002	52	10	15	2	0	3	10	7	6	2	0	1	.288	.393	.500	.893
2003	162	28	40	5	1	6	25	25	36	0	4	5	.247	.353	.401	.754
2004	259	33	75	16	1	10	28	27	54	2	3	7	.290	.358	.475	.833
2005	574	82	151	34	3	19	71	67	97	4	4	13	.263	.344	.432	.776
2006	165	18	43	12	0	4	18	18	19	0	1	3	.261	.340	.406	.746
2007	109	13	27	7	0	4	12	11	11	0	1	1	.248	.325	.422	.747
2008	669	114	202	46	4	36	107	77	127	4	6	17	.302	.376	.544	.920

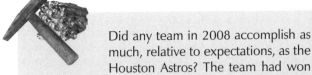

Did any team in 2008 accomplish as much, relative to expectations, as the Houston Astros? The team had won only 73 games in 2007. They signed no significant free agents, the team is getting older, and, as is well known, their farm system has fallen and cannot reach its life-alert bracelet. They are generally conceded to have had the weakest farm system in the majors in recent years, and were picked by many of us to finish last in the division. Yes, they did make a deal for Miguel Tejada, but at the time, the reaction of the press was "What are they thinking of?"

So what did they do? They competed into the last week of the season. I'm sure there are legitimate ways to explain that that would use words like "courage" and "determination," but another thing we could point to is that the team was remarkably good at winning when they scored 3 or 4 runs. They were 25-18 in games when they scored three or four runs.

Houston Astros – 2008
Record by Runs Scored and Allowed

	Scored	Allowed
10 runs or more	6 - 0	1 - 16
9 runs	5 - 0	0 - 7
8 runs	7 - 1	0 - 7
7 runs	9 - 5	3 - 5
6 runs	15 - 6	4 - 9
5 runs	14 - 7	5 - 11
4 runs	12 - 7	15 - 9
3 runs	13 - 11	16 - 6
2 runs	5 - 16	14 - 5
1 run	0 - 16	15 - 0
0 runs	0 - 6	13 - 0
Total	86 - 75	86 - 75

Pitch Load

by Bill James

Suppose that you have a strikeout pitcher and a non-strikeout pitcher, otherwise equal, pitching the same number of innings. How many extra pitches does the strikeout pitcher throw, over the course of a season, because it takes more pitches to get an out by a strikeout?

The best answer to that question, in my opinion, is "near zero". There are different ways to interpret the data, however, depending on exactly what you mean by "otherwise equal", so I will put the data that I have on record and let you make what you will of it.

I got interested in this issue because of a discussion with John Dewan about one of his Stat-of-the-Week items where he suggests that striking out batters leads to higher pitch counts because a strikeout requires more pitches.

To study the issue, I decided to form groups of pitchers, and to look at the number of pitches thrown by each group. The groups of pitchers are:

High Strikeout High Walk
High Strikeout Medium Walk
High Strikeout Low Walk

Medium Strikeout High Walk
Medium Strikeout Medium Walk
Medium Strikeout Low Walk

Low Strikeout High Walk
Low Strikeout Medium Walk
Low Strikeout Low Walk

How to form such groups? I took all pitchers from the years 2002-2007, selecting those years because those are the years for which Bill James Online has pitch data. I then trimmed this group to the 1102 pitchers pitching the most innings.

Why 1102, you asked? I wanted to have a substantial number of pitchers in each pool—300—and I wanted to have "dead zones" between them so that something more than one strikeout or one walk separated the groups of pitchers. I aimed for 1100, but there was a

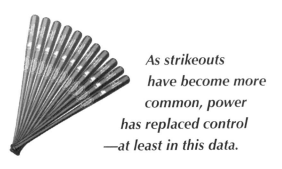

As strikeouts have become more common, power has replaced control —at least in this data.

tie at the 1100 spot, so I included the two extras.

I then figured for each pitcher his strikeouts as a percentage of batters faced, and ranked the pitchers 1 through 1102 in terms of strikeouts as a percentage of batters faced. The top 300 were "1", the next 101 (301-401) were "2", the next 300 (402-701) were "3", the next 101 (702-802) were "4", and the final 300 (803-1102) were "5". I then did the same for walks as a percentage of batters faced, again sorting the pitchers in groups 1 through 5:

High Strikeout High Walk was pitchers in group 1-1
High Strikeout Medium Walk was pitchers in group 1-3
High Strikeout Low Walk was pitchers in group 1-5

Medium Strikeout High Walk was pitchers in group 3-1
Medium Strikeout Medium Walk was pitchers in group 3-3
Medium Strikeout Low Walk was pitchers in group 3-5

Low Strikeout High Walk was pitchers in group 5-1
Low Strikeout Medium Walk was pitchers in group 5-3
Low Strikeout Low Walk was pitchers in group 5-5

Pitchers in groups "2" and "4", either in walks or strikeouts, were excluded from the study. "High strikeout/High Walk" pitchers thus were in the top 27% of all pitchers both in strikeouts and walks as a percentage of batters faced.

I then sorted each group of pitchers by the number of batters faced, and took the 40 pitchers from each group who faced the most batters. For those 40 pitchers in each group (360 total) I looked up the number of pitches thrown during the season. (I initially did the study with 25 pitchers in each group, but the process of gathering the pitch data was fairly quick and painless, so I expanded it to 40, although 25 seemed to be adequate to provide stable data.)

Peripheral Analysis

Of course, the pitchers with the better strikeout-to-walk performance got better results.

This is the average performance of the 1,102 pitchers as a whole—9-9 record, .506 winning percentage, 4.41 ERA, 16% strikeouts, 8% walks:

Count	G	W	L	WPct	IP	SO	BB	H	HR	BFP	ERA	SO %	BB %
1102	34	9	9	.506	154	107	52	157	18	658	4.41	.16	.08

This is the average performance of the pitchers sorted into high strikeout, medium strikeout and low strikeout groups:

Count	G	W	L	WPct	IP	SO	BB	H	HR	BFP	ERA	SO %	BB %
300	37	11	8	.566	161	148	54	145	17	673	3.74	.22	.08
300	33	9	9	.501	152	102	52	158	18	645	4.53	.16	.08
300	31	8	9	.459	147	73	49	165	19	642	4.91	.11	.08

The strikeout pitchers had a .566 winning percentage, 3.74 ERA; the low-strikeout pitchers had a .459 winning percentage, 4.91 ERA. The high strikeout pitchers struck out 22% of the batters they faced, 148 batters on average; the low strikeout pitchers struck out only 11%, 73 on average.

This chart sorts the pitchers into groups with high, medium and low walk frequencies:

Count	G	W	L	WPct	IP	SO	BB	H	HR	BFP	ERA	SO %	BB %
300	35	7	8	.470	130	96	63	129	15	573	4.69	.17	.11
300	34	9	9	.500	158	109	53	163	19	677	4.46	.16	.08
300	33	11	9	.548	174	118	39	179	20	726	4.06	.16	.05

The pitchers with the highest walk rates had a .470 winning percentage with a 4.69 ERA. The pitchers with the best control had a .548 winning percentage, with a 4.06 ERA.

There are two things about this data so far that are interesting. First, **strikeouts have more impact on the quality of performance than walks**. I did not expect this. I would have anticipated that differences in walk rates would be more significant in driving pitcher effectiveness than strikeouts, and I would predict that if we did the same study for some earlier year—pre-1980—then walks would be the more important. If my understanding is correct, then think what a historic shift we have undergone, as strikeouts have become more common. It was always true—I believe—that the most important thing for a pitcher was control. No more; as strikeouts have become more common, power has replaced control—at least in this data.

Second, **strikeouts and walks are not closely related**. The walk percentage was actually 8.4% for the high-strikeout pitchers, 8.1% for the mid-group and 7.9% for the low-strikeout pitchers. It shows at 8% all along; it was actually higher with the high-strikeout pitchers, but not much higher. When sorted by walks, we have 16.7% strikeouts for the high-walk group, 16.1% strikeouts for the mid-walk group, and 16.0% for the low-walk group. There is a connection between strikeouts and walks, but not much of a connection. They're pretty much independent variables.

How many extra pitches does the strikeout pitcher throw, over the course of a season, because it takes more pitches to get an out by a strikeout? The best answer to that question, in my opinion, is "near zero".

This data summarizes the performance of the pitchers in each of the nine groups; 1-1 is the High Strikeout/High Walk group, and 5-5 is the Low Strikeout/Low Walk group:

Group	Count	G	W	L	WPct	IP	SO	BB	H	HR	BFP	ERA	SO %	BB %
1-1	103	39	8	8	.507	137	128	65	120	15	587	4.04	.22	.11
1-3	72	37	10	7	.573	159	146	52	144	16	662	3.66	.22	.08
1-5	79	33	14	8	.623	196	176	42	179	20	796	3.38	.22	.05
3-1	81	34	8	8	.484	134	92	66	137	15	592	4.80	.16	.11
3-3	92	33	9	9	.486	153	103	52	161	19	661	4.59	.16	.08
3-5	73	32	11	8	.551	169	111	38	175	19	707	4.12	.16	.05
5-1	72	31	6	8	.414	120	61	58	130	16	535	5.24	.11	.11
5-3	82	32	9	10	.460	158	79	54	178	20	690	5.00	.11	.08
5-5	85	30	9	9	.499	163	79	37	186	21	699	4.61	.11	.05

The high-strikeout/low walk pitchers were 14-8 on average, .623 winning percentage, 176-42 strikeout/walk ratio. The opposite-end group was 6-8 on average. .414 winning percentage, 5.24 ERA, 61-58 strikeout/walk ratio.

That data is from the entire group of 1102 pitchers, excluding those who fall into one of the borderline categories.

This is the same data, but only for the 40 pitchers selected from each group:

Group	G	W	L	WPct	IP	SO	BB	H	HR	BFP	ERA	SO %	BB %
1-1	32	12	10	.554	191	179	86	165	21	813	3.93	.22	.11
1-3	32	13	9	.591	196	177	64	179	20	821	3.67	.22	.08
1-5	34	16	10	.625	229	205	48	212	24	933	3.40	.22	.05
3-1	31	10	11	.474	172	119	82	178	19	761	4.84	.16	.11
3-3	32	13	11	.549	199	133	68	205	23	852	4.23	.16	.08
3-5	33	14	10	3583	210	137	46	213	23	875	3.85	.16	.05
5-1	30	8	10	.442	143	72	69	156	18	641	5.11	.11	.11
5-3	33	11	12	.496	193	99	66	215	24	842	4.79	.12	.08
5-5	32	12	11	.527	202	99	46	225	24	861	4.33	.11	.05

There are some differences due to the fact that this second group includes only the pitchers who pitched more innings, thus there is a "quality screening" effect.

At this point I added to the data the numbers of pitches thrown by each pitcher. **The pitchers throwing the most pitchers per batter and the fewest pitchers per batter in a season, among the 360 pitchers in the study, were:**

Most		Least	
1. Al Leiter, 2004	4.33	1. Greg Maddux, 2007	3.26
2. Al Leiter, 2005	4.25	2. Greg Maddux, 200	3.27
3. Chris Young, 2006	4.12	3. Greg Maddux, 2005	3.31
4. Chris Young, 2007	4.09	4. Carlos Silva, 2006	3.32
5. Geremi Gonzalez, 2003	4.08	5. Carlos Silva, 2004	3.33
6. Scott Kazmir, 2007	4.07	6. Josh Towers, 2005	3.37
7. Gil Meche, 2006	4.04	7. Jason Johnson, 2005	3.38
8. Daniel Cabrera, 2006	4.05	8. David Wells, 2003	3.38
9. Gil Meche, 2005	4.04	9. Roy Halladay, 2003	3.39
10. Matt Cain, 2006	4.04	10. Chien-Ming Wang, 2006	3.39

Thus, we realize that throwing a large number of pitches (or a small number of pitches) per batter is a very pitcher-specific trait. Gil Meche has quite ordinary strikeout and walk numbers, nothing remarkable about them. He just uses a ton of pitches to do it. There are other pitchers who have strikeout and walk numbers much higher than Leiter and Chris Young; they just do it with fewer pitches. One suspects that Meche, Young and Leiter must be (or must have been) inclined to nibble on an 0-1 pitch or a 1-2 pitch, or inclined to simply waste a pitch down and away. Otherwise it is hard to understand why they would throw so many pitches.

Analysis Central to the Research

Strikeout pitchers, on average, throw no more pitches per inning than do non-strikeout pitchers, at least within this data. The average number of pitches per inning for the pitchers in these nine groups was:

High Strikeout High Walk 16.72
High Strikeout Medium Walk 16.06
High Strikeout Low Walk 15.16

Medium Strikeout High Walk 16.88
Medium Strikeout Medium Walk 16.03
Medium Strikeout Low Walk 14.97

Low Strikeout High Walk 16.55
Low Strikeout Medium Walk 15.96
Low Strikeout Low Walk 15.27

Pitches per inning vary substantially with walks, but vary with strikeouts only to a small degree. The data above can be re-stated as follows:

High Strikeout Total 15.98
Medium Strikeout Total 15.96
Low Strikeout Total 15.93

High Walk Total 16.72
Medium Walk Total 16.01
Low Walk Total 15.13

How can this be, since we all know that a strikeout requires more pitches to accomplish than another out? According to Pat Quinn of Baseball Info Solutions, the average strikeout requires 4.80 pitches, whereas the average non-strikeout at bat requires 3.53 (data is the same for either 2007 or the 2002-2007 period.)

But that's a relatively small difference to begin with—a difference of 26% (3.53 ÷ 4.80 = .74), or a difference of 1.27 pitches. But that difference applies only to the strikeouts themselves. Even the high-strikeout pitchers strike out only 22% of the batters they face—and even the low-strikeout pitchers strike out 11% of the batters they face. The difference is not 1.27 pitches per batter, but 1.27 x .11 pitches per batter, or .140 pitches per batter.

But this effect is offset, on a per-inning basis, by the fact that the strikeout pitchers are more effective, and thus are able to complete their innings while facing fewer batters. *The net effect is that strikeout pitchers throw no more pitches per inning than do non-strikeout pitchers.*

One can see a difference, as noted, in pitches per batter. Repeating the charts above, but with **pitches per batter** replacing pitches per inning, we have:

High Strikeout High Walk 3.92
High Strikeout Medium Walk 3.83
High Strikeout Low Walk 3.71

Medium Strikeout High Walk 3.82
Medium Strikeout Medium Walk 3.74
Medium Strikeout Low Walk 3.59

Low Strikeout High Walk 3.69
Low Strikeout Medium Walk 3.65
Low Strikeout Low Walk 3.59

High Strikeout Total 3.82
Medium Strikeout Total 3.72
Low Strikeout Total 3.64

High Walk Total 3.81
Medium Walk Total 3.74
Low Walk Total 3.63

Stated per batter, the effect of strikeouts in driving pitch counts upward is essentially the same as the effect of walks. Since walks, of course, have no "out value", they are simply an addition to the load when stated on a per-inning basis, which causes walk totals to dominate the data stated by innings.

So if what you mean by "other things being equal" is that you have two pitchers who each face the same number of batters, then yes, the strikeout pitcher will throw some extra pitches. How many? About 100 to 150 extra pitches per year, for a healthy starting pitcher. I don't

Strikeout pitchers throw no more pitches per inning than do non-strikeout pitchers.

think that is what most people mean by "other things be-ing equal". I think when we think of a pitcher with 220 inning pitched, we tend to think of that as being equal to another pitcher who pitched 220 innings, not to a pitcher who pitched 205 innings but faced the same number of batters.

By the way, John Dewan did some research as well and found this:

Using the top five starters on each team (based on games started), we get 150 Major League Baseball pitch-ers from 2007. We divide them into three groups of 50 based on their Strikeouts Per Nine ratio. Here is how it comes out:

	Innings	BB/9	K/9	Pitches/Inning
High Strikeouts	8,716	3.1	8.1	16.28
Medium Strikeouts	7,442	3.0	6.2	16.19
Low Strikeouts	7,332	2.8	4.6	15.81

So there is a pattern. Strikeout pitchers do throw more pitches. But it's minimal. Over the course of 7 innings, the high strikeout group throws 114 pitches, medium throws 113 and low throws 111. That's a difference of only three pitches per game from the top group to the bottom. Which, interestingly coincides pretty much with the extra pitches thrown on the 3-4 extra strikeouts those pitchers get.

So, we're back to where we started. Strikeout pitch-ers do throw extra pitches, but not very many, and not anywhere near as many as most baseball observers might think.

It's a matter of perspective, I suppose. From now on, when I hear somebody say that strikeout pitchers throw more pitches because the strikeout requires three pitches to get an out, I plan to say, "That's really not true." If you want to interpret the data differently, I guess that's up to you.

Appendix: Control Problems

Another comment made by John Dewan is that "strike-out pitchers are more prone to control problems." His-torically, this has been true, and it remains true now if you focus on pitchers pitching a limited number of innings.

In modern baseball, however, when you are talking about pitchers pitching 150 or more innings, there is little connection between strikeouts and control problems. I looked at all pitchers pitching 150 or more innings:

a) from 1920 to 1935,
b) from 1950 to 1965,
c) from 1998 to 2007.

From 1920 to 1935 there were 1,140 such pitchers. Comparing the top 20% of those pitchers in strikeouts/nine innings to the bottom 20%, the top strikeout pitch-ers walked 20% more hitters (20.1%, as a percentage of batters faced).

From 1950 to 1965 there were 1,053 such pitchers. Comparing the top 20% of those in strikeouts/nine innings to the bottom 20%, the top strikeout pitchers walked 16% more hitters (15.5%).

From 1998 to 2007 there were 975 such pitchers. Comparing the top 20% of those in strikeouts to the bot-tom 20%, the top strikeout pitchers walked 8% more hit-ters (7.8%).

So...yes, strikeouts *do* connect to walks, but not really, in the modern game; not the way they did when you and I were young, Maggie. It used to be that there were *some* pitchers who were playing for strikeouts, and those pitch-ers sometimes walked batters because they were trying to strike them out. In the modern power vs. power game, it is more true that *everybody* is playing for strikeouts, and thus that walk rates simply represent control. It used to be an option; now that's just the way the game is played.

If you want to interpret the data differently, I guess that's up to you.

Kansas City Royals

Kansas City Royals – 2008
Team Overview

Description		Ranking
Won-Lost Record	75-87	
Place	4th of 5 in American League Central	
Runs Scored	691	24th in the majors
Runs Allowed	781	21st in the majors
Home Runs	120	24th in the majors
Home Runs Allowed	159	8th in the majors
Batting Average	.269	9th in the majors
Batting Average Allowed	.264	18th in the majors
Walks Drawn	392	28th in the majors
Walks Given	515	11th in the majors
OPS For	.717	25th in the majors
OPS Against	.743	15th in the majors
Stolen Bases	79	18th in the majors
Stolen Bases Allowed	78	9th in the majors

Key Players

Pos	Player	G	AB	R	H	2B	3B	HR	RBI	SB	CS	BB	SO	Avg	OBP	Slg	OPS	WS
C	John Buck	109	370	48	83	23	1	9	48	0	3	38	96	.224	.304	.365	.669	8
1B	Ross Gload	122	388	46	106	18	1	3	37	3	4	23	39	.273	.317	.348	.664	5
2B	Mark Grudzielanek	86	331	36	99	24	0	3	24	2	1	19	41	.299	.345	.399	.743	10
3B	Alex Gordon	134	493	72	128	35	1	16	59	9	2	66	120	.260	.351	.432	.783	15
SS	Mike Aviles	102	419	68	136	27	4	10	51	8	3	18	58	.325	.354	.480	.833	17
LF	Jose Guillen	153	598	66	158	42	1	20	97	2	1	23	106	.264	.300	.438	.738	10
CF	David DeJesus	135	518	70	159	25	7	12	73	11	8	46	71	.307	.366	.452	.818	22
RF	Mark Teahen	149	572	66	146	31	4	15	59	4	3	46	131	.255	.313	.402	.715	11
DH	Billy Butler	124	443	44	122	22	0	11	55	0	1	33	57	.275	.324	.400	.724	8

Key Pitchers

Pos	Player	G	GS	W	L	Sv	IP	H	R	ER	SO	BB	BR/9	ERA	WS
SP	Gil Meche	34	34	14	11	0	210.1	204	98	93	183	73	11.85	3.98	14
SP	Zack Greinke	32	32	13	10	0	202.1	202	87	78	183	56	11.65	3.47	15
SP	Brian Bannister	32	32	9	16	0	182.2	215	127	117	113	58	13.80	5.76	2
SP	Kyle Davies	21	21	9	7	0	113.0	121	57	51	71	43	13.22	4.06	7
SP	Luke Hochevar	22	22	6	12	0	129.0	143	84	79	72	47	13.60	5.51	3
CL	Joakim Soria	63	0	2	3	42	67.1	39	13	12	66	19	8.55	1.60	17
RP	Ron Mahay	57	0	5	0	0	64.2	61	27	25	49	29	12.66	3.48	6
RP	Ramon Ramirez	71	0	3	2	1	71.2	57	23	21	70	31	11.05	2.64	9

G Whiz

Gathright, Gordon, Gload, Grudzielanek, German, Gobble, Greinke...what is this? Shouldn't you guys be concentrating on getting better hitters, rather than getting guys whose names started with "G"? It's a shame you let Ruben Gotay get away from you. And now Joey Gathright is with the Cubs.

The Groyals 9th place hitters (Gathright, German and Gpena) drove in only 42 runs in 2008—lowest total in the American League, and lower than six National League teams. A key reason for this: Joey Gathright probably bunts more often than any other major league player, and certainly bunts more often than any other major league player who can't actually bunt worth a hoot. The Major League leaders in Bunt Attempts:

Name	Team	PA	Bunts	Bunt Outs
Gomez,Carlos	Twins	614	66	36
Taveras,Willy	Rockies	538	59	37
Gathright,Joey	**Royals**	**315**	**54**	**39**
Casilla,Alexi	Twins	437	37	21
Blanco,Gregor	Braves	519	36	21
Bourn,Michael	Astros	514	34	21
Pierre,Juan	Dodgers	406	32	21
Aybar,Erick	Angels	375	29	20
Patterson,Corey	Reds	392	27	17
Cabrera,Asdrubal	Indians	418	23	19

Getting the Job Done, Somehow (or, Production without Production)

The Royals had baseball's worst OPS of any major league team from the cleanup spot (.718, 14 points lower than any other team), but still got 126 RBI out of the spot, more than all but five other teams.

Kansas City Royals – 2008
Productivity by Batting Order Position

Pos	Players	Avg	OBP	Slg	OPS
1	DeJesus (105 G), Aviles (30 G), Gathright (20 G)	.313	.358	.437	.796
2	Aviles (56 G), Grudzielanek (55 G), German (20 G)	.294	.343	.409	.752
3	Gordon (67 G), Teahen (35 G), DeJesus (24 G)	.248	.327	.372	.700
4	Guillen (117 G), Butler (31 G)	.252	.292	.426	.718
5	Butler (49 G), Teahen (49 G), Grudzielanek (21 G)	.284	.331	.448	.779
6	Gordon (46 G), Teahen (43 G), Butler (28 G)	.286	.339	.451	.790
7	Gload (60 G), Buck (37 G), Olivo (25 G)	.245	.288	.364	.652
8	Buck (60 G), Gload (35 G)	.252	.310	.357	.667
9	Pena (49 G), Gathright (43 G), German (20 G)	.233	.281	.285	.566
	Total	.269	.320	.397	.717

The Royals may have been the streakiest team in the majors last year—in both directions. They lost 12 games in a row in late May, then won 11 of 12 in June.

Their record from August 12th until the end of the season was also topsy-turvy. Breaking the season into home/road segments, they went 3-15 from the 12th of August to the 31st, 8-5 from September 2nd through the 14th, and 10-3 until the end of the season.

Kansas City Royal – 2008
Tracking the Season by Segments

	W-L	R	PG	Avg	OR	PG	ERA	W-L
Road Trip, March 31 to April 6	4-2	23	3.8	.256	16	2.7	2.67	4-2
Homestand, April 8 to 13	3-3	15	2.5	.258	16	2.7	2.50	7-5
Road Trip, April 14 to 20	2-5	25	3.6	.264	45	6.4	6.83	9-10
Homestand, April 22 to 27	2-4	19	3.2	.233	36	6.0	5.50	11-14
Road Trip, April 29 to May 4	3-2	25	5.0	.266	20	4.0	4.19	14-16
Homestand, May 5 to 15	5-5	39	3.9	.282	36	3.6	3.60	19-21
Road Trip, May 16 to 26	2-9	35	3.2	.230	65	5.9	6.00	21-30
Homestand, May 27 to June 1	2-4	26	4.3	.295	26	4.3	4.03	23-34
Road Trip, June 3 to 9	2-5	30	4.3	.238	42	6.0	5.85	25-39
Homestand, June 10 to 12	1-2	16	5.3	.305	22	7.3	6.00	26-41
Road Trip, June 13 to 19	5-1	29	4.8	.286	11	1.8	1.66	31-42
Homestand, June 20 to 29	6-3	53	5.9	.276	47	5.2	4.44	37-45
Road Trip, June 30 to July 7	3-5	34	4.3	.252	51	6.4	6.17	40-50
Homestand, July 8 to 13	3-3	28	4.7	.277	25	4.2	3.41	43-53
Road Trip, July 18 to 20	2-1	22	7.3	.248	17	5.7	5.88	45-54
Homestand, July 21 to 27	2-5	22	3.1	.236	46	6.6	6.14	47-59
Road Trip, July 28 to 30	3-0	13	4.3	.248	7	2.3	2.25	50-59
Homestand, August 1 to 10	4-5	42	4.7	.294	48	5.3	4.71	54-64
Road Trip, August 12 to 21	1-8	26	2.9	.232	70	7.8	6.84	55-72
Homestand, August 22 to 27	1-5	17	2.8	.260	25	4.2	3.67	56-77
Road Trip, August 29 to 31	1-2	18	6.0	.333	13	4.3	3.24	57-79
Homestand, September 2 to 7	4-2	26	4.3	.289	25	4.2	3.60	61-81
Road Trip, September 9 to 14	4-3	40	5.7	.305	38	5.4	5.61	65-84
Homestand, September 15 to 21	5-2	35	5.0	.287	19	2.7	2.71	70-86
Road Trip, September 22 to 28	5-1	33	5.5	.315	15	2.5	2.21	75-87

If Brian Bannister could just pitch against below-average teams, he'd be an All-Star. His career ERA is 3.17 against sub-.500 teams—but almost twice as high against teams with winnng records.

Brian Bannister
Career Records Against Quality of Opposition

Opponent	G	IP	W	L	SO	BB	ERA
.600 teams	1	6.2	0	1	3	2	6.75
.500 - .599 teams	36	197.1	8	20	106	28	6.25
.400 - .499 teams	30	181.2	15	5	100	54	3.17

Joakim Soria in 2008 had 36 1-2-3 innings—the most by any major league reliever. K-Rod had only 22, and Brad Lidge converted 41 of 41 Save chances with only 25 1-2-3 innings.

Joakim Soria – 2008
Inning Analysis

Innings Pitched	67.1
Runs Allowed	13
Innings Started	66
Runs in Those Innings	10
Shutout Innings	58
One-Run Innings	6
Two-Run Innings	2
Got First Man Out	53
Runs Scored in Those Innings	6
Runs/9 Innings	1.02
First Man Reached	13
Runs Scored in Those Innings	4
Runs/9 Innings	2.77
1-2-3 Innings	36
10-pitch Innings (or less)	12
Long Innings (20 or more pitches)	11
Failed to Finish Inning	2

Francisco Rodriguez – 2008
Inning Analysis

Innings Pitched	68.1
Runs Allowed	21
Innings Started	65
Runs in Those Innings	19
Shutout Innings	53
One-Run Innings	8
Two-Run Innings	1
Three-Run Innings	3
Got First Man Out	43
Runs Scored in Those Innings	4
Runs/9 Innings	.84
First Man Reached	22
Runs Scored in Those Innings	15
Runs/9 Innings	6.14
1-2-3 Innings	22
10-pitch Innings (or less)	14
Long Innings (20 or more pitches)	20
Failed to Finish Inning	4

Brad Lidge – 2008
Inning Analysis

Innings Pitched	69.1
Runs Allowed	17
Innings Started	69
Runs in Those Innings	17
Shutout Innings	58
One-Run Innings	10
Seven-Run Innings	1
Got First Man Out	51
Runs Scored in Those Innings	6
Runs/9 Innings	1.06
First Man Reached	18
Runs Scored in Those Innings	11
Runs/9 Innings	5.50
1-2-3 Innings	25
10-pitch Innings (or less)	4
Long Innings (20 or more pitches)	23
Failed to Finish Inning	1

Mike Aviles – 2008
Pitch Analysis

Overall		
Pitches Seen	1501	
Taken	721	48%
Swung At	780	52%
Pitches Taken		
Taken for a Strike	265	37%
Called a Ball	456	63%
Pitches Taken by Pitch Location		
In Strike Zone	265	37%
High	105	15%
Low	144	20%
Inside	82	11%
Outside	125	17%
Swung At		
Missed	122	16%
Fouled Off	295	38%
Put in Play	363	47%
Swung At by Pitch Location		
In Strike Zone	541	69%
High	85	11%
Low	48	6%
Inside	27	3%
Outside	79	10%

Treetops Lover

Mike Aviles chased 44.7% of the high pitches he saw last year, sixth-highest among hitters who batted 300 times. Perhaps not coincidentally, 12.7% of the pitches thrown to Aviles were up and out of the strike zone, highest in baseball among hitters who batted 300 times.

Jose Guillen hit .264 with an on-base percentage of .300, and slugged .438 last year, with 20 home runs. That's pretty good (except for the on-base percentage) but it's still a bit surprising that he managed to rank 13th in the league with 97 RBIs. The key is that he came to bat with runners in scoring position 179 times, the 7th-highest figure in the majors.

Here's a list of the top ten batters with the most at-bats with runners in scoring position, as well as their batting averages in those situations:

David Wright	189	.243
Garrett Atkins	187	.225
Carlos Beltran	185	.286
Justin Morneau	181	.348
Michael Young	181	.298
James Loney	181	.304
Jose Guillen	179	.279
Josh Hamilton	177	.311
Jeff Francoeur	177	.192
Miguel Cabrera	176	.294

The Angels were the AL's only .600 team last year, and Gil Meche beat them the only time he faced them. He is now 7-1 in 9 career starts against .600+ teams.

Gil Meche
Career Records Against Quality of Opposition

Opponent	G	IP	W	L	SO	BB	ERA
.600 teams	9	57.1	7	1	37	17	2.35
.500 - .599 teams	101	587.2	35	35	459	227	4.69
.400 - .499 teams	62	350.2	18	22	258	132	4.23
sub .400 teams	12	74.2	6	2	53	25	4.22

Alex Gordon has had 215 career at-bats against pitchers with an ERA of 3.50 or lower, and Billy Butler has had 157. In those at-bats, neither player has hit a single homer, and each has produced just seven RBI.

Alex Gordon – 2007-2008
Batting Performance by Quality of Opposing Pitcher

	AB	H	HR	RBI	Avg	OPS
Pitcher with ERA <= 3.50	215	44	0	7	.205	.564
Pitcher with ERA 3.51 to 4.25	259	63	11	35	.243	.777
Pitcher with ERA 4.26 to 5.25	317	76	9	37	.240	.707
Pitcher with ERA over 5.25	245	79	11	40	.322	.951

Billy Butler – 2007-2008
Batting Performance by Quality of Opposing Pitcher

	AB	H	HR	RBI	Avg	OPS
Pitcher with ERA <= 3.50	157	34	0	7	.217	.540
Pitcher with ERA 3.51 to 4.25	185	55	7	28	.297	.806
Pitcher with ERA 4.26 to 5.25	232	69	5	35	.297	.771
Pitcher with ERA over 5.25	198	60	7	37	.303	.854

David DeJesus was moved to left field last year to make room for Joey Gathright. That experiment failed, and DeJesus spent some time in center after all. But he'll go back to left in 2009 while Coco Crisp mans center.

As a center fielder, DeJesus was average at best. But he was the seventh-best left fielder in the majors last year, as rated by the Plus/Minus system, even though he only played about a third of the season there. Given an entire season in left field, he could put up some outstanding fielding numbers.

David DeJesus – 2008
Left Field Plus/Minus Data

Year	Team	Inn	THROWING					PLAYS		PLUS/MINUS		
			Opps To Advance	Extra Bases	Kills	Pct	Rank	Expected Outs	Outs Made	Total	Enhanced	Rank
2006	KC	544.2	90	27	3	.300	4	140	138	-2	-2	23
2008	KC	482.2	44	16	0	.364		132	136	+4	+8	7

David DeJesus – 2008
Center Field Plus/Minus Data

Year	Team	Inn	THROWING					PLAYS		PLUS/MINUS		
			Opps To Advance	Extra Bases	Kills	Pct	Rank	Expected Outs	Outs Made	Total	Enhanced	Rank
2006	KC	479.2	45	29	4	.644		150	149	-1	+1	22
2007	KC	1351.1	135	75	2	.556	15	401	400	-1	-1	19
2008	KC	507.0	49	35	1	.714	37	156	151	-5	-11	26

Los Angeles Angels

Los Angeles Angels – 2008
Team Overview

Description		Ranking
Won-Lost Record	100-62	
Place	1st of 4 in American League West	
Runs Scored	765	14th in the majors
Runs Allowed	697	8th in the majors
Home Runs	159	16th in the majors
Home Runs Allowed	160	9th in the majors
Batting Average	.268	10th in the majors
Batting Average Allowed	.261	14th in the majors
Walks Drawn	481	23rd in the majors
Walks Given	457	4th in the majors
OPS For	.743	18th in the majors
OPS Against	.729	8th in the majors
Stolen Bases	126	5th in the majors
Stolen Bases Allowed	109	18th in the majors

Key Players

Pos	Player	G	AB	R	H	2B	3B	HR	RBI	SB	CS	BB	SO	Avg	OBP	Slg	OPS	WS
C	Jeff Mathis	94	283	35	55	8	0	9	42	2	2	30	90	.194	.275	.318	..593	7
1B	Casey Kotchman	100	373	47	107	24	0	12	54	2	1	18	23	.287	.327	.448	.774	12
2B	Howie Kendrick	92	340	43	104	26	2	3	37	11	4	12	58	.306	.333	.421	.754	15
3B	Chone Figgins	116	453	72	125	14	1	1	22	34	13	62	80	.276	.367	.318	.685	12
SS	Erick Aybar	98	346	53	96	18	5	3	39	7	2	14	45	.277	.314	.384	.699	15
LF	Garret Anderson	145	557	66	163	27	3	15	84	7	4	29	77	.293	.325	.433	.758	19
CF	Torii Hunter	146	551	85	153	37	2	21	78	19	5	50	108	.278	.344	.466	.810	21
RF	Vladimir Guerrero	143	541	85	164	31	3	27	91	5	3	51	77	.303	.365	.521	.886	22
DH	Gary Matthews Jr.	127	426	53	103	19	3	8	46	8	3	45	95	.242	.319	.357	.675	8

Key Pitchers

Pos	Player	G	GS	W	L	Sv	IP	H	R	ER	SO	BB	BR/9	ERA	WS
SP	Ervin Santana	32	32	16	7	0	219	198	89	85	214	47	10.40	3.49	19
SP	Joe Saunders	31	31	17	7	0	198	187	82	75	103	53	11.18	3.41	18
SP	Jon Garland	32	32	14	8	0	196.2	237	116	107	90	59	13.91	4.90	9
SP	John Lackey	24	24	12	5	0	163.1	161	71	68	130	40	11.63	3.75	13
SP	Jered Weaver	30	30	11	10	0	176.2	173	88	85	152	54	11.87	4.33	11
CL	Francisco Rodriguez	76	0	2	3	62	68.1	54	21	17	77	34	11.85	2.24	16
RP	Scot Shields	64	0	6	4	4	63.1	56	29	19	64	29	12.36	2.70	8
RP	Justin Speier	62	0	2	8	0	68	69	41	38	56	27	13.50	5.03	2

Los Angeles Angels – 2008
Record by Runs Scored and Allowed

	Scored	Allowed
10 runs or more	12 - 0	3 - 10
9 runs	5 - 1	0 - 7
8 runs	2 - 1	0 - 6
7 runs	15 - 1	1 - 5
6 runs	14 - 6	3 - 8
5 runs	15 - 4	11 - 6
4 runs	16 - 11	16 - 8
3 runs	11 - 9	20 - 7
2 runs	6 - 16	18 - 4
1 run	4 - 7	18 - 1
0 runs	0 - 6	10 - 0
Total	100 - 62	100 - 62

Making Your Runs Work

The Angels had the best record in baseball in 2008, but their record when they only scored one to four runs was remarkable. The Angels were slightly under .500 (37-43) and were 10 games better than the average of the seven other playoff teams (24-50). Here are the records for the playoff teams:

Playoff Team	Record when scoring 1-4 runs
Philadelphia	24-49
Chicago Cubs	20-46
LA Dodgers	23-57
Milwaukee	31-55
Tampa Bay	30-47
Boston	17-47
Chicago White Sox	22-49
LA Angels	37-43

Don't you just love the picture of Vlad Guerrero sliding on the cover of this book? We did—that's why we put it there. That's a nice slide in the picture, but the real question is, is he any good as a baserunner? Answer: Not even close. Over the last three years his baserunning Net Gain has been -15, -21 and -20. Generally, that means he's averaging around 20 fewer baserunning bases per year than an average baserunner.

Vladimir Guerrero Baserunning Analysis

Year	1st to 3rd Adv	1st to 3rd Opp	2nd to Home Adv	2nd to Home Opp	1st to Home Adv	1st to Home Opp	DP Opp	GIDP	Bases Taken	BR Outs	BR Gain	SB Gain	Net Gain
2002	6	15	9	16	2	4	140	20	26	3	3	0	3
2003	3	18	7	14	1	5	94	18	11	4	-21	-1	-22
2004	9	21	16	19	6	8	146	19	9	10	-18	9	-9
2005	10	32	9	16	6	8	133	16	8	6	-11	11	0
2006	6	21	10	17	2	6	121	16	17	10	-20	5	-15
2007	15	32	9	16	2	8	162	19	20	12	-17	-4	-21
2008	9	25	13	22	1	6	122	27	15	6	-19	-1	-20
Totals	58	164	73	120	20	45	918	135	106	51	-102	19	-83
		35%		61%		44%		15%					

The 2008 Angels won 14 games in which their starting pitcher had a Game Score under 40; they were 14-29 under those conditions, best in the majors. The Rockies, despite playing in a park where it might be thought to be easier to erase a deficit, were 5-48 in the same situation.

Los Angeles Angels – 2008
Performance by Quality of Start

Game Score	#	ERA	W - L
80 and above	5	0.60	5 - 0
70 to 79	25	0.98	21 - 1
60 to 69	21	2.03	16 - 5
50 to 59	37	3.16	28 - 9
40 to 49	31	4.22	16 - 15
30 to 39	24	6.78	9 - 15
20 to 29	12	8.41	3 - 9
Below 20	7	10.14	2 - 15

Don't Go There

Once again, Vlad Guerrero saw the lowest percentage of pitches in the strike zone of any hitter in the majors, and once again, it wasn't even close. Only 40.4% of the pitches he saw were in the strike zone; among hitters who batted 300 times, Prince Fielder was next-lowest at 44.7%. It was the fourth year in a row that Guerrero had seen the lowest percentage of strikes of any major league hitter.

Vladimir Guerrero – 2008
Pitch Analysis

Overall		
Pitches Seen	1964	
Taken	803	41%
Swung At	1161	59%
Pitches Taken		
Taken for a Strike	146	18%
Called a Ball	657	82%
Pitches Taken by Pitch Location		
In Strike Zone	146	18%
High	120	15%
Low	199	25%
Inside	118	15%
Outside	220	27%
Swung At		
Missed	213	18%
Fouled Off	480	41%
Put in Play	468	40%
Swung At by Pitch Location		
In Strike Zone	648	56%
High	84	7%
Low	163	14%
Inside	131	11%
Outside	135	12%

Joe Saunders belongs to an elite pitching club: nine pitchers whose fastballs averaged at least 90 mph last year, but who relied on both their curve and changeup at least 10% of the time. These are pitchers with a lot of weapons at their disposal, and the list includes some of the best pitchers in baseball, such as Cole Hamels and Tim Lincecum.

Name	CB%	CH%	FBv
Tim Lincecum	14%	19%	94.1
Justin Verlander	21%	16%	93.6
Manny Parra	17%	13%	92.4
Matt Cain	10%	11%	92.4
Gil Meche	18%	11%	92.3
Javier Vazquez	13%	11%	91.7
Joe Saunders	11%	21%	91.0
Cole Hamels	14%	32%	90.4

In 2007 a typical hitter against Ervin Santana was Eddie Murray, but with more power. Murray had a career batting average of .287, on-base percentage of .357, slugging of .476: the average hitter against Santana in 2007 hit .288 with a slugging percentage of .497.

Last year, a typical hitter against Ervin Santana was Andujar Cedeno. Cedeno had a career average of .236, .292 OBP, .366 slugging.

Ervin Santana
Record of Opposing Batters

Season	AB	R	H	2B	3B	HR	RBI	BB	SO	SB	CS	GIDP	Avg	OBP	Slg	OPS
2005	523	73	139	34	5	17	66	47	99	8	5	9	.266	.333	.447	.781
2006	751	106	181	41	6	21	95	70	141	5	9	19	.241	.311	.395	.707
2007	604	103	174	38	5	26	91	58	126	11	3	13	.288	.357	.497	.854
2008	834	89	198	32	4	23	85	47	214	16	4	10	.237	.283	.368	.651

Ervin Santana, when he was getting pasted in 2007 threw 9% curveballs.

Last year, when he was good, he threw 1% curves.

Ervin Santana – 2007
Pitch Type Analysis

Overall		
Total Pitches	2577	
Fastball	1572	61%
Curveball	221	9%
Changeup	139	5%
Slider	609	24%
Pitchout	4	0%
Not Charted	32	1%

Ervin Santana – 2008
Pitch Type Analysis

Overall		
Total Pitches	3428	
Fastball	2078	61%
Curveball	26	1%
Changeup	133	4%
Slider	1146	33%
Pitchout	9	0%
Not Charted	36	1%

Mike Napoli has a secret weapon. He's really good at getting hits off his groundballs. It's not that he hits a lot of groundballs—he doesn't. Over his career, 33% of his batted balls have been groundballs—the major league average is around 44%. But when he hits them, they make it through the infield at a pretty good clip. Napoli has a lifetime .293 batting average on groundballs. The major league average was .236 last year.

Napoli doesn't exactly fit the stereotype of a groundball hitter (think Juan Pierre or Ichiro, of course). He's a catcher, listed at 215 pounds. But you can see one of the secrets to his success here: Napoli pulls groundballs with a vengeance. Only 7% of his grounders were hit to the opposite field. When you pull groundballs, you're more likely to hit them hard, which means they're more likely to scoot through the infield before a fielder can reach them. It's an approach that seems to be working quite well for him.

Mike Napoli – Career
Hitting Analysis

Batting Right-Handed										1B	-	2B	-	3B	-	HR
Total on Ground Balls	167	Outs	118	Hits	49	Average	.293	Hit Type		43	-	6	-	0	-	0
Total on Line Drives	82	Outs	21	Hits	61	Average	.763	Hit Type		45	-	14	-	1	-	1
Total on Fly Balls	251	Outs	184	Hits	67	Average	.278	Hit Type		8	-	13	-	1	-	45

A man with no strike zone is hard to pitch to.

Vladimir Guerrero – 2008
Batting Performance by Quality of Opposing Pitcher

	AB	H	HR	RBI	Avg	OPS
Pitcher with ERA <= 3.50	139	39	8	21	.281	.869
Pitcher with ERA 3.51 to 4.25	130	36	10	31	.277	.904
Pitcher with ERA 4.26 to 5.25	145	49	5	18	.338	.893
Pitcher with ERA over 5.25	127	40	4	21	.315	.879

Young stud reliever Jose Arredondo won 10 games in just 61 innings pitched last year. Among pitchers who have won at least ten games, that's the lowest number of innings pitched in major league history.

Jose Arredondo – 2008
Decision Analysis

Group	G	IP	W	L	Pct	H	R	SO	BB	ERA
Wins	10	14	10	0	1.000	9	2	11	6	1.29
Losses	2	1	0	2	.000	4	3	1	3	27.00
Blown Saves	7	8	3	2	.600	13	9	6	6	5.63
Holds	16	17.1	0	0	—	11	0	14	5	0.00
No Decisions	22	27	0	0	—	15	6	28	8	2.00

Who will close for the Angels next year? After breaking the season record for saves, Francisco Rodriguez fled via free agency to New York, and the Angels signed erstwhile Rockie closer Brian Fuentes. Plus, they have Scot Shields, a setup man *par excellence*.

But the best closer candidate may be youngster Jose Arredondo, who compiled the best record last year among all four candidates—particularly from the batter's perspective.

	BA	OBP	Slg	OPS
Arredondo	.190	.266	.267	.533
Fuentes	.205	.277	.293	.569
K-Rod	.216	.314	.316	.630
Shields	.236	.323	.346	.669

You might think that southpaw Darren Oliver is a "LOOGY"—John Sickels' acronym for a "left-handed one-out guy". But over the last three years, Oliver has limited right-handed hitters to a .242 average, almost the same as lefties (.239).

How does he do it? Against left-handers in 2008, Oliver threw 49% fastballs, 51% offspeed. But against right-handers—and most of the batters he faced were right-handers—he threw 72% fastballs, only 28% offspeed.

Oliver's fastball comes in at 89, and, on the modern guns, mold has been clocked growing at 46. It is surprising that a pitcher can get out hitters who have the platoon advantage with that fastball, but he has.

The 2008 Clutch Hitter of the Year

by Bill James

A reader tells me that I have taken so many positions on the issue of clutch hitting that he has given up hope of following me. Well, for the sake of clarity, I have had only two positions on this issue.

First, in following the lead of other researchers, I thought that there was no such thing as an ability to hit in clutch situations. Second, thinking more about the issue, I decided that we had jumped the gun in reaching that conclusion—thereby introducing bias into our research—and that we should have waited and studied the issue more carefully.

Whether any hitter has an ability to hit in clutch situations is a debatable issue on which I have no position. In any season, however, it is clear that some players come through more often in clutch situations, if only because of luck. Last year we introduced an "Award"—one of our mythical awards with no trophy, but you can bring it up in an arbitration case if you want to—for the major league Clutch Hitter of the Year. The winner was Brad Hawpe of the Colorado Rockies.

Hawpe had another good year in the clutch in 2008, by the way; he hit .290 with 4 homers and 22 RBI in clutch situations. No other Rockies' hitter had more than 13 clutch RBI.

What, exactly, is a clutch situation?

A general definition of a clutch at bat is "any at bat which occurs in a situation in which one can see, as the at bat starts, that a hit in this situation would likely have a much greater-than-normal impact on the success of the team." We consider six factors in determining whether or not an at bat is a clutch at bat:

> The Score.
> The Inning.
> The Runners on Base.
> The Outs.
> The Opponent.
> The Standings.

Exactly how all of these things are combined is explained in Bill James Online, in an article which is exactly like this one except that it spells out in detail how all of

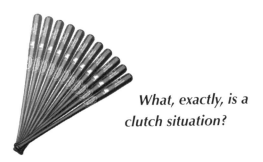

What, exactly, is a clutch situation?

these things are weighted and combined. That goes on for about two pages and is as interesting as a technical manual on the construction of ballpoint pens, so we'll leave that out of the book.

In the first game of the 2008 season, with Oakland playing the Red Sox in Tokyo on March 25, the Red Sox trailed 2-0 in the sixth inning. Manny Ramirez hit a two-run double, tying the score. The game went into the tenth inning, now tied 4-4. Ramirez hit another two-run double, putting the Red Sox ahead.

On April 12 at Fenway Park, the Red Sox trailed the Yankees 2-1 in the bottom of the sixth. (Ramirez had homered earlier for the one Red Sox run.) Ramirez hit another two-run double, giving the Red Sox the lead.

Two days later in Cleveland, the Red Sox were tied 4-4 with two out in the ninth inning. Boom. Two-run homer. Red Sox win, 6-4.

On April 17 at Yankee Stadium, Ramirez homered twice and drove in three runs, leading the Red Sox to a 7-5 win.

Two days later, playing the Rangers in Fenway Park, the game was tied 3-3 in the bottom of the 8th, Ramirez at bat, man on first. Home Run. 5-3.

After that incredible run of clutch hits early in the season, Ramirez did not have another really big hit until July. On July 7 at Fenway, the Sox and Twins played scoreless ball into the bottom of the 8th. Ramirez singled, driving in Pedroia, and the Sox won 1-0.

The next day the Red Sox trailed the Twins 5-3 in the bottom of the eighth, runner on second base. Ramirez homered, tying the game. The Sox won, 6-5.

Manny was injured shortly after that, or something, and that was the last big hit he would get as a member of the Red Sox.

Ramirez' heroics with the Dodgers are so well-chronicled that we may not need to recount them here but briefly: a .396 average with 17 homers, 53 RBI in 53 games. The Dodgers, 54-54 before Manny arrived, won their division, with Ramirez hitting .500 and .533 in two rounds of playoff games, adding four more homers and 10 more RBI in eight post-season games.

For the season (and not including the playoffs), Manny hit .405 in the season's most important at bats, 34 for 77, with half of the hits being for extra bases (10 doubles, 7 homers). He drove in 40 runs in clutch situations, tying Carlos Pena for the major league lead. His OPS in clutch situations was 1.279 (.505 on-base percentage, .774 slugging).

Diverging into Pena...in 2007, when Pena had a career year, he hit very poorly in clutch situations, just .167 with 10 RBI in 42 clutch at bats. Last year, although he was not as devastating overall, he hit 8 clutch homers, averaged .293, and drove in 40 clutch runs, same as Manny and more than anybody else.

Another guy who had a really good year in the clutch is a player who had a similar winter, Adam Dunn. Dunn had just 59 clutch at bats and hit just .288 in clutch situations—but 14 of 17 clutch hits were for extra bases, including a major-league leading 9 bombs. Think about it this way: The Atlanta Braves didn't have anyone on their team with more than one clutch homer, and the team total was 5. Adam Dunn had 9. That's a bunch.

Back to our award winner. Manny is an unusual person and an unusual player, and, as has been well documented, you can love him or you can loathe him. Sometimes Manny pursues his self-interest to the point of self-destruction. I have been a little too close to the situation to speak wistfully of Manny, but this is a factual, nuts-and-bolts analysis. The fact is, nobody had more big hits in 2008 than Manny Ramirez.

A clutch at bat is "any at bat which occurs in a situation in which one can see, as the at bat starts, that a hit in this situation would likely have a much greater-than-normal impact on the success of the team."

Past Clutch Hitters of the Year

Year	Player	Team
2007	Brad Hawpe	Colorado Rockies
2006	Albert Pujols	St. Louis Cardinals
2005	Andruw Jones	Atlanta Braves
2004	David Ortiz	Boston Red Sox
2003	David Oritz	Boston Red Sox

Los Angeles Dodgers

Los Angeles Dodgers – 2008
Team Overview

Description		Ranking
Won-Lost Record	84-78	
Place		1st of 5 in National League West
Runs Scored	700	23rd in the majors
Runs Allowed	648	2nd in the majors
Home Runs	137	19th in the majors
Home Runs Allowed	123	1st in the majors
Batting Average	.264	14th in the majors
Batting Average Allowed	.252	5th in the majors
Walks Drawn	543	15th in the majors
Walks Given	480	7th in the majors
OPS For	.732	21st in the majors
OPS Against	.691	2nd in the majors
Stolen Bases	126	6th in the majors
Stolen Bases Allowed	82	10th in the majors

Key Players

Pos	Player	G	AB	R	H	2B	3B	HR	RBI	SB	CS	BB	SO	Avg	OBP	Slg	OPS	WS
C	Russell Martin	155	553	87	155	25	0	13	69	18	6	90	83	.280	.385	.396	.781	20
1B	James Loney	161	595	66	172	35	6	13	90	7	4	45	85	.289	.338	.434	.772	14
2B	Jeff Kent	121	440	42	123	23	1	12	59	0	1	25	52	.280	.327	.418	.745	9
3B	Blake DeWitt	117	368	45	97	13	2	9	52	3	0	45	68	.264	.344	.383	.728	12
SS	Angel Berroa	84	226	26	52	13	1	1	16	0	0	20	41	.230	.304	.310	.614	3
LF	Juan Pierre	119	375	44	106	10	2	1	28	40	12	22	24	.283	.327	.328	.655	9
CF	Matt Kemp	155	606	93	176	38	5	18	76	35	11	46	153	.290	.340	.459	.799	19
RF	Andre Ethier	141	525	90	160	38	5	20	77	6	3	59	88	.305	.375	.510	.885	23

Key Pitchers

Pos	Player	G	GS	W	L	Sv	IP	H	R	ER	SO	BB	BR/9	ERA	WS
SP	Chad Billingsley	35	32	16	10	0	200.2	188	76	70	201	80	12.38	3.14	16
SP	Derek Lowe	34	34	14	11	0	211.0	194	84	76	147	45	10.24	3.24	16
SP	Hiroki Kuroda	31	31	9	10	0	183.1	181	85	76	116	42	11.29	3.73	10
SP	Clayton Kershaw	22	21	5	5	0	107.2	109	51	51	100	52	13.54	4.26	5
SP	Brad Penny	19	17	6	9	0	94.2	112	68	66	51	42	14.93	6.27	0
CL	Takashi Saito	45	0	4	4	18	47.0	40	14	13	60	16	11.11	2.49	9
RP	Joe Beimel	71	0	5	1	0	49.0	50	11	11	32	21	13.59	2.02	7
RP	Jonathan Broxton	70	0	3	5	14	69.0	54	29	24	88	27	10.96	3.13	10

Nomar Garciaparra had the third best walk rate of his career, and the second lowest strikeout rate of his career.

In a couple of years, we project that Derek Lowe will be throwing 140% sliders:

Derek Lowe threw:

No sliders in 2002
2% sliders in 2003
4% sliders in 2004
14% sliders in 2005
18% sliders in 2006
19% sliders in 2007
31% sliders in 2008

Lowe has remained remarkably consistent on the mound while gradually re-building his toolkit. His curve, which he used to throw more than 10% of the time, has disappeared, while his fastball and change have also waxed and waned.

Nomar Garciaparra – 2008
Pitch Analysis

Overall		
Pitches Seen	602	
Taken	307	51%
Swung At	295	49%
Pitches Taken		
Taken for a Strike	76	25%
Called a Ball	231	75%
Pitches Taken by Pitch Location		
In Strike Zone	76	25%
High	56	18%
Low	83	27%
Inside	42	14%
Outside	50	16%
Swung At		
Missed	32	11%
Fouled Off	109	37%
Put in Play	154	52%
Swung At by Pitch Location		
In Strike Zone	210	71%
High	5	2%
Low	23	8%
Inside	10	3%
Outside	47	16%

Derek Lowe – 2008
Pitch Type Analysis

Overall		
Total Pitches	3137	
Fastball	1883	60%
Changeup	213	7%
Slider	975	31%
Pitchout	17	1%
Not Charter	49	2%

Joe Beimel's 2.02 ERA in 2008 was probably the most misleading ERA in the major leagues. Beimel was charged with only 11 earned runs allowed, but gave up 26 RBI. If the run was charged to the pitcher who actually allows the run to score, rather than the pitcher who puts the runner on base, Beimel's ERA would have been 4.78.

Dodger reliever Jonathan Broxton had a strikeout to walk ratio against right-handed hitters of 60 to 5—but against lefties, of 28 to 22.

Most Valuable Half and Half

Four of the very best players in baseball in 2008 weren't serious contenders for the MVP Award or the Cy Young Award, because they split their seasons between the two leagues.

CC Sabathia, 17-10 with 251 strikeouts and a 2.70 ERA, didn't win the Cy Young Award in either league because he made 18 starts in one league and 17 in the other.

Mark Teixeira hit .308 with 33 homers, 97 walks, 121 RBI, 41 doubles and eye-popping glove work at first base, but wasn't a serious MVP candidate in either league because he split his time between the leagues.

Manny Ramirez hit .332 with 37 homers, 121 RBI (same as Teixeira), 87 walks and a .601 slugging percentage, but he, too, had one foot in each league.

And Jason Bay, while no one seems to have anything to say about him except that he is no Manny Ramirez, hit .286 with 35 doubles, 31 homers, 101 RBI, 111 runs scored, 81 walks and 10-for-10 base stealing. A lot of guys have won MVP Awards doing less, but Bay, again, was a half-and-half.

Here's a question for you: In all of baseball history up to 2007, are there four players that good who were out of the awards picture for either league because they split their duty between the leagues? I'm not sure there are. I know for certain that if you took all of baseball history up until about 1990, you couldn't find four guys like that.

These split seasons have become more common in recent years, of course, because cross-league deadline trades have come into the game. Carlos Beltran in 2004 had a monster two-league season (38 homers, 42 stolen bases), and Randy Johnson in 1998 struck out 329 batters in the two leagues. Still. . .four in one season is, I am pretty sure, unprecedented.

Do we need an award for these guys? They're MVP candidates, after all; they merely need legal standing. Are there going to be four of these guys every year, from now on, or was it a one-year aberration?

I don't know. I just hadn't heard anybody talk about it, so I thought I would.

The back end of the Dodger bullpen was very effective in limiting home runs. Takashi Saito, Joe Beimel, and Jonathan Broxton threw 165 innings in relief for Los Angeles and allowed only three home runs.

Matt Kemp and Russell Martin

Russell Martin was the Dodgers' most displined hitter last year, drawing 90 walks with 83 strikeouts, while Matt Kemp had a strikeout-to-walk ratio of 153 to 46. A closer look at their data shows:

1) Martin took 60% of the pitches thrown to him. Kemp took 48%, swung at 52%.

2) 75% of the pitches Martin swung at were strikes, vs. 71% for Kemp. It's a small percentage difference, but it's bigger than it looks, because the effects multiply as the strikes pile up.

3) When Martin swung, he put the ball in play 47% of the time. Kemp put the ball in play on only 36% of his swings.

Cory Wade threw his first pitch to a batter for a strike 67% of the time. In the National League, only Arizona's Chad Qualls had a higher percentage (68%).

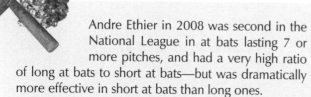

Andre Ethier in 2008 was second in the National League in at bats lasting 7 or more pitches, and had a very high ratio of long at bats to short at bats—but was dramatically more effective in short at bats than long ones.

We need to be careful about drawing inferences from this. It would be easy to say that Ethier is most effective when he gets his work done quickly, therefore he might benefit from having more of those at bats. The reality may well be that he is effective in short at bats precisely **because** he is a fairly selective hitter—therefore, the only way he has a short at bat is if the pitcher makes a mistake early in the count. He is just not, at this point, handling his long at bats as well as he will later in his career.

Andre Ethier – 2008
Short and Long AB

	AB	H	HR	RBI	Avg	OBP	Slg	OPS
One and done	52	19	3	5	.365	.377	.635	1.012
Short	222	77	12	38	.347	.356	.595	.950
Long	303	83	8	39	.274	.394	.436	.830
7 Up	57	12	0	7	.211	.384	.246	.629

Andre Ethier had the second highest percentage of line drives on balls put in play of any player in the majors at 27%. Jerry Hairston led the majors at 27.5%

Andre Ethier – 2008
Hitting Analysis

Batting Left-Handed								1B	-	2B	-	3B	-	HR	
Total on Ground Balls	184	Outs	138	Hits	46	Average	.250	Hit Type	38	-	7	-	1	-	0	41%
Total on Line Drives	118	Outs	40	Hits	78	Average	.667	Hit Type	55	-	21	-	2	-	0	27%
Total on Fly Balls	142	Outs	106	Hits	36	Average	.265	Hit Type	4	-	10	-	2	-	10	32%

Milwaukee Brewers

Milwaukee Brewers – 2008
Team Overview

Description		Ranking
Won-Lost Record	90-72	
Place	2nd of 6 in National League Central	
Runs Scored	750	16th in the majors
Runs Allowed	689	5th in the majors
Home Runs	198	5th in the majors
Home Runs Allowed	175	16th in the majors
Batting Average	.253	25th in the majors
Batting Average Allowed	.256	8th in the majors
Walks Drawn	550	14th in the majors
Walks Given	528	13th in the majors
OPS For	.757	14th in the majors
OPS Against	.729	9th in the majors
Stolen Bases	108	10th in the majors
Stolen Bases Allowed	71	7th in the majors

Key Players

Pos	Player	G	AB	R	H	2B	3B	HR	RBI	SB	CS	BB	SO	Avg	OBP	Slg	OPS	WS
C	Jason Kendall	151	516	46	127	30	2	2	49	8	3	50	45	.246	.327	.324	.651	19
1B	Prince Fielder	159	588	86	162	30	2	34	102	3	2	84	134	.276	.372	.507	.879	23
2B	Rickie Weeks	129	475	89	111	22	7	14	46	19	5	66	115	.234	.342	.398	.740	16
3B	Bill Hall	128	404	50	91	22	1	15	55	5	6	37	124	.225	.293	.396	.689	8
SS	J.J. Hardy	146	569	78	161	31	4	24	74	2	1	52	98	.283	.343	.478	.821	20
LF	Ryan Braun	151	611	92	174	39	7	37	106	14	4	42	129	.285	.335	.553	.888	23
CF	Mike Cameron	120	444	69	108	25	2	25	70	17	5	54	142	.243	.331	.477	.809	17
RF	Corey Hart	157	612	76	164	45	6	20	91	23	7	27	109	.268	.300	.459	.759	16

Key Pitchers

Pos	Player	G	GS	W	L	Sv	IP	H	R	ER	SO	BB	BR/9	ERA	WS
SP	Ben Sheets	31	31	13	9	0	198.1	181	74	68	158	47	10.39	3.09	15
SP	Jeff Suppan	31	31	10	10	0	177.2	207	110	98	90	67	14.08	4.96	5
SP	Manny Parra	32	29	10	8	0	166.0	181	91	81	147	75	13.99	4.39	8
SP	David Bush	31	29	9	10	0	185.0	163	92	86	109	48	10.75	4.18	8
SP	CC Sabathia	17	17	11	2	0	130.2	106	31	24	128	25	9.30	1.65	15
CL	Salomon Torres	71	0	7	5	28	80.0	75	35	31	51	33	12.60	3.49	12
RP	Brian Shouse	69	0	5	1	2	51.1	46	19	16	33	14	10.52	2.81	6
RP	Guillermo Mota	58	0	5	6	1	57.0	52	28	26	50	28	12.63	4.11	4

Whenever a pitcher gets out of a bases-loaded, no-out situation without allowing a run, we count that as a "Houdini." Brewer pitchers in 2008 pulled off seven Houdinis—two more than any other major league team.

Here's the list of each Houdini:

Player	Date	Inning	Foe
Mitch Stetter	Apr 27	Top 7	Fla
David Riske	May 6	Bot 6	Fla
David Bush	Aug 11	Top 5	Was
CC Sabathia	Aug 13	Bot 5	SD
Eric Gagne	Aug 20	Top 8	Hou
Guillermo Mota	Aug 24	Top 12	Pit
David Bush	Sep 8	Top 4	Cin

Prince Fielder takes 53% of the pitches thrown to him, and swings at 47%, the same percentages in each of the last three years. In 2006, however, 31% of the pitches he DIDN'T swing at were called strikes. That has dropped sharply over the last two years.

Prince Fielder
Multi-Year Pitch Analysis

Season	Pitches	Pitches Taken	%	Swung at	%	Taken Strikes	%	Taken Balls	%	Swung & Missed	%	Fouled Off	%	Put in Play	%
2005	239	111	.46	128	.54	42	.38	69	.62	37	.29	48	.38	43	.34
2006	2321	1231	.53	1090	.47	381	.31	850	.69	257	.24	381	.35	452	.41
2007	2510	1318	.53	1192	.47	385	.29	933	.71	283	.24	453	.38	456	.38
2008	2635	1403	.53	1232	.47	348	.25	1055	.75	298	.24	470	.38	464	.38
Total	7705	4063	.53	3642	.47	1156	.28	2907	.72	875	.24	1352	.37	1415	.39

Brian Shouse's slider is what makes him such an effective lefty specialist, but his inability to use it against right-handed hitters is what prevents him from filling a larger role. It's a heck of a weapon against left-handed hitters—he threw it to them 41% of the time, but they got only four hits off it all year. However, it's virtually useless against right-handed hitters, probably because it often winds up in the right-handed hitters' batter's box. Seeing mostly fastballs, right-handed hitters hit over .300 against him and struck out only five times in 108 plate appearances.

Brian Shouse – 2008
Pitch Type Analysis

Overall		
Total Pitches	731	
Fastball	519	71%
Curveball	1	0%
Changeup	24	3%
Slider	166	23%
Not Charted	21	3%

	Vs. RHB		Vs. LHB	
Total Pitches	373		358	
Outs Recorded	67		87	
Fastball	323	87%	196	55%
Curveball	0	0%	1	0%
Changeup	14	4%	10	3%
Slider	21	6%	145	41%
Not Charted	15	4%	6	2%

"Hardy" and "Braun"… are those great names for athletes, or what?

Who is a better baserunner: Brewer shortstop J. J. Hardy, or left fielder Ryan Braun?

Braun, by far.

Hardy in 2008 was 4-for-23 at moving first-to-third on a single. Braun was 9-for-26.

Hardy was 5-for-10 at scoring from second on a single. Braun was 11-for-12.

Hardy batted 132 times in double-play situations, and grounded into 18 double plays. Braun batted 129 times in double-play situations, and grounded into 13 double plays.

Hardy moved up 10 bases on the five types of events we call "Bases Taken"—Wild Pitches, Passed Balls, Balks, Sac Flies and Defensive Indifference. Braun moved up 11 bases on those events.

Hardy ran into six outs on the bases, including five times that he was thrown out trying to take an extra base or move up an extra base on somebody else's hit. Braun ran into only two outs on the bases.

Braun was 14-for-18 as a base stealer; Hardy was 2-for-3.

If you add it all up, Hardy was 17 bases worse than an average major league baserunner. Braun was 16 bases better than average. The difference—33 bases—is roughly equivalent to eight runs.

J.J. Hardy – 2005-2008
Baserunning Analysis

Year	1st to 3rd Adv	Opp	2nd to Home Adv	Opp	1st to Home Adv	Opp	DP Opp	GIDP	Bases Taken	BR Outs	BR Gain	SB Gain	Net Gain
2005	6	16	11	12	1	2	83	10	6	1	+6	0	+6
2006	1	5	2	5	0	1	22	4	2	1	-5	-1	-6
2007	4	21	8	14	2	6	100	13	14	6	-12	-4	-16
2008	4	23	5	10	3	5	132	18	10	6	-17	0	-17
Totals	15	65	26	41	6	14	337	45	32	14	-27	-5	-32
		23%		63%		43%		13%					

Ryan Braun – 2007-2008
Baserunning Analysis

Year	1st to 3rd Adv	Opp	2nd to Home Adv	Opp	1st to Home Adv	Opp	DP Opp	GIDP	Bases Taken	BR Outs	BR Gain	SB Gain	Net Gain
2007	3	13	9	15	2	2	96	13	19	2	+9	+5	+14
2008	9	26	11	12	3	5	129	13	11	2	+10	+6	+16
Totals	12	39	20	27	5	7	225	26	30	4	+19	+11	+30
		31%		74%		71%		11%					

Remember when Jason Kendall was a good hitter? Seriously. From 1998 through 2000, Kendall hit .327, .332 and .320. Just two years ago, Kendall had a nice .295 batting average. What happened?

Kendall stopped hitting line drives, the essence of his batting game. His line drive percentage over the last seven years is:

2002	24.1%
2003	25.3%
2004	22.0%
2005	22.0%
2006	23.7%
2007	18.5%
2008	17.7%

The Cubs were the only team to beat Ben Sheets twice last year. They also were the NL's only .600 team. Sheets now has a career record of 3-13 against .600+ teams, and is the only active pitcher who's 10 games under .500 against them (dating back to 2002). In July the Brewers traded for CC Sabathia. At the time, he had dropped 9 of 10 career decisions to .600+ teams. The Brewers lost each of his first two starts against the Cubs, but he beat them on three days' rest on the last day of the season to help put them in the playoffs. The victory brought his career record against .600 teams to 2-10.

Ben Sheets
Career Records Against Quality of Opposition

Opponent	G	IP	W	L	SO	BB	ERA
.600 teams	19	112.0	3	13	98	31	5.06
.500 - .599 teams	91	595.0	34	35	527	113	3.60
.400 - .499 teams	79	520.0	35	23	449	115	3.39
sub .400 teams	7	49.2	3	2	38	6	2.54

CC Sabathia
Career Records Against Quality of Opposition

Opponent	G	IP	W	L	SO	BB	ERA
.600 teams	16	106.0	2	10	65	40	4.58
.500 - .599 teams	84	555.1	31	32	460	166	3.81
.400 - .499 teams	84	567.0	45	20	479	154	3.25
sub .400 teams	37	250.2	22	6	218	68	3.30

Ben Sheets easily led the majors in percentage of pitches thrown that were curveballs, using his hook 32% of the time. A.J. Burnett was next on the list at 29%. Ricky Nolasco was the only other pitcher who qualified for the ERA title who used his curve more than 25% of the time.

Ben Sheets – 2008
Pitch Type Analysis

Overall		
Total Pitches	3054	
Fastball	1844	60%
Curveball	984	32%
Changeup	154	5%
Pitchout	1	0%
Not Charted	71	2%

	Vs. RHB		Vs. LHB	
Total Pitches	1497		1557	
Outs Recorded	301		294	
Fastball	920	61%	924	59%
Curveball	489	33%	495	32%
Changeup	47	3%	107	7%
Pitchout	1	0%	0	0%
Not Charted	40	3%	31	2%

Re-Considering the Playoffs

by Bill James

When I started doing sabermetrics in the mid-1970s, it was an easy decision to essentially ignore post-season play. We ignored post-season play for two reasons:

1. It was very small. I think that all of post-season history, at that time, was about 500 games, and only a handful of players had played in as many as 25 of them. If you had five homers in post-season play, you were among the all-time leaders.

2. There was a lack of equal access. To the extent that sabermetrics is about comparing players one to another, it is problematic to base evaluations on areas of performance that are only available on some of the players.

This became, I think, more or less the standard practice—to evaluate player careers as if the post-season didn't exist. The world has changed, however, and we need to seriously review this policy. The number of post-season games has changed so dramatically that the role of post-season games in the making of a great career is just not the same as it was in 1975. John Smoltz is who he is in substantial part because of his post-season success. So is Derek Jeter, and Mariano Rivera, and Curt Schilling.

There are players now who have played 100+ post-season games. It is a matter of time until the post-season totals of some players start to pass the markers that identify entire outstanding individual seasons...100 RBI, 200 hits, 100 runs scored, 20 wins. In a few years, people are going to start hitting those numbers for post-season play. By ignoring postseason play in our analysis, we're now ignoring an entire season of a player's career—and not just *any* season, but the most important games of his career.

I know that the equal-access problem is still with us, and I don't really have a solution for that. But I don't think we can go on discussing who should be in the Hall of Fame, or how the top 100 shortstops of all time rate, or much of anything else, with no reference or with minimal reference to post-season play.

The world has changed, and we need to seriously review this policy.

While we're sort-of on the subject...why do the leagues exclude the division series and the league championship series from Cy Young and MVP voting? Does that really make sense? I understand why the World Series is excluded, and I agree that it should be. But it seems to me that the logic of the honoring groups in 1969 was simply "If the World Series doesn't count, these games shouldn't count, either." Should that really be the controlling logic?

The League Championship Series *is* a part of the league. I agree that there *might* be a problem with some people over-valuing or over-weighting the post-season games, but I still don't really get the logic of excluding the league's most critical games from the consideration of who is the league's Most Valuable Player or the league's Best Pitcher.

Anyway, to get the ball rolling on including postseason play statistics, we included the lifetime postseason stats (including World Series play) in the player registers in *The Bill James Handbook 2009* and will continue to do so in the future. Of course, because that book comes out on November 1 each year, we can't include the current postseason stats. We haven't gotten *that* good in our player projections. Yet.

We haven't gotten that good in our player projections. Yet.

The Ten Commandments of Sabermetrics

by Bill James

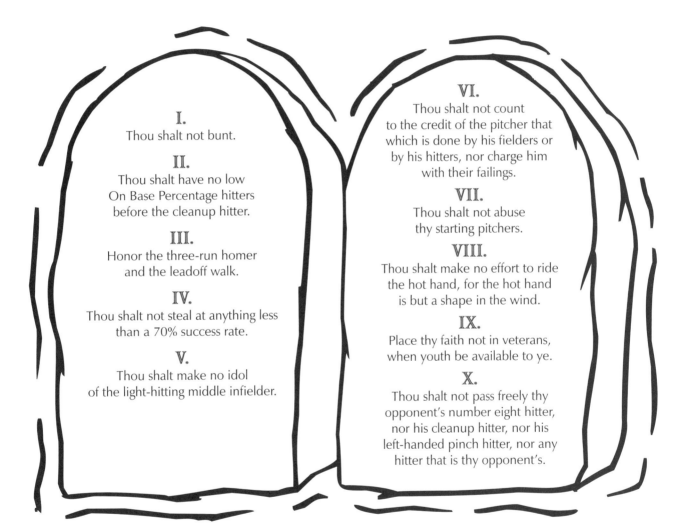

I.
Thou shalt not bunt.

II.
Thou shalt have no low
On Base Percentage hitters
before the cleanup hitter.

III.
Honor the three-run homer
and the leadoff walk.

IV.
Thou shalt not steal at anything less
than a 70% success rate.

V.
Thou shalt make no idol
of the light-hitting middle infielder.

VI.
Thou shalt not count
to the credit of the pitcher that
which is done by his fielders or
by his hitters, nor charge him
with their failings.

VII.
Thou shalt not abuse
thy starting pitchers.

VIII.
Thou shalt make no effort to ride
the hot hand, for the hot hand
is but a shape in the wind.

IX.
Place thy faith not in veterans,
when youth be available to ye.

X.
Thou shalt not pass freely thy
opponent's number eight hitter,
nor his cleanup hitter, nor his
left-handed pinch hitter, nor any
hitter that is thy opponent's.

Minnesota Twins

Description		Ranking
Won-Lost Record	88-75	
Place	2nd of 5 in American League Central	
Runs Scored	829	4th in the majors
Runs Allowed	745	15th in the majors
Home Runs	111	26th in the majors
Home Runs Allowed	183	18th in the majors
Batting Average	.279	4th in the majors
Batting Average Allowed	.274	23rd in the majors
Walks Drawn	529	20th in the majors
Walks Given	406	1st in the majors
OPS For	.748	17th in the majors
OPS Against	.756	18th in the majors
Stolen Bases	102	11th in the majors
Stolen Bases Allowed	69	5th in the majors

Key Players

Pos	Player	G	AB	R	H	2B	3B	HR	RBI	SB	CS	BB	SO	Avg	OBP	Slg	OPS	WS
C	Joe Mauer	146	536	98	176	31	4	9	85	1	1	84	50	.328	.413	.451	.864	30
1B	Justin Morneau	163	623	97	187	47	4	23	129	0	1	76	85	.300	.374	.499	.873	28
2B	Alexi Casilla	98	385	58	108	15	0	7	50	7	2	31	45	.281	.333	.374	.707	9
3B	Brian Buscher	70	218	29	64	9	0	4	47	0	2	19	42	.294	.340	.390	.730	8
SS	Brendan Harris	130	434	57	115	29	3	7	49	1	1	39	98	.265	.327	.394	.721	11
LF	Delmon Young	152	575	80	167	28	4	10	69	14	5	35	105	.290	.336	.405	.741	13
CF	Carlos Gomez	153	577	79	149	24	7	7	59	33	11	25	142	.258	.296	.360	.657	13
RF	Denard Span	93	347	70	102	16	7	6	47	18	7	50	60	.294	.387	.432	.819	16
DH	Jason Kubel	141	463	74	126	22	5	20	78	0	1	47	91	.272	.335	.471	.805	12

Key Pitchers

Pos	Player	G	GS	W	L	Sv	IP	H	R	ER	SO	BB	BR/9	ERA	WS
SP	Scott Baker	28	28	11	4	0	172.1	161	66	66	141	42	10.76	3.45	13
SP	Glen Perkins	26	26	12	4	0	151.0	183	81	74	74	39	13.41	4.41	7
SP	Nick Blackburn	33	33	11	11	0	193.1	224	102	87	96	39	12.57	4.05	10
SP	Kevin Slowey	27	27	12	11	0	160.1	161	74	71	123	24	10.61	3.99	10
SP	Livan Hernandez	23	23	10	8	0	139.2	199	93	85	54	29	14.76	5.48	3
CL	Joe Nathan	68	0	1	2	39	67.2	43	13	10	74	18	8.38	1.33	16
RP	Dennys Reyes	75	0	3	0	0	46.1	40	12	12	39	15	11.07	2.33	6
RP	Matt Guerrier	76	0	6	9	1	76.1	84	47	44	59	37	14.27	5.19	2

The Minnesota Twins are known for using pitchers who do not walk batters. In 2008 they lost two pitchers who had been in the rotation in Minnesota for several seasons, Johan Santana and Carlos Silva. They also traded Matt Garza who had been a part-time starter the last two seasons. They brought in veteran starter Livan Hernandez. When these players changed organizations what happened to their walk rates?

From 2004 thru 2007 Carlos Silva walked 1.19 batters per nine innings (not including intentional walks). After moving to Seattle his walk rate increased to 1.76 batters walked per nine innings.

From 2004 thru 2007 Johan Santana walked 1.94 batters per nine innings. After moving to the Mets his walk rate increased to 2.23 batters walked per nine innings.

Livan Hernandez pitched for Montreal/Washington and Arizona from 2004 to 2007. He unintentionally walked 2.87 batters per nine innings during this period. He also walked 30 batters intentionally during those years, which is exactly equal to the number of intentional bases on balls Silva and Santana have issued in their careers combined.

Upon joining Minnesota his walk rate dropped to 1.68 per nine innings, less than half of his walk rate the prior season in Arizona.

In the 40.1 innings he pitched for Colorado last season after leaving the Twins, his walk rate was 2.90 per nine innings pitched.

Matt Garza's walk rates have declined each of his three seasons in the majors, from 4.14 per nine innings as a rookie to 3.04 in 2007, to 2.78 in 2008 when he moved to Tampa Bay.

Is Delmon Young the new Vladimir Guerrero? Well, not yet, but Young in 2008 swung at 80% of pitches that were in the strike zone, the same percentage as Guerrero, and higher than anybody else. Young, however, swung at "only" 40% of pitches outside the strike zone, fourth-highest in the majors. Guerrero led the majors, by far, at 46%.

Francisco Liriano's 2008 ERA was higher than it was in 2006, but that wasn't the most striking difference in the pitcher's performance after Tommy John surgery:

- In 2006, his average fastball averaged nearly 95 miles per hour; in 2008, it was 91 mph.
- In 2006, he threw his slider about 37% of the time; in 2008, he threw it just 26% of the time.
- In 2006, 26% of the batted balls he allowed were flyballs; in 2008, 40% were flyballs.

Delmon Young – 2008 Pitch Analysis

Overall		
Pitches Seen	2190	
Taken	915	42%
Swung At	1275	58%
Pitches Taken		
Taken for a Strike	219	24%
Called a Ball	696	76%
Pitches Taken by Pitch Location		
In Strike Zone	219	24%
High	131	14%
Low	257	28%
Inside	105	11%
Outside	203	22%
Swung At		
Missed	301	24%
Fouled Off	498	39%
Put in Play	476	37%
Swung At by Pitch Location		
In Strike Zone	848	67%
High	68	5%
Low	142	11%
Inside	107	8%
Outside	110	9%

Joe Mauer was the best baserunner in the majors in 2008 among players with less than five stolen base attempts. We rate him at +19, meaning 19 bases better than average. He scored from first base on a double a major-league-leading nine times.

Joe Mauer – 2004-2008
Baserunning Analysis

Year	1st to 3rd Adv	Opp	2nd to Home Adv	Opp	1st to Home Adv	Opp	DP Opp	GIDP	Bases Taken	BR Outs	BR Gain	SB Gain	Net Gain
2004	1	3	2	3	0	1	22	1	4	1	2	1	3
2005	9	24	10	15	1	3	97	9	17	5	5	11	16
2006	8	32	18	27	2	6	136	24	23	2	4	2	6
2007	8	18	9	17	2	6	96	11	15	3	4	5	9
2008	13	34	14	26	9	13	137	21	30	2	20	-1	19
Totals	39	111	53	88	14	29	488	66	89	13	35	18	53
		35%		60%		48%		13%					

Joe Mauer swung at only 36% of his pitches last year, the second-lowest figure in the majors. And when he did swing, he made contact over 90% of the time, one of the ten highest rates.

Joe Mauer – 2008
Pitch Analysis

Overall		
Pitches Seen	2545	
Taken	1634	64%
Swung At	911	36%
Pitches Taken		
Taken for a Strike	569	35%
Called a Ball	1065	65%
Pitches Taken by Pitch Location		
In Strike Zone	569	35%
High	157	10%
Low	359	22%
Inside	136	8%
Outside	412	25%
Swung At		
Missed	85	9%
Fouled Off	328	36%
Put in Play	498	55%
Swung At by Pitch Location		
In Strike Zone	670	74%
High	62	7%
Low	48	5%
Inside	76	8%
Outside	55	6%

The Ultimate Mismatch

Joe Nathan has given up a total of three earned runs in 54.1 career innings against sub-.400 teams.

Joe Nathan – 2002-2008
Career Records Against Quality of Opposition

Opponent	G	IP	W	L	SO	BB	ERA
.600 teams	20	18.1	1	2	22	2	2.95
.500 - .599 teams	182	188.2	13	6	225	65	2.29
.400 - .499 teams	168	171.1	13	6	199	48	2.10
sub .400 teams	54	54.1	5	0	68	16	0.50

The Twins had 64 bunt hits last year, far more than any other major league team (the Reds were next with 39). Carlos Gomez himself had more bunts hits (30) than all but four other major league teams. The leaders in Twins bunt hits (and their batting average on bunt hit attempts) were:

Name	Bunt Hits	Bunt Batting Average
Carlos Gomez	30	.469
Alexi Casilla	16	.667
Nick Punto	6	.600
Joe Mauer	4	.800
Matt Tolbert	3	.750
Denard Span	2	.222
Matthew Macri	2	1.000
Mike Lamb	1	1.000

The Twins scored the fourth-most runs in the majors last year, despite...

- Finishing 7th in on-base percentage,
- Finishing 20th in slugging percentage,
- Finishing 26th in home runs, and
- Batting Carlos Gomez (with the .296 OBP) in the leadoff position 90 times.

How did they do it? Somehow, they managed to get their hitters up to bat with runners on base 2,517 times, the seventh-highest number in the majors, and 1,491 times with runners in scoring position, the fifth-highest number in the majors. And to cap it off, they were much better than any other major league team at "impact batting." The top five teams in batting average with runners in scoring position were:

MIN	.305
BAL	.287
TEX	.287
KC	.286
BOS	.280

Justin Morneau in 2008 led the majors in driving in runners other than himself. Most RBI leaders are home run leaders too, but Morneau was second in the league in RBI with only 23 home runs. His advantages were that:

1) He led the majors in at-bats with runners on base, and

2) He hit .330 with runners on base, as opposed to .266 with the bases empty.

He also led the league in RBI doubles (30), and most RBI per home run (2.00), among batters with 20 or more home runs.

Justin Morneau – 2008
RBI Analysis

Hits		RBI Hits		RBI Total		Drove In	
Home Runs:	23			RBI on Home Runs:	46	Scott Baker	1
Triples:	4	RBI Triples:	3	RBI on Triples:	5	Brian Buscher	1
Doubles:	47	RBI Doubles:	23	RBI on Doubles:	30	Alexi Casilla	17
Singles:	111	RBI Singles:	27	RBI on Singles:	30	Adam Everett	1
		Other RBI: Walks	1	Sacrifice Flies:	10	Carlos Gomez	17
		Other RBI: Ground Outs	7			Brendan Harris	7
				Total Other:	8	Joe Mauer	28
						Nick Punto	7
				Total RBI:	129	Mike Redmond	1
						Denard Span	19
						Matt Tolbert	6
						Delmon Young	1
						His Own Bad Self	23
						Total	129

New York Mets

New York Mets – 2008
Team Overview

Description		Ranking
Won-Lost Record	89-73	
Place		2nd of 5 in National League East
Runs Scored	799	8th in the majors
Runs Allowed	715	10th in the majors
Home Runs	172	12th in the majors
Home Runs Allowed	163	11th in the majors
Batting Average	.266	12th in the majors
Batting Average Allowed	.254	7th in the majors
Walks Drawn	619	4th in the majors
Walks Given	590	22nd in the majors
OPS For	.761	12th in the majors
OPS Against	.729	8th in the majors
Stolen Bases	138	3rd in the majors
Stolen Bases Allowed	.66	3rd in the majors

Key Players

Pos	Player	G	AB	R	H	2B	3B	HR	RBI	SB	CS	BB	SO	Avg	OBP	Slg	OPS	WS
C	Brian Schneider	110	335	30	86	10	0	9	38	0	0	42	53	.257	.339	.367	.707	10
1B	Carlos Delgado	159	598	96	162	32	1	38	115	1	1	72	124	.271	.353	.518	.871	23
2B	Luis Castillo	87	298	46	73	7	1	3	28	17	2	50	35	.245	.355	.305	.660	8
3B	David Wright	160	626	115	189	42	2	33	124	15	5	94	118	.302	.390	.534	.924	27
SS	Jose Reyes	159	688	113	204	37	19	16	68	56	15	66	82	.297	.358	.475	.833	28
LF	Fernando Tatis	92	273	33	81	16	1	11	47	3	0	29	59	.297	.369	.484	.853	13
CF	Carlos Beltran	161	606	116	172	40	5	27	112	25	3	92	96	.284	.376	.500	.876	29
RF	Ryan Church	90	319	54	88	14	1	12	49	2	3	33	83	.276	.346	.439	.785	10

Key Pitchers

Pos	Player	G	GS	W	L	Sv	IP	H	R	ER	SO	BB	BR/9	ERA	WS
SP	Johan Santana	34	34	16	7	0	234.1	206	74	66	206	63	10.49	2.53	21
SP	Oliver Perez	34	34	10	7	0	194.0	167	100	91	180	105	13.13	4.22	8
SP	Mike Pelfrey	32	32	13	11	0	200.2	209	86	83	110	64	12.83	3.72	12
SP	John Maine	25	25	10	8	0	140.0	122	70	65	122	67	12.41	4.18	7
SP	Pedro Martinez	20	20	5	6	0	109.0	127	70	68	87	44	14.61	5.61	1
CL	Billy Wagner	45	0	0	1	27	47.0	32	17	12	52	10	8.04	2.30	10
RP	Joe Smith	82	0	6	3	0	63.1	51	28	25	52	31	12.22	3.55	6
RP	Pedro Feliciano	86	0	3	4	2	53.1	57	24	24	50	26	14.51	4.05	3

Through the first three innings, the Mets were baseball's best team, and it wasn't even close: They were 23.5 games over .500, 10 full games better than any other team. From that point onward, they did a long, slow fade, holding fewer leads and facing more deficits each inning, ultimately finishing eight games over .500 and just short of making the postseason.

New York Mets – 2008
Innings Ahead Behind Tied

Inning	1	2	3	4	5	6	7	8	9	Extra	Final
Ahead	55	69	89	88	86	86	83	85	80	9	89
Behind	34	41	42	45	49	54	60	62	64	9	73
Tied	73	52	31	29	27	22	19	15	18	24	—

Jose Reyes led off 317 innings for the Mets in 2008—by far the largest number of leadoff innings in the majors. He was the Mets leadoff man, of course, and then it just happened that a lot of innings ended with Reyes due up next.

Reyes also led the majors in times reached base leading off an inning (118), although not by such a wide margin.

New York Mets – 2008
Led Off Innings Reaching Base

Player	Reached Base
Jose Reyes	118
Ichiro Suzuki	114
Hanley Ramirez	113
Brian Roberts	106
Grady Sizemore	104
Akinori Iwamura	102
Skip Schumaker	96
Johnny Damon	95
Orlando Cabrera	90
Ian Kinsler	86

Jose Reyes – 2008
Performance as Leadoff Man

Innings Led Off:	317		
Team Scored:	239	Runs	.75 per inning
Reached Base Leading Off:	118		
Team Scored:	142	Runs	1.20 per inning
Did Not Reach:	199		
Team Scored:	97	Runs	.49 per inning
Other Innings for Team:	1143		
Team Scored:	560	Runs	.49 per inning

The Santana twins (Ervin and Johan) both finished 16-7, and had nearly identical batting averages, on-base percentages, slugging percentages and OPS allowed:

Batting averages: .237 and .232.
On-Base Percentages: .283 and .286.
Slugging Percentages: .362 and .368.

They allowed 23 homers apiece, struck out about the same number of batters.

Johan's ERA was almost a run better (2.53 vs. 3.49), but that doesn't track with any other category.

Johan Santana pitched a brilliant, must-win game on the penultimate day of the Mets' season, but he's always pitched well against the best. His ERA against teams that are better than .600 is almost as good as his ERA against teams that are worse than .400.

Johan Santana
Career Record Against Quality of Opposition

Opponent	G	IP	W	L	SO	BB	ERA
.600 teams	18	102.1	8	2	121	34	2.29
.500 - .599 teams	104	604.0	37	29	609	159	3.07
.400 - .499 teams	79	486.0	39	14	531	107	3.00
sub .400 teams	39	221.0	22	3	234	57	2.24

David Wright drove in Jose Reyes 42 times last year, the second-highest figure for a pair of teammates in the last six years.

Only Gary Sheffield and Rafael Furcal reached a higher total—Sheffield drove in Furcal 49 times in 2003.

David Wright – 2008
RBI Analysis

Hits		RBI Hits		RBI Total		Drove In	
Home Runs:	33			RBI on Home Runs:	53	Marlon Anderson	1
Triples:	2	RBI Triples:	1	RBI on Triples:	1	Luis Castillo	11
Doubles:	42	RBI Doubles:	14	RBI on Doubles:	20	Ramon Castro	1
Singles:	112	RBI Singles:	26	RBI on Singles:	28	Endy Chavez	6
		Other RBI: Walks	4	Sacrifice Flies:	11	Ryan Church	8
		Other RBI: Ground Outs	4			Carlos Delgado	1
				Total Other:	11	Damion Easley	2
						Nick Evans	5
				Total RBI:	124	John Maine	1
						Daniel Murphy	4
						Angel Pagan	1
						Mike Pelfrey	1
						Oliver Perez	1
						Jose Reyes	42
						Argenis Reyes	1
						Johan Santana	3
						Brian Schneider	2
						His Own Bad Self	33
						Total	124

Among players who batted at least 200 times last year, Luis Castillo was the major leagues' most patient hitter by far. He took 68% of the pitches he saw; no other hitter took more than 64%.

Duaner Sanchez returned in 2008, after fracturing his shoulder and missing a year and a half of baseball. He pitched well, but he wasn't the Sanchez of old. His fastball was slower and he relied on his changeup more often.

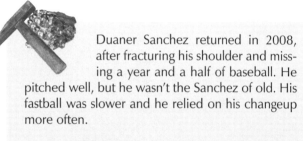

	% Fastballs	FB speed	% Changeups
2005	56%	93	16%
2006	49%	93	23%
2008	45%	90	30%

Carlos Delgado led the majors in line-drive home runs in 2008, with 8.

After posting a disappointing 5.21 ERA in 2008, several commentators wondered if Heilman's increasing emphasis on a slider impacted his performance. However, his weakness last year played out against left-handed batters, who were rarely thrown a slider. After three straight years of equal effectiveness against righties and lefties, Heilman's batting average against left-handed batters jumped to .308.

	RHB	LHB
2005	.236	.208
2006	.231	.231
2007	.218	.234
2008	.222	.308

Luis Castillo – 2008
Pitch Analysis

Overall		
Pitches Seen	1530	
Taken	1047	68%
Swung At	483	32%
Pitches Taken		
Taken for a Strike	409	39%
Called a Ball	638	61%
Pitches Taken by Pitch Location		
In Strike Zone	409	39%
High	111	11%
Low	211	20%
Inside	104	10%
Outside	212	20%
Swung At		
Missed	31	6%
Fouled Off	180	37%
Put in Play	272	56%
Swung At by Pitch Location		
In Strike Zone	391	81%
High	16	3%
Low	20	4%
Inside	28	6%
Outside	28	6%

Aaron Heilman – 2008
Pitch Type Analysis

Overall		
Total Pitches	1485	
Fastball	921	62%
Changeup	346	23%
Slider	173	12%
Pitchout	1	0%
Not Charted	44	3%

	Vs. RHB		Vs. LHB	
Total Pitches	843		642	
Outs Recorded	139		89	
Fastball	516	61%	405	63%
Changeup	154	18%	192	30%
Slider	158	19%	15	2%
Pitchout	1	0%	0	0%
Not Charted	14	2%	30	5%

Catcher Pride Points

by Bill James

This is not about the Red Sox, but Jason Varitek was the point of departure for the train of thought that led to this research. When Varitek caught Jon Lester's no-hitter on May 19, 2008, this was his fourth no-hitter, which was widely reported to be a record. (Apparently it ties the record, but this is wandering afield.)

I was thinking about the career that Varitek has had. He has caught four no-hitters; he has been the starting catcher on two World Championship teams. He has caught five 20-game winners (Pedro twice, Schilling, Derek Lowe and Josh Beckett), and two Cy Young Award winners. He has won a Gold Glove, played in the All-Star game, caught rookies who had outstanding seasons. Everything that a catcher might do that he can point to with pride, it seemed to me, Varitek has done.

What are all the things a catcher might do that he might take pride in?

This led me to ask,

a) "OK, what are all the things a catcher might do that he might take pride in?" and

b) "Who has done these things most often?"

I don't mean Johnny Bench-type things, hitting 45 homers and leading the league in RBI; I mean defensive things. Things that you might not see when you open the Encyclopedia and turn to the player's batting record.

Eventually I identified 13 things that a catcher might do that he could point to with pride, which are:

1) Catching a no-hitter.
2) Catching a 20-game winner.
3) Catching a Cy Young Award winner.
4) Working with a rookie pitcher who has a good season.
5) Working with a pitcher who has a breakthrough season.
6) Being the catcher for a team that leads the league in ERA.
7) Winning a World Series.
8) Being in a World Series.
9) Catching a team that has a good year. (That is, the catcher can say to himself, or others say about the team, "OK, we didn't get into the Series, but we had a good year".)

10) Leading the league in Fielding Percentage.
11) Leading the league in Assists.
12) Playing in an All-Star game.
13) Winning the Gold Glove at catcher.

I then made up a list of "catchers of interest"—a list that eventually grew to 107 names—and I started counting how often these catchers had done each of these things. A word to the wise: don't start a project like this unless you have some time on your hands. I must have spent 70 to 100 hours on this project, and the results may not be all that compelling. But anyway, taking these one at a time:

1) Catching a no-hitter

I posted a note on SABR asking for a list of catchers who had caught no-hitters, and four people wrote to help me out with that—Chuck Rosciam, Joel Tscheme, Mike Emeigh and Joe Krupnick—so let me begin by thanking those four gentlemen.

Of the 107 catchers on my list, 37 never caught a no-hitter, including Carlton Fisk, Bill Dickey, Mickey Cochrane and Gabby Hartnett. 35 had caught one no-hitter, 22 had caught two no-hitters, 11 had caught three, and two—Varitek and Ray Schalk—had caught four.

In the "Catcher Pride Points" system that eventually evolved I gave the catcher two points for each no-hitter that he signaled for.

2) Catching a twenty-game winner

Jim Hegan, catcher for the Cleveland Indians from 1941 through 1957, was the primary receiver for 18 twenty-game winners—Bob Feller in 1946, 1947 and 1951, Bob Lemon in 1948, 1949, 1950, 1952, 1953, 1954 and 1956, Gene Bearden in 1948, Early Wynn in

1951, 1952, 1954 and 1956, Mike Garcia in 1951 and 1952, and Herb Score in 1956.

Hegan also caught Bob Feller in 1941 (25-13) and Sam Jones in 1959 (21-15), but he doesn't get credit for those because he was not the primary receiver for those pitchers. Actually, figuring out whether somebody was the primary receiver for such-and-such a pitcher turned out to be a nightmare, involving a great deal of guesswork and supposition.

To begin with, I had to eliminate from the list of twenty-game winners a number of early pitchers who clearly didn't deserve to be celebrated as heroes. Adonis Terry in 1884 went 20-35; so did Pud Galvin in 1880. Obviously, 20-35 is not what we mean when we say "twenty-game winner", but what about Deacon Phillippe in 1899, when he went 21-17. Is that a distinguished accomplishment, or a throwaway like Galvin and Terry?

I decided to count all pitchers who had 20 or more wins except those who

    a)   pitched in the 19th century,

    b)   had winning percentages under .600, and

    c)   did not win 30 games.

This eliminated a little less than a hundred "twenty-game winners"—including Phillippe in 1899—but left more than a thousand on the list, each of whom had to be assigned to some catcher.

A few of those pitchers, I knew, had "personal catchers", and if a pitcher had a personal catcher and I knew about it, I credited him to the personal catcher, obviously. But there were, no doubt, also some times when a pitcher had a personal catcher and I didn't know about it, and I no doubt credited some of these to the wrong mask. When this study is re-done in 15 years by somebody with more programming skills than I have, there will be a data base you can run to get each pitcher's record with each catcher, so there's something you will be able to improve on.

When a pitcher did *not* have a personal catcher (or I didn't know about it), I simply credited the season to the team's "regular" catcher. Except that, in the history of baseball, there are many, many, many teams that have no easily identifiable "regular" catcher. And many of those teams had multiple twenty-game winners, or had one twenty-game winner and one rookie pitcher having a good season and one pitcher having a breakthrough season. Like, to pick one example at random out of 400, the Brooklyn Dodgers of 1939. Their catchers were Babe Phelps (92 games, 361 putouts) and Al Todd (73 games, 284 putouts). They had a twenty-game winner on the staff (Luke Hamlin), but they also had a rookie pitcher have a very good year (Hugh Casey). Do we credit *all* of their success to Phelps, because he is the "regular" catcher, or do we split them between Phelps and Todd?

In theory, I could dig into the box scores, find out who worked with Hamlin and who worked with Casey, and credit each to the "correct" catcher. I'd have to give up

my day job, but I could do it. But I just tried to be fair. If a team had a clearly identifiable "regular" catcher—somebody who caught two-thirds of the time or more—I credited all of the team's pitchers to him, unless I knew there was a personal catcher thing going on there. If a team had only one successful pitcher to be assigned to somebody, I assigned that to the catcher with the most putouts. If a team had multiple catchers and multiple pitchers—which happened very, very often—I tried to apportion credit to the catchers in proportion to their playing time, as nearly as possible. It was time-consuming and it wasn't perfect, but I did the best I could.

So anyway, Jim Hegan worked with 18 twenty-game winners, which was the most of any pitcher in my study. Wilbert Robinson worked with 16, Mickey Cochrane with 15, and five catchers (all of them pre-1925) worked with 14. 98 of the 107 catchers in the study had worked with at least one twenty-game winner, all the exceptions except one being post-1955—Gus Triandos, Ernie Whitt, Mike Piazza, Manny Sanguillen, Terry Kennedy, Charles Johnson, Sandy Alomar Jr., and Jason Kendall. I'll get to the other guy later.

I gave four points, in the Catcher Pride Points system, for working with a twenty-game winner.

3) Catching a Cy Young Award winner

John Roseboro caught four Cy Young Award winners—Don Drysdale, and three guys named Sandy Koufax. Dave Duncan caught three (Vida Blue, and Jim Palmer twice), and Jerry Grote caught three (Seaver, Seaver, Seaver). Damian Miller also caught three, although he wasn't in our study. Javier Lopez would have had four, but Maddux used Charlie O'Brien as a personal catcher in '95. On the other hand, 70 of the 107 catchers on our list never worked with a Cy Young Award winner.

Some of you are no doubt poised to object that the use of the Cy Young Award biases the study toward the later catchers (post-1956), since catchers before 1956 had no opportunity to work with a Cy Young Award winner. In fact, there is a time-line bias in the study, but it goes the other way. The addition of the Cy Young Award doesn't begin to compensate the latter-day catchers for the declining number of twenty-game winners. Between 1900 and 1909, with 152 major league teams, there were 135 twenty-game winners—essentially one per team. Between 2000 and 2007, with 240 major league teams, there were 30 twenty-game winners—one for eight teams.

I gave a catcher four points for working with a Cy Young Award winner.

4) Working with a rookie pitcher who has a good season

What is a "Good Rookie Season", you ask? I defined a "good rookie season" as a Season Score of 75 or higher. These are the pitchers who just barely made it—the worst rookies that I counted as "good rookies":

Pitcher	Catcher	Team	Lg	Year	G	W	L	Pct	IP	SO	BB	Sv	ERA
Oyster Burns	Bill Traffley	Bal	AA	1885	20	7	4	.636	106	30	21	3	3.58
Cy Young	Chief Zimmer	Cle	NL	1890	23	9	7	.563	148	38	30	0	3.47
Nixey Callahan	Malachi Kittridge	Chi	NL	1897	23	12	9	.571	190	52	55	0	4.03
Three Finger Brown	Jack O'Neill	StL	NL	1903	26	9	13	.409	201	83	59	0	2.60
Jim Winford	Bruce Ogrodowski	StL	NL	1936	26	11	10	.524	192	72	68	3	3.80
Bill McCahan	Buddy Rosar	Phi	AL	1947	26	10	5	.667	165	47	62	0	3.33
Julio Navarro	Bob Rodgers	LA	AL	1963	27	4	5	.444	90	53	32	12	2.90
Dennis Higgins	John Romano	Chi	AL	1966	26	1	0	1.000	93	86	33	5	2.52
John Hiller	Bill Freehan	Det	AL	1967	29	4	3	.571	65	49	9	3	2.63
Mike Torrez	Tim McCarver	StL	NL	1969	22	10	4	.714	108	61	62	0	3.59
Bruce Berenyi	Joe Nolan	Cin	NL	1981	26	9	6	.600	126	106	77	0	3.50
Bill Long	Carlton Fisk	Chi	AL	1987	27	8	8	.500	169	72	28	1	4.37
Jeff Montgomery	Mike Macfarlane	KC	AL	1988	26	7	2	.778	63	47	30	1	3.45
Mike Schooler	Scott Bradley	Sea	AL	1988	25	5	8	.385	48	54	24	15	3.54
Carlos Silva	Mike Lieberthal	Phi	NL	2002	23	5	0	1.000	84	41	22	1	3.21

Bill Dickey in his career worked with ten rookies who had good seasons—the most of any catcher in our study. The ten were Johnny Allen, 1932 (17-4, 3.70 ERA), Russ Van Atta, 1933 (12-4, 4.18), Johnny Murphy, 1934 (14-10, 3.12), Johnny Broaca, 1934 (12-9, 4.17), Vito Tamulis, 1935 (10-5, 4.08), Atley Donald, 1939 (13-3, 3.71), Marius Russo, 1939 (8-3, 2.41), Tiny Bonham, 1941 (9-3, 1.90), Hank Borowy, 1942 (15-4, 2.53), and Butch Wensloff, 1943 (13-11, 2.54). I have written before that Joe McCarthy had an unusual tolerance for rookie pitchers, and almost certainly used more rookie pitchers than any other manager in history, and this is no doubt a reflection of that fact. Behind Dickey in our study were Bob Boone, Roy Campanella, Carlton Fisk, Johnny Kling and Ray Schalk—each worked with eight rookie pitchers who had good seasons.

By my standards there have been 872 rookie pitchers in history who have had "good" rookie seasons. 360 of those were working with one of the 107 catchers in our study. Only six catchers in our study (Roger Bresnahan, Spud Davis, Rollie Hemsley, Dave Duncan, Gene Tenace and Terry Steinbach) never worked with a rookie pitcher who had a good season. I gave a catcher 3 points for working with a rookie pitcher who had a good year.

Gary Carter in his career worked with 19 pitchers who had breakthrough seasons—more than any other catcher in our study.

5) Working with a pitcher who has a breakthrough season

I defined a "breakthrough" season by a pitcher as

a) a Season Score of at least 100 points,
b) which is at least 50 points better than the pitcher's previous best season,
c) and is not a rookie season.

Some pitchers have more than one "breakthrough" season—that is, they establish a new level in 2006, establish another even better new level in 2007. That's fine; what I was counting was pitchers who, working with this catcher, accomplished more than they ever had before. You're limited to one rookie season, but you're not limited to one "new career best" season.

Gary Carter in his career worked with 19 pitchers who had breakthrough seasons—more than any other catcher in our study. The 19 pitchers who had breakthrough seasons working with Carter were Steve Rogers, 1977 and again in 1982, Dan Schatzeder, 1979, Scott Sanderson, 1979 and again in 1980, Jeff Reardon, 1982, Charlie Lea, 1982, Dwight Gooden, 1985, Ron Darling, 1985, Sid Fernandez, 1985 and again in 1986, Bob Ojeda, 1986, Roger McDowell, 1986, Terry Leach, 1987, David Cone, 1988, Randy Myers, 1988, Ken Hill, 1992, John Wetteland, 1992, and Mel Rojas, 1992.

After Carter, the leaders in working with breakthrough pitchers were Benito Santiago (16), Carlton Fisk (15), Ramon Hernandez (14, not including this season), Roy Campanella (13) and Johnny Bench (13). Every catcher in our study worked with at least one pitcher who had a breakthrough season except Emil Gross, a 19th-century catcher, and I'm really not sure why I included Emil Gross in this study to begin with.

The leaders are all recent catchers…well, reasonably recent. There are more breakthrough pitchers now because pitching staffs are much larger now. This, again, helps to offset the bias in the data toward earlier catchers, caused (among other things) by the fact that the earlier catchers worked with many, many more 20-games winners.

I gave each catcher 3 points for each breakthrough pitcher that he worked with. In baseball history there have been 1,579 breakthrough seasons by pitchers, of which 723 occurred while working with one of the catchers included in this study.

6) Being the catcher for a team that leads the league in ERA

Bill Dickey was the regular catcher on nine teams that led the league in ERA, Johnny Kling for seven, Jim Hegan and Javier Lopez for six. I gave the catcher four points for being the regular receiver on a team that led the league in ERA.

7) Being the regular catcher on a team that wins the World Series

Dickey and Berra were the regular catchers on seven teams each that won the World Series, no one else more than three. Altogether, the catchers in our study have won 78 World Series…actually, more than that, but 78 on which one of them was the #1 catcher.

In an earlier version of the point system, I gave a catcher twelve points for winning the World Series, figuring that the catcher would be much more proud of winning the World Series than of any other accomplishment. But this seemed to distort the totals and make them less convincing, and I decided to keep everything within a range of two to five points, reasoning that "how proud" the catcher was of this accomplishment was not a perfect standard for how much weight it should be given. Winning a World Series is something that is accomplished by 25 players and hundreds of off-field supporters, and, while we're all extremely proud of it, the reality is that each person's share of the trophy is limited. It gets five points—the only accomplishment that does—but it shouldn't be allowed to dominate the system.

8) Being the regular catcher on a team that reaches the World Series

Four points, not redundantly counted with Rule 7.

Roy Campanella and Chief Meyers were the regular catchers on four teams that lost the World Series, Wally Schang, Elston Howard and Steve Yeager on three.

9) Being the regular catcher on a team that has a good year

I defined "having a good year" as

a) winning 90 or more games, or

b) winning your division or league.

Three points. Thus, I credited these three points to teams that won their division but didn't make the World

Series, to teams that won 90 games but didn't make the playoffs, and teams that won leagues (like the Federal League and the 19th century leagues)—which had no World Series to go to. I did not count any of the 19th century post-season series as being "World Series", since they weren't, and I did not give any credit to teams that won a wild card slot but with less than 90 wins, unless they were able to fight their way into the World Series.

Combining points 7, 8, and 9, the top point-earners for team performance were:

1	Bill Dickey	48
2	Yogi	46
3	Jorge Posada	38
4	Mickey Cochrane	32
5	Bench	30
6	Roy Campanella	27
and	Javy Lopez	27
8	Bob Boone	26
9	Jason Varitek	25
10 tie	Jim Hegan	24
10 tie	John Roseboro	24
10 tie	Johnny Kling	24

While seven catchers in the study had zeroes: Rick Ferrell, Rollie Hemsley, Sammy White, Mike Tresh, Frankie Hayes, Emil Gross and Hank DeBerry.

10) Leading the league in Fielding Percentage

This category, again, biases the study against the modern catchers, since there are many fewer "league leaders per team" in modern baseball. Up until 1960, one catcher for each eight teams led the league in fielding percentage. Now it is one in 14 or one in 16.

Charlie Bennett, the 19th-century catcher for whom Bennett Park in Detroit was named, led his league in fielding percentage seven times, while Ray Schalk, Gabby Hartnett and Jim Sundberg did it six times each. I gave the catcher three points for the accomplishment.

11) Leading the league in Assists

My intention, when I started this project, was to give these points to the catcher who led the league in baserunner throw-out percentage, where the data was available on that issue. I found, however, that while a great deal of related statistical evidence was available, I could not find it in a way that was organized and useful.

We know, through the wonders of Retrosheet, that Gus Triandos in 1957 threw out 42 of 63 would-be base stealers, which is the highest percentage known. We know that in 1929 the most difficult *team* to steal against was

The catcher with the most Catcher Pride Points in his career, by my accounting, is Bill Dickey, with 203 points.

the Washington Senators (regular catchers, Bennie Tate, Muddy Ruel and Roy Spencer) and in 1926 the most difficult team to steal against was the White Sox (regular catchers Ray Schalk, Buck Crouse and Johnny Grabowski). However, if you phrase the question this way—"Who led the American League in throw-out percentage in 1971?"—the answer is not all that easy to find. You can find it by flipping from catcher to catcher in *Retrosheet*, and you could probably find it at baseball-reference. com, if you knew where to look, which I don't. Anyway, I couldn't find the data, so I wound up just giving three points to the catcher who led the league in assists, which is Gus Triandos in 1957, but it doesn't always work.

Hartnett, Sundberg, Del Crandall and Bob Boone led the league six times each in assists, Gary Carter five times. When this study is redone in fifteen or twenty years this will be something that you'll be able to improve. The advancement of databases will make it simple to see who led the league in caught stealing percentage for most leagues, and you'll be able to increase this to a four-point category and improve the reliability of who gets the points. But at the same time, a catcher might reasonably point with pride to the fact that he led the league in assists in a certain year.

12) Playing in an All-Star game

I gave a player two points for appearing in an All-Star game, maximum one All-Star game per season. The problem with making it more than that is that this is essentially a study of defensive accomplishments, while the All-Star team is determined to a large extent by hitting. Also, since a few catchers go to the All-Star game year after year after year, if you give very many points to this accomplishment it pushes you strongly in the direction of the conclusion that the catchers who have the most "Point to with Pride" type accomplishments are the big stars, which is of course where we are headed anyway, to an extent, but I don't want to needlessly increase that extent. Yogi and Pudge played in 14 All-Star games each…actually 15 for Yogi, but that includes two in 1960.

13) Winning the Gold Glove

I made this a four-point accomplishment. The catchers with five or more Gold Gloves are Ivan Rodriguez (13), Bench (10), Bob Boone (7), Sundberg (6), and Bill Freehan (5).

AND THE WINNER IS

The catcher with the most Catcher Pride Points in his career, by my accounting, is Bill Dickey, with 203 points. The top ten are:

1.	Bill Dickey	203
2.	Yogi Berra	189
3.	Jim Hegan	184
4.	Ivan Rodriguez	183
5.	Gary Carter	178
6.	Ray Schalk	177
7.	Johnny Kling	176
8.	Johnny Bench	167
and	Mickey Cochrane	167
10.	Del Crandall	160

You might think that Dickey wins simply because he played for all of those great teams, and there is an argument for this position, but it isn't necessarily true. Dickey has 48 points for team performance (rules 7, 8 and 9)—less than a quarter of his total. If you take those points away from Dickey, while allowing other catchers to keep theirs, Dickey would still be in eleventh place all-time. If you take the team performance points away from everybody, the leader would be Ivan Rodriguez (165), based on his enormous numbers of Gold Gloves and All-Star games, but Dickey would be only ten points off the lead (165-155).

Dickey, of course, has no Gold Gloves or points for working with a Cy Young Award winner, since those awards didn't exist when he was playing, and even the All-Star game didn't start until he was in mid-career. The system is certainly not biased in favor of catchers from his era, as we will see in a moment. Dickey never caught a no-hitter.

Dickey, however, has the following items to point to with pride—setting aside his seven World Series rings, which only Yogi can approach:

- He caught ten twenty-game winners (Red Ruffing and Lefty Gomez four times each, Tiny Bonham and Spud Chandler once each.) He got 40 points for that.
- His teams, more famous for their power than for

their pitching, led the league in ERA nine times—more than anyone else in history. We gave him 36 points for that.

- He caught more rookies who had good seasons (ten) than any other catcher. We gave him 30 points for that.
- He led his league four times in fielding percentage, three times in assists, earning him a total of 21 points for those accomplishments.
- He played in 8 All-Star games (16 points).
- He caught four pitchers who had breakthrough seasons (12 points).

I have always been sort of low man on the totem poll in evaluating Dickey—insisting at length that he was no Yogi Berra, for example—but you have to admit, it's a pretty impressive resume.

You remember Yogi's Yogiism when asked how he became the catcher that he was: "Bill Dickey learned me all of his experiences." Dickey took the lead in converting from an outfielder to a catcher not only Yogi, but also Elston Howard, who also did very well in our survey (117 points in a fairly short career.) If you combine that with the large number of rookie pitchers, it creates an argument that Dickey did have an unusual ability to work with others and to bring out the best in them, which is central to what we are trying to measure here.

Let me note a couple of other things in Dickey's favor. I have puzzled, in the past, about the fact that when Red Ruffing pitched with the Boston Red Sox in the late 1920s, his winning percentage was actually worse than the team's winning percentage (which was terrible), but when he joined the Yankees, his winning percentage became better than the Yankees' winning percentage. What happened to Ruffing, when he was sold to New York, that made him what he was? Bill Dickey is one answer to that.

Also, while we do not have catcher throwout percentages from Dickey's years, we do have it from the World Series. In 38 World Series games Dickey threw out 11 of 17 would-be base stealers—an extremely impressive accomplishment. It's a better record in World Series play than Yogi, Cochrane, Bench or Campanella, although all of them also had very good World Series throwout percentages. The Yankees' record against base stealers in Dickey's years is also generally very good; the Yankees' were generally near the bottom in stolen bases allowed, and near the top in stolen base throwout percentage.

I have always been skeptical about Dickey's stature in history, but I am, to an extent, convinced by my own study. I think he was probably better, defensively, than I have given him credit for being.

Other notes of interest on the top dogs. Gary Carter and Johnny Bench have fairly similar career batting statistics. While both are in the Hall of Fame, Bench is universally ranked higher, in part because his defense was more

impressive. Carter was a converted outfielder who won a few Gold Gloves, but Bench was the Ivan Rodriguez of his time, the gold standard for catcher's defense. It is interesting to note, if not entirely persuasive, that Carter out-points Bench in our survey. While Bench has a huge advantage in Gold Gloves (10-3, or 40-12) and advantages in All Star games, World Series wins and World Series appearances, Carter beats him in things like leading the league in ERA (3 to 0), catching twenty-game winners (3 to 2), catching Cy Young winners (1 to 0), and catching pitchers who had breakthrough seasons (19 to 13).

Among the many light-hitting defensive wizards of baseball history (John Roseboro, Malachi Kittridge, Mickey Owen, Steve Yeager, Bob Boone, Al Lopez, Rick Dempsey, Luke Sewell), the most consistent point-producer in our analysis is Jim Hegan. Hegan, who never won a Gold Glove or worked with a Cy Young winner, because those awards came in just as he was going out, and who played in only two All-Star games because of Yogi and Sherm Lollar and his low batting average, produces points all along the system—twenty-game winners, three times leading the league in ERA, seven teams that won 90 or more games—and winds up near the top of our survey.

Yogi said, "Bill Dickey learned me all of his experiences."

THE HIGHEST AND LOWEST RATES PER GAME PLAYED

The question *really* is; "Who isn't there?" You see those names above…Bill Dickey, you think "Sure; he's obvious"; Yogi, of course; Jim Hegan, he's famous for that stuff; Mickey Cochrane, Bench, Pudge, Carter, of course. This only becomes meaningful when you look at who doesn't do so well in the same survey. For that, we have to look at points per game played.

In terms of points earned per game played, most of the highest totals go to 19th-century catchers. In very early major league baseball, when the schedule was short and catchers didn't wear gloves, you have "regular" catchers who might have caught 40 games in a season. Most of the famous 19th-century catchers caught only a few hundred games in their careers. Buck Ewing, the most famous of 19th–century catcher, caught 636 games. These are the leaders, in my study of 107 catchers, in terms of points earned per game caught, with 130 games considered a "season":

	Catcher	G	Pts	Points Per Season
1.	Lew Brown	248	52	27.3
2.	Tom Daly	308	54	22.8
3.	Silver Flint	727	118	21.1
4.	Johnny Kling	1168	176	19.6
5.	Elrod Hendricks	600	85	18.4
6.	Charlie Bennett	954	126	17.2
7.	Jack Boyle	544	61	17.0
8.	Roy Campanella	1183	151	16.6
9.	Bill Dickey	1708	203	15.5
10.	Chief Meyers	911	108	15.4

Brown, Daly, Flint , Bennett and Boyle were all 19th-century players, having short careers as catchers (except Bennett) in a world where mediocre pitchers went 30-27 and you could lead the league in Fielding Percentage fielding .880. I believe that these were all very good defensive catchers, but their presence on this list is just a reminder that the 19th-century game was very different.

Among 20th- and 21st-century catchers in points per "season" played, the leaders are:

	Catcher (Years)	G	Pts	Points Per Season
1.	Johnny Kling (1900-1913)	1168	176	19.6
2.	Elrod Hendricks (1968-1979)	600	85	18.4
3.	Roy Campanella (1948-1957)	1183	151	16.6
4.	Bill Dickey (1928-1946)	1708	203	15.5
5.	Chief Meyers (1909-1917)	911	108	15.4
6.	Bill Killefer (1909-1921)	1005	119	15.4
7.	Bill Carrigan (1906-1916)	649	75	15.0
8.	Mickey Cochrane (1925-1937)	1451	167	15.0
9.	Lou Criger (1896-1912)	984	112	14.8
10.	Jim Hegan (1941-1960)	1629	184	14.7

This is another "good list", containing four of the same names (Dickey, Hegan, Kling and Cochrane), but substituting players with short careers for Bench, Berra, Gary Carter and others. But the method, as you can see, clearly does not discriminate in favor of the more recent catchers, despite the addition of points for the Cy Young catcher (post-1956) and the Gold Gloves (post-1957). Only one catcher from the Cy Young/Gold Glove era—Elrod Hendricks—cracks the list of the most productive catchers, which is dominated by catchers from before 1920.

What I was trying to get to, though, is "Who *doesn't* come out well in this system?" The number one and two "non-productive" catchers in baseball history are Blimp Hayes and Spud Davis. Frankie Hayes became the regular catcher for the Philadelphia A's in 1934 when he was just 19 years old, after Connie Mack had sold Mickey Cochrane to Detroit.

Hayes had an impressive career in many respects. He had some good years with the bat, hitting .291 in 1938, .283 with 20 homers, 83 RBI in 1939, and .308 with 16 homers, 70 RBI in 1940. In 1944, on a 154-game schedule, he caught 155 games, a major league record at the time, and still tied for the American League record. He was mentioned in the MVP voting in 1939, 1940, 1941, 1944 and 1945, and he played in four All-Star games.

But in terms of the things that a catcher can point to with pride, he's got nothin'. He was the one catcher in our study, pre-1955, who never worked with a twenty-game winner (or never got credit for it. Actually he caught part of the season for the Indians in 1946, when Feller had a monster season.) He gets:

2 points for catching a no-hitter

6 points for working with 2 rookie pitchers who had good years

9 points for working with 3 pitchers who had breakthrough seasons

3 points for leading the AL in assists in 1944

8 points for appearing in 4 All-Star games

A total of 28 points, in a career that is a couple of years longer than Roy Campanella's, longer than Thurman Munson's, or Steve Yeager's, or Manny Sanguillen's. Per 130 games played he is credited with only 2.8 Catcher Pride Points—the poorest ratio of any catcher in our study.

Just ahead of him is Spud Davis. Spud Davis played in the majors from 1928 to 1945, making him an exact contemporary of Bill Dickey. He was a very good hitter—a lifetime .308 hitter—and he was the regular catcher for the 1934 St. Louis Cardinals, who won the World Series with Dizzy Dean winning 30 games.

He gets 12 points for that—five for the World Series win, four for Dizzy being a 20-game winner, and 3 more for Dizzy having a breakthrough season—and man, does he need them. Other than those 12 points, he has a career total, in a long career, of 22 Catcher Pride Points.

He was never a regular on any other team that had a good year, no other team winning 90 or more games. He caught only one other 20-game winner (Dizzy Dean in '36). He led the league a couple of times in fielding percentage, once in assists. When the old catchers get together up yonder and start to brag about their earthly deeds, he doesn't bring much to the cloud.

Spud Davis lost his starting job in '35 to Bill Delancey, who Branch Rickey used to say wistfully was the best catcher he ever saw. Delancey was forced out of the game very early by tuberculosis, which finally killed him on his 35th birthday in 1946. Delancey's illness put Davis back in the starting lineup, but, despite his .300+ batting averages, he wasn't really a first-division catcher.

These are the weakest catchers, in terms of points per "season" played:

	Catcher (Years)	G	Pts	Points Per Season
1.	Frankie Hayes (1933-1947)	1311	28	2.8
2.	Spud Davis (1928-1945)	1282	34	3.4
3.	Bob O'Farrell (1915-1935)	1338	40	3.9
4.	Terry Kennedy (1978-1991)	1378	45	4.2
5.	Deacon McGuire (1884-1912)	1611	55	4.4
6.	Rollie Hemsley (1928-1947)	1482	51	4.5
7.	Sammy White (1951-1962)	1027	36	4.6
8.	Jason Kendall (1996-2007)	1774	63	4.6
9.	Gene Tenace (1969-1983)	892	32	4.7
10.	Rick Ferrell (1929-1947)	1806	68	4.9

What do you notice there? First of all, four players on this list are very direct contemporaries of Bill Dickey (1928-1946). Bill Dickey actually comes from an era which is discriminated *against* by this system, an era that this system doesn't much like. I tried to make the system balance reasonably across time, and it does, but...the catchers from the Bill Dickey era, other than Dickey and Cochrane, really did not score well.

Second, while there are some players on this list who had poor defensive reputations anyway (Gene Tenace,

Terry Kennedy, Jason Kendall, Spud Davis) at least two catchers on this list generally have good defensive reputations. Bob O'Farrell was voted the Most Valuable Player in the National League in 1926, when the Cardinals won their first World Series. But, as was true of Spud Davis, that world championship with the Cardinals was his only good team. He caught a no-hitter, but he worked with only three twenty-game winners—in a long career, in an era when winning twenty games was far more common than it is now. He worked, in his long career, with only one rookie pitcher who had a good season—Art Reinhart in 1925. Of course, he was a backup catcher for most of his career, and it may be that the system discriminates against him unfairly for that reason.

But what do we say about Rick Ferrell? Ferrell was voted into the Hall of Fame in 1984

a) as a testament to exactly how badly the Hall of Fame's selection system can screw up sometimes, and

b) upon the belief that he was an outstanding defensive catcher.

Of course, virtually nobody believes that Ferrell belongs in the Hall of Fame, anyway; it was a totally absurd and arbitrary selection, even if we assume that Ferrell was a defensive genius. But if he was a defensive genius, the evidence of it largely escapes our research. Ferrell

a) never caught a no-hitter,

b) was the regular catcher for one team that led the league in ERA, the 1945 Washington Senators,

c) caught six 20-game winners, which is a decent total and earns him 24 points, but

d) caught only three rookie pitchers who had good years,

e) caught only six pitchers who had breakthrough seasons, an unimpressive total,

f) was never the regular catcher for any team that won 90 games or won any kind of championship,

g) led his league once in fielding percentage, twice in assists, and

h) played in two All-Star games.

Adding it all up, we credit him with just 68 points, catching 1,806 games. The raw total ranks well behind guys like Alan Ashby, Terry Steinbach and Dan Wilson, in much shorter careers. The per-game ratio is one of the poorest in our study.

Other catchers who did well in our study, albeit not well enough to make the leader boards: Buck Ewing, Chief Zimmer, Billy Sullivan, Ramon Hernandez, John Roseboro, Elston Howard, Wilbert Robinson, Dave Duncan, Walker Cooper, Jason Varitek, Tim McCarver, Bill Freehan, Gabby Hartnett, Thurman Munson, Earl Battey, Tom Haller.

Mid-range numbers, not notably good or notably bad: Mike Scioscia, Steve Yeager, Smoky Burgess, Sherm Lollar, Jerry Grote, Jim Sundberg, Bob Boone, Dan Wilson, Jorge

Posada, Charles Johnson, Hall of Famer Roger Bresnahan. Bresnahan, like Ferrell, was elected to the Hall of Fame mostly on the basis of the theory that he was a great defensive catcher. His point ratio, for the era in which he played, is actually very unimpressive.

Carlton Fisk comes in at a not-too-awesome 8.3 points per season…not quite low enough to make the Dud list, but not anything to get excited about. Rick Dempsey is at just 8.1, Brad Ausmus at 7.9, Benito Santiago at 7.7, and Lance Parrish at 7.7.

Below that, you're talking about guys who just honestly do not have a whole lot of markers on their side. These include some Gold Glove winners: Ray Fosse, Tony Pena (four Gold Gloves and a couple of World Series losses are basically all that he has to brag about) and Sandy Alomar

Jr. Alomar narrowly misses the "bottom ten" list, ranking just two slots above Rick Ferrell—despite the help of *six* All-Star selections. Without the All-Star selections he'd be down around Spud Davis. Other guys who don't do well in our survey include Mike Piazza, Ernie Lombardi, Luke Sewell, Al Lopez, Ted Simmons, Manny Sanguillen, Bo Diaz, Ernie Whitt and Rich Gedman.

I want to stop short of saying that any of those men was not a good defensive catcher, or that our system proves that Johnny Kling and Chief Meyers were great defensive catchers. It's not proof. I just thought it would be interesting to look at this issue in this way, and I hope it was worth my time to do the research and your time to read it. I'll try to keep what I learned here in mind the next time I rank catchers.

I just thought it would be interesting to look at this issue in this way, and I hope it was worth my time to do the research and your time to read it. I'll try to keep what I learned here in mind the next time I rank catchers.

New York Yankees

Description		Ranking
Won-Lost Record	89-73	
Place	3rd of 5 in American League East	
Runs Scored	789	9th in the majors
Runs Allowed	727	12th in the majors
Home Runs	180	9th in the majors
Home Runs Allowed	143	4th in the majors
Batting Average	.271	6th in the majors
Batting Average Allowed	.267	19th in the majors
Walks Drawn	535	17th in the majors
Walks Given	489	8th in the majors
OPS For	.769	8th in the majors
OPS Against	.733	11th in the majors
Stolen Bases	118	8th in the majors
Stolen Bases Allowed	113	20th in the majors

Key Players

Pos	Player	G	AB	R	H	2B	3B	HR	RBI	SB	CS	BB	SO	Avg	OBP	Slg	OPS	WS
C	Jose Molina	100	268	32	58	17	0	3	18	0	0	12	52	.216	.263	.313	.576	9
1B	Jason Giambi	145	485	68	113	19	1	32	96	2	1	76	111	.247	.373	.502	.876	14
2B	Robinson Cano	159	597	70	162	35	3	14	72	2	4	26	65	.271	.305	.410	.715	12
3B	Alex Rodriguez	138	510	104	154	33	0	35	103	18	3	65	117	.302	.392	.573	.965	23
SS	Derek Jeter	150	596	88	179	25	3	11	69	11	5	52	85	.300	.363	.408	.771	18
LF	Johnny Damon	143	555	95	168	27	5	17	71	29	8	64	82	.303	.375	.461	.836	23
CF	Melky Cabrera	129	414	42	103	12	1	8	37	9	2	29	58	.249	.301	.341	.641	5
RF	Bobby Abreu	156	609	100	180	39	4	20	100	22	11	73	109	.296	.371	.471	.843	22
DH	Hideki Matsui	93	337	43	99	17	0	9	45	0	0	38	47	.294	.370	.424	.795	10

Key Pitchers

Pos	Player	G	GS	W	L	Sv	IP	H	R	ER	SO	BB	BR/9	ERA	WS
SP	Mike Mussina	34	34	20	9	0	200.1	214	85	75	150	31	11.37	3.37	17
SP	Andy Pettitte	33	33	14	14	0	204.0	233	112	103	158	55	13.01	4.54	10
SP	Chien-Ming Wang	15	15	8	2	0	95.0	90	44	43	54	35	12.13	4.07	7
SP	Darrell Rasner	24	20	5	10	0	113.1	135	74	68	67	39	14.21	5.40	3
SP	Sidney Ponson	16	15	4	4	0	80.0	99	53	52	33	32	15.30	5.85	2
CL	Mariano Rivera	64	0	6	5	39	70.2	41	11	11	77	6	6.24	1.40	20
RP	Edwar Ramirez	55	0	5	1	1	55.1	44	25	24	63	24	11.55	3.90	5
RP	Jose Veras	60	0	5	3	0	57.2	52	23	23	63	29	13.11	3.59	5

For the six years prior to 2008, the Yankees were a superior baserunning team. Their average Net Gain per year was +47 (meaning, in essence, about 47 extra bases taken on the basepaths each year, compared to an average team). In 2008 they were -4.

New York Yankees – 2002-2008
Baserunning Analysis

Year	1st to 3rd Adv	1st to 3rd Opp	2nd to Home Adv	2nd to Home Opp	1st to Home Adv	1st to Home Opp	DP Opp	GIDP	Bases Taken	BR Outs	BR Gain	SB Gain	Net Gain
2002	77	250	137	196	18	54	1281	150	158	24	+7	+24	+31
2003	70	233	132	193	27	63	1387	154	153	29	-6	+32	+26
2004	62	236	125	188	15	64	1325	156	159	36	-7	+18	+11
2004	96	281	127	206	18	51	1391	125	151	41	+50	+30	+80
2006	62	247	131	228	18	57	1328	139	167	35	+16	+69	+85
2007	73	263	154	246	31	72	1418	138	159	48	+6	+43	+49
2008	62	230	110	192	28	64	1207	149	150	48	-44	+40	-4
Totals	502	1740	916	1449	155	425	9337	1011	1097	261	+23	+256	+279
		29%		63%		36%		10%					

Close to you

15.4% of the pitches thrown to Alex Rodriguez were off the plate inside, easily the highest percentage of any hitter in baseball (Adrian Beltre was second at 13.5%). It was the third time in four years that A-Rod had seen the highest percentage of inside pitches; Vlad Guerrero edged him out in 2007.

Alex Rodriguez – 2008
Pitch Analysis

Overall		
Pitches Seen	2288	
Taken	1245	54%
Swung At	1043	45%
Pitches Taken		
Taken for a Strike	371	30%
Called a Ball	874	70%
Pitches Taken by Pitch Location		
In Strike Zone	371	30%
High	141	11%
Low	281	23%
Inside	297	24%
Outside	155	12%
Swung At		
Missed	254	24%
Fouled Off	391	37%
Put in Play	398	38%
Swung At by Pitch Location		
In Strike Zone	789	76%
High	29	3%
Low	102	10%
Inside	56	5%
Outside	67	6%

Moose

Mike Mussina retired over the winter, apparently because he just got tired of making American League hitters look stupid. At one time Mussina had a larger menu to choose from than Applebee's; he had a fastball, curve, change, slider, knuckle curve— and he could put them on the third line of your shoelaces if that was where he wanted to put them. At the end his repertoire had been reduced to smoke and mirrors, only the "smoke" drifted toward the plate as if it was being paid by the hour. It was more like haze and tinsel. He should have taken the mound wearing a top hat and a big cloak, with a rabbit in his underwear and the seven of spades in his hat. Pick a pitch, my friend; any pitch. If you decide it's a change-up, I'll turn it into a curve; call it a fastball, I'll pull the string on it the instant you start to swing.

How Mussina won 20 games last year nobody will ever know, particularly since he could never do that when he was young and could actually pitch. Mussina could go 17-8 with both legs in traction. At the end, hitters couldn't wait to step into the batter's box against him. His fastball arrived inside a double white envelope, RSVP second base. His curveball was a sugary confection; anybody could hit that thing—usually a mile high and 250 feet deep. His changeup wore pink lipstick and had a tattoo just over the panty line: Hit me, baby. Hit me hard. Man, I was one millisecond from hitting that thing on a line into center field. *Just* got a little bit ahead of it.

Mussina struck out 150 batters last year, 149 of whom had to wash out their mouths with soap afterward. He walked, by actual count, eight batters who later came around to score. I've seen Daniel Cabrera do that by the third inning.

Mike Mussina could still throw 90, but you had to add two or three pitches together to get there. He used to break your bats; anymore he just breaks your balls. He'll give you a single anytime if you promise not to go anywhere.

Mussina graduated from Stanford without taking any classes in Exercise Science, Sports Facility Management or the Sociological Implications of TV sitcoms. He loves to do Crossword puzzles. So do I, but mine have clues like "Jamie Spears' sister" and "Prevaricate or deceive, three letters." His have clues like "protagonist in Flaubert short story" and "leader of the Maurya- as between Chandragupta and Ashoka." To which the answer, by the way, is "Bindusara"; don't look it up, it took me an hour. I Bindusara I brought it up.

The Yankees' new $160-million pitcher has been in the majors since 2001 and has had a winning record every year, overall 117-73 for the eight seasons. Mussina has had a winning record every year, too, and he totals up to 123-72. Of course, Mussina hasn't had a better record in a single season than the big guy has since…well, last year, I guess, but before that you have to go all the way back to 2006.

It's hard to imagine a pitcher retiring with a record like that, but Mussina was always hard to figure. At the start of his career he was firing bullets; by the end of the line he was firing up marshmallows, but still getting about the same results. You ever hit a marshmallow with a bat? It's hard to get much distance.

Not since Koufax has anybody left the game with a better exit line. Koufax left, of course, because he wanted to keep using all four extremities. Mussina left because he reached a point where even he couldn't imagine getting hitters out with pastry and noodles anymore. Mike Mussina won more games than Bob Feller, Carl Hubbell, Bob Gibson, Herb Pennock, Waite Hoyt, Luis Tiant or Jim Bunning—and lost fewer than any of them. He won 50 more games than Catfish Hunter and 60 more than Don Drysdale—and lost fewer. He'll go into the Hall of Fame some day, perhaps with a rabbit in his top hat, the 7 of spades up his sleeve and a crossword puzzle in his pocket. He'll have the only plaque in Cooperstown that cites the influences of Harry Houdini, Albus Dumbledore and Milton Friedman.

He was a handsome man who pitched with a sour grimace on his face, as if he was trying to remember how exactly to make a baserunner vanish without creating an unexplained discrepancy on the scorecards. He looked at the world with what the world took to be disdain, although maybe we just weren't getting it. The Yankees are hoping he left his wand and spellbook in his locker; Ian Kennedy and Philip Hughes could really use them.

He wasn't the pitcher, at the end of his career, that he was in the beginning; he had gotten a little bit lucky. But how many guys, when they get a little bit lucky, are smart enough to know what the score really is? Most guys go 20-9, they'll call their agent and start the auction. You can complain about the modern athlete all you want to, but show me the old-timer who had Mike Mussina's moxie. He could have stayed to fight for 300 wins, but he didn't need them to know how good he was. Once he won twenty, he had made his point, and it was time for him to go.

Bobby Abreu became only the second player to have a season of exactly 100 RBI and 100 runs scored in a season.

Kip Selbach, a leftfielder for Washington in the National League in 1896, is the only other player to finish the season with exactly 100 in each category.

There is more than one way to skin a pitcher. Vladimir Guerrero and Bobby Abreu are both all-time great right fielders now in their mid-thirties. Both are career .300 hitters, with power. Both throw well, and both ran well when they were younger. Between them they have driven in 100 runs in a season sixteen times, and scored 100 runs fourteen times.

And a more dramatic contrast in approaches to an at-bat, you could not invent. Vladimir swung at the first pitch last year 47% of the time, highest in the majors. Abreu swung at the first pitch 6% of the time, lowest in the majors.

Guerrero had 117 one-pitch at-bats. Abreu had 19.

Guerrero had 209 long at-bats (four pitches or more.) Abreu had 380.

Bobby Abreu – 2008
Short and Long AB

	AB	H	HR	RBI	Avg	OBP	Slg	OPS
One and done	19	8	1	6	.421	.421	.789	1.211
Short	229	75	9	53	.328	.330	.546	.876
Long	380	105	11	47	.276	.393	.425	.818
7 Up	46	10	2	8	.217	.368	.383	.751

Vladimir Guerrero – 2008
Short and Long AB

	AB	H	HR	RBI	Avg	OBP	Slg	OPS
One and done	117	39	8	23	.333	.339	.622	.961
Short	332	110	20	64	.331	.337	.591	.928
Long	209	54	7	27	.258	.406	.400	.806
7 Up	32	14	2	6	.438	.550	.656	1.206

Over the last seven years, Derek Jeter's batting average on groundballs has gotten steadily higher:

Year	Avg
2002	.239
2003	.251
2004	.234
2005	.274
2006	.269
2007	.282
2008	.291

Melky Cabrera's problem as a hitter can be explained in two words: flyballs. He hits lots of flyballs, and they don't do anything; they don't leave the park, they don't go off the wall; they're just outs. In 2007 he hit 28% flyballs (flyballs as a percentage of balls in play), and he hit .154 on them. In 2008 he increased that to 34% flyballs, and the average went down to .123. To succeed as a hitter, he has either got to stop hitting so many flyballs, or else make them **do** something, one of the two.

We like to track the number of flyballs that don't make it beyond the infield baselines, because they are caught for outs 99% of the time, making them as effective as a strikeout. Among all major league pitchers with at least 50 innings pitched last year, Mariano Rivera had the highest proportion of flyballs that didn't make it out of the infield.

Pitcher	IP	IF/F
Mariano Rivera	70.7	25%
Logan F Kensing	55.3	22%
Joe Nelson	54	21%
Ramon Ramirez	71.7	20%
Chris Young	102.3	19%

Digital Reliever

Mariano Rivera went the entire season without allowing an opponent to put up a crooked number against him.

Mariano Rivera – 2008
Inning Analysis

Innings Pitched	70.2
Runs Allowed	11
Innings Started	66
Runs in Those Innings	10
Shutout Innings	56
One-Run Innings	10
Got First Man Out	47
Runs Scored in Those Innings	1
Runs/9 Innings	0.19
First Man Reached	19
Runs Scored in Those Innings	9
Runs/9 Innings	4.26
1-2-3 Innings	34
10-pitch Innings (or less)	14
Long Innings (20 or more pitches)	8
Failed to Finish Inning	1

Oakland Athletics

Oakland Athletics – 2008
Team Overview

Description		Ranking
Won-Lost Record	75-86	
Place	3rd of 4 in American League West	
Runs Scored	646	26th in the majors
Runs Allowed	690	6th in the majors
Home Runs	125	22nd in the majors
Home Runs Allowed	135	3rd in the majors
Batting Average	.242	30th in the majors
Batting Average Allowed	.253	6th in the majors
Walks Drawn	574	10th in the majors
Walks Given	576	19th in the majors
OPS For	.686	30th in the majors
OPS Against	.720	7th in the majors
Stolen Bases	88	13th in the majors
Stolen Bases Allowed	70	6th in the majors

Key Players

Pos	Player	G	AB	R	H	2B	3B	HR	RBI	SB	CS	BB	SO	Avg	OBP	Slg	OPS	WS
C	Kurt Suzuki	148	530	54	148	25	1	7	42	2	3	44	69	.279	.346	.370	.716	17
1B	Daric Barton	140	446	59	101	17	5	9	47	2	1	65	99	.226	.327	.348	.674	9
2B	Mark Ellis	117	442	55	103	20	3	12	41	14	2	53	65	.233	.321	.373	.694	13
3B	Jack Hannahan	143	436	48	95	27	0	9	47	2	0	55	131	.218	.305	.342	.647	5
SS	Bobby Crosby	145	556	66	132	39	1	7	61	7	3	47	96	.237	.296	.349	.645	10
LF	Jack Cust	148	481	77	111	19	0	33	77	0	0	111	197	.231	.375	.476	.851	17
CF	Carlos Gonzalez	85	302	31	73	22	1	4	26	4	1	13	81	.242	.273	.361	.634	6
RF	Emil Brown	117	402	48	98	14	2	13	59	4	2	27	65	.244	.297	.386	.682	7
DH	Frank Thomas	55	186	20	49	6	1	5	19	0	0	28	44	.263	.364	.387	.751	4

Key Pitchers

Pos	Player	G	GS	W	L	Sv	IP	H	R	ER	SO	BB	BR/9	ERA	WS
SP	Dana Eveland	29	29	9	9	0	168.0	172	82	81	118	77	13.98	4.34	8
SP	Justin Duchscherer	22	22	10	8	0	141.2	107	45	40	95	34	9.47	2.54	13
SP	Greg Smith	32	32	7	16	0	190.1	169	92	88	111	87	12.25	4.16	9
SP	Rich Harden	13	13	5	1	0	77.0	57	21	20	92	31	10.40	2.34	8
SP	Joe Blanton	20	20	5	12	0	127.0	145	74	70	62	35	12.83	4.96	3
CL	Huston Street	63	0	7	5	18	70.0	58	29	29	69	27	11.06	3.73	10
RP	Santiago Casilla	51	0	2	1	2	50.1	60	22	22	43	20	14.84	3.93	3
RP	Alan Embree	70	0	2	5	0	61.2	59	36	34	57	30	13.28	4.96	2

2008 was the first season in Billy Beane's 12 years as GM that the Athletics were out-walked by their opponents. While the margin was slight—they drew only two fewer than they handed out —they had become accustomed to enjoying a sizable advantage in walks. Over the previous 11 seasons, they out-walked their opponents by an average of more than 100 per year. Last year also was the first time in a decade that the Athletics were out-homered by their opponents.

Are You Guys Trying to Lose?

That low rumble you hear is Rickey Henderson rolling over in his retirement. The 2008 Oakland A's were last in the American League in runs scored; in fact, they scored the fewest runs of any American League team since the Tigers in 2003. A big reason for this: .285 on-base percentage by their leadoff men. It was their worst on-base percentage from any batting order position. Second-worst was the Nine spot, which you would expect, but third-worst was the Two spot; the A's Number Two hitters also had a .306 on-base percentage. The A's were last in the majors in runs scored by leadoff hitters (78), and also in runs scored by Number Two hitters (68).

Oakland Athletics – 2008
Runs and RBI by Batting Order

Pos	Players	Runs	RBI
1	Ellis (38 G), Buck (25 G), Davis (24 G)	78	62
2	Crosby (34 G), Ellis (33 G), Suzuki (24 G)	68	58
3	Cust (62 G), Sweeney (21 G), Barton (18 G)	80	69
4	Cust (46 G), Thomas (41 G), Brown (24 G)	87	76
5	Brown (44 G), Suzuki (24 G), Cust (22 G)	83	81
6	Crosby (43 G), Gonzalez (19 G)	73	69
7	Hannahan (37 G), Crosby (24 G), Barton (21 G)	77	73
8	Barton (29 G), Hannahan (27 G)	52	66
9	Hannahan (19 G), Barton (17 G)	48	56
	Total	646	610

Oakland Athletics – 2008
Productivity by Batting Order Position

Pos	Players	Avg	OBP	Slg	OPS
1	Ellis (38 G), Buck (25 G), Davis (24 G)	.218	.285	.327	.613
2	Crosby (34 G), Ellis (33 G), Suzuki (24 G)	.245	.306	.360	.667
3	Cust (62 G), Sweeney (21 G), Barton (18 G)	.228	.331	.358	.688
4	Cust (46 G), Thomas (41 G), Brown (24 G)	.234	.332	.400	.732
5	Brown (44 G), Suzuki (24 G), Cust (22 G)	.274	.327	.411	.738
6	Crosby (43 G), Gonzalez (19 G)	.258	.333	.396	.729
7	Hannahan (37 G), Crosby (24 G), Barton (21 G)	.253	.326	.403	.729
8	Barton (29 G), Hannahan (27 G)	.241	.327	.360	.688
9	Hannahan (19 G), Barton (17 G)	.225	.292	.301	.593
	Total	.242	.318	.369	.686

Brad Ziegler had an amazing rookie season, posting a 1.06 ERA in 47 appearances, but his most incredible stat may be this: He induced 20 ground-ball double plays in only 59.2 innings, for a rate of 3.0 per nine innings, a full 50% more than any other pitcher who threw at least 50 innings. Texas reliever Josh Rupe was second at 2.0 GDPs per nine innings.

Brad Ziegler – 2008
Record of Opposing Batters

Season	AB	R	H	2B	3B	HR	RBI	BB	SO	SB	CS	GIDP	Avg	OBP	Slg	OPS
2008	199	8	47	8	2	2	12	22	30	1	0	20	.236	.311	.327	.638

Which would you rather have: a second baseman who hits .300 and is average in the field, or a second baseman who hits .233 but is great in the field?

Mark Ellis hit .233 in 2008, but our estimate is that he made 26 plays more than an average second baseman would probably have made. He's +26 in the field.

At bat, he would have had to get 133 hits to hit .300. He had 103 hits, so he's minus 30. So, by our math, you may be better off with the .300 hitter—but it's close.

Mark Ellis
Fielding Bible Plus/Minus

| | | | GROUND DP | | | | PLAYS | | | | PLUS/MINUS | | | | | |
| | | | | | | Expected Outs | | Outs Made | | | | | | | | |
Year	Team	Inn	GIDP Opps	GIDP	Pct	Rank	GB	Air	GB	Air	To His Right	Straight On	To His Left	GB	Air Total	Rank
2006	Oak	1070	152	89	.586	6	270	107	280	110	-3	+8	+5	+10	+3 +13	7
2007	Oak	1322	177	95	.537	12	410	131	426	134	0	+5	+11	+16	+3 +19	4
2008	Oak	1012	131	81	.618	3	255	93	277	96	+9	+7	+5	+22	+3 +25	2

Oakland rookie Greg Smith finished 7-16—but his ERA in his seven wins was 0.94.

Greg Smith – 2008
Decision Analysis

Group	G	IP	W	L	Pct	H	R	SO	BB	ERA
Wins	7	47.2	7	0	1.000	33	5	20	19	0.94
Losses	16	92.2	0	16	.000	97	67	53	50	6.31
No Decisions	9	50.0	0	0	—	39	20	38	18	3.24
Quality Starts: 6 in Wins, 2 in Losses, 5 in no-decisions										

Jack Cust was the only American League player to reach base more often without hitting the ball than by hitting it. He had 111 hits, 113 walks and a hit by pitch.

Jack Cust knocked in 77 runs last year, 46 of them on home runs. That's 60%. On the other hand, he knocked in three runs just from drawing walks. That's the kind of thing that happens when you basically do three things: strike out, walk and hit home runs.

Jack Cust – 2008
RBI Analysis

Hits		RBI Hits		RBI Total		Drove In	
Home Runs:	33			RBI on Home Runs:	46	Daric Barton	1
Triples:	0	RBI Triples:	0	RBI on Triples:	0	Emil Brown	2
Doubles:	19	RBI Doubles:	6	RBI on Doubles:	8	Travis Buck	1
Singles:	59	RBI Singles:	14	RBI on Singles:	15	Bobby Crosby	9
		Other RBI: Walks	3	Sacrifice Flies:	4	Rajai Davis	2
		Other RBI: Ground Outs	0			Mark Ellis	6
				Total Other:	4	Carlos Gonzalez	1
						Jack Hannahan	2
				Total RBI:	77	Donnie Murphy	1
						Cliff Pennington	1
						Gregorio Petit	1
						Kurt Suzuki	5
						Mike Sweeney	1
						Ryan Sweeney	9
						Frank Thomas	2
						His Own Bad Self	33
						Total	77

Missed It by That Much

If he could have pitched another three games or so and managed another 20.1 innings, Justin Duchscherer would have reached the 162 innings pitched level for qualification on pitching leaderboards. Assuming his continued excellence, here's how he would have finished in each of these key pitching categories in the American League:

ERA	2.54	2nd	Justin's 2.541 would be just behind Cliff Lee's 2.539
Opposing Batting Average	.210	1st	Just ahead of Dice-K's .211
Opposing On-Base Pct.	.268	1st	Ahead of Roy Halladay's .276
Opposing Slugging	.322	1st	Edges out Dice-K again (.324)
Opposing OPS	.590	1st	Beats Halladay's .621

Last year Justin Duchscherer was the only starter in baseball (min. 20 GS) who retired the side in order in more than half the innings he started.

Justin Duchscherer – 2008
Inning Analysis

Innings Pitched	141.2
Runs Allowed	45
Innings Started	146
Runs in Those Innings	45
Shutout Innings	117
One-Run Innings	20
Two-Run Innings	5
Three-Run Innings	2
Four-Run Innings	1
Fice-Run Innings	1
Got First Man Out	113
Runs Scored in Those Innings	29
Runs/9 Innings	2.31
First Man Reached	33
Runs Scored in Those Innings	16
Runs/9 Innings	4.36
1-2-3 Innings	74
10-pitch Innings (or less)	39
Long Innings (20 or more pitches)	26
Failed to Finish Inning	8

Every major league team in 2008 had at least one regular infielder who hit at least .270—except the A's. The A's four regular infielders hit .226, .233, .218 and .237—all below .270, .260, .250, and .240.

There was at least one positive development for the A's last year: Kurt Suzuki established himself as one of the better catchers in the American League. In addition to ranking in the top half among all catchers in plate discipline, hitting for average and running, he accrued the second-most fielding Win Shares among all A.L. catchers (8).

Kurt Suzuki – 2008
Skills Assessment

Plate Discipline:	73rd percentile	76th percentile among catchers
Hitting for Average:	44th percentile	71st percentile among catchers
Running:	35th percentile	63rd percentile among catchers
Hitting for Power:	18th percentile	15th percentile among catchers

Triple Crowns

by Bill James

An odd concept, the Triple Crown. It's kind of like a Grand Slam with a leg missing. Does a Triple Crown mean that you led the league in triples?

Tennis has a Grand Slam, meaning that you win four titles. Golf has that, too. Nobody ever wins it. Horse racing has a Triple Crown. Baseball has one true Triple Crown, for leading the league in Home Runs, RBI and Batting Average, and then people make up other ones…Triple Crowns for pitchers and such. Hat Tricks…a Hat Trick is three, also. Why? Why doesn't Denny's have a Hat Trick breakfast? "Uneasy lies the head that wears the crown," wrote Shakespeare, but just imagine if you had three of them.

The Triple Crown, like the Triple Double in basketball or Hitting for the Cycle in baseball, is a concept so arbitrary it can almost be called capricious. What about leading the league in Runs Scored, RBI, and OPS? Wouldn't that be just as good? What about leading in Hits, Walks and Homers, or Batting, On-Base Percentage and Slugging? Wouldn't that be just as legitimate a three-pronged accomplishment? Maybe it just needs a cool name: the Golden Fork. As in, "Barry Bonds was the last man to win the historic Golden Fork, leading the National League in Batting, On-Base Percentage and Slugging Percentage in 2004 and also in 2002. Other than Bonds, however, no player has won the magic Golden Fork since Todd Helton in 2000."

Or how about The Magic Troika?

There are thirteen or fourteen Triple Crowns in baseball history, depending on whether you recognize Jimmie Foxx as the batting champion in 1932. We haven't had one since 1967, however, and at one point I assumed that the reason for this was expansion. When you increase the number of players competing for each "crown", you make it more difficult to win all three.

Research, however…nasty habit, research…research proved that this was untrue. This was ten years ago, maybe fifteen. I remember that Frank Thomas was young, so it may have been thirty years ago. Anyway, in order to demonstrate that the reason for the disappearance of Triple Crown winners was expansion, I set

My guess is that we will see another Triple Crown winner in the next ten years.

out to demonstrate that the number of players leading their own **team** in all three categories was the same as it has always been. If you take two teams, three teams, four teams, eight teams, you still get the same number of players leading in all categories. It's just a lot harder to lead fourteen teams than it is eight.

Unfortunately, this turned out on examination to be entirely untrue; it's not the same as it has always been, at all. John Dewan had some new data on this for one of his Stat of the Week entries: the percentage of teams which had one player leading his team in all three categories nose-dived between the early 1950s and the mid-1980s.

Since the mid-1980s this number has gone back up. It's not back where it was in the early fifties, but it's pretty close. I would explain why this happened, why this number went down and then why it went back up, but…don't have a clue. Somebody would have to explain it to me first.

I have been playing around with Triple Crown data here for a while. I started with the batting records of all players in baseball history, and then I eliminated those who
a) played before 1900, or
b) had less then 450 plate appearances.

I sorted the remaining players by decade, so that all of the players from the 1930s, let's say, were "competing" for the Triple Crown with all of the other players from the 1930s. I then started re-arranging players into competing "leagues" of players to see how often one player would win the Triple Crown.

I did this for several days, and there is a whole lot of stuff I didn't learn. However, I did emerge from this gigantic waste of time with a few definite conclusions. I will put a few of these in question-and-answer form, to create the illusion that this was stuff that somebody actually wanted to know, rather than just stuff that floated to the top while I was messing around with the data. Here goes:

1) What was the greatest Triple Crown season of all Time?

Beyond any question, the greatest Triple Crown season since 1900, in terms of its probability of leading the league in all three categories, given the norms of the era, was by Nap Lajoie in 1901. Lajoie's .426 batting average was the highest of that decade and, depending on your source and qualifications, may have been the highest ever. His 125 RBI were the highest total of the 1900-1909 era with one exception (Honus Wagner drove in 126, also in 1901.) His 14 home runs were exceeded by only two players in the years 1900-1909 (Sam Crawford in 1900 and Socks Seybold in 1902.)

Lajoie's season had an 72 to 89% probability of winning the Triple Crown, given the standards of his era—72 to 89%, depending on what assumptions you use about how many players will be competing for the championship and what the group of years is that represents Lajoie's peer group. Probably no other season in baseball history is over 50%. Certainly no other season is close to Lajoie in 1901.

Second on the list is Mickey Mantle in 1956. Mantle hit .353 with 52 homers, 130 RBI. Those are impressive numbers. Given the standards of that era, those are the second most-impressive Triple Crown numbers since 1900.

However, it was still probably less than 50% likely that, given those numbers, Mantle would win the Triple Crown. 52 homers…no problem; that was the most homers any player hit in that decade, so that number in that era has a 100% chance of leading the league.130 RBI, on the other hand…not so much. There were nine players in the years 1950-1959 who drove in more than 130 runs. If history wasn't a sample of one…if we could re-run the season and Mantle had the same numbers but everybody else was scrambled…there's a very good chance that his 130 RBI would not lead the league.

And even if he did, somebody else might edge him out in batting average. Billy Goodman hit .354 in 1950. Harvey Kuenn hit .353 in 1959—a higher .353 than Mantle's .353. Hank Aaron hit .355, and Musial did, too, and Ted Williams hit .388. One of these players could have done it head to head with Mantle.

Research, however…nasty habit, research…research proved that this was untrue.

2) Who had the greatest Triple Crown Numbers but DIDN'T win it?

Stan Musial, 1948. The four greatest Triple Crown seasons of all time, given the norms of the era, are Lajoie in 1901, Mantle in 1956, Hornsby in 1922, and Musial in 1948. The first three won. Musial missed by one home run.

3) What was the weakest Triple Crown season that DID win?

By far, the weakest of the "actual" Triple Crown seasons was Chuck Klein in 1933. Klein led the National League with 28 homers and with 120 RBI—a long odds accomplishment.

It is the assumption of my studies that what happened did not *have* to happen; it could have happened some other way. That's kind of an arbitrary assumption, of course; only you know how you feel about fate. But 28 home runs would have finished third in the National League in 1932, fourth in 1934. It was a pitcher's year in the NL, and, more to the point, a year in which most of the big hitters had injuries or bad years. Klein found a little crease there where 28 homers and 120 RBI would lead the NL, and he slid into it.

Setting actual history aside, Klein was much more likely to have won the Triple Crown in 1929, 1930 or 1932 than he was in 1933. Frank Robinson was much more likely to have won in 1962 than in 1966. There is a flaw in the assumptions of my research; there is always a flaw in the assumptions of research, because the real world is always more complicated than the research. Anyway, I have assumed that the standards of offensive production are constant throughout each decade. Using that assumption, Frank Robinson in 1966 (49 homers, 122 RBI, .316) clearly has much less chance of winning a Triple Crown than Mickey Mantle in 1961 (54 homers, 128 RBI, .317), since all of Mantle's numbers are higher.

But, of course, 1961 was not 1966. They re-defined the strike zone in 1963, with very poor results, and for a few years the major leagues were hit-challenged and run-impaired. Still, winning a batting title with a .316 average was a kind of a fluke. He wouldn't have led the league with that batting average in 1965 or 1967. The Pittsburgh Pirates that same year had four outfielders who hit .315 or better, but they were in the other league. The normal batting champions of that era, Tony Oliva and Carl Yastrzemski, had down years. Robby was in the right place at the right time.

Robinson, on the other hand, was much more likely to win a Triple Crown in 1962 than he was in 1966. In 1962 he hit .342 with 39 homers, 136 RBI—not leading in any of the three categories (as Mantle didn't in 1961). But 136 RBI in the 1960s…that would normally be a league-leading figure. .342 is a batting average that would very often be a league-leading total. Leading the league in home runs with 39 is uncommon, but not nearly as uncommon as leading the league in batting average at .316.

These are the top 40 Triple Crown seasons of all time, by my math (actual Triple Crown seasons marked with an asterisk):

Player	Year	HR	RBI	Avg	Chance		
Nap Lajoie*	1901	14	125	.426	72	to	89%
Mickey Mantle*	1956	52	130	.353	17	to	50%
Rogers Hornsby*	1922	42	152	.401	9	to	39%
Stan Musial	1948	39	131	.376	9	to	35%
Chuck Klein	1930	40	170	.386	7	to	25%
Elmer Flick	1900	11	110	.367	7	to	35%
Lou Gehrig	1930	41	174	.379	6	to	29%
Ted Williams	1949	43	159	.343	5	to	14%
Norm Cash	1961	41	132	.361	4	to	13%
Rogers Hornsby*	1925	39	143	.403	4	to	20%
Jimmie Foxx*?	1932	58	169	.364	4	to	13%
Larry Walker	1997	49	130	.366	4	to	14%
Ted Williams*	1942	36	137	.356	3	to	19%
Charlie Hickman	1902	11	110	.361	3	to	22%
Babe Ruth	1931	46	163	.373	3	to	18%
Babe Ruth	1921	59	171	.378	3	to	6%
Hack Wilson	1930	56	191	.356	3	to	5%
Todd Helton	2001	49	146	.336	2	to	10%
Todd Helton	2000	42	147	.372	2	to	5%
Lou Gehrig*	1934	49	165	.363	2	to	9%
Hank Greenberg	1940	41	150	.340	2	to	7%
Fred Lynn	1979	39	122	.333	2	to	14%
Ty Cobb*	1909	9	107	.377	2	to	7%
Cy Seymour	1905	8	121	.377	2	to	5%
George Foster	1977	52	149	.320	1	to	3%
Lou Gehrig	1927	47	175	.373	1	to	3%
Hank Aaron	1971	47	118	.327	1	to	5%
Frank Robinson	1962	39	136	.342	1	to	5%
Al Simmons	1930	36	165	.381	1	to	6%
Manny Ramirez	1999	44	165	.333	1	to	3%
Gavvy Cravath	1913	19	128	.341	1	to	2%
Jim Rice	1979	39	130	.325	1	to	3%
Al Rosen	1953	43	145	.336	1	to	3%
Billy Williams	1972	37	122	.333	1	to	5%
Billy Williams	1970	42	129	.322	1	to	2%
Honus Wagner	1908	10	109	.354	1	to	4%
Ted Williams	1941	37	120	.406	1	to	2%
Rogers Hornsby	1929	39	149	.380	1	to	4%
Babe Ruth	1930	49	153	.359	0	to	2%
Jimmie Foxx*	1933	48	163	.356	0	to	3%

There are five other actual Triple Crown seasons—Yastrzemski, 1967 (54th on my list of likely Triple Crown seasons), Frank Robinson, 1966 (80th), Joe Medwick, 1937 (91st), Ted Williams, 1947 (116th), and Chuck Klein, 1933 (239th).

Of the fourteen Triple Crowns (counting Foxx in 1932), twelve were won in leagues with eight teams, while the other two were won in leagues with ten teams. One of the central questions I was trying to study, then, is "exactly how much of this difference was caused by the expansion?"

Players in the eight-team leagues competed for the Triple Crown in a context of 64 eligible spots (8 x 8), which normally produced about 50 eligible combatants. Modern players compete in 14-team and 16-team leagues with 126 or 128 eligible spots (14 x 9 or 16 x 8), and about 100 eligible hitters. I thus studied this issue by sorting batting records into groups of 50 and groups of 100, seeing how often one player would lead all 50 or all 100 in all three Silver Trident categories.

I sorted all seasons in baseball history, by decade, into 50- and 100-player groups, and repeated this experiment 100 times. Using 50-player groups, I got 646 Triple Crowns. Using 100-player groups, I got 237. This would suggest that doubling the number of players in each group reduces the number of Triple Crowns by something more than 50%…63%, actually.

You can't help but notice, however, that even using 50-player groups I got far fewer Triple Crowns (per test) than actual history. I got six Triple Crowns per trial, in major league history, using the 50-player grouping. There are actually fourteen, and would be more than that if we had stayed with eight-team teams. The reason for this discrepancy may be the flawed assumption I talked about before—the assumption that batting norms are constant throughout the decade—or it may be something else, some other flaw in my assumptions. That's why I have the wide ranges in my estimates…I'm not really on solid ground here.

In any case, there are a couple of other things that are pretty clear. One is that Triple Crowns disappeared from history post-1970 for some reason other than expansion. In the 1980s, there simply are no Triple Crown-type seasons. In re-sorting 1980s seasons 100 times into 100-player groups—creating something more than 1500 100-player groups (since there are about 15 100-player groups from the 1980s in each trial), I got *no* Triple Crown seasons from the 1980s. Doing the same thing with 50-player groups, I got only *three* Triple Crown seasons from the 1980s.

There simply aren't any players in the 1980s who have Triple Crown numbers. The best Triple Crown season from the 1980s was by Don Mattingly in 1985—35 homers, 145 RBI, .324. The 145 RBI was the highest total from the 1980s, so that's a sure winner. But one's chance of leading a league in home runs with 35, in the 1980s, was around 8%, and a .324 batting average is around 3%. Altogether, that's about a one-in-four-hundred shot at a Triple Crown—from the best Triple Crown season of the decade.

Our instinct in this situation is to try to explain this by some change in the game…something happened in the nature of the game which made Triple Crown-type hitters more scarce in that generation. But let me point out that there is an equally reasonable explanation which has nothing at all to do with the nature of baseball in 1980s. Triple Crown-type hitters are very rare. There are only maybe 50 players in baseball history who routinely put up big numbers in all three categories.

When you take 50 players and you sprinkle them across baseball history, you're not going to get an even distribution. You're going to get random clusters—Mays, Mantle, Robinson and Aaron all born 1931-1934, and then nobody born 1954-1963. That just happens. So it is possible that there is nothing going on here except a random clustering of talent.

Whatever, the Triple Crown-type numbers began to re-appear in the 1990s, often in Colorado, and have continued to pop up throughout the current decade. As it happens, no one *has* won the Triple Crown in this decade—but there have been numerous people who *could have*. Albert Pujols, if healthy, is a legitimate Triple Crown threat every year, as much as Mays or Aaron were. Todd Helton was, and Manny Ramirez was. Vladimir Guerrero, Carlos Delgado, Barry Bonds and Larry Walker all had very legitimate shots at the Triple Crown.

My guess is that we will see another Triple Crown winner in the next ten years. The historical trend lines are heading in that direction. That doesn't necessarily mean anything, since, as I said, the historical trend lines may be simply a result of a random clustering of talent. It's difficult, and it hasn't happened for a long time, but it has **not** become impossible for some player to win the Triple Crown.

It is the assumption of my studies that what happened did not **have to happen;** *it could have happened some other way. That's kind of an arbitrary assumption, of course; only you know how you feel about fate.*

Philadelphia Phillies

Philadelphia Phillies – 2008
Team Overview

Description		Ranking
Won-Lost Record	92-70	
Place		1st of 5 in National League East
Runs Scored	799	8th in the majors
Runs Allowed	680	4th in the majors
Home Runs	214	2nd in the majors
Home Runs Allowed	160	9th in the majors
Batting Average	.255	23rd in the majors
Batting Average Allowed	.260	12th in the majors
Walks Drawn	586	8th in the majors
Walks Given	533	14th in the majors
OPS For	.770	7th in the majors
OPS Against	.739	12th in the majors
Stolen Bases	136	4th in the majors
Stolen Bases Allowed	109	18th in the majors

Key Players

Pos	Player	G	AB	R	H	2B	3B	HR	RBI	SB	CS	BB	SO	Avg	OBP	Slg	OPS	WS
C	Carlos Ruiz	117	320	47	70	14	0	4	31	1	2	44	38	.219	.320	.300	.620	5
1B	Ryan Howard	162	610	105	153	26	4	48	146	1	1	81	199	.251	.339	.543	.881	24
2B	Chase Utley	159	607	113	177	41	4	33	104	14	2	64	104	.292	.380	.535	.915	30
3B	Pedro Feliz	133	425	43	106	19	2	14	58	0	0	33	54	.249	.302	.402	.705	8
SS	Jimmy Rollins	137	556	76	154	38	9	11	59	47	3	58	55	.277	.349	.437	.786	24
LF	Pat Burrell	157	536	74	134	33	3	33	86	0	0	102	136	.250	.367	.507	.875	20
CF	Shane Victorino	146	570	102	167	30	8	14	58	36	11	45	69	.293	.352	.447	.799	20
RF	Jayson Werth	134	418	73	114	16	3	24	67	20	1	57	119	.273	.363	.498	.861	17

Key Pitchers

Pos	Player	G	GS	W	L	Sv	IP	H	R	ER	SO	BB	BR/9	ERA	WS
SP	Jamie Moyer	33	33	16	7	0	196.1	199	85	81	123	62	12.47	3.71	13
SP	Cole Hamels	33	33	14	10	0	227.1	193	89	78	196	53	9.78	3.09	18
SP	Kyle Kendrick	31	30	11	9	0	155.2	194	103	95	68	57	15.32	5.49	3
SP	Brett Myers	30	30	10	13	0	190.0	197	103	96	163	65	12.69	4.55	7
SP	Adam Eaton	21	19	4	8	0	107.0	131	71	69	57	44	15.22	5.80	1
CL	Brad Lidge	72	0	2	0	41	69.1	50	17	15	92	35	11.16	1.95	15
RP	Ryan Madson	76	0	4	2	1	82.2	79	29	28	67	23	11.21	3.05	8
RP	J.C. Romero	81	0	4	4	1	59.0	41	18	18	52	38	12.81	2.75	7

Hit, Pitch, Stay Healthy

The three National League teams that had the highest percentage of games started by Opening Day starters all made the playoffs.

Rank	NL Team	Games Started	%
1	Philadelphia	1042	80%
2	Milwaukee	981	76%
3	Chicago	972	75%
8	Los Angeles	879	68%

Over the past several years, the Phillies have been the best baserunning club in the majors. Last year, they gained a net 114 bases on the basepaths, including a +86 from stolen bases, which means Phillies baserunners contributed 114 more bases than the average major league team. Jimmy Rollins is their baserunning leader, but he's just the tip of the iceberg. Shane Victorino has been +34 two years in a row, Jayson Werth was +28 last year, and Chase Utley was +21. Even the slow guys weren't as bad as you might think: Pat Burrell was only –3 and Ryan Howard was –7.

Philadelphia Phillies
Team Baserunning Analysis

Year	1st to 3rd Adv	1st to 3rd Opp	2nd to Home Adv	2nd to Home Opp	1st to Home Adv	1st to Home Opp	DP Opp	GIDP	Bases Taken	BR Outs	BR Gain	SB Gain	Net Gain
2002	66	210	107	159	18	61	1196	129	141	26	-10	18	8
2003	51	218	121	210	28	61	1223	119	166	32	-14	14	0
2004	64	223	110	174	24	72	1266	123	147	40	1	46	47
2005	64	226	128	227	17	65	1269	107	161	47	13	62	75
2006	64	222	107	180	36	70	1261	114	159	36	50	42	92
2007	53	214	117	193	34	81	1258	125	168	36	35	100	135
2008	55	195	98	163	29	55	1107	108	142	36	28	86	114
Totals	417	1508	788	1306	186	465	8580	825	1084	253	103	368	471
	28%		60%		40%			9%					

Speaking of baserunning, the Phillies stole bases at an 84.5% clip. The only team that has ever had a better stolen base percentage was the 2007 Phillies, with an 87.9%. The overall major league stolen base percentage was 73%.

J.C.Romero – 2008
Pitch Type Analysis

Overall		
Total Pitches	1034	
Fastball	700	68%
Curveball	2	0%
Changeup	127	12%
Slider	182	18%
Not Charted	23	2%

	Vs. RHB		Vs. LHB	
Total Pitches	592		442	
Outs Recorded	85		92	
Fastball	305	52%	395	89%
Curveball	1	0%	1	0%
Changeup	122	21%	5	1%
Slider	142	24%	40	9%
Not Charted	22	4%	1	0%

Oddball

Unlike most lefty specialists, J.C. Romero does not attack left-handed hitters with breaking balls. He does it mostly with his fastball, which he threw them 89% of the time last year. You certainly can't argue with the results, as he held them to a .102 average.

Pat Burrell followed Chase Utley in the Phillies' lineup about 20 times last year. Fielders must have gotten out of breath running from one end of the field to the other, because the lefty and righty batters were two of the most extreme hitters in the majors.

Utley hit only 81 balls to left field, the lowest proportion of any qualified major league hitter (16%). Burrell hit only 85 balls to right field; that was 21% of all his batted balls, one of the ten lowest percentages in the majors.

Chase Utley – 2008
Hitting Analysis

Batting Left-Handed								1B -	2B -	3B -	HR
Total Hit to Left	81	Outs	62	Hits	19	Average	.235	Hit Type 12 -	7 -	0 -	0
Total Hit to Center	167	Outs	109	Hits	58	Average	.356	Hit Type 37 -	9 -	2 -	10
Total Hit to Right	262	Outs	162	Hits	100	Average	.388	Hit Type 50 -	25 -	2 -	23
All Balls in Play	512	Outs	335	Hits	177	Average	.352	Hit Type 99 -	41 -	4 -	33

Pat Burrell – 2008
Hitting Analysis

Batting Right-Handed								1B -	2B -	3B -	HR
Total Hit to Left	211	Outs	128	Hits	83	Average	.395	Hit Type 37 -	16 -	1 -	29
Total Hit to Center	110	Outs	79	Hits	31	Average	.287	Hit Type 19 -	8 -	1 -	3
Total Hit to Right	85	Outs	65	Hits	20	Average	.244	Hit Type 9 -	9 -	1 -	1
All Balls in Play	406	Outs	272	Hits	134	Average	.335	Hit Type 65 -	33 -	3 -	33

Back in 2005, Pat Burrell had one of the 15 lowest contact rates in the majors, making contact when he swung only about 75% of the time. Since then, however, he has improved his contact rate to about the league average.

I suspect that this is a common syndrome, although we don't really have enough linear data to study it. In 2001 (before we have data) Burrell struck out 162 times, in 2002 153 times. He still strikes out a lot, but not as much—which seems to be a common pattern. The new guy who breaks the strikeout record is usually in his second or third year in the league, like Mark Reynolds in 2008. I suspect that most players, like Adam Dunn and Ryan Howard, gradually begin to improve their contact rates after about 10,000 swings and misses.

Season	Contact Rate
2002	75%
2003	74%
2004	79%
2005	75%
2006	79%
2007	81%
2008	81%

Jimmy Rollins led all shortstops in fielding plus/minus in 2008 with a total of +23. Rollins' total is not nearly as large as the past two seasons' top totals. In 2007 Troy Tulowitzki was +35, and in 2006 Adam Everett was +41. The second place finishers in both 2007 and 2006, John McDonald and Clint Barmes, also had higher plus/minus totals than Rollins did this year.

Jimmy Rollins – 2008
Leaderboard, Shortstop

Player	+/-
Jimmy Rollins	+23
Yunel Escobar	+21
J.J. Hardy	+19
Cesar Izturis	+19
Jack Wilson	+16
Cristian Guzman	+15
Mike Aviles	+15
Marco Scutaro	+12
Omar Vizquel	+9
Jed Lowrie	+8

Brad Lidge's dramatic recovery last year came about in part from using his slider earlier in the count, rather than saving it for a strikeout pitch. He used the slider more than he ever had before and more than any major league reliever except Mike Wuertz of the Cubs.

Year	Slider %
2003	27%
2004	39%
2005	43%
2006	42%
2007	36%
2008	55%

Greg Dobbs was a superb pinch hitter last year, batting .355 in 67 pinch-hit appearances. Pinch hitters often excel in short plate appearances, and Dobbs was no exception. He was best in appearances that only lasted three pitches or less (labeled "short" plate appearances below).

Greg Dobbs – 2008
Short and Long AB

	AB	H	HR	RBI	Avg	OBP	Slg	OPS
Short	127	43	5	23	.339	.344	.559	.903
Long	99	25	4	17	.253	.327	.396	.723

Scotch Tape Award

In 2007, the Cincinnati Reds went just 8-13 when they sent Kyle Lohse to the mound, and were ready to part ways with him in mid-season. The Phillies picked him up, went 9-2 in the games that Lohse started, and the Phillies chased down the Mets from behind.

In 2008, the Oakland A's went just 6-14 when they sent Joe (the Pitcher) Blanton to the mound, and were ready to let him go in mid-season. The Phillies took him on, went 9-4 in the games that Blanton started, and the Phillies chased down the Mets from behind.

Philadelphia Phillies – 2007
Performance by Starting Pitcher

Games Started By	GS	RS	RA	Won	Lost
Moyer, Jamie	33	174	168	18	15
Eaton, Adam	30	150	166	15	15
Hamels, Cole	28	149	107	19	9
Kendrick, Kyle	20	129	91	13	7
Lieber, Jon	12	50	72	3	9
Lohse, Kyle	11	65	52	9	2
Garcia, Freddy	11	60	62	5	6
Durbin, J.D.	10	83	61	6	4
Myers, Brett	3	14	22	0	3
Happ, J.A.	1	3	8	0	1
Team Totals	162	892	821	89	73

Philadelphia Phillies – 2008
Performance by Starting Pitcher

Games Started By	GS	RS	RA	Won	Lost
Moyer, Jamie	33	172	129	22	11
Hamels, Cole	33	152	114	19	14
Kendrick, Kyle	30	178	142	18	12
Myers, Brett	30	130	143	12	18
Eaton, Adam	19	75	86	8	11
Blanton, Joe	13	73	59	9	4
Happ, J.A.	4	19	7	4	0
Team Totals	162	799	680	92	70

Pittsburgh Pirates

Pittsburgh Pirates – 2008
Team Overview

Description		Ranking
Won-Lost Record	67-95	
Place	6th of 6 in National League Central	
Runs Scored	735	18th in the majors
Runs Allowed	884	28th in the majors
Home Runs	153	18th in the majors
Home Runs Allowed	176	17th in the majors
Batting Average	.258	22nd in the majors
Batting Average Allowed	.287	28th in the majors
Walks Drawn	474	24th in the majors
Walks Given	657	27th in the majors
OPS For	.723	24th in the majors
OPS Against	.816	28th in the majors
Stolen Bases	57	25th in the majors
Stolen Bases Allowed	104	17th in the majors

Key Players

Pos	Player	G	AB	R	H	2B	3B	HR	RBI	SB	CS	BB	SO	Avg	OBP	Slg	OPS	WS
C	Ryan Doumit	116	431	71	137	34	0	15	69	2	2	23	55	.318	.357	.501	.858	20
1B	Adam LaRoche	136	492	66	133	32	3	25	85	1	1	54	122	.270	.341	.500	.841	16
2B	Freddy Sanchez	145	569	75	154	26	2	9	52	0	1	21	63	.271	.298	.371	.669	11
3B	Jose Bautista	107	314	38	76	15	0	12	44	1	1	38	77	.242	.325	.404	.729	8
SS	Jack Wilson	87	305	24	83	18	1	1	22	2	2	13	27	.272	.312	.348	.659	7
LF	Jason Bay	106	393	72	111	23	2	22	64	7	0	59	86	.282	.375	.519	.894	17
CF	Nate McLouth	152	597	113	165	46	4	26	94	23	3	65	93	.276	.356	.497	.853	24
RF	Xavier Nady	89	327	50	108	26	1	13	57	1	0	25	55	.330	.383	.535	.919	14

Key Pitchers

Pos	Player	G	GS	W	L	Sv	IP	H	R	ER	SO	BB	BR/9	ERA	WS
SP	Paul Maholm	31	31	9	9	0	206.1	201	89	85	139	63	11.91	3.71	9
SP	Ian Snell	31	31	7	12	0	164.1	201	107	99	135	89	15.99	5.42	2
SP	Zach Duke	31	31	5	14	0	185.0	230	111	99	87	47	13.82	4.82	3
SP	Tom Gorzelanny	21	21	6	9	0	105.1	120	79	78	67	70	16.32	6.66	0
SP	Phil Dumatrait	21	11	3	4	0	78.2	82	48	46	52	42	14.42	5.26	1
CL	Matt Capps	49	0	2	3	21	53.2	47	20	18	39	5	9.06	3.02	7
RP	Tyler Yates	72	0	6	3	1	73.1	72	39	38	63	41	14.11	4.66	3
RP	John Grabow	74	0	6	3	4	76.0	60	25	24	62	37	11.61	2.84	6

In 2008 the Pittsburgh Pirates were the only team to have a losing record (13-14) when hitting two homers in a game.

Pittsburgh Pirates – 2008
Record by Home Runs

Home Runs	W	-	L
0 homers	19	-	48
1 homer	23	-	31
2 homers	13	-	14
3 or more homers	12	-	2

The Pittsburgh Pirates led the National League in double plays and groundball double plays in 2008, although their primary shortstop (Jack Wilson) and primary second baseman (Freddy Sanchez) were **not** particularly good at turning the double play. There were four reasons for this:

1) Pirate pitchers threw a lot of groundballs,

2) The Pirate pitchers also led the league in walks,

3) While Wilson was not particularly effective at turning the double play—he turned double plays on 60% of his opportunities—the Pirates other shortstops were much better. Brian Bixler, who was the Pirate shortstop in April and some of September, but spent much of summer out somewhere else because he didn't hit, turned double plays on 68% of his opportunities, while backup Luis Rivas turned two on 67%.

4) While Sanchez turned double plays on only 51% of his opportunities, Rivas, backing him up as well, converted 61% of his (as a second baseman.)

The Pirates led the majors in 2008 in

1) Starts by left-handed pitchers (94), and

2) Assists by the defense (1830).

These two facts are related. The great majority of "assists" by fielders—which is a horrible name, because recording an "assist" in the field has absolutely nothing to do with "assisting" any other player—but the great majority of assists by fielders are on groundballs. Left-handed pitchers tend often to be groundball pitchers.

The Pirates had the best extra-inning record in the majors last year, 12-6, thanks primarily to their pitching staff. Pirate pitchers held opposition hitters to a .183 batting average in extra innings.

Zach Duke has led the majors in doubles allowed in two of the last three years—58 doubles given up in 2008, 60 in 2006.

When the Pittsburgh Pirates play the New York Mets, do you know what you have in center field?

Perhaps the two most remarkable percentage base stealers in baseball history.

Nate McLouth, four years into his career, has stolen 57 bases and been caught stealing only 5 times—a 92% success rate. It almost goes without saying that, were he able to sustain this over the course of a longer career, that would be the highest stolen base percentage ever.

The greatest percentage base stealer ever, given a longer career, is Carlos Beltran, who has an 88% success rate over 300+ attempts.

I tried to research the question of whether any player has *ever* had a 92% stolen base percentage over a period of several years and with 50 or more steals. This issue is very difficult to research, because stolen base data for much of baseball history is spotty. However, the only other player that I could find with a similar stolen base percentage over several years was Carlos Beltran, 2000 to 2004. Beltran was caught stealing 8 times in 1999, but then stole 162 bases in 177 attempts over the following five seasons—92%.

Ian Snell made 13 quality starts last year. That's not a lot, but what really hurts is that seven of them resulted in losses. Snell was the only pitcher in the majors who had over half of his quality starts result in losses (minimum of ten quality starts).

Ian Snell – 2008
Decision Analysis

Group	G	IP	W	L	Pct	H	R	SO	BB	ERA
Wins	7	43.1	7	0	1.000	39	13	44	10	2.28
Losses	12	66.0	0	12	.000	85	47	55	41	5.73
No Decisions	12	55.0	0	0	—	77	47	36	38	7.53
Quality Starts: 5 in Wins, 7 in Losses, 1 in no-decisions										

Only 26% of Ian Snell's innings were 1-2-3 innings, and 28% of Zach Duke's innings were 1-2-3 innings. Those were the two lowest percentages of all major league pitchers who pitched at least 162 innings.

	Snell	Duke
Innings Pitched	164.1	185.0
1-2-3 Innings	42	51
10-pitch Innings (or less)	16	38
Long Innings (20 or more pitches)	55	45
Failed to Finish Inning	9	10

Pirate catcher Ryan Doumit had a breakthrough season in 2008 although his batting average on Ground Balls (.215) and his batting average on Line Drives (.761) were both the **worst** of his four-year career. He had his best year because:

1) He hit more line drives than usual (23%).

2) His batting average on flyballs has surged by a hundred points over the last two years.

3) (And most importantly) he dramatically reduced his strikeout rate.

He cut his strikeouts basically in half—from a strikeout percentage (Strikeouts/At bats) of .282 in 2006 and .234 in 2007 to .128 in 2008.

What all of these facts suggest is that he cut down his swing…reduced his bat speed. When you cut down your bat speed your groundballs and flyballs won't be hit as hard, so the average on those will drop—but you may come out ahead because you have a lot more solid contact, and solid contact is where you make your money. His batting average on flyballs went up, almost certainly, because more of them were what John Dewan calls "Fliners"—halfway between a fly and a liner.

Ryan Doumit – 2005-2008
Batting Average on Fly Balls

2005	Batting on Ground Balls	22	for	92	.239
2006	Batting on Ground Balls	11	for	50	.220
2007	Batting on Ground Balls	21	for	81	.259
2008	Batting on Ground Balls	34	for	158	.215
2005	Batting on Line Drives	27	for	33	.844
2006	Batting on Line Drives	14	for	18	.778
2007	Batting on Line Drives	32	for	40	.800
2008	Batting on Line Drives	67	for	89	.761
2005	Batting on Fly Balls	10	for	59	.169
2006	Batting on Fly Balls	6	for	41	.154
2007	Batting on Fly Balls	16	for	73	.222
2008	Batting on Fly Balls	36	for	134	.277

Ryan Doumit batted .407 with runners in scoring position, the third-highest total among all major leaguers with at least 100 at-bats with runners in scoring position. David DeJesus (.419) and Ian Kinsler (.413) were the two batters with higher averages.

Paul Maholm had nine quality starts in his no-decisions, which tied Johan Santana for the major league lead. He also was one of only 10 major league starters who had a quality start in every single one of their victories (minimum 7 wins).

Paul Maholm – 2008
Decision Analysis

Group	G	IP	W	L	Pct	H	R	SO	BB	ERA
Wins	9	68.2	9	0	1.000	51	16	32	13	1.97
Losses	9	50.2	0	9	.000	71	46	38	20	7.64
No Decisions	13	87.0	0	0	—	79	27	69	30	2.79
Quality Starts: 9 in Wins, 1 in Losses, 9 in no-decisions										

As pointed out in this year's *Hardball Times Season Preview*, Matt Capps has struck out 159 batters and walked only 33 in the past three years—but 15 of those walks have been intentional. Capps' ratio of strikeouts to unintentional walks is 159/18, or 8.8 strikeouts per walk. Over the same period of time, only Mariano Rivera has a better ratio, at 9.0, and the next highest ratio is Jonathan Papelbon's at 6.9.

In his three-year career, Matt Capps has pitched much better against better competition.

Matt Capps – 2005-2008
Career Records Against Quality of Opposition

Opponent	G	IP	W	L	SO	BB	ERA
.600 teams	6	9.0	0	0	10	0	1.00
.500 - .599 teams	98	101.0	4	4	73	13	1.96
.400 - .499 teams	103	99.2	11	6	76	19	4.42
sub .400 teams	7	7.2	0	1	3	1	2.35

Adam LaRoche hit only six groundballs to the opposite field last year. No qualified left-handed batter hit less, and right-hander Mike Cameron was the only batter to hit less groundballs to the opposite field.

Adam LaRoche – 2008
Hitting Analysis

Batting Left-Handed									1B	2B	3B	HR
Ground Balls to Left	6	Outs	4	Hits	2	Average	.333	Hit Type	2 -	0 -	0 -	0
Ground Balls to Center	35	Outs	25	Hits	10	Average	.286	Hit Type	10 -	0 -	0 -	0
Ground Balls to Right	98	Outs	82	Hits	16	Average	.163	Hit Type	14 -	2 -	0 -	0
All Balls in Play	376	Outs	243	Hits	133	Average	.359	Hit Type	73 -	32 -	3 -	0

What I Have Learned About Fly Balls and Such

by Bill James

I understand now something that I didn't understand at all two years ago, and I thought I would try to explain this to you.

Basically, there is no such thing as a Fly Ball Hitter or a Line Drive Hitter. OK, this is an overgeneralization; I am stating as an absolute truth something that is only generally true. I'll have a paragraph in a moment, "Qualifications and Apologies", but let me make my point first.

For every five balls in play… leave strikeouts out of it…for every five balls in play, a hitter hits two fly balls, two ground balls, and one line drive. The ratio isn't exactly the same for every hitter, of course, and the ratio isn't exactly 2-1-2, of course. But still, the statement is a lot more true than it is false.

I had this idea, before I had actual data, that there were some hitters who hit mostly fly balls, and there were some hitters who hit mostly ground balls, and then there were the great hitters, who hit mostly line drives. I believe, based on the things that people say, that that's what most baseball fans think.

It's not true.

The reason it is not true is simple.

Hitting a baseball is really, really hard. You've got a baseball moving 90, 95 miles an hour, and you've got a wooden stick moving at a comparable speed, and you're trying to bring them together so that they meet squarely.

Most of the time, you miss.

If you swing a little bit too low, that's a fly ball (including pop ups as fly balls).

If you swing a little bit too high, that's a ground ball.

If you hit it square, that's a line drive.

If you're behind the pitch, you'll pop it up.

If you're ahead of the pitch, you'll roll the ball to an infielder.

If you time it perfectly, that's a line drive.

Everybody—and I mean everybody—is a little bit off most of the time.

I am stating as an absolute truth something that is only generally true.

Almost everybody swings a little bit too low about as often as they swing a little bit too high. Thus, almost everybody hits about twice as many ground balls as line drives, and most hitters hit about as many fly balls as ground balls. A 2-1-2 ratio.

Qualifications and Apologies

Of course, there are some hitters who chop down on the ball, trying to hit ground balls, and there are some hitters who try to hit the ball in the air. However:

1) There really aren't very many of them, on either side of that, and

2) It generally doesn't work, and

3) It doesn't have much to do with why or how one hitter is different from another.

Most of the guys who do *either* of the above—chop down on the ball or concentrate on lofting the ball—are marginal players who have little impact on the game, or catchers or shortstops who are just trying to hang in the game. There are two good hitters who chop down on the ball—Jeter and Ichiro—and Joe Mauer is a good hitter and a ground ball hitter. I don't think there are any really good hitters who have a huge uppercut.

There's a simple reason for this. It's too hard. Trying to center your bat on the ball is hard enough. When you try to do something *more* than that, you're making it harder.

If you hit a line drive, you hit .700—actually about .725. The math goes something like this: for every 10 at bats that you don't strike out, you're going to have about 8 fly balls and ground balls, and you're going to hit about .250 on those, so that's 2 hits. You'll hit two line drives and hit .700 on those, that's 3.4 hits for each ten at bats you don't strike out—a .340 average. The actual average of major league hitters who didn't strike out last year was

.329; we're a little off, but we're speaking in generalities, rather than calculating decimals.

But if you chop down on the ball, you're just creating more ground balls—on which your batting average is going to be low, even if you run like Rickey Henderson—and your line drives will be weak, so you'll lose 75 points on those.

If you uppercut more than a little bit you'll strike out more, and you will wind up hitting a lot of pop outs and fly outs.

No hitter actually hits fly balls on 50% of his at bats, over time, but some hitters are close to that number, and sometimes a hitter will stray over 50% for a single season. I believe the only major league regular last year who hit fly balls on 50% of his balls in play was Kevin Millar. You know what his batting average was when he hit a fly ball? It was .181. Yes, that included all of his home runs, but even so, that's .181 with a .496 slugging percentage (on his fly balls), which becomes .147 with a .412 slugging percentage if you figure that half of his strikeouts are attributable to the uppercut.

Alfonso Soriano has a big uppercut. His career batting average, when he does put the ball in the air, is .271—not adjusted for the strikeouts. Most of the people you think of as "fly ball hitters", like Jim Thome and David Ortiz and Mark Teixeira and Ryan Howard and Lance Berkman and Albert Pujols, really are not. Most of them hit more ground balls than fly balls. A few of them hit slightly more fly balls than ground balls. For the most part, they have the same 4-2-4 ratio as everybody else. Albert Pujols has an absolutely normal ratio of ground balls to fly balls to line drives. So does Dustin Pedroia. It has nothing at all to do with why Albert Pujols is Albert Pujols or why Dustin Pedroia is Dustin Pedroia.

What makes hitters different, one from another is:
1) How HARD they hit the ball,
2) How often they swing and miss,
3) How many pitches they take, and
4) How often they pull the ball.
Those things are really different, one hitter to another.

There are two good hitters who chop down on the ball—Jeter and Ichiro—and Joe Mauer is a good hitter and a ground ball hitter. I don't think there are any really good hitters who have a huge uppercut.

And, to an extent, of course, the fly ball/ground ball mix does figure into it. Let's look at those one at a time.

Fly Balls, and Fly Ball Hitters

Fly balls are actually not 40% of balls in play, but more like 37-39%.

There is tremendous variation, among hitters, in what happens when they hit a fly ball. There is relatively little variation in batting average among hitters when they hit a ground ball, and there is relatively little variation in batting average among hitters when they hit a line drive. There is tremendous variation in batting average among hitters when they hit a fly ball. Ryan Howard hits .450 when he hits the ball in the air, with most of the hits being home runs. Juan Pierre hits .120, and most of the hits are singles and doubles. Lots of guys hit less than .150 on balls hit in the air. It's a big difference.

For this reason, fly balls are, in a sense, the dominant element in the triangle. Everybody hits .240 when they hit a ground ball, more or less, and everybody hits .725 when they hit a line drive. But when they hit the ball in the air, everybody's got his own number—so it is that number that gives shape to the player's overall ability.

When they hit a ball in the air **and pull it**, a lot of the big hitters hit .500, .600, even .700. Of course, they don't pull it all that often. What makes Howard unique is that he hits the ball out of the park very regularly to all fields. Nobody else does.

Most hitters actually hit more ground balls than fly balls—not a lot more, but a few. The vast majority of hitters, for every ten balls in play, hit four ground balls, two line drives and four fly balls—the 4-2-4 ratio. Some of the guys who chop down on the ball, like Juan Pierre and Willy Taveras, are 6-2-2, and some of the guys who really uppercut are 3-2-5. Almost all of the good hitters are 4-2-4; the "fly ball" minority among them are guys who hit 4.2 or 4.3 fly balls per ten balls in play. If all you mean by the term "fly ball hitter" is guys who hit more fly balls than average, obviously there are hitters like that. The average is about 37-39%; you can call anybody who hits 40-46% a fly ball hitter, I guess.

But not everybody that you might think of as a fly ball hitter meets even that standard. Richie Sexson? He hits more ground balls than fly balls. Always has. Even in 2003, when he hit 45 homers, he hit far more ground balls than flies (215-154). Andruw Jones, the year he hit 51 homers, hit 202 ground balls, 202 fly balls, and 77 line drives. A lot of guys who hit 30, 40 homers still hit more ground balls than fly balls.

So does Ryan Howard. When I first saw Ryan Howard, I thought that he was the second coming of David Ortiz. They have obvious similarities as players—but when you profile them as hitters, they're actually not even similar. Very, very different. David is something of a fly ball hitter—45% fly balls. Howard fly ball percentage is actually

Most of the people you think of as "fly ball hitters", like Jim Thome and David Ortiz and Mark Teixeira and Ryan Howard and Lance Berkman and Albert Pujols, really are not.

a little low. Ortiz doesn't strike out a lot, by the standards of modern hitters. Howard does.

But Ryan Howard hits the ball so phenomenally hard—and remember, we're contrasting him with David Ortiz, who can crush a baseball himself—but Howard hits the ball so hard that he doesn't need to pull it to get it to go out. In his career, he's hit 66 home runs to the opposite field, 57 to center, 54 to right. David hits six times as many homers to right field as he does to left—actually a little more than six. Radically different hitters—different strikeout rates, different ground ball rates, different pull rates, different bat speed.

Good hitters concentrate on trying to square up on the pitch, center the bat on the ball. When you center the bat on the ball and have outstanding bat speed, what happens is:

1) You get a good share of line drives, and
2) Your batting average on fly balls is good, because the fly balls often leave the park.

But when a hitter concentrates on hitting the ball in the air, what happens is:

1) He strikes out more, and
2) His batting average on fly balls goes down, dragging his batting average down further.

The difference is the difference between Carlos Pena in 2007 and Carlos Pena in 2008. In 2007, Pena had a normal ratio of ground balls to line drives to fly balls (133-64-158). He hit .420 on fly balls.

Last year he lapsed, to an extent, into his habit of trying to loft everything. His fly ball ratio went up (104-59-165), but his batting average on fly balls dropped to .340. Not that there's anything wrong with that; he was still an extremely effective hitter, but—the more fly balls you hit, the less effective they become.

Ryan Ludwick, a fly ball hitter, had a great year in 2008, but Ludwick hit 105 line drives. That was very unusual—he had almost as many line drives (105) as ground balls (109). It's questionable whether that is a sustainable performance model. We'll see. My guess is that in 2009, his line drive percentage drops, and his batting average falls 30-40 points.

Again, I didn't know any of this stuff two years ago, and this is my job. I always assumed that there were guys who hit 400 fly balls a year. It's not that way.

Line Drives, and Line Drive Hitters

Moe Drabowsky was a quotable relief pitcher who had been around the majors a long time before he was a teammate of Joe Torre in 1971, when Torre won the MVP Award. I'm going to have to give you this quote from memory, so it's probably not exactly right, but Drabowsky after the '71 season said something like "Joe Torre had the greatest year I ever saw. I've been around a lot of great hitters. I was a teammate of Ernie Banks when he won two straight MVP Awards, a teammate of Hank Aaron in '61, Rocky Colavito for a couple of years, Frank Robinson when he hit 49 homers and won the Triple Crown in '66, Boog Powell when he won the MVP Award last year. But Joe Torre this year hit three or four line drives every day. I've never seen anybody else do that."

Torre had a fantastic year, and I have no doubt that he hit a huge number of line drives. But if you hit *one* line drive a day—one—that's a huge number. Dustin Pedroia won the MVP Award last year; he hit 129 line drives.

Almost everybody hits 19 to 22% line drives. Pedroia last year hit 21%. Kevin Youkilis hit 22% line drives, Teixeira 21%, Ryan Howard 22%. Juan Pierre has a career average, in the years since we have been tracking this (dating back to 2002) of 22%; Barry Bonds is at 21%. Jim Thome's at 20%. Chipper Jones hits 22%. Jeter's at 21%.

What makes the difference, then? Well, first of all, striking out. When you hit a line drive, it's usually a hit. When you strike out, it's never a hit. Fewer strikeouts means more line drive hits.

Second, there's a difference in how hard different players hit the ball. The average hitter hits about .725 when he hits a line drive. Pedroia, who hits the ball quite hard, hit .746 last year (on his line drives). Ryan Howard in his MVP year hit .795 when he hit a line drive.

Third, since line drives are mostly hits, even small variations in the percentage of line drives become significant.

And fourth, some guys do hit more line drives. There are two players that I know of who hit 25% line drives: Todd Helton and Michael Young. Young gets 200 hits every year for a reason: he centers the bat on the ball better than anybody else, at least now that Helton is older and not as quick as he used to be.

The weirdest line drive data of 2008 was Rickie Weeks'. First of all, Weeks hit exceptionally few line drives—15%.

His bat was either just under the ball or just over it, just ahead of it or just behind it. Second, his batting average on line drives was just .527—about as low as I have ever seen. He clearly was not entirely "right", as a hitter—but he also was hitting in tough luck.

It is not unreasonable to describe some guys as "Line Drive Hitters", as long as you remember what you're talking about. You're talking about guys who hit 23-25% line drives, as opposed to the norm of 19-22%.

Ground Balls, and Ground Ball Hitters

Now, there *are* "Ground Ball Hitters" Early in the article I said that there is really no such thing as a Line Drive Hitter or a Fly Ball hitter, but I didn't say there is no such thing as a Ground Ball Hitter. There are hitters who deliberately hit ground balls, and who hit the ball on the ground more than 50% of the time.

Ground ball hitters have very recognizable ground ball patterns, quite different from the norms. They are guys who hit .100-.150 when they hit the ball in the air—as many hitters do—so they figure "what's the percentage in that?" One of the things you read very often about Ichiro is that he is tremendously strong, and when he chooses to turn on a ball he can hit it out. This may be true, but Ichiro's career batting average when he hits the ball in the air is .184.

Ichiro since 2002 has hit 2300 ground balls, 900 line drives, 996 fly balls. That's a normal split for these guys; that's almost the exact ratio that all of these guys have—closer to a 5-2-2 ratio than 6-2-2, and, even though they chop down on the ball, they usually hit more fly balls than line drives:

	GB	LD	FB
Ichiro	2300	900	996
Jeter	1977	747	833
Juan Pierre	2086	820	822
Willy Taveras	784	270	410
Gregor Blanco	151	73	80
Tony Pena	348	112	162
Joey Gathright	568	137	128
Willie Bloomquist	497	210	309

My general feeling about Ground Ball Hitters is: You can have them. There are a few guys who make it work for them. Ryan Theriot. Skip Schumacher, last year at least. A few guys make it work. Joe Mauer is a great player.

But the typical Ground Ball Hitter is...well, Juan Pierre. Do you know what Juan Pierre's batting average is, when he hits a ground ball? It's .237. Since 2002, Pierre's batting average on ground balls is .237—and that's almost all singles.

You can understand what he is doing; he hits .122 on fly balls, so what's the point in that? He's trying to elimi-

nate that ".122" sector from his batting average.

But...237, all singles? Who wants *that*, either? And that's one of three problems. The other two are:

1) He is *not* significantly increasing his percentage of line drives. Pierre has a career mark of 22% Line Drives, not much different than anybody else, and

2) When he does hit a line drive, he doesn't hit it very hard, so his batting average on line drives is lower than the norm. Pierre has a career batting average, on line drives, of .666, which sounds good but isn't. It's 50, 60 points below the norm.

Most of these guys are below the norm—Taveras .648, Pena .627, Gathright .693, Bloomquist .684. Jeter, Mauer, Ichiro—those guys hit the ball hard, and they hit .720-.750 on line drives. That's great. The other guys...they're just trying to stay in the league, and they've got an idea of how to do it, and they're still in the league so I guess it must be working for them.

Some guys drive their ground ball percentage up by bunting. Bunting for a hit is a good play, if you can do it. But if you don't hit the ball hard, the theory of "chop the ball and run" really doesn't work. You remember what I was saying before, that power hitters hit .350, .400 or more when they hit the ball in the air, but singles hitters hit .150 when the hit the ball in the air? People think that speed is like that for ground ball hitters, that ground ball hitters hit for a high average when they hit the ball on the ground.

Well, yes. Sort of. Fast guys hit for a higher average on ground balls than slow guys do.

The thing is, Jacoby Ellsbury hit .264 on ground balls last year—and it's all singles. Joey Gathright hit .269 on ground balls. Yeah, that is better than the slow guys do; the slow guys hit .190 or .210 on ground balls. Adam Dunn in 2006 hit .136 on ground balls. But still, .260 and it's all singles...what's that really worth? Not very much.

Well, I'm wandering now into things that I've known all along. Before I had the data, maybe I would have bought into that slap-and-run theory, at least for some players. Before I had the data, I would have thought that maybe some hitters hit 60% line drives. Before I had the data, I thought there were true "fly ball hitters". There aren't.

Until the last year, I never knew that almost everybody really hits about 40% fly balls, 40% ground balls and 20% line drives. I didn't realize that a lot of players hit .150 when they hit the ball in the air, while others hit .370 and up. I am glad to know these things, and I wanted to share.

Hitting a baseball is really, really hard.

St. Louis Cardinals

St. Louis Cardinals – 2008
Team Overview

Description		Ranking
Won-Lost Record	86-76	
Place	4th of 6 in National League Central	
Runs Scored	779	11th in the majors
Runs Allowed	725	11th in the majors
Home Runs	174	10th in the majors
Home Runs Allowed	163	11th in the majors
Batting Average	.281	2nd in the majors
Batting Average Allowed	.270	20th in the majors
Walks Drawn	577	9th in the majors
Walks Given	496	10th in the majors
OPS For	.783	5th in the majors
OPS Against	.764	20th in the majors
Stolen Bases	73	21st in the majors
Stolen Bases Allowed	49	2nd in the majors

Key Players

Pos	Player	G	AB	R	H	2B	3B	HR	RBI	SB	CS	BB	SO	Avg	OBP	Slg	OPS	WS
C	Yadier Molina	124	444	37	135	18	0	7	56	0	2	32	29	.304	.349	.392	.740	15
1B	Albert Pujols	148	524	100	187	44	0	37	116	7	3	104	54	.357	.462	.653	1.114	34
2B	Adam Kennedy	115	339	42	95	17	4	2	36	7	1	21	43	.280	.321	.372	.692	8
3B	Troy Glaus	151	544	69	147	33	1	27	99	0	1	87	104	.270	.372	.483	.856	20
SS	Cesar Izturis	135	414	50	109	10	3	1	24	24	6	29	26	.263	.319	.309	.628	9
LF	Skip Schumaker	153	540	87	163	22	5	8	46	8	2	47	60	.302	.359	.406	.765	16
CF	Rick Ankiel	120	413	65	109	21	2	25	71	2	1	42	100	.264	.337	.506	.843	13
RF	Ryan Ludwick	152	538	104	161	40	3	37	113	4	4	62	146	.299	.375	.591	.966	24

Key Pitchers

Pos	Player	G	GS	W	L	Sv	IP	H	R	ER	SO	BB	BR/9	ERA	WS
SP	Kyle Lohse	33	33	15	6	0	200.0	211	88	84	119	49	11.84	3.78	12
SP	Todd Wellemeyer	32	32	13	9	0	191.2	178	84	79	134	62	11.60	3.71	12
SP	Braden Looper	33	33	12	14	0	199.0	216	101	92	108	45	12.30	4.16	11
SP	Adam Wainwright	20	20	11	3	0	132.0	122	51	47	91	34	10.84	3.20	11
SP	Joel Pineiro	26	25	7	7	1	148.2	180	89	85	81	35	13.14	5.15	3
CL	Ryan Franklin	74	0	6	6	17	78.2	86	34	31	51	30	13.61	3.55	8
RP	Russ Springer	70	0	2	1	0	50.1	39	14	13	45	18	10.37	2.32	6
RP	Ron Villone	74	0	1	2	1	50.0	45	27	26	50	37	15.12	4.68	2

The Cardinals were 20-2, the best record in the majors, when they scored five runs. The average major league team was 12-7 when they scored five runs.

St. Louis Cardinals – 2008
Record by Runs Scored and Allowed

	Scored	Allowed
10 runs or more	13 - 1	0 - 8
9 runs	6 - 1	0 - 5
8 runs	10 - 1	2 - 8
7 runs	8 - 1	3 - 10
6 runs	13 - 2	6 - 4
5 runs	20 - 2	5 - 9
4 runs	8 - 10	17 - 16
3 runs	6 - 18	22 - 12
2 runs	2 - 19	13 - 4
1 run	0 - 16	11 - 0
0 runs	0 - 5	7 - 0
Total	86 - 76	86 - 76

If games had ended after six innings in the 2008 season, the Cardinals would have won the NL Central by seven full games and finished 8 games ahead of the third-place Cubs.

St. Louis Cardinals – 2008
Innings Ahead Behind Tied

Inning	1	2	3	4	5	6	7	8	9	Extra	Final
Ahead	49	62	78	78	82	87	87	81	80	6	86
Behind	28	45	51	60	59	58	56	62	64	12	76
Tied	85	55	33	24	21	17	19	19	18	15	—

The Marlins leadoff position scored more runs than any other batting position. The Boston Red Sox 2nd place in the batting order was tied for second in runs scored, with the St. Louis Cardinals number two hitters.

The Red Sox 2nd slot in the order was chiefly filled by Dustin Pedroia. The Cardinals slot was most frequently filled by Aaron Miles and Ryan Ludwick, neither of which ever had "MVP" chanted at them.

The Cardinals number two batters also had the highest RBI total in that batting order position.

St. Louis Cardinals – 2008
Runs and RBI by Batting Order

Pos	Players	Runs	RBI
1	Schumaker (110 G), Izturis (17 G)	111	58
2	Miles (34 G), Ludwick (30 G), Ankiel (17 G)	128	99
3	Pujols (143 G)	113	126
4	Ludwick (67 G), Ankiel (56 G), Glaus (29 G)	102	113
5	Glaus (109 G)	80	114
6	Molina (63 G), Duncan (27 G), Kennedy (18 G)	69	79
7	Molina (42 G), LaRue (32 G), Kennedy (28 G)	64	59
8	Wellemeyer (31 G), Looper (31 G), Lohse (31 G)	41	56
9	Izturis (81 G), Ryan (33 G)	71	40
	Total	779	744

Of all the St. Louis big boppers, Ryan Ludwick was the one who performed best against elite pitchers. He batted .282 with a .916 OPS against pitchers with ERAs of 3.50 or less. Against the same category of pitchers, Pujols batted .243/.866, Glaus batted .185/.655 and Ankiel batted .183/.581.

Ryan Ludwick
Batting Performance by Quality of Opposing Pitcher

	AB	H	HR	RBI	Avg	OPS
Pitcher with ERA <= 3.50	124	35	9	22	.282	.916
Pitcher with ERA 3.51 to 4.25	157	44	8	26	.280	.880
Pitcher with ERA 4.26 to 5.25	145	44	14	33	.303	1.044
Pitcher with ERA over 5.25	112	38	6	32	.339	1.041

Games With 6 Hits 2008

Player	Games
Johnny Damon	1
Skip Schumaker	1

Damon's big day came against the Royals on June 7, when he had a double and five singles. His four RBI and helped the Yanks to a 12-11 win.

Schumaker had six singles in eight plate appearances in the Cardinals 14 inning, 10-8 win over the Mets on July 26.

One of the most remarkable baseball stories of 2008 was the Cardinals' outfield—three first-time regulars who were 28, 28 and 29 years old. Two of them (Ryan Ludwick and Skip Schumacher) were sort of knockaround professionals, minor-league journeyman, while the other, Rick Ankiel, is a real-time novel. So far he's had a Steve Blass chapter, a Steve Cauthen chapter, a Roy Hobbs chapter, and a Jose Canseco chapter. Will the real Rick Ankiel please stand up?

And then they turned out to be…oh, I don't know, maybe the best outfield in baseball? Cardinal outfielders hit 83 homers, drove in 285 runs, and scored 330. These are the stats for the three positions:

Position	AB	R	H	2B	3B	HR	RBI	BB	SO	Avg	OBP	Slg
Left	632	101	169	25	3	23	77	74	134	.267	.348	.426
Center	665	105	195	37	5	28	94	61	117	.293	.353	.490
Right	650	124	192	42	6	32	114	74	156	.295	.369	.526

Ludwick, the primary right fielder, had the highest flyball ratio in the National League (186 flyballs, 109 groundballs.) Schumacher, who played all three outfield spots, had the lowest flyball rate in the majors (279 groundballs, 97 flies.)

Ryan Franklin came up with the Mariners ten years ago, 1999, and pitched OK in a limited role for a couple of years. Moving into the rotation, he went 11-13 in 2003, 4-16 in 2004, and 8-15 in 2005.

In the old days, before I can remember baseball, there were pitchers like that who would hang around for years, just getting the hell beat out of them. Milt Gaston finished with a career record of 97-164, Jack Russell was 85-141, Si Johnson was 101-165. Jack Fisher, who I actually do remember, was 86-139.

In modern baseball, since teams have farm systems and bullpens, they figure they can find somebody else to go 8-15 every year, so you do that for a couple of years and they move you to the bullpen. When you move the pitcher to the bullpen all he has to do is throw hard for a couple of innings, and many times this makes these pitchers dramatically more effective as relievers than they were as starters.

So I hear that the Cardinals are using Ryan Franklin as their closer, and my first thought was "really?" Because I remember the Ryan Franklin of several years ago, the guy you'd get mad if he beat you. But very often, after a year or two in the bullpen, guys figure out a new pitch.

In Franklin's case, it was a splitter. Franklin, who didn't throw a splitter at all a few years ago, now throws it 20% of the time against lefties.

Ryan Franklin – 2008
Pitch Type Analysis

Overall		
Total Pitches	1320	
Fastball	670	51%
Curveball	123	9%
Changeup	15	1%
Slider	301	23%
Split Finger	137	10%
Knuckleball	5	0%
Cut Fastball	42	3%
Pitchout	6	0%
Not Charted	21	2%

	Vs. RHB		Vs. LHB	
Total Pitches	793		527	
Outs Recorded	142		94	
Fastball	443	56%	227	43%
Curveball	23	3%	100	19%
Changeup	2	0%	13	2%
Slider	271	34%	30	6%
Split Finger	32	4%	105	20%
Knuckleball	5	1%	0	0%
Cut Fastball	5	1%	37	7%
Pitchout	6	1%	0	0%
Not Charted	6	1%	15	3%

In 2007 Kyle Lohse finished 9-12 with a 4.62 ERA. In 2008 he was 15-6 with a 3.78.

The entire difference between the seasons was: in 2008 he got the first man out. The batting average of the leadoff hitters each inning against Lohse in 2007 was .321. In 2008 it was .247. The batting average of the first hitter in the game, in 2007, was .382. In 2008 it was .129. After that...he was the same pitcher in 2008 that he had been in 2007.

Too bad Albert Pujols is such a lousy baserunner.

Albert Pujols – 2008
Skills Assessment

Hitting for Power:	100th percentile	100th percentile among first basemen
Fielding:		100th percentile among first basemen
Hitting for Average:	100th percentile	100th percentile among first basemen
Plate Discipline:	97th percentile	95th percentile among first basemen
Running:	40th percentile	71st percentile among first basemen

San Diego Padres

San Diego Padres – 2008
Team Overview

Description		Ranking
Won-Lost Record	63-99	
Place	5th of 5 in National League West	
Runs Scored	637	29th in the majors
Runs Allowed	764	18th in the majors
Home Runs	154	17th in the majors
Home Runs Allowed	165	12th in the majors
Batting Average	.250	28th in the majors
Batting Average Allowed	.263	16th in the majors
Walks Drawn	518	22nd in the majors
Walks Given	561	17th in the majors
OPS For	.707	27th in the majors
OPS Against	.741	14th in the majors
Stolen Bases	36	26th in the majors
Stolen Bases Allowed	168	25th in the majors

Key Players

Pos	Player	G	AB	R	H	2B	3B	HR	RBI	SB	CS	BB	SO	Avg	OBP	Slg	OPS	WS
C	Nick Hundley	60	198	21	47	7	1	5	24	0	0	11	52	.237	.278	.359	.636	3
1B	Adrian Gonzalez	162	616	103	172	32	1	36	119	0	0	74	142	.279	.361	.510	.871	24
2B	Tadahito Iguchi	81	303	29	70	14	1	2	24	8	1	26	75	.231	.292	.304	.595	4
3B	Kevin Kouzmanoff	154	624	71	162	31	4	23	84	0	0	23	139	.260	.299	.433	.732	14
SS	Khalil Greene	105	389	30	83	15	2	10	35	5	1	22	100	.213	.260	.339	.599	4
LF	Chase Headley	91	331	34	89	19	2	9	38	4	1	30	104	.269	.337	.420	.757	8
CF	Jody Gerut	100	328	46	97	15	4	14	43	6	4	28	52	.296	.351	.494	.845	13
RF	Brian Giles	147	559	81	171	40	4	12	63	2	2	87	52	.306	.398	.456	.854	20

Key Pitchers

Pos	Player	G	GS	W	L	Sv	IP	H	R	ER	SO	BB	BR/9	ERA	WS
SP	Jake Peavy	27	27	10	11	0	173.2	146	57	55	166	59	10.88	2.85	13
SP	Greg Maddux	26	26	6	9	0	153.1	161	80	68	80	26	11.27	3.99	5
SP	Chris Young	18	18	7	6	0	102.1	84	46	45	93	48	11.70	3.96	5
SP	Cha Seung Baek	22	20	6	9	0	111.0	118	60	57	77	30	12.24	4.62	3
SP	Randy Wolf	21	21	6	10	0	119.2	123	69	63	105	47	13.39	4.74	2
CL	Trevor Hoffman	48	0	3	6	30	45.1	38	19	19	46	9	9.33	3.77	7
RP	Heath Bell	74	0	6	6	0	78.0	66	31	31	71	28	11.19	3.58	6
RP	Cla Meredith	73	0	0	3	0	70.1	79	34	32	49	24	13.31	4.09	3

The Padres scored the least runs in the league, but their leadoff hitters were among the most powerful. They batted in 80 runs (2nd in the league) and hit 30 home runs (3rd in the league) from the #1 spot in the lineup. Top three Padre batters in the leadoff position:

	GS	PA	HR	RBI	Avg	OBP	Slg	OPS
J. Gerut	57	261	11	30	.296	.352	.492	.844
B. Giles	48	229	6	24	.308	.402	.482	.884
S. Hairston	41	186	12	19	.294	.346	.612	.958

The Padres stole only 36 bases, easily the lowest team total in the majors last year and the second-lowest total over a full season since 1984. Oakland stole 31 bases in 2005.

A Double Play When You Least Can Afford It

Kevin Kouzmanoff hit into 14 double plays last year, but six of them came in clutch situations. That's 43% of his season double play total in the clutch, the highest ratio in baseball.

Kevin Kouzmanoff – 2008
Clutch Hitting

Season	AB	H	2B	3B	HR	RBI	BB	SO	GIDP	Avg	OBP	Slg
2006	4	1	0	0	0	0	0	0	0	.250	.250	.250
2007	81	22	3	0	4	20	6	18	1	.272	.326	.457
2008	87	19	4	0	2	12	4	21	6	.218	.266	.333
Totals	172	42	7	0	6	32	10	39	7	.244	.295	.390

Adrian Gonzalez finished third in the National League with 119 RBI, batting in 19% of San Diego's total runs. That was the highest percentage in the majors. Ryan Howard batted in 18% of the Phillies' runs.

Gonzalez raised his batting average with runners in scoring position by 68 points (compared to his batting with no one on base) and his slugging percentage by 152 points.

	Avg	Slg
No one on	.257	.448
Runners in scoring position	.325	.600

Jake Peavy started 174 innings last year and pitched a total of 173.2 innings. In other words, he finished every inning he started except one. The next lowest number of unfinished innings among qualified major league starters was five (Dan Haren and John Lannan).

Jake Peavy – 2008
Inning Analysis

Innings Pitched	173.2
Runs Allowed	57
Innings Started	174
Runs in Those Innings	57
Shutout Innings	137
One-Run Innings	22
Two-Run Innings	10
Three-Run Innings	5
Got First Man Out	118
Runs Scored in Those Innings	25
Runs/9 Innings	1.91
First Man Reached	56
Runs Scored in Those Innings	32
Runs/9 Innings	5.14
1-2-3 Innings	64
10-pitch Innings (or less)	26
Long Innings (20 or more pitches)	43
Failed to Finish Inning	1

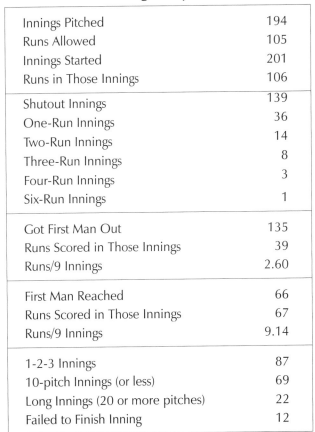

Still Efficient
After All These Years

Greg Maddux led the majors in 10-pitch innings with 69, five more than anyone else.

Greg Maddux – 2008
Inning Analysis

Innings Pitched	194
Runs Allowed	105
Innings Started	201
Runs in Those Innings	106
Shutout Innings	139
One-Run Innings	36
Two-Run Innings	14
Three-Run Innings	8
Four-Run Innings	3
Six-Run Innings	1
Got First Man Out	135
Runs Scored in Those Innings	39
Runs/9 Innings	2.60
First Man Reached	66
Runs Scored in Those Innings	67
Runs/9 Innings	9.14
1-2-3 Innings	87
10-pitch Innings (or less)	69
Long Innings (20 or more pitches)	22
Failed to Finish Inning	12

Brian Giles:

1) Had only 68 swings-and-misses all season in 2008, the lowest percentage of any major league hitter, and

2) Swung at only 40% of the pitches he saw. Not the lowest percentage in the majors, but one of the lowest.

Brian Giles – 2008
Pitch Analysis

Overall		
Pitches Seen	2417	
Taken	1456	60%
Swung At	961	40%
Swung At		
Missed	68	7%
Fouled Off	381	40%
Put in Play	512	53%
Swung At by Pitch Location		
In Strike Zone	742	77%
High	43	4%
Low	65	7%
Inside	26	3%
Outside	85	9%

Cla Meredith is an extreme groundball pitcher. But when he gets the ball up, it's about 50% more likely to be a home run than the average major league pitcher's. Last year, he had the highest groundball percentage of any National League reliever, and he had the sixth-highest home run per flyball rate.

	Ground Balls	HR per Fly Ball
2006	68.8%	14.3%
2007	72.0%	17.1%
2008	66.8%	15.8%

When the at-bat lasted longer than three pitches, Khalil Greene's batting average dropped from .313 to .126.

Khalil Greene – 2008
Short and Long AB

	AB	H	HR	RBI	Avg	OBP	Slg	OPS
Short At Bats	182	57	10	28	.313	.321	.516	.837
Long At Bats	207	26	0	7	.126	.220	.168	.388

U Scores

by Bill James

In recent years there has been some talk about "suspicious numbers" for aging baseball players.

I should say, in my opening words, that I want nothing to do with the concept of forensic sabermetrics. The problem with indicting baseball players based on shady statistics is that we lack the ability to reach that which is the goal of all forensics: certainty. Those are his fingerprints or they or not; we don't need to know that they *could* be. That is her blood or it is not; those are his tire tracks or they are not; that is her handwriting or it is not. We need clear answers, not expert speculation. Saying that a player's numbers are "suspicious" is dirtying a player's reputation based on guesswork and inference.

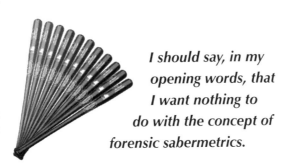

I should say, in my opening words, that I want nothing to do with the concept of forensic sabermetrics.

I'm not talking about that; I am not suggesting that any player's statistics indicate on any level a likelihood of performance enhancing drug use. We do, however, have other levels of deviance from the norm. There is a "hierarchy of departure from the norm" which would go something like this:

A) Criminal,
B) Suspicious,
C) Unusual,
D) Normal.

We certainly cannot conclude, based on statistical analysis, that any player has engaged in criminal conduct, and I would regard it as reckless to say, based on the statistics, that anyone's statistics are suspicious.

We can, however, observe that certain statistical events are unusual. Davey Johnson hit 43 homers in 1973 after having played in the majors for several years, hitting no more than 18. That's unusual. Zack Wheat had a career-high 221 hits in 1925 at the age of 37. That's unusual. It doesn't mean that either of them was using steroids, but it's unusual.

Well, how unusual is it? That's what I'm trying to get here. I'm working on a system to "score" how unusual the things are that any player does, with the goal in mind of being able to say, with a measure of objectivity, that "this player's career is highly unusual, or moderately unusual," or that it is "not unusual at all".

The $64,000 question is, "What is unusual?" Many things are unusual. It's unusual to hit more triples in a season than doubles. It is unusual to have a higher on-base percentage than slugging percentage. It is unusual to have more walks than hits. It is unusual to drive in twice as many runs as you score. None of these things is suspicious, but they are unusual.

In the process of this research I isolated and studied as many "unusual" types of accomplishments as I could. However, first let me note two things that I do not regard as unusual:

1) Excellence itself is not unusual. Willie Mays is not "unusual" because he is great.

2) Unusual consistency is not unusual (meaning, of course, that unusual consistency is not what we are trying to identify with this research).

What is unusual is a long list, and we probably won't get to everything, but let's begin:

U1) It is unusual to have more triples in a season than doubles.

I gave five "U points" for each triple that any player hit in a season above his doubles total. Harry Davis in 1897 hit 10 doubles, 28 triples, the most unusual relationship between those two categories in baseball history. I gave him 90 points for that.

U2) It is unusual to have extra base hits on more than one-half or less than one-ninth of your hits.

I gave a player five points for each extra-base hit that his extra-base hit total was

a) below one-ninth of his total hits (minimum 18 hits), or

b) above one-half of his hits (minimum 10 hits).

Juan Pierre in 2000 had 62 hits, of which only 2 were doubles, none triples and none home runs. That's unusual. Pierre gets 24.4 points for that—62 divided by 9 is 6.889, minus 2 is 4.889, times five is 24.4.

I'm working on a system to "score" how unusual the things are that any player does, with the goal in mind of being able to say, with a measure of objectivity, that "this player's career is highly unusual, or moderately unusual," or that it is "not unusual at all".

Unusual combinations on that end used to be more common. Willie Keeler in 1898 had 216 hits, of which 206 were singles, and Roy Thomas in 1900 had 168 hits, of which 161 were singles. Altogether there are 1,062 players in my data base who qualify for points on U2-a, including eleven in 2008. Willie Bloomquist had highly unusual ratios in both 2007 and 2008.

In modern baseball it is more common (though still quite uncommon) to see a player with more extra-base hits than singles (U2-b). There are 366 players in my database who have more extra base hits than singles, led by Barry Bonds, 2001 (107 extra base hits, 49 singles) and Babe Ruth, 1921 (119 extra base hits, 85 singles). Bonds is 29 hits above one-half of his hits, thus gets 145 points on this account. There have been players getting points on this account since 1883.

U3) It is unusual to have more walks in a season than hits.

There were 42,000 players in my data, of whom 41,000 have at least as many hits as walks, and about 1,000 have more walks than hits. Jack Crooks in 1892 had 95 hits, 136 walks, which stood as the record for its type until Barry Bonds came along. I gave each player one point for each walk that they had in excess of their hit total.

U4) It is unusual to have twice as many RBI in a season as runs scored.

I awarded two points under U4 for the player's RBI, times .6, minus runs scored.

Vic Wertz in 1960 had 45 runs scored, 103 RBI—the most "unusual" ratio of all time. That's worth 33.6 points (103, times .6, minus 45, times 2.) Washington catcher Jesus Flores in 2008 drove in 59 runs, scored only 23—one of the fifteen most unusual ratios of all time.

U5) It is unusual for a player to increase his career high in home runs after the age of 30.

86% of players have their career high in home runs by age 30. For those who didn't I gave them:

- One point for each Home Run by which they increased their career high at age 31.
- Two points for each additional Home Run at age 32.
- Three points at age 33, etc.

Hank Sauer at age 30 had a career high in home runs of 5. At age 31 he hit 35 home runs, increasing his career high by 30, and earning 30 points under U5. Four years later he increased his career high to 37, earning him an additional 10 points (5 * 2 or, if you prefer, (35 – 30) * (37 – 35)). Two years after that he increased his career high in home runs by an additional four, earning him another 28 points (7 * 4 or, if you prefer, (37-30) * (41 – 37)).

Given the experience of the last fifteen years, it is noteworthy how few players set late-in-life career home run records in 2008. The only significant late-in-life home run accomplishment of 2008 was Mark DeRosa, age 33, hitting 21 home runs after a previous career high of 13. That's a "U Score" of 24, but it's nothing compared to what we have seen in the last ten years.

U6) It is unusual for a player to significantly increase or significantly decrease his home run frequency after establishing a major league baseline.

To factor that in, I figured each player's career home runs per plate appearance at the end of the season in which the player played his 500th career game (S-500). I then figured an "expected career home runs" for each player based on his career plate appearances and his career home run rate through S-500. I then gave the player one point for each two home runs *greater than ten* that his career home run rate was different from his expected.

Al Dark, for example, played his 500th game in 1951. At the end of that season he had hit 36 career home runs in 2,507 plate appearances. He finished his career with 7,829 career plate appearances. We thus could have expected him to hit 112 home runs—actually, 112.42. We thus treat any number between 102.42 and 122.42 as "normal", and Dark would get no points under U6 if he were between those points. But he hit 126 career home runs—3.58 more than we would regard as normal deviation. For this, he gets 1.79 points.

Some people will object that U5 and U6 are redundant measures of the same trait. Yes, that's true, they are—as is U9 and, to an extent, U8. We have imperfect measures of these unusual career paths.

My belief is that by measuring this "late in life Home Run growth" in different ways we get a better approximation of the underlying events than if we simply make one kind of flawed and arbitrary measurement.

U7) It is unusual for players to have seasons in which their OPS is more than 150 points (.150) distant from their career norm.

Norm Cash in 1961 had an OPS of 1.148. His career OPS was .862—a discrepancy of 286 points (.286).

In this category I ignored discrepancy occurring in 100 plate appearances or less, and credited points for discrepancies larger than .150 in more than 100 plate appearances. These were credited by the formula:

Career OPS

Minus Season OPS

Minus .150 (set to zero if total is less than zero)

Times Plate Appearances minus 100

Divided by 1.5.

For Norm Cash, 1961, this is 1.148, minus .862, minus .150, equaling .136. Cash had 672 plate appearances, so we multiply this by 572, making 77.8. Divided by 1.5, making 51.8. Cash's 51.8 "U point season score" in 1961 is the 7th highest of all time.

You are no doubt asking how I arrive at these contorted and arbitrary formulas. The answer is: I have too much time on my hands. No, seriously…I'm trying to give essentially equal weight to each type of "oddness". I am trying to get essentially the same number of seasons labeled as "unusual" and the same number of points awarded for unusualness in each category. I fool around with the parameters until I get results in which

a) about the same number of points are awarded, and

b) the results seem reasonable.

A system in which Norm Cash, Luis Gonzalez, Brady Anderson and Jim Hickman are listed among the players having the most unusual seasons in history seems like a reasonable system.

U8) It is unusual for players to have prime seasons at ages before 24 and after 30.

Not *terribly* unusual, but 72% of prime seasons are between the ages of 24 and 30.

How do we measure this? I'm only dealing with position players here, not pitchers. I figured the "season score" for each season, and identified all seasons which exceeded .800 of the player's career high season score as a prime season. I then subtracted .800 times the player's career high season score from each season which exceeded .800 of the career high.

This then was multiplied by:

7 if the player was 18 years old

6 if he was 19

5 if he was 20

4 if he was 21

3 if he was 22

2 if he was 23

But zero if he was 24.

This was done, of course, because it is *more* unusual to have a prime season at a very early age.

On the other end, this was multiplied by:

1 if he was 31

1.5 if he was 32

2 if he was 33

2.5 if he was 34

3 if he was 35

Etc.

And then the product of that was divided by 12.

OK, Bob Horner, 1980. Season score, 225. His career high was 260. .800 times 260 is 208. 225 minus 208 is 17. Horner's 1980 is a prime season because it exceeds 80% of his career norm, and it exceeds 80% of his career norm by 17 points.

Horner was 22 years old, so we multiply the 17 points by 3, and divide by 12. Horner winds up with 4 "U points" for having a prime season at age 22.

U9) It is unusual for a player to increase his career high in Home Runs after playing more than 500 games.

This, of course, is an amalgam of points 5 and 6, which attempted awkwardly to measure the same thing. In this category, we simply award one point for each Home Run that the player increases his career best in homers, after the season in which he plays his 500th game. Davey Johnson, for example, gets 33 points because his career high in home runs at the end of the season in which he played his 500th game was 10, and he subsequently improved that to 43. Hank Sauer, on the other hand, gets only 6 points in this category because, while his home runs were hit late by age, he did hit 35 home runs in his first season as a regular.

U10) It is unusual for a player to have an on-base percentage which is 15% higher or 33% lower than his slugging percentage.

In this category I ignored players who had less than 100 plate appearances. For players whose on-base percentage was 15% higher than their slugging percentage, I subtracted 1.15 times the slugging percentage from the on-base percentage, and multiplied the difference by Plate Appearances minus 100.

Bill North in 1980 had an on-base percentage of .373, a slugging percentage of just .292. His on-base percentage was 37 points higher than 15% more than his slugging percentage. He had 500 plate appearances. Multiplying .037 times 400, then, North receives 15 points for having an unusual ratio between his on-base percentage and his slugging percentage.

On the other end, players are credited with "U points" if their on-base percentage is less than two-thirds of their slugging percentage. Same process, reversed; two-thirds of slugging percentage, minus on-base percentage, times 100 less than plate appearances.

Victor Diaz in 2007 had a .259 on-base percentage, a .538 slugging percentage, which is the most extreme ratio ever between those two stats (in 100 or more plate appearances, although there are a few players not included in my data). Two-thirds of his slugging percentage is .359, minus his on-base percentage leaves .100. He had only 108 plate appearances, however, so he is credited with only 8/10 of one "U point".

The most unusual ratios of 2008 were by Ryan Braun and Mike Jacobs, on the high end (very high slugging percentages relative to on-base percentages), and Willie Bloomquist and Gregor Blanco on the other end. Ryan Braun was credited with 19 points for his odd ratio.

OK, that's all I have so far. There are many, many other kinds of "unusual" accomplishments for hitters, and, if I get time, I'll add points for other unusual career progressions or unusual combinations of events. I hope you will tell me at www.billjamesonline.com what things you would regard as unusual occurrences for hitters and (later) for pitchers, and I hope that I'll get time to incorporate some of those things into the system.

But right now, let me summarize the results of points U1 to U10 through the 2008 season.

U1 is points awarded for having more triples in a season than doubles. The top ten seasons in this area are:

Rank	Player	YEAR	U1
1	Harry Davis	1897	90
2	Chief Wilson	1912	85
3	Duff Cooley	1895	55
4	Bill Kuehne	1885	50
5	Heinie Reitz	1894	45
6	Hughie Jennings	1899	45
7	Deion Sanders	1992	40
8	Edd Roush	1916	40
9	Tommy Leach	1902	40
10	Eleven Tied with		35

A total of 9,501 points have been awarded (through 2008) under rule U1.

Victor Diaz in 2007 had a .259 on-base percentage, a .538 slugging percentage, which is the most extreme ratio ever between those two stats.

U2 is points awarded for having extra base hits on more than one-half or less than one-ninth of the player's total hits. The top ten seasons in this area are:

Rank	Player	YEAR	U2	High/Low
1	Barry Bonds	2001	145	High
2	Babe Ruth	1921	85	High
3	Albert Belle	1995	82.5	High
4	Mark McGwire	1998	75	High
5	Mark McGwire	1999	72.5	High
6	Willie Keeler	1898	69.88	Low
7	Babe Ruth	1920	65	High
8	Willie Stargell	1973	60	High
9	Roy Thomas	1900	58.24	Low
10	Jim Edmonds	2003	57.5	High

A total of 10,611 points are awarded under rule U2.

U3 is points awarded to players with more walks in a season than hits. The top ten players seasons in this area are:

Rank	Player	YEAR	U3
1	Barry Bonds	2004	291
2	Barry Bonds	2002	147
3	Jack Crooks	1892	123
4	Barry Bonds	2007	114
5	Jimmy Wynn	1976	102
6	Roy Cullenbine	1947	99
7	Eddie Yost	1956	96
8	Yank Robinson	1890	93
9	Ferris Fain	1955	81
10	Wes Westrum	1951	75

A total of 10,124 points are awarded under U3.

U4 is points awarded to hitters whose Runs Scored are less than 60% of their RBI. The top ten seasons in this area are:

Rank	Player	YEAR	U4
1	Vic Wertz	1960	33.6
2	Earl Sheely	1931	32.4
3	Larry McLean	1910	31.2
4t	Bob Oliver	1974	24.8
4t	John Bateman	1963	24.8
4t	Smoky Burgess	1965	24.8
7	Chief Meyers	1910	24.4
8t	Doc Miller	1914	23.6
8t	Rusty Staub	1983	23.6
8t	Smead Jolley	1931	23.6
8t	Terry Kennedy	1983	23.6

A total of 10,025 points are awarded under rule U4.

U5 is points awarded to hitters who establish new career highs in home runs at age 31 or later. The top seasons in this area are:

Rank	Player	YEAR	U5
1	Barry Bonds	2001	144
2	George Crowe	1957	96
3	Luke Easter	1950	92
4t	Andres Galarraga	1996	80
4t	Bob Thurman	1957	80
6	Luis Gonzalez	2001	78
7	Carlton Fisk	1985	77
8	Terry Steinbach	1996	76
9	Cy Williams	1923	75
10	John Vander Wal	2000	72

Bonds in 2001 established a new career high in home runs by 24 (73 vs. 49), at the age of 36. That's 144 points—easily the highest total in baseball history. A total of 8,622 points are awarded under rule U5. George Crowe and Bob Thurman, 2nd and 4th on the list, were teammates on the 1957 Cincinnati Reds, both of them veterans of the Negro Leagues.

U6 is points awarded to hitters who increase or decrease their home run rates after the season in which they played their 500th career game. All of the players in the top ten increased their home run rate, although many players—Eddie Mathews, for example—do lose home runs as they age:

Rank	Player	U6
1	Barry Bonds	154
2	Rafael Palmeiro	153
3	Sammy Sosa	131
4	Ken Griffey Jr.	109
5	Stan Musial	108
6	Steve Finley	102
7	Rogers Hornsby	88
8	Lou Whitaker	88
9	Gary Sheffield	80
10	Robin Yount	76

A total of 10,468 points are awarded under rule U6. These points, of course, are awarded only once in a career, as opposed to being potentially awarded in multiple seasons.

U7 is points awarded to hitters who have an OPS 150 points higher or lower than their career norm. The top seasons in this area are:

Rank	Player	YEAR	U7
1	Barry Bonds	2002	94
2	Barry Bonds	2004	76
3	Hugh Duffy	1894	73
4	Barry Bonds	2001	67
5	Sammy Sosa	2001	60
6	Tip O'Neill	1887	57
7	Norm Cash	1961	52
8	Luis Gonzalez	2001	49
9	Barry Bonds	1989	48
10	Fred Dunlap	1884	44

U8 is points awarded to players who have prime seasons at ages before 24 and after 30. In 1929, Mel Ott hit .328 with 42 home runs, 151 RBI. He was 20 years old, and these were easily the best raw numbers that he was ever to have. This is the most remarkable peak season at an off-prime age of all time. The top ten seasons in this area are:

Rank	Player	YEAR	U8
1	Mel Ott	1929	47
2	Barry Bonds	2001	42
3	Barry Bonds	2002	40
4	Barry Bonds	2004	40
5	Joe Jackson	1911	35
6	Al Kaline	1955	33
7	Jim O'Rourke	1890	32
8	Alex Rodriguez	1996	32
9	Eddie Mathews	1953	31
10	Joe Kelley	1894	31

A total of 10,371 points are awarded under rule U8.

U9 are points awarded to hitters who increase their career-best home run total after the season in which they play their 500th game. The top ten increases of all time are:

Rank	Player	U9
1	Barry Bonds	48
2	Luis Gonzalez	42
3	Rogers Hornsby	34
4t	Rafael Palmeiro	33
4t	Sammy Sosa	33
4t	Davey Johnson	33
7	Tilly Walker	31
8t	Ken Griffey Jr.	29
8t	Brady Anderson	29
10t	Cy Williams	28
10t	Steve Finley	28

U10 is points awarded for an unusual relationship between on-base percentage and slugging percentage. The top ten seasons in this area are:

Rank	Player	YEAR	OBA	SPct	U10
1	Roy Thomas	1900	.451	.335	38
2	Yank Robinson	1890	.434	.281	35
3	Sammy Sosa	1999	.367	.635	35
4	Goat Anderson	1907	.343	.225	34
5	Sammy Sosa	1998	.377	.647	34
6	Matt Williams	1994	.319	.607	33
7	Sammy Sosa	2001	.437	.737	33
8	Dave Kingman	1979	.343	.613	32
9	Jack Crooks	1890	.357	.254	32
10	Javier Lopez	2003	.378	.687	32

A total of 10,845 points are awarded under rule U10, which are about evenly split between players with high on-base percentages and players with high slugging percentages.

Summarizing these ten categories of performance, you might guess that Barry Bonds would score as having the most unusual career of all time. In fact, you might suspect that I have set up the system so that Bonds always comes to the fore. I certainly did not. I doubt that it would be possible to measure these type of unusual accomplishments in such a way that any player other than Bonds would come to the front. You could measure them to get different totals, different rankings, but these are the 25 most unusual players of all time by my system so far:

Rank	Player	Pl Tot
1	Barry Bonds	1974
2	Mark McGwire	803
3	Sammy Sosa	521
4	Babe Ruth	511
5	Roy Thomas	393
6	Yank Robinson	323
7	Max Bishop	303
8	Andres Galarraga	293
9	Ken Griffey Jr.	293
10	Luis Gonzalez	288
11	Rogers Hornsby	288
12	Cy Williams	283
13	Jack Crooks	278
14	Rafael Palmeiro	268
15	Brady Anderson	262
16	Hank Aaron	246
17	Eddie Yost	244
18	Willie Keeler	240
19	Gene Tenace	237
20	Ken Caminiti	237
21	Albert Belle	237
22	Jack Clark	228
23	Edgar Martinez	227
24	Willie McCovey	222
25	Juan Gonzalez	212

These are all players who had longer careers. At some point, when I have done more research, I would need to compare the player's "U Score"—his total of odd accomplishments—against his games played. I will look at more things, or anyway I plan to. I will also look at pitchers. Perhaps some of the 1990s/turn-of-the-century players will slide down the list a little. But it is hard to imagine Barry Bonds sliding out of the position of having had the most unusual career of all time. The Kansas City Royals in this off-season have picked up arguably the two most unusual players in the majors. First Baseman Mike Jacobs had the highest U-Score of 2008 (38 points) based on (1) having more than half of his hits for extra bases, and (2) having an unusual ratio of slugging percentage to on-base percentage. With a .299 on-base percentage and .514 slugging, Jacobs was only the second player in major league history to qualify for the batting title with a slugging percentage over .500 and an on-base percentage under .300. The other was Dave Kingman in 1976.

And Jacob's exact opposite is the player who will be playing beside him on opening day—Royals' new second baseman Willie Bloomquist. Bloomquist, batting only 165 times, still ranked as the sixth most-unusual player of the year, based on not getting any extra-base hits and having a much higher on-base percentage than slugging percentage.

The ten most Unusual Players of 2008, by my admittedly quirky method:

1. Mike Jacobs
2. Russell Branyan
3. Taylor Teagarden
4. Mark DeRosa
5. Ryan Howard
6. Willie Bloomquist
7. Jesus Flores
8. Bengie Molina
9. Adam Dunn
10. Pat Burrell

Teagarden should get extra points for being named "Teagarden".

You are no doubt asking how I arrive at these contorted and arbitrary formulas. The answer is: I have too much time on my hands.

San Francisco Giants

San Francisco Giants – 2008
Team Overview

Description		Ranking
Won-Lost Record	72-90	
Place	4th of 5 in National League West	
Runs Scored	640	28th in the majors
Runs Allowed	759	16th in the majors
Home Runs	94	27th in the majors
Home Runs Allowed	147	5th in the majors
Batting Average	.262	20th in the majors
Batting Average Allowed	.258	10th in the majors
Walks Drawn	452	25th in the majors
Walks Given	652	26th in the majors
OPS For	.703	28th in the majors
OPS Against	.745	16th in the majors
Stolen Bases	108	10th in the majors
Stolen Bases Allowed	99	16th in the majors

Key Players

Pos	Player	G	AB	R	H	2B	3B	HR	RBI	SB	CS	BB	SO	Avg	OBP	Slg	OPS	WS
C	Bengie Molina	145	530	46	155	33	0	16	95	0	0	19	38	.292	.322	.445	.767	19
1B	John Bowker	111	326	31	83	14	3	10	43	1	1	19	74	.255	.300	.408	.708	7
2B	Ray Durham	87	263	43	77	23	0	3	32	6	2	38	49	.293	.385	.414	.799	8
3B	Jose Castillo	112	394	42	96	28	4	6	35	2	2	25	71	.244	.290	.381	.671	5
SS	Omar Vizquel	92	266	24	59	10	1	0	23	5	4	24	29	.222	.283	.267	.550	5
LF	Fred Lewis	133	468	81	132	25	11	9	40	21	7	51	124	.282	.351	.440	.791	13
CF	Aaron Rowand	152	549	57	149	37	0	13	70	2	4	44	126	.271	.339	.410	.749	14
DH	Randy Winn	155	598	84	183	38	2	10	64	25	2	59	88	.306	.363	.426	.790	19

Key Pitchers

Pos	Player	G	GS	W	L	Sv	IP	H	R	ER	SO	BB	BR/9	ERA	WS
SP	Tim Lincecum	34	33	18	5	0	227.0	182	72	66	265	84	10.78	2.62	25
SP	Matt Cain	34	34	8	14	0	217.2	206	95	91	186	91	12.57	3.76	14
SP	Jonathan Sanchez	29	29	9	12	0	158.0	154	90	88	157	75	13.44	5.01	6
SP	Barry Zito	32	32	10	17	0	180.0	186	115	103	120	102	14.60	5.15	5
SP	Kevin Correia	25	19	3	8	0	110.0	141	80	74	66	47	15.71	6.05	0
CL	Brian Wilson	63	0	3	2	41	62.1	62	32	32	67	28	13.43	4.62	9
RP	Jack Taschner	67	0	3	2	0	48.0	57	27	26	39	24	15.56	4.88	2
RP	Tyler Walker	65	0	5	8	0	53.1	47	29	27	49	2	11.64	4.56	4

The Giants played almost .500 ball (63-65) in games started by their top four starting pitchers (Lincecum, Zito, Sanchez and Cain), but went 9-25 in games started by their fifth starters.

San Francisco Giants – 2008
Performance by Starting Pitcher

Games Started By	GS	RS	RA	Won	Lost
Cain, Matt	34	108	151	14	20
Lincecum, Tim	33	149	118	21	12
Zito, Barry	32	114	152	13	19
Sanchez, Jonathan	29	136	146	15	14
Correia, Kevin	19	75	103	5	14
Misch, Pat	7	27	46	0	7
Hennessey, Brad	4	18	21	2	2
Palmer, Matt	3	11	21	1	2
Valdez, Merkin	1	2	1	1	0
Team Totals	162	640	759	72	90

Not counting players with one or zero home runs, the only two major league players in 2008 with identical triple crown numbers were Fred Lewis of the Giants and Adam Lind of the Blue Jays. Both players hit .282 with 9 homers and 40 RBI.

Veteran Leadership

Barry Zito walked 102 batters; 27 of them ultimately scored, the most in the majors. Youngster Jonathan Sanchez—perhaps following his elder teammate's lead—gave out 26 free passes that came back to haunt him, which tied for second-most.

Barry Zito – 2008
Runs Allowed Analysis

Reached by Single:	125	Scored:	41	33%
Reached by Double:	40	Scored:	19	48%
Reached by Triple:	5	Scored:	2	40%
Reached by Homer:	16			
Reached by Walk:	102	Scored:	27	26%
Reached by HBP:	4	Scored:	1	25%
Reached by Error:	10	Scored:	7	70%
Reached by FC - All Safe:	3	Scored:	1	33%
Reached by FC - Out:	24	Scored:	1	4%
Total On Base	329	Scored:	115	35%
Stolen Bases Allowed:	6	Scored:	4	67%
Caught Stealing:	4	Scored:	0	0%
Steal Attempts:	10	Scored:	4	40%
Intentional Walks:	10	Scored:	1	10%

Jonathan Sanchez – 2008
Runs Allowed Analysis

Reached by Single:	98	Scored:	29	30%
Reached by Double:	39	Scored:	15	38%
Reached by Triple:	3	Scored:	2	67%
Reached by Homer:	14			
Reached by Walk:	75	Scored:	26	35%
Reached by HBP:	7	Scored:	2	29%
Reached by Error:	5	Scored:	0	0%
Reached by FC - Out:	14	Scored:	2	14%
Reached by Other:	1	Scored:	0	0%
Total On Base	256	Scored:	90	35%
Stolen Bases Allowed:	19	Scored:	9	47%
Caught Stealing:	3	Scored:	0	0%
Steal Attempts:	22	Scored:	9	41%
Intentional Walks:	1	Scored:	0	0%

There were 20 major league pitchers in 2008 who had 20 or more Quality Starts. Every one of them had a winning record except Matt Cain, who finished 8-14. Mark Buehrle (15-12) had the second-worst winning percentage in the group.

In the 47 innings led off by Emmanuel Burris, the Giants scored 42 runs, or .89 per inning, or 8.04 per nine innings. No one else on the team was above .61 per inning (or 5.49 per nine innings).

Emmanuel Burris – 2008
Performance as Leadoff Man

Innings Led Off:	47		
Team Scored:	42	Runs	.89 per inning
Reached Base Leading Off:	23		
Team Scored:	30	Runs	1.30 per inning
Did Not Reach:	24		
Team Scored:	12	Runs	.50 per inning
Other Innings for Team:	1410		
Team Scored:	598	Runs	.42 per inning

Brian Wilson's career ERA against winning teams (5.46) is 76% higher than it is against losing teams (3.11).

Brian Wilson
Career Records Against Quality of Opposition

Opponent	G	IP	W	L	SO	BB	ERA
.600 teams	3	3.1	0	1	2	4	8.10
.500 - .599 teams	59	57.2	4	5	50	22	5.31
.400 - .499 teams	40	39.0	2	1	41	22	3.46
sub .400 teams	16	16.0	0	0	15	8	2.25

Among all major league pitchers pitching 30 or more innings, Brad Hennessey of the Giants had the highest opposition batting average (.358), the highest opposition on-base percentage (.409), the highest opposition slugging percentage (.602), and (it would go without saying) the highest opposition OPS (1.012). Not only was no other pitcher over 1.000 OPS allowed, but nobody else was over .900.

Obviously Tim Lincecum was the Giants' best player in 2008, but who was the second-best, and the third-best, and the fourth?

Randy Winn, Matt Cain and Fred Lewis. I have a method that attempts to state everything that a player does at bat, in the field or on the mound as a part of a win—a "share" of a win. For each game won by the team there should be about three Win Shares, and for each loss, about three Loss Shares.

Lincecum in 2008 had a personal won-lost record of 26-6, making him one of the best players in the major leagues. The Giants had two other players of championship quality. Right fielder Randy Winn, who hit over .300 with 38 doubles and 25 stolen bases, was 16-8 as a hitter (16 wins, 8 losses), plus 3-3 in the field, making him 19-11 overall—one of the league's better right fielders. And Matt Cain, although stuck with an ugly "official" won-lost record, pitched very well, as he had in 2007.

The chart below summarizes the won-lost contributions of all the Giants of 2008. Players not listed were 0-0.

First	Last	Batting W	L	Fielding W	L	Pitching W	L	Total W	L	Winning Percentage
Tim	Lincecum	2	2			24	5	26	6	.810
Randy	Winn	16	8	3	3			19	11	.625
Matt	Cain	2	2			15	12	17	13	.563
Bengie	Molina	10	12	3	2			14	14	.495
Aaron	Rowand	10	13	3	2			14	16	.461
Fred	Lewis	12	8	1	3			13	11	.537
Jonathon	Sanchez	1	2			9	12	10	14	.409
Rich	Aurilia	7	11	1	3			8	14	.372
Barry	Zito	1	2			7	15	8	17	.326
Brian	Wilson	0	0			8	6	8	6	.567
Ray	Durham	7	4	1	2			7	6	.548
Jose	Castillo	5	13	2	2			7	15	.321
John	Bowker	6	9	1	2			6	11	.374
Emmanuel	Burris	5	6	1	1			6	7	.453
Pablo	Sandoval	4	2	1	1			4	3	.609
Alex	Hinshaw	0	0			4	2	4	2	.689
Keeichi	Yabu	0	0			4	4	4	4	.507
Omar	Vizquel	2	10	2	1			4	12	.246
Eugenio	Velez	4	8	0	3			4	11	.252
Billy	Sadler	0	0			3	3	3	3	.498
Tyler	Walker	0	0			3	4	3	4	.445
Sergio	Romo	0	0			3	1	3	1	.722
Jack	Taschner	0	0			3	3	3	3	.479
Kevin	Correia	0	1			2	11	3	12	.182
Travis	Ishikawa	2	2	0	1			2	2	.512
Dave	Roberts	2	3	1	0			2	4	.399
Nate	Shierholtz	2	1	0	0			2	1	.643
Steve	Holm	2	2	0	0			2	2	.468
Merkin	Valdez	0	0			2	0	2	0	.796

First	Last	Batting W	L	Fielding W	L	Pitching W	L	Total W	L	Winning Percentage
Pat	Misch	0	0			1	6	2	6	.208
Brian	Horwitz	1	1	1	0			1	1	.667
Ivan	Ochoa	0	6	1	1			1	6	.160
Scott	McClain	1	0	0	0			1	1	.660
Vinnie	Chulk	0	0			1	3	1	3	.288
Geno	Espinelli	0	0			1	1	1	1	.446
Travis	Denker	1	1	0	0			1	1	.513
Daniel	Ortmeier	1	2	0	0			1	3	.261
Erick	Threets	0	0			1	1	1	1	.597
Brian	Bocock	0	4	1	0			1	4	.158
Brad	Hennessey	0	0			0	5	1	5	.099
Osiris	Matos	0	0			0	2	0	3	.082
Ryan	Rohlinger	0	2	0	1			0	3	.000
Rajai	Davis	0	1	0	0			0	1	.000
Matt	Palmer	0	0			0	2	0	2	.000
Eliezer	Alfonzo	0	1	0	0			0	1	.000
		105	139	22	30	92	98	220	267	.451

Southpaw Jeremy Affeldt throws his curveball against right-handed batters almost as often as he throws it against lefties, with strong results. Righties batted .255 against him last year, fourteen points lower than lefties (.269).

Jeremy Affeldt – 2008
Pitch Type Analysis

	Vs. RHB		Vs. LHB	
Total Pitches	882		421	
Outs Recorded	149		86	
Fastball	537	61%	273	65%
Curveball	255	29%	145	34%
Changeup	77	9%	1	0%

Sergio00000000000000000000000000

Sergio Romo completed a scoreless inning in 23 of the 27 innings he started. He retired the first batter 22 of 27 times.

Sergio Romo – 2008
Inning Analysis

Innings Pitched	34.0
Runs Allowed	13
Innings Started	27
Runs in Those Innings	13
Shutout Innings	23
One-Run Innings	1
Three-Run Innings	1
Four-Run Innings	1
Five-Run Innings	1
Got First Man Out	22
Runs Scored in Those Innings	3
Runs/9 Innings	1.23
First Man Reached	5
Runs Scored in Those Innings	10
Runs/9 Innings	18.00
1-2-3 Innings	15
10-pitch Innings (or less)	6
Long Innings (20 or more pitches)	4
Failed to Finish Inning	1

Seattle Mariners

Seattle Mariners – 2008
Team Overview

Description		Ranking
Won-Lost Record	61-101	
Place	4th of 4 in American League West	
Runs Scored	671	25th in the majors
Runs Allowed	811	23rd in the majors
Home Runs	124	23rd in the majors
Home Runs Allowed	161	10th in the majors
Batting Average	.266	13th in the majors
Batting Average Allowed	.276	26th in the majors
Walks Drawn	417	27th in the majors
Walks Given	626	24th in the majors
OPS For	.707	26th in the majors
OPS Against	.784	24th in the majors
Stolen Bases	90	12th in the majors
Stolen Bases Allowed	92	13th in the majors

Key Players

Pos	Player	G	AB	R	H	2B	3B	HR	RBI	SB	CS	BB	SO	Avg	OBP	Slg	OPS	WS
C	Kenji Johjima	112	379	29	86	19	0	7	39	2	0	19	33	.227	.277	.332	.609	8
1B	Richie Sexson	74	252	27	55	8	0	11	30	1	0	37	76	.218	.315	.381	.696	3
2B	Jose Lopez	159	644	80	191	41	1	17	89	6	3	27	67	.297	.322	.443	.764	18
3B	Adrian Beltre	143	556	74	148	29	1	25	77	8	2	50	90	.266	.327	.457	.784	13
SS	Yuniesky Betancourt	153	559	66	156	36	3	7	51	4	4	17	42	.279	.300	.392	.691	8
LF	Raul Ibanez	162	635	85	186	43	3	23	110	2	4	64	110	.293	.358	.479	.837	21
CF	Jeremy Reed	97	286	30	77	18	1	2	31	2	3	18	38	.269	.314	.360	.674	4
RF	Ichiro Suzuki	162	686	103	213	20	7	6	42	43	4	51	65	.310	.361	.386	.747	19
DH	Jose Vidro	85	308	28	72	11	0	7	45	2	1	18	36	.234	.274	.338	.612	2

Key Pitchers

Pos	Player	G	GS	W	L	Sv	IP	H	R	ER	SO	BB	BR/9	ERA	WS
SP	Felix Hernandez	31	31	9	11	0	200.2	198	85	77	175	80	12.83	3.45	13
SP	Jarrod Washburn	28	26	5	14	1	153.2	174	87	80	87	50	13.53	4.69	5
SP	Erik Bedard	15	15	6	4	0	81.0	70	38	33	72	37	12.33	3.67	6
SP	Carlos Silva	28	28	4	15	0	153.1	213	114	110	69	32	14.62	6.46	0
SP	Miguel Batista	44	20	4	14	1	115.0	135	89	80	73	79	17.22	6.26	0
CL	J.J. Putz	47	0	6	5	15	46.1	46	20	20	56	28	14.76	3.88	5
RP	Sean Green	72	0	4	5	1	79.0	80	47	41	62	36	13.90	4.67	4
RP	Mark Lowe	57	0	1	5	1	63.2	78	44	38	55	34	16.40	5.37	1

The Seattle Mariners last year had a man on second base, no one out 116 times, and scored only 111 runs in those innings. They were the only major league team to score less than one run an inning when they had a leadoff hitter at second base.

Only When It Counts

Jeff Clement went 10-for-21 (.476) with six extra-base hits in the clutch. (In his other 182 at-bats he batted .198 and slugged .286.) In 2007, he went 2-for-3 with 2 homers and a walk in the clutch.

Jeff Clement – 2007-2008
Clutch Hitting

Season	AB	H	2B	3B	HR	RBI	BB	SO	GIDP	Avg	OBP	Slg
2007	3	2	0	0	2	3	1	0	0	.667	.750	2.667
2008	21	10	3	1	2	9	3	6	1	.476	.542	1.000
Totals	24	12	3	1	4	12	4	6	1	.500	.571	1.208

The Mariners in 2006 drafted Brandon Morrow with the #5 pick in the draft, rather than local favorite Tim Lincecum, who went to San Francisco with the tenth pick. This is something that people talk about, but—just my opinion—in the long run, I don't think anybody is going to regret drafting Brandon Morrow. I think he's tremendous.

Morrow had a 3.34 ERA last year, but there are several signals that he may be a better pitcher even than that. Batters hit .174 against him, which is Randy Johnson territory. He made a mid-season conversion from relief to starting, which probably didn't help his numbers any, and he gave up 10 home runs with just 47 fly outs. A ratio like that is probably a fluke, since the pitcher doesn't really control the percentage of fly-balls against him that become home runs.

He may not be a starting pitcher. In five starts in September he walked 19 men, which is too many; even Randy couldn't succeed as a starter issuing that many free passes. He may have to go back to the bull-pen. And I'm not saying he is Tim Lincecum, but....I think he's a guy who has Cy Young ability.

Brandon Morrow – 2007-2008
Career Records Against Quality of Opposition

Opponent	G	IP	W	L	SO	BB	ERA
.600 teams	3	6.0	0	1	5	5	3.00
.500 - .599 teams	48	55.1	3	3	59	41	3.74
.400 - .499 teams	51	63.2	3	4	75	38	3.96
sub .400 teams	3	3.0	0	0	2	0	0.00

Yuniesky Betancourt was the only major league starter who had twice as many short at-bats as long at-bats, and no one else even came close. Bengie Molina, who was closest, would have needed 25 more short at-bats to join the 2-to-1 club.

Yuniesky Betancourt – 2008
Short and Long AB

	AB	H	HR	RBI	Avg	OBP	Slg	OPS
One and done	84	26	2	16	.310	.310	.465	.775
Short	376	116	7	42	.309	.312	.445	.757
Long	183	40	0	9	.219	.285	.270	.555
7 Up	16	2	0	2	.125	.263	.235	.498

The average hitter, facing Carlos Silva in 2008, hit about like Dustin Pedroia or Ian Kinsler.

Carlos Silva – 2002-2008
Record of Opposing Batters

Season	AB	R	H	2B	3B	HR	RBI	BB	SO	SB	CS	GIDP	Avg	OBP	Slg	OPS
2002	312	34	88	21	2	4	39	22	41	4	5	12	.282	.334	.401	.735
2003	329	43	92	19	3	7	54	37	48	4	1	14	.280	.365	.419	.785
2004	823	100	255	48	4	23	86	35	76	7	6	28	.310	.342	.462	.804
2005	730	83	212	33	1	25	73	9	71	7	4	35	.290	.300	.441	.741
2006	759	130	246	44	2	38	114	32	70	10	2	16	.324	.354	.538	.892
2007	797	99	229	41	7	20	87	36	89	8	7	24	.287	.319	.432	.751
2008	643	114	213	42	5	20	105	32	69	8	2	18	.331	.363	.505	.868

Over the last three years Raul Ibanez has driven in Ichiro Suzuki 100 times—30 times in 2006, 28 in 2007, and 42 times last year.

No other major league combination has produced as many ribbies. Ryan Howard driving in Chase Utley is in second place, with 89.

Last year, we mentioned that Felix Hernandez had thrown his slider more often in 2007. In 2008, he changed his pattern again, throwing fastballs more often than anytime in his major league career, and de-emphasizing the slider and curveball.

Year	Fastball	Slider	Curve	Change
2005	55%	3%	20%	13%
2006	55%	7%	20%	15%
2007	55%	20%	12%	10%
2008	64%	12%	8%	13%

What happened to Yuniesky Betancourt's glove? His fielding plus/minus figures have dropped each of the past two years, and he was last among all major league shortstops last year. He has particularly lost range on groundballs up the middle.

Yuniesky Betancourt
Fielding Bible Plus/Minus

			SECOND BASE													
			GROUND DP				PLAYS				PLUS/MINUS					
							Expected Outs		Outs Made								
Year	Team	Inn	GIDP Opps	GIDP	Pct	Rank	GB	Air	GB	Air	To His Right	Straight On	To His Left	GB	Air	Total	Rank
2006	Sea	1374.1	141	88	.624	9	377	128	377	125	+4	0	-4	0	-3	-3	22
2007	Sea	1302.1	174	104	.598	22	376	97	366	97	-11	+6	-5	-10	0	-10	27
2008	Sea	1325.1	150	93	.620	7	356	109	335	111	+7	-7	-21	-21	+2	-19	35

When Kenji Johjima hit the ball, he generated the usual number of groundballs, line drives and flyballs. The problem was what happened after he hit them. If he had accrued enough plate appearances to qualify, Johjima would have had the fifth-worst batting average on groundballs, fifth-worst batting average on line drives, and sixth-worst batting average on flyballs.

Kenji Johjima – 2008
Hitting Analysis

Batting Right-Handed									1B		2B		3B		HR
Ground Balls to Left	100	Outs	84	Hits	16	Average	.160	Hit Type	13	-	3	-	0	-	0
Ground Balls to Center	35	Outs	29	Hits	6	Average	.171	Hit Type	6	-	0	-	0	-	0
Ground Balls to Right	22	Outs	17	Hits	5	Average	.227	Hit Type	5	-	0	-	0	-	0
Line Drives to Left	42	Outs	15	Hits	27	Average	.643	Hit Type	16	-	10	-	0	-	1
Line Drives to Center	14	Outs	6	Hits	8	Average	.571	Hit Type	7	-	1	-	0	-	0
Line Drives to Right	17	Outs	8	Hits	9	Average	.529	Hit Type	7	-	2	-	0	-	0
Fly Balls to Left	49	Outs	39	Hits	10	Average	.208	Hit Type	2	-	2	-	0	-	6
Fly Balls to Center	30	Outs	26	Hits	4	Average	.138	Hit Type	3	-	1	-	0	-	0
Fly Balls to Right	37	Outs	36	Hits	1	Average	.027	Hit Type	1	-	0	-	0	-	0
Total on Ground Balls	157	Outs	130	Hits	27	Average	.172	Hit Type	24	-	3	-	0	-	0
Total on Line Drives	73	Outs	29	Hits	44	Average	.603	Hit Type	30	-	13	-	0	-	1
Total on Fly Balls	116	Outs	101	Hits	15	Average	.132	Hit Type	6	-	3	-	0	-	6
Total Hit to Left	191	Outs	138	Hits	53	Average	.279	Hit Type	31	-	15	-	0	-	7
Total Hit to Center	79	Outs	61	Hits	18	Average	.231	Hit Type	16	-	2	-	0	-	0
Total Hit to Right	76	Outs	61	Hits	15	Average	.197	Hit Type	13	-	2	-	0	-	0
Bunts	3	Outs	3	Hits	0	Average	.000	Hit Type	0	-	0	-	0	-	0
All Balls in Play	349	Outs	263	Hits	86	Average	.249	Hit Type	60	-	19	-	0	-	7

Although he's often overlooked, Adrian Beltre is one of the best third basemen in baseball. He is at the top of the list in fielding and below average in only one category, plate discipline. He has also been very durable, and his skill set is actually very similar to one of baseball's saints: Brooks Robinson.

Adrian Beltre – 2008
Skills Assessment

Fielding:		100th percentile among third basemen
Hitting for Power:	85th percentile	83rd percentile among third basemen
Running:	65th percentile	74th percentile among third basemen
Hitting for Average:	54th percentile	55th percentile among third basemen
Plate Discipline:	23rd percentile	31st percentile among third basemen

Adrian Beltre – 2008
Leaderboard, Third Base

Adrian Beltre finally won the third base fielding plus/minus title in 2008 after finishing second twice and third once in the past five seasons. In 2003, Beltre was +30, finishing second behind Hank Blalock's +34. In 2004 Beltre was again +30 but finished second again behind Scott Rolen's +37.

Player	+/-
Adrian Beltre	+32
Jack Hannahan	+21
Marco Scutaro	+17
Scott Rolen	+13
Joe Crede	+13
Chone Figgins	+11
Blake DeWitt	+11
Evan Longoria	+11
Chipper Jones	+10
Ryan Zimmerman	+10

Whoppers

by Bill James

This article is in response to a column by Roel Torres in Bill James Online about the firing during spring training in 1999 of Toronto manager Tim Johnson for lying about his military service in Vietnam and other things.

Let's start with Roel's piece. He wrote:

I'm guessing most people think I shouldn't feel bad for him. But I do. Tim Johnson was a baseball lifer. He played minor league ball. He played major league ball. He scouted. He was a minor league manager. He was a major league bench coach. Then, when he finally realized a dream and became a surprisingly successful major league manager, he was fired after a single season. Because he lied. Well, okay, lots of managers lie. Baseball people lie all the time. The difference was, Tim Johnson lied about things that you are not allowed to lie about. And in the blink of an eye, he was exiled to the Mexican Baseball League, a pariah in the sport he loved so very much….

It is common behavior, particularly among adolescent boys, to tell Whoppers.

Who gets forgiven? Who gets to redeem themselves? Who gets the chance to walk away from the wreckage of their mistakes? Former Dodgers closer Steve Howe was suspended from baseball for drug abuse. Seven times! After his sixth suspension, they didn't kick him out the door and ship him out to the Mexican League. No. After his sixth suspension, they gave him a contract, a glove, and welcomed him back to the majors with open arms. He had a problem. A disease. He was struggling with his inner demons. People understood.

Tim Johnson? Different story. Tim Johnson wasn't lucky enough to get a seventh chance.

When I was a kid, I would make stuff up. Constantly. I remember the time in third grade that my mom came home from her first parent-teacher conference since moving to the States. The kids in my class had been asking me if I was related to the Red Sox pitcher, Mike Torrez. I didn't really know who he was. I was new to the country and we didn't follow baseball in the Philippines. I told them, "Yes." It was crazy. Our names weren't even spelled the same way. Torrez, Torres. I said "Yes", then forgot about it. I had no idea my teacher, Mrs. Hardy, had even heard about it. But of course she had. And she asked my mom about it. Which of course caught my mom flustered and unprepared. She was prepared for a conversation about how her son was adjusting to the American elementary school system. She did not expect to be answering questions about imaginary relatives pitching in the majors. When my mom got home, she confronted me about it. She wasn't mad at me. Not really. I'm sure she was embarrassed, probably a little surprised. But I was nine years old. What did she expect? That's what nine year-olds do. They make stuff up. Right?

My mom asked me not to spread lies to my classmates. More specifically, she asked me to stop telling people we were related to Mike Torrez. Okay. No problem. He was a relatively mediocre starting pitcher anyway.

Looking back, it would be easy to justify my tendency to stretch the truth as a sign of creativity, the mark of a vivid imagination. And I think there's something to that. But deep down, I know the real reason I used to lie so often.

I wanted to be liked. I wanted to impress people. I wanted people to think I was cool. I was an overweight nine year-old son of an illegal alien, I didn't speak English as my first language, and I had immigrated to the United States nine months earlier. That was reality. But lying could change that. Lying could alter the facts. Lying could make me better than I was.

(How much damage do you think has been done by insecure young men trying to impress someone? How much havoc has been caused by misfits and outsiders trying to find a way to make people think they were cool? And conversely, how much peace of mind do you achieve that moment when you realize that it doesn't matter whether people are impressed or not? That it doesn't matter if anyone thinks you're cool? Wouldn't it be great if we could quantify all of that somehow? Measurements like, "Throughout history, insecure young men have wasted so much energy trying to impress people that, if harnessed, it could power a million suns....")

Major league managers lie all the time. I think we all know this and accept it. If your centerfielder shows up hung-over and smelling like sex because he spent the night club-hopping and getting hammered while chasing skirts, you're allowed to tell the press you're giving him a day off because it's a long season and you're trying to preserve his health. And if your shortstop and your starting pitcher hate each other with a burning animosity, you're allowed to lie through your teeth and tell the media that everyone gets along in the clubhouse. Sure.

Whenever the government embarks on a large-scale public works project, they calculate the number of deaths that will come as a direct result of building the final product. They're inevitable. They're called "acceptable losses" and everyone recognizes that they come with the territory. By the same measure, we have "acceptable lies." White lies. Harmless ones. We're all adults here. We get it. We know the rules of the game. It's only when someone oversteps the unspoken, invisible boundary lines that we end up staring at the ground uncomfortably, shuffling our feet, trying to figure out how to extricate ourselves from the suddenly awkward situation.

We expect major league managers to motivate their team. I don't know why, exactly. You would think that athletes playing at the highest level of the game for the highest compensation and the greatest stakes would do just fine motivating themselves. The players motivated themselves in Little League, in high school, in college, in the Cape League, in the minors, in the Arizona Fall League, in the Dominican Winter League, and finally the majors. And these players need someone to fire them up? Can't we assume their natural competitive tendencies will serve them just fine? And even if they aren't all fired up, does it really matter?

Isn't a supremely talented slugger who's just going about his business going to dominate due to his superior natural talent when compared to an undersized utility infielder who's always scrappy and fiery and hustles down to first on a routine ground ball? It sure seems like it to me. It sure seems like talent wins. I don't put a lot of stock in motivational speeches, inner fire, and scrappiness. Your mileage may vary.

Still, there are societal expectations on a Major League manager. It's not enough for him to maximize his bullpen resources, or to exploit the opposition's extreme platoon splits. He's supposed to motivate the troops. I mean, have you ever seen a mainstream sports movie where the head coach doesn't give a big game speech to fire up the team? Hell, in some movies, such as Any Given Sunday, the en-

tire point of the movie seems to be about the big speech. Motivating the guys. It's what leaders do. That's Hollywood for you.

Tim Johnson tried to motivate his team. As manager of the 1998 Toronto Blue Jays, he had a tall task ahead of him. He played in the same division as historic super powers Boston and New York. The team had only won 72 games the previous year, good for fifth place in the division. It was his first season ever as a Major League manager. He needed to find a way to turn things around. He needed to find a way to help his guys believe. He needed an edge.

So he lied. Some lies; none too egregious. He told his players he was a star basketball player who turned down a scholarship to UCLA. That seemed reasonable. After all, Tim Johnson was a good enough athlete to be the starting shortstop for the Milwaukee Brewers in 1973. It wasn't too big a stretch for him to claim he could make the cut for a Division I college basketball program. No worries. No harm done.

Tim Johnson also claimed that he killed people in the Vietnam War. Which he did not. He never served in combat in Vietnam. But he told his players that he did. And when the truth came out as he was about to begin his second season at the helm for Toronto, he was fired in the middle of spring training.

I've told many lies in my life. Lies to people I barely knew. Lies to the people closest to me. Lies about how much money I've made. Lies about the girls I've slept with. Lies about how happy I am with my life. I even lie to myself sometimes, and if I do it well enough, I can almost re-shape my past, rearrange my memories into a manner more convenient for me. The power of self-delusion. It's almost infinite.

I'm not here to tell you that lying is fine. And I'm not here to tell you that I had excellent reasons to justify my own lies. No. No, I'm not. But I am here to tell you that no matter how wild and implausible and prolific my lies were, no matter how habitual or damaging—I was always given a chance to make up for them. Always given a chance to make the truth more substantial than the lies. Always given a chance to make good. And for every exaggeration I told to make me look like a caring and compassionate person, I had countless opportunities to step up to the plate and actually prove it. And I'm appreciative for that.

In the end, I feel like we should judge people not by their words, but by their deeds. Don't pay attention to what a man says, but what he does. Does he claim to be a good man, or does he actually do good things? The difference is everything.

Tim Johnson took over a fifth-place club in the American League East and helped them improve by sixteen wins in a season. He has a .543 lifetime winning percentage as a manager in the majors. That's better than Terry Francona, Jim Leyland, or Tony LaRussa. His players competed hard and his team won games. Tim Johnson proved he could *manage in the big leagues and succeed.*

But he lied. He lied about killing people. In Vietnam. And in a league that accepts drunken drivers, 'Roid users, and cocaine addicts back into the fold, he crossed that unspoken, invisible boundary line which makes us stare at the ground uncomfortably, shuffling our feet, trying to figure out how to extricate ourselves from the suddenly awkward situation. It makes us feel dirty. So someone has to pay. For how long? That remains to be seen.

As for me, I've already forgiven Tim Johnson. I have. I figure it's the least I could do, considering the way the world has forgiven me.

It is common behavior, particularly among adolescent boys, to tell Whoppers. A Whopper can be distinguished from a venal lie in this way: that whereas the purpose of a venal lie is to deny guilt or failings, the purpose of a Whopper is to inflate one's image with imaginary attributes.

Most people discover through life experience that the telling of Whoppers erodes their respect from others, and they gradually learn to live with the dreary realities of their personal history. Some people miss the memo. Those people who do not learn this lesson are generally excluded from the better jobs, which rely more on trust and decorum.

So anyway, Roel Torres argues for forgiveness for Tim Johnson, based on his own failings, and I find this a very moving argument. I believe, in general, that one of the greatest problems of the modern world is our inability to forgive one another and move on. Our politics are composed of two parties, both of which believe that it is entirely appropriate for them to exaggerate the failings of those on the other side. The fact that they all agree about this does not make them right—nor, for that matter, is it even necessarily an effective position from a selfish standpoint. I believe in forgiveness. Who speaks for me? Who represents me on this?

Both sides of the political debate make frenzied efforts to attract my support—by exaggerating the failings of the other side. The problem is, I don't believe in exaggerating the failings of one's opponents, and I don't support anybody who does.

And I'm not really unusual. Studies show that more and more people refuse to identify themselves as either Republicans or Democrats. Why? I would argue that one of the reasons that many of us will not identify ourselves as either Republican or Democrat is the sense that both Republicans and Democrats are selfish and immature, and that neither really speaks for values.

Set aside politics; try journalism. People say stupid stuff every day, but twice a month, somebody says The Wrong Thing, and a scandal results. In sports we have had the Jimmie the Greek Scandal, and the Al Campanis Scandal, and the Marge Schott Scandal, and the Bill Singer Scandal, and…I don't know. I don't keep a calendar. In the broader world we have them all the time…Trent Lott, and Don Imus, and the guy who played Kramer.

And, because we have these Scandals, we have tempests, which we are watching to see if they will develop into Scandals, rather as one watches a wart to see whether it will develop into cancer. For every Scandal, there are 25 tempests, building toward a Scandal.

Journalists, in some sense, are pretending to speak for values by pointing out the moral failings of senators and other sinners. But my question is, who speaks for forgiveness?

Roel has hit the nail on the head in this way: that the refusal of forgiveness is a type of self-righteousness. We don't want to say "OK, I forgive you for lying, because I lie, too." We don't want to say, "I forgive you for having mean and petty and unworthy notions about other groups of people, because I have mean and petty and unworthy notions about other groups of people, too." We want to say, "Oh, I'm better than that. I don't have any little Nazis in *my* subconscious mind."

Oh, you don't?

Somehow I don't believe you.

It takes real courage to do what Roel did, to raise your hand and say, "I'm a liar, too." But the fact is, none of us is that different from the others. We all want other people to think we're a little bit bigger and a little bit grander than we really are. We want others to think that inside of us is a bottomless lake of pure compassion, without pettiness or selfishness or any inappropriate kind of lust.

I am not suggesting that it is wrong of journalists to find out that someone has lied, or to point this out. What I am questioning is what happens after that—this ritual of turning, teeth bared, on the person whose depravity has been exposed, and snarling at him and driving him out of the circle. He is unworthy of us.

What I am really trying to get to is this: that it is very difficult to *organize* people around the principle of compassion, because compassion requires the acknowledgement of our own guilt. It was, for centuries, the role of the church to organize the communal acknowledgement of our guilt, but as the church is being driven out of public life, how do we replace that?

The journalists are organized, in a sense, in their ruthless exposure of people who betray a racist wart, but how do we organize forgiveness? The political parties are or-

We all want other people to think we're a little bit bigger and a little bit grander than we really are.

ganized in their relentless exaggeration of the failings of their opponents, but how do we organize on behalf of tolerance?

We have to do what Roel did. We have to admit that we're *not* any better. I'm *not* any better than Bill Singer, and I'm *not* any better than Al Campanis, and I'm not any better than Marge Schott.

That, it seems to me, is what is missing from the Barry Bonds debate: forgiveness. I'm not any better than Barry Bonds, and I'm not any better than Mark McGwire, and I'm not any better than Roger Clemens, and I'm not any better than Pete Rose, either. You give me the opportunity to earn $22 million a year by taking steroids, I'll shoot the pharmacist if I have to. I'm not saying it's right. I'm not saying I shouldn't be punished for shooting the pharmacist. I am saying it is self-righteous to pretend that I don't have the same human failings that these guys do, and further, if you are insisting that *you* don't have them, *I don't believe you*. When you fire Al Campanis to show us that his failings are not your failings, I don't believe you. When you fire the next Al Campanis to show us that you are morally superior to him, I don't buy it. I don't believe you are morally superior to him; you're just a self-righteous asshole who is refusing to forgive his human failings.

Look, am I saying that Tim Johnson should not have been fired for telling some Whoppers to his players? Not exactly. Tim Johnson was not asking to be a *member* or the group; he was asking to be the *leader* of the group. It's a little different. He did the things that adolescent boys do, well after his adolescence was over with.

Is it a sham to say, "I forgive him, but he has to be fired anyway?" I don't know. I don't have the answer to that one. If you cheat on your wife it is not self-righteous for her to divorce you. If you cheat in the game, it is not self-righteous for the umpire to call you out, or to throw you out. Where trust is necessary, it is necessary to speak for values.

But when it comes to Roger Clemens, for example, is it necessary for us to punish his failings? Or are we doing it to demonstrate to one another that we are better than he is, that we wouldn't have taken a dollar that we couldn't earn with the talent God gave us, and that we'd have kicked Mindy McCready out of bed before she could get her shoes off?

Yeah, right, buddy. Sure you would have. It's just a shame that God didn't give more talent to good people like you, but that was Her decision, and we'll just have to live with it.

Roel Torres argues for forgiveness for Tim Johnson, based on his own failings, and I find this a very moving argument.

Tampa Bay Rays

Tampa Bay Rays – 2008
Team Overview

Description		Ranking
Won-Lost Record	97-65	
Place		1st of 5 in American League East
Runs Scored	774	12th in the majors
Runs Allowed	671	3rd in the majors
Home Runs	180	9th in the majors
Home Runs Allowed	166	13th in the majors
Batting Average	.260	21st in the majors
Batting Average Allowed	.246	3rd in the majors
Walks Drawn	626	3rd in the majors
Walks Given	526	12th in the majors
OPS For	.762	10th in the majors
OPS Against	.715	5th in the majors
Stolen Bases	142	1st in the majors
Stolen Bases Allowed	76	8th in the majors

Key Players

Pos	Player	G	AB	R	H	2B	3B	HR	RBI	SB	CS	BB	SO	Avg	OBP	Slg	OPS	WS
C	Dioner Navarro	120	427	43	126	27	0	7	54	0	4	34	49	.295	.349	.407	.757	17
1B	Carlos Pena	139	490	76	121	24	2	31	102	1	1	96	166	.247	.377	.494	.871	22
2B	Akinori Iwamura	152	627	91	172	30	9	6	48	8	6	70	131	.274	.349	.380	.729	21
3B	Evan Longoria	122	448	67	122	31	2	27	85	7	0	46	122	.272	.343	.531	.874	19
SS	Jason Bartlett	128	454	48	130	25	3	1	37	20	6	22	69	.286	.329	.361	.690	14
LF	Carl Crawford	109	443	69	121	12	10	8	57	25	7	30	60	.273	.319	.400	.718	11
CF	B.J. Upton	145	531	85	145	37	2	9	67	44	16	97	134	.273	.383	.401	.784	23
RF	Gabe Gross	127	302	40	73	13	3	13	38	2	2	40	75	.242	.333	.434	.767	9
DH	Cliff Floyd	80	246	32	66	13	0	11	39	1	0	28	58	.268	.349	.455	.804	6

Key Pitchers

Pos	Player	G	GS	W	L	Sv	IP	H	R	ER	SO	BB	BR/9	ERA	WS
SP	James Shields	33	33	14	8	0	215.0	208	94	85	160	40	10.88	3.56	15
SP	Andy Sonnanstine	32	32	13	9	0	193.1	212	105	94	124	37	11.82	4.38	10
SP	Edwin Jackson	32	31	14	11	0	183.1	199	91	90	108	77	13.65	4.42	10
SP	Matt Garza	30	30	11	9	0	184.2	170	83	76	128	59	11.45	3.70	12
SP	Scott Kazmir	27	27	12	8	0	152.1	123	61	59	166	70	11.64	3.49	12
CL	Troy Percival	50	0	2	1	28	45.2	29	26	23	38	27	11.23	4.53	6
RP	Trever Miller	68	0	2	0	2	43.1	39	21	20	44	20	13.08	4.15	3
RP	Dan Wheeler	70	0	5	6	13	66.1	44	25	23	53	22	8.95	3.12	12

Among the four American League playoff teams in 2008, none had a particularly good leadoff man. The Rays were 8th in the league in OPS by their leadoff men, the White Sox 9th, the Angels 10th, and the Red Sox 13th.

Tampa Bay in 2008 scored only 71 first-inning runs, one of the lowest totals in the majors. They were outscored in the first inning 83-71, and were behind more often than they were ahead after one inning. They were still behind more often than they were ahead after five innings; after five innings they were ahead 68 times, behind 73.

Akinori Iwamura, although he had a fine year, did very poorly when leading off the game, hitting .243 with few walks when leading off the first inning.

The Rays had a great year because they dominated the late innings—both offensively and defensively. While many teams score more runs in the first inning than any other, Tampa Bay scored 85, 89 and 96 runs in the 6th, 7th and 8th innings.

Tampa Bay Rays – 2008
Innings Ahead Behind Tied

Inning	1	2	3	4	5	6	7	8	9	Extra	Final
Ahead	34	52	69	68	68	74	80	86	87	10	97
Behind	37	55	63	69	73	66	66	59	59	6	65
Tied	91	55	30	25	21	22	16	17	16	22	—

Matt Garza may well have been the Rays best pitcher in 2008—but the Rays, who went 22-11 with Shields on the mound, 20-12 with Sonnanstine and 19-8 with Kazmir, had a losing record with Garza. When Garza was good, he was very, very good, posting a 0.64 ERA in games that he won—the best in the majors.

Tampa Bay Rays – 2008
Performance by Starting Pitcher

Games Started By	GS	RS	RA	Won	Lost
Shields, James	33	163	135	22	11
Sonnanstine, Andy	32	149	147	20	12
Jackson, Edwin	31	156	125	17	14
Garza, Matt	30	128	121	14	16
Kazmir, Scott	27	140	103	19	8
Hammel, Jason	5	19	22	2	3
Niemann, Jeff	2	8	11	1	1
Talbot, Mitch	1	7	5	1	0
Price, David	1	4	2	1	0
Team Totals	162	774	671	97	65

RWI

Last year Carlos Pena had *nine* bases-loaded walks. If that sounds impossibly, insanely high, that's because it is. It's a full 50% more than anyone has had in a single season any time in the last 20 years, except for one year when D'Angelo Jimenez had seven.

Carlos Pena – 2008
RBI Analysis

Hits		RBI Hits		RBI Total		Drove In	
Home Runs:	31			RBI on Home Runs:	52	Willy Aybar	1
Triples:	2	RBI Triples:	1	RBI on Triples:	1	Rocco Baldelli	1
Doubles:	24	RBI Doubles:	9	RBI on Doubles:	12	Jason Bartlett	2
Singles:	64	RBI Singles:	15	RBI on Singles:	17	Carl Crawford	16
		Other RBI: Walks	9	Sacrifice Flies:	9	Gabe Gross	1
		Other RBI: Ground Outs	2			Nathan Haynes	1
				Total Other:	11	Michel Hernandez	1
						Eric Hinske	4
				Total RBI:	102	Akinori Iwamura	18
						Evan Longoria	1
						Fernando Perez	3
						Shawn Riggans	3
						B.J. Upton	15
						Ben Zobrist	4
						His Own Bad Self	31
						Total	102

Tough League

Over the past two years, Edwin Jackson is the only starter in baseball who's made more than two-thirds of his starts against teams that finished the year at .500 or better. In both 2007 and 2008, 22 of his 31 starts came against non-losing teams. Those included 13 starts against playoff-bound teams in 2007, and 8 in 2008.

Edwin Jackson – 2007-2008
Career Records Against Quality of Opposition

Opponent	G	IP	W	L	SO	BB	ERA
.600 teams	3	15.0	2	1	10	11	3.00
.500 - .599 teams	68	299.0	13	20	215	143	4.85
.400 - .499 teams	32	124.0	8	9	74	68	6.60
sub .400 teams	3	18.0	2	0	12	7	2.00

82% of the pitches B.J. Upton swung at last year were in the strike zone. Only Marco Scutaro had a higher percentage (83%).

Scott Kazmir threw one-half as many sliders last year as he did in 2007 and one-third as many as he threw in 2006.

Year	Fastball	Slider
2005	63%	21%
2006	55%	28%
2007	69%	19%
2008	75%	9%

B.J. Upton – 2008
Pitch Analysis

Overall		
Pitches Seen	2575	
Taken	1527	59%
Swung At	1048	41%
Pitches Taken		
Taken for a Strike	443	29%
Called a Ball	1084	71%
Pitches Taken by Pitch Location		
In Strike Zone	443	29%
High	168	11%
Low	371	24%
Inside	251	16%
Outside	294	19%
Swung At		
Missed	201	19%
Fouled Off	440	42%
Put in Play	407	39%
Swung At by Pitch Location		
In Strike Zone	856	82%
High	25	2%
Low	57	5%
Inside	55	5%
Outside	55	5%

Over half of the flyballs Evan Longoria pulled to left field were home runs last year—22 of 43. No other qualified major league batter can say the same thing.

Evan Longoria – 2008
Hitting Analysis

Batting Right-Handed									1B		2B		3B		HR
Fly Balls to Left	43	Outs	19	Hits	24	Average	.600	Hit Type	0	-	2	-	0	-	22
Fly Balls to Center	52	Outs	40	Hits	12	Average	.240	Hit Type	2	-	6	-	1	-	3
Fly Balls to Right	44	Outs	40	Hits	4	Average	.095	Hit Type	0	-	2	-	1	-	1
All Balls in Play	334	Outs	212	Hits	122	Average	.374	Hit Type	62	-	31	-	2	-	27

Grant Balfour in 2008 cut the batting average of opposing hitters to less than half of what it was in 2007. Batters hit .316 against him in 2007, .143 in 2008, with on-base and slugging percentages around .230.

Grant Balfour – 2003-2004, 2007-2008
Record of Opposing Batters

Season	AB	R	H	2B	3B	HR	RBI	BB	SO	SB	CS	GIDP	Avg	OBP	Slg	OPS
2003	98	12	23	5	0	4	14	14	30	2	1	1	.235	.327	.408	.736
2004	147	19	35	1	1	4	19	21	42	2	2	2	.238	.341	.340	.681
2007	95	21	30	4	3	2	21	20	30	3	1	2	.316	.429	.484	.913
2008	196	10	28	8	0	3	16	24	82	2	1	0	.143	.233	.230	.463

Texas Rangers

Texas Rangers – 2008
Team Overview

Description		Ranking
Won-Lost Record	79-83	
Place	2nd of 4 in American League West	
Runs Scored	901	1st in the majors
Runs Allowed	967	29th in the majors
Home Runs	194	6th in the majors
Home Runs Allowed	176	17th in the majors
Batting Average	.283	1st in the majors
Batting Average Allowed	.288	29th in the majors
Walks Drawn	595	6th in the majors
Walks Given	625	23rd in the majors
OPS For	.816	1st in the majors
OPS Against	.817	29th in the majors
Stolen Bases	81	16th in the majors
Stolen Bases Allowed	114	21st in the majors

Key Players

Pos	Player	G	AB	R	H	2B	3B	HR	RBI	SB	CS	BB	SO	Avg	OBP	Slg	OPS	WS
C	Gerald Laird	95	344	54	95	24	0	6	41	2	4	23	63	.276	.329	.398	.727	9
1B	Chris Davis	80	295	51	84	23	2	17	55	1	2	20	88	.285	.331	.549	.880	8
2B	Ian Kinsler	121	518	102	165	41	4	18	71	26	2	45	67	.319	.375	.517	.892	24
3B	Ramon Vazquez	105	300	44	87	18	3	6	40	0	1	38	66	.290	.365	.430	.795	10
SS	Michael Young	155	645	102	183	36	2	12	82	10	0	55	109	.284	.339	.402	.741	20
LF	David Murphy	108	415	64	114	28	3	15	74	7	2	31	70	.275	.321	.465	.786	11
CF	Josh Hamilton	156	624	98	190	35	5	32	130	9	1	64	126	.304	.371	.530	.901	26
RF	Marlon Byrd	122	403	70	120	28	4	10	53	7	2	46	62	.298	.380	.462	.842	12
DH	Milton Bradley	126	414	78	133	32	1	22	77	5	3	80	112	.321	.436	.563	.999	19

Key Pitchers

Pos	Player	G	GS	W	L	Sv	IP	H	R	ER	SO	BB	BR/9	ERA	WS
SP	Vicente Padilla	29	29	14	8	0	171.0	185	100	90	127	65	14.0	4.74	8
SP	Kevin Millwood	29	29	9	10	0	168.2	220	104	95	125	49	14.7	5.07	6
SP	Scott Feldman	28	25	6	8	0	151.1	161	103	89	74	56	13.5	5.29	4
SP	Matt Harrison	15	15	9	3	0	83.2	100	57	51	42	31	14.3	5.49	3
SP	Kason Gabbard	12	12	2	3	0	56.0	64	36	30	33	39	16.7	4.82	2
CL	C.J. Wilson	50	0	2	2	24	46.1	49	35	31	41	27	15.2	6.02	2
RP	Jamey Wright	75	0	8	7	0	84.1	93	57	48	60	35	14.5	5.12	3
RP	Frank Francisco	58	0	3	5	5	63.1	47	24	22	83	26	10.4	3.13	6

Closer C.J. Wilson notched 24 saves for the Rangers in 2008 in 28 opportunities, a respectable save percentage. However, his 6.02 ERA was the highest of any relief pitcher in baseball with seven or more saves. Plus it was the second-highest ERA among all relief pitchers with 50-plus appearances (Jamie Walker, Baltimore, 6.87 in 59 games). Wilson appeared in 50 games.

MVP Whoever

What team/position hit the most home runs in 2008?

Philadelphia first basemen. Ryan Howard led the majors with 48 homers; Philadelphia first basemen hit 48 homers. The three positions for which a team had 40 homers were Philadelphia first basemen (Ryan Howard), White Sox left fielders (Carlos Quentin) and Florida first basemen (Mike Jacobs).

Who drove in the most runs?

Philadelphia first basemen again. Ryan Howard drove in 146 runs; Philadelphia first basemen drove in 146.

That was just to get you to understand the concept; now we can deal with the fun stuff. What team/position had the most hits? Guess.

No.

No.

No.

It was actually Washington Nationals' shortstops. Cristian Guzman had 183 hits, and whoever else played shortstop for them chipped in another 37 hits, total of 220. That edged out Boston second basemen, 218 (Pedroia) and Atlanta third basemen, 215 (Chipper).

Who hit the fewest home runs?

Every team/position except pitcher had at least one home run. San Francisco and St. Louis shortstops had only one.

Most runs scored was 133, by Florida shortstops (Hanley Ramirez). Most doubles was 56, by Boston second basemen (Pedroia) and also Baltimore second basemen (Brian Roberts). Most walks was Tampa Bay first basemen (Carlos Pena), highest batting average Atlanta third basemen (duh), highest OPS was St. Louis first basemen (duhh!)

OK, here's the one I was trying to get to. What team had the most extra-base hits?

It's actually Texas right fielders; Texas right fielders had 90 extra-base hits in 2008.

The trick is, Texas didn't really have a right fielder in 2008. Nobody played more than 56 games there. David Murphy played 56, Marlon Byrd 39, Josh Hamilton 34, Nelson Cruz 31, Milton Bradley 19, and then three other guys played a few innings.

But whoever they put out there, it worked. Murphy, Hamilton and Milton Bradley all hit much better when playing right field than when playing their other positions, Marlon Byrd didn't hit any worse, and Nelson Cruz, of course, was dynamite in his 31 games. Texas regular right fielder Wesley Whoever had 202 hits including 52 doubles, 34 homers, a .317 average, and drove in 134 runs.

Gerald Laird has done a disproportionate amount of damage against below-average pitchers for his entire career.

Gerald Laird – 2008
Batting Performance by Quality of Opposing Pitcher

	AB	H	HR	RBI	Avg
Pitcher with ERA <= 4.25	584	116	5	37	.199
Pitcher with ERA over 4.25	641	196	20	97	.306

Gerald Laird "bunted" .545 last year (six hits in 11 at-bats). He's bunted 49 times over the last three years, going 23-for-39 (.590) with 10 sacrifices.

Gerald Laird – 2008
Hitting Analysis

Batting Right-Handed									1B	-	2B	-	3B	-	HR
Bunts	15	Outs	9	Hits	6	Average .545	Hit Type		6	-	0	-	0	-	0
All Balls in Play	289	Outs	194	Hits	95	Average .338	Hit Type		65	-	24	-	0	-	6

Offense without End, Amen, Amen

The Texas Rangers' 7th, 8th and 9th place hitters all led the major leagues in runs scored—94 by the 7th place hitters, 94 by the 8th place, 83 by the 9th place. The 8 and 9 hitters also led the majors in RBI by those positions.

Texas Rangers – 2008
Runs and RBI by Batting Order

Pos	Players	Runs	RBI
1	Kinsler (120 G), Arias (20 G)	125	87
2	Young (118 G), Catalanotto (22 G)	110	87
3	Hamilton (124 G), Young (36 G)	105	130
4	Bradley (114 G), Hamilton (31 G)	112	104
5	Murphy (64 G), Byrd (51 G), Blalock (33 G)	92	93
6	Byrd (41 G), Boggs (34 G), Blalock (23 G)	86	103
7	Davis (29 G), Laird (26 G), Cruz (23 G)	94	80
8	Laird (41 G), Davis (37 G), Saltalamacchia (32 G)	94	105
9	Vazquez (56 G), Duran (28 G)	83	78
	Total	901	867

In his recently-released autobiography *Beyond Belief*, Josh Hamilton wrote that during his rookie year of 2007, his baserunning wasn't up to his standards. He also wrote that he worked out during the 2007-08 offseason in order to become stronger and faster. In 2008 he improved his baserunning across the board, and was, by our estimate, one of the 12 best baserunners in baseball.

Josh Hamilton – 2007-2008
Baserunning Analysis

Year	1st to 3rd Adv	Opp	2nd to Home Adv	Opp	1st to Home Adv	Opp	DP Opp	GIDP	Bases Taken	BR Outs	BR Gain	SB Gain	Net Gain
2007	6	13	3	8	1	3	55	6	8	2	+1	-3	-2
2008	13	32	11	18	7	11	147	8	13	0	+25	+7	+32
Totals	19	45	14	26	8	14	202	14	21	2	+25	+4	+29
		42%		54%		57%		6%					

Texas Rangers – 2008
Performance by Starting Pitcher

Games Started By	GS	RS	RA	Won	Lost
Millwood, Kevin	29	132	154	14	15
Padilla, Vicente	29	178	156	19	10
Feldman, Scott	25	121	140	8	17
Harrison, Matt	15	120	100	10	5
Gabbard, Kason	12	79	58	8	4
Mendoza, Luis	11	56	104	3	8
Ponson, Sidney	9	70	61	5	4
Jennings, Jason	6	16	41	0	6
Nippert, Dustin	6	22	32	3	3
McCarthy, Brandon	5	31	34	2	3
Hurley, Eric	5	20	22	1	4
Mathis, Doug	4	21	28	2	2
Hunter, Tommy	3	12	23	1	2
Murray, A.J.	2	18	10	2	0
Madrigal, Warner	1	5	4	1	0
Team Totals	162	901	967	79	83

Matt Harrison posted a 9-3 record in 2008 despite a 5.49 ERA (with a team record of 10-5 in his 15 starts). The Rangers scored 8.0 runs per game with Harrison as the starting pitcher, and scored ten or more runs in five of his fifteen starts. By comparison, the Houston Astros scored ten or more runs only six times all season.

Strong Cup of Coffee

In his 47 at-bats with the big club, rookie Taylor Teagarden hit 14 flyballs. Seven of them went for extra bases, including six that left the park.

Taylor Teagarden – 2008
Hitting Analysis

Batting Right-Handed									1B	-	2B	-	3B	-	HR
Fly Balls to Left	5	Outs	2	Hits	3	Average	.600	Hit Type	0	-	0	-	0	-	3
Fly Balls to Center	7	Outs	3	Hits	4	Average	.570	Hit Type	0	-	1	-	0	-	3
Fly Balls to Right	2	Outs	2	Hits	0	Average	.000	Hit Type	0	-	0	-	0	-	0
All Balls in Play	28	Outs	13	Hits	15	Average	.540	Hit Type	4	-	5	-	0	-	6

The Texas Rangers had the largest baserunning gain of any major league team. They were led by Josh Hamilton, who was in the MLB top 10 at +25, and Ian Kinsler at +19. Hank Blalock was the only Ranger who had a really poor performance, at –16.

Texas Rangers – 2008
Special Baserunning Summary

	Baserunning Gain	Stolen Base Gain	Net Gain	At-Bats
Josh Hamilton	+25	+7	+32	624
Ian Kinsler	+19	+22	+41	518
Michael Young	+8	+10	+18	645
Marlon Byrd	+7	+3	+10	403
Nelson Cruz	+5	+1	+6	115
German Duran	+4	-1	+3	143
Ramon Vazquez	+4	-2	+2	300
Ben Broussard	+3	0	+3	82
Jarrod Saltalamacchi	+3	-4	-1	198
Chris Shelton	+3	+1	+4	97
Brandon Boggs	+2	-1	+1	283
Frank Catalanotto	+2	-1	+1	248
Taylor Teagarden	+2	0	+2	47
Jason Ellison	+1	0	+1	13
Joaquin Arias	0	+2	+2	110
Jason Botts	0	0	0	38
Adam Melhuse	0	0	0	20
David Murphy	0	+3	+3	415
Max Ramirez	0	0	0	46
Ryan Roberts	0	0	0	1
Milton Bradley	-2	-1	-3	414
Travis Metcalf	-2	0	-2	56
Gerald Laird	-4	-6	-10	344
Chris Davis	-6	-3	-9	295
Hank Blalock	-16	+1	-15	258

Our baserunning analysis measures a hitter's overall contribution on the bases, his basestealing, avoidance of the double play, and success at taking the extra base while avoiding being thrown out. Here are the definitions for each category:

Baserunning Gain (or Loss if a negative number) is the total of all the types of extra baserunning advances, minus the (triple) penalty for all the baserunning outs, compared with what would be expected based on the MLB averages. (Zero is average.) Plus numbers are above-average and negative numbers are below-average.

Stolen Base Gain. Stolen Base attempts must be successful greater than about two-thirds of the time to have a positive result on the number of runs scored.

For a summary of each runner, look at the far right column (above) called Net Gain. It combines Baserunning Gain and Stolen Base Gain.

The Texas Rangers jumped out to more first inning leads than any other team in the American League.

The percentage of the games they led fell from .546 to .466 between the end of the 6th and 8th innings.

Texas Rangers – 2008
Innings Ahead Behind Tied

Inning	1	2	3	4	5	6	7	8	9	Extra	Final
Ahead	52	63	70	74	72	77	73	69	74	5	79
Behind	41	59	61	66	65	64	72	79	77	6	83
Tied	69	40	31	22	25	21	17	14	11	14	—

Getting Milled

Last year Kevin Millwood lowered his ERA from 2007 just a bit (from 5.16 to 5.07). However, opposing batters have feasted on his offerings with increasing zeal over his three seasons with Texas. Opponents have hit .272, .301 and .312 over the three years with an increasing OPS as well (.735, .812, .823).

Kevin Millwood – 2002-2008
Record of Opposing Batters

Season	AB	R	H	2B	3B	HR	RBI	BB	SO	SB	CS	GIDP	Avg	OBP	Slg	OPS
2002	809	83	186	33	3	16	75	65	178	21	1	20	.230	.292	.337	.630
2003	841	103	210	45	7	19	95	68	169	41	4	19	.250	.307	.388	.695
2004	557	81	155	41	2	14	73	51	125	12	1	8	.278	.345	.434	.780
2005	733	72	182	36	3	20	67	52	146	33	6	19	.248	.300	.387	.688
2006	839	114	228	42	6	23	101	53	157	10	3	21	.272	.317	.418	.735
2007	708	111	213	40	3	19	100	67	123	14	5	18	.301	.366	.446	.812
2008	705	104	220	40	6	18	94	49	125	26	4	10	.312	.361	.462	.823

One Is All It Takes

Josh Hamilton led the majors in one-pitch at-bats (118), but he sure put them to good use—he finished second in the majors with 13 first-pitch homers, and also ranked in the top 25 among major league starters in both batting average and slugging percentage on the first pitch.

Josh Hamilton – 2008
Short and Long AB

	AB	H	HR	RBI	Avg	OBP	Slg	OPS
One and done	118	54	13	41	.458	.462	.882	1.345
Short	330	119	28	93	.361	.368	.694	1.062
Long	294	71	4	37	.241	.382	.333	.716
7 Up	49	10	1	4	.204	.391	.300	.691

A What-If Fantasy

by Bill James

I recently received an eight-page letter from an Oakland A's fan disgruntled with the leadership of A's GM Billy Beane. At times he mixed up his arguments a little bit, arguing one moment that Beane was arrogant and the next moment that he was a poor judge of talent. His long list of Billy's mistakes would give one the impression that the A's probably hadn't made the playoffs since Connie Mack died. Having said that, the man's writing was clear, his research exhaustive, his use of the language varied and impressive, his presentation flawless. He gave every impression of being a highly intelligent, organized, successful person who happened to be powerfully disenchanted with Billy Beane's stewardship of his favorite baseball team. There was, unfortunately, nothing whatsoever that he could do with his irritation other than write letters to other people who couldn't do anything about it either.

I'm not here to argue about Billy Beane; if Billy were on trial on a charge of arrogance I wouldn't want to be his lawyer, and if he were on trial for his ability as a GM he would scarcely need one. What struck me about the letter was the ironic impotence of it: Here you have a man, who is probably just as intelligent as Billy Beane or anyway just as intelligent as most General Managers, who cares passionately about his subject, who wants the Oakland A's to succeed, and yet who has no access whatsoever to the levers that control his team. I got to thinking: wouldn't it be interesting if he did have a way to seek power within the organization? What if he could simply declare himself a candidate for the Oakland A's General Managers' position, present to the Oakland fan base the arguments that he has presented to me, and stand for election against Billy Beane?

Philosophically, I believe that almost everything that exists is an accident of history…that we could as reasonably run the bases clockwise as counter-clockwise, that there could as easily be seven bases as four, that the pitcher could as reasonably throw from 150 feet as from 60, that umpires could as easily wear gold as blue, that the roster limit could as easily be eleven as twenty-five and that the Dodgers could just as easily play in New Orleans as in LA. Fundamentally, there is very little about the game that has to be the way it is. This article is an examination of the alternative universe fantasy suggested by the gentleman's letter.

The Union Democratic Association was founded in 1968 by an unhappy Chicago Cub fan living in Indianapolis. John Adrian Folger had made a fortune from a 1946 patent on disposable diapers, and had spent much of the 1960s trying to purchase a major league baseball team—the Cubs, preferably, but that failing any team except the Cardinals. Although he was wealthy enough to buy half a dozen teams he could never seem to meet the right people at the right time. When a team was for sale he was always showing up a day late and a dollar long.

Finally, on May 18, 1968, he made the announcement of his intention to launch a competing league. How exactly the decision was made that each franchise should operate as a mini-democracy is a subject of some dispute. Certainly there are countless histories that asso-

Fundamentally, there is very little about the game that has to be the way it is.

ciate this decision with the 1960s slogan "Power to the People", but Mr. Folger was hardly a leftist radical, and it appears more likely that he was influenced by the mid-sixties dominance of the Green Bay Packers, a football team more or less publicly owned by the citizens of a small Wisconsin city. Folger had used Lamar Hunt's courage in founding the AFL as an inspiration for his project, and also to convince prospective owners that they could succeed.

Each roster in the Association has twenty-two players, twelve of whom are employees of the team, and the other ten of whom are actually employed by the league, although assigned to play for the team.

In any case it was decided that the professionals in each city were to be directly answerable to the fans. The Union Democratic Association consists of twelve teams—Indianapolis, Buffalo, Jacksonville, Charlotte, New Orleans and Memphis in the East, and Sacramento, Salt Lake City, San Jose, Las Vegas, San Antonio and Portland in the West. Each roster in the Association has twenty-two players, twelve of whom are employees of the team, and the other ten of whom are actually employed by the league, although assigned to play for the team. There is also a four-team developmental league centered in western Texas; more on that later.

The league starts play on or about April 1, with a pre-season tournament played out in three-game series. The teams that finished one and two in each division the previous year get first-round byes, and then the number three team in one division plays the number six team in the other division, while the number four team plays the number five. After that they play three more rounds of three-game series, always on the home field of the higher-seeded team. The winner of the tournament wins the Jefferson Cup, which is the league's most prized championship. Very large bonuses are paid to the players and coaches for each series win in the Jefferson Cup games. A gigantic replica of a loving cup, more than sixty feet high, is displayed in the winner's park throughout the season.

After that they take a two-week break to celebrate the Jefferson Cup series and cement the winner's position in history, and then league play starts about May 10. The teams each play a 135-game schedule (75 games in the division, 60 out), and wrap that up about September 25. Each team is required to schedule at least ten double-headers during the season. Games that cannot be played when they are scheduled are never made up, except for the Jefferson Cup games; they simply disappear from the schedule, so that sometimes, before the development of modern drain-through surfaces, teams in the Union would complete their schedule having played less than 120 games.

After each season there are a series of three elections to steer the course for each franchise. On October 15 there is a referendum on the manager. The manager (unless he resigns) runs unopposed, in an up-or-down vote of the fans. If he fails the vote of confidence, the responsibility to hire a new manager falls to the General Manager—the incoming General Manager, not the outgoing General Manager. Almost 90% of managers win the vote of confi-

dence and are retained for the following season, but this is true in large part because those managers whose jobs would be in jeopardy generally resign rather than face defeat at the ballot box.

The General Manager stands for election one week after the national Election Day—the second Tuesday after the first Monday in November. Anyone can stand for election as General Manager—anyone. There is no clearing committee, no age requirement, no experience requirement; anyone can run. Often these elections turn into wild, rambunctious contests involving dozens of participants. Many times people campaign for these positions for years, or even decades. Kevin Neulander, current GM of the San Jose Tremors, starting running for election to that position in 1974, when he was sixteen years old, and stood for election every year until 1983, never earning more than three percent of the vote. He started his own business in 1984, sold the business in 1998 for $182 million, and was elected GM of the Tremors in 2000. He was ousted by Peter Melton in 2003, but won back the position in 2004.

To be elected GM you must win an actual majority of the vote. If no one wins a majority of the vote in the first round there will be a second round vote the next day. The same people will be on the ballot the second day, except that candidates who received less than one percent of the vote are eliminated. This can result in the second-day ballot being the same as the original ballot, although it rarely does; there are almost always people on the ballot who no one really wants to see as the GM. After the Wednesday vote the lowest vote-getter is eliminated from the ballot, and, if necessary, they vote again on Thursday, and on Friday, and on Saturday.

In general, however, the election is almost always decided by the second or third day. It may be, for example, that on the first day of the election a not-very-popular incumbent GM will win 38% of the vote in a field including several former players from the team, none of whom wins more than 20%. But on the second day of the vote almost everyone who wants to throw the bums out will coalesce behind the leading vote-getter among the ex-players, and he may have a majority. Candidates who get less than five or ten percent of the vote in the first round often drop out at that point, and in fact it is not uncommon for the incumbent GM to resign if he gets less than 35% in the first round, since experience has shown that an incumbent GM almost never gains significant ground after the first-round vote. Although there was once an election which took eight days to complete, in Jacksonville in 1993, more than ninety-five percent of elections are over by the third day.

The final election, the vote on the team's players for the next season is staged sometime shortly after New Year's Day, also on a Tuesday. First, the players are asked to file whether they would like to return to the same team the next year. Ordinarily the great majority of players do file to return to the team, since the "Full Team" positions are better paid than the "League Staff" and "Team Staff" positions. All 22 members of the team are eligible to stand for election to the ten Full Team positions. The fans vote "yes" or "no" on each player who files to return, and the ten highest vote-getters win the Full Team positions.

Initially the Full Team positions were paid $13,000 a year, while the League Staff positions and the two Team Staff positions paid $10,000 a year. As salaries have exploded over the years the numbers have gone up to $1.3 million and $1 million, but the same ratio has been retained, so that you don't have superstars in the league making seventy times as much as their teammates, as you do in the National and American leagues. A player can make another $500,000 more if his team wins the Jefferson Cup, but that, again, is the same for all the members of the team.

After the Player's Election, the General Manager can elect to retain two more players for his team, the Team Staff positions, so that each team retains at least twelve players from year to year. As a consequence of this there is much more stability in the association than in the National or American leagues. Many, many players remain with one team for fifteen or twenty years. It does sometimes happen that a popular veteran will be re-elected for several years after his playing skills have diminished, and this is thought to be a weakness of the democratic system. Veteran players who file to return to the team but don't win a position in their mid-thirties often retire at that time, rather than returning in a League Staff position that could see them playing in some other city, far from their home. In this way the league is thought to be better for a family man than the so-called "Organized Baseball" leagues. There are no trades in the league, so an established player will not have his life disrupted in that way.

Anyway, twelve players are designated to return to their team by the end of January, ten by election and two by selection. The league then hires another 200 players, 120 who will eventually make the roster of a team, and the other 80 who will go to the developmental program operated east of El Paso. In the first week of February there is a reverse-order draft of these 200 players, the weakest team from the season before getting the first draft pick. Each team picks 16 or 17 players, and each team then goes to spring training with 28 or 29 players, from whom the 22-man roster is chosen. The Full Team and Team Staff players have the team made, and the others compete for the ten League Staff positions on each roster.

Those who make a roster this year will earn $1,000,000 a year; those who go to the developmental program will earn $100,000 a year, but will still accumulate service time in the pension plan at the same level as those chosen for a roster. For those players, the value of the pension benefits often outweighs their salary. It is not uncommon for players to retire (or be released) after fifteen- or seventeen-year careers, spent almost entirely in the developmental program.

After the rosters are announced on March 25, there will be one opportunity each month for the General Manager to adjust the roster. After the game is played on the last day of each month, April through August, the General Manager may release one League Staff player back to the developmental program, and claim one player from the developmental program. These decisions are hotly debated on the talk shows around the Union cities, and thousands of fans from every team will make the journey to west Texas to personally check out the available players. The General Managers, unless they have great faith in their scouts, basically live in west Texas the last week of each month. And there is an old saying in the league: You don't want to slump in August. If a player is released at the end of July, he may be picked up at the end of August by a team that has abandoned the pennant chase and is re-stocking for the following year. But if a player is released to the developmental program at the end of August he is not on anyone's roster at the end of the season, and thus cannot file for a Full Team position.

In the first year of the Union's play, 1969, total attendance for the league was 2.1 million fans, or about 175,000 fans per team—less than 2,000 per game. There might have been less than a thousand core fans for each team, but those thousand got to be involved in the decisions of the team, and so they tended to stay involved and draw others in around them. Attendance grew to 189,000 per team in 1970, to 483,000 per team by 1980, 1.1 million per team by 1990, 1.9 million per team in 2000, and 2.7 million per team today. In cities like San Jose, which compete pretty directly with the American and National Leagues, attendance at the Union games has exploded whenever Organized Baseball" has gone on strike.

There are 20,000 "season seats" available on each team; league rules limit them to 20,000, and all twelve

There are no trades in the league, so an established player will not have his life disrupted in that way.

teams have long since sold out. The 20,000 are the season-ticket holders, and they are the voting block in the elections. No one can hold more than one seat, and the right to a seat cannot be transferred from one person to another; only from the team to the individual. Those who own seats do, however, have the right to re-sell tickets to individual games, and there are some fans who own seats but never or virtually never go to the games; they just sell off the "game passes", as they call them, and retain the voting rights. You can't leave the seat to someone else in your will when you die—all lawsuits on that issue were decided in the league's favor—so there are always some seats available each year. Seats on the popular teams have sold for as much as $450,000. The sale of new seats reduces the annual fees to the established seat holders.

The money from the "seats"—the season tickets—goes to the teams, and the team is responsible to pay the full salaries of the Full Team players, as well the team General Manager, the scouts, the ticket managers, the manager and coaches, the Team Staff players, the promotion directors, the PA announcer, etc. The team is responsible to procure a stadium to play in. There are no "owners" in the Union anymore; there were original owners, but the system was set up so that the original owners would be gradually "bought out" by the seat holders—bought out at a nice profit. But once each team had sold out the 20,000 seats, the ownership position disappeared.

The money from the sale of "game passes"—that is, tickets beyond the 20,000 "seats"—is split evenly between the home team, the visiting team and the league. All broadcasting revenue beyond expenses goes directly to the league, and the league is responsible for paying the salaries of the League Staff players, the players in the developmental program, the umpires, league officials, and, interestingly enough, hotel rooms. The transportation costs are borne by the teams, but the league maintains hotel rooms or apartments where visiting players stay. The league pays for promotional events, and the league maintains press boxes. The league, not the team, controls access to the press box.

What is perhaps most interesting about the Union Democratic Association is the way that these different operating arrangements have shaped the ethics and behavior of the people who are part of the league. Perhaps most striking is the attitude of the Union players toward hustle and showboating. The things you see sometimes in the other leagues, where players may stand and watch home runs leave the park or take thirty seconds to round the bases after a home run…these things would simply never happen in the Union. The players clearly understand that anything that will get you booed will get you fired. Anything that causes the fans to dislike a player is not tolerated…not only by the fans *but by the other players*. The players are very well paid, but they are not well enough insulated that they can forget who is paying their salary.

There is a certain range of anti-fan attitudes among Organized Baseball players, and I don't mean to make this seem worse than it is, because many sportswriters do in fact exaggerate these failings by the players and do represent them as much worse than they really are. But there are certain levels of insensitivity toward the fans among those players which are notably absent in the Union. There is a thing the Organized Baseball players do sometimes, if you are (let us say) a Dodger fan and you are talking to a Dodger player and you refer to a game that "we" won. The player may say, "You got a mouse in your pocket?" Meaning: Who is this "we"? You don't play for the team.

It's very rude, and it's very common in Organized Baseball. That would never, ever, happen in the Union Democratic Association, because it really *is* "we". The fan is a part of the Union team, a part of the decision-making process. There is a sense that we're in this together. The players rarely hear boos. The players are much, much more co-operative with the media, because they are, in a sense, always running for re-election. But at the same time the media is a little less judgmental, a little less harsh, on Union players because they're *not* dealing with arrogant and hostile players, and also because their fan base has different expectations from the media.

The managers in the Union Democratic Association actually have more power than they do in Organized Baseball. In part this is because the General Manager can't fire the manager; the new manager is hired by the GM, but once hired he serves at the pleasure of the fans. That's not the only reason the manager has more power; there is a more subtle reason. The manager is one of the main information conduits to the public. The manager has his daily five-minute radio show, just as in the AL and the NL, and he has his post-game briefings and all of the other everyday chances to talk to the press.

What is perhaps most interesting about the Union Democratic Association is the way that these different operating arrangements have shaped the ethics and behavior of the people who are part of the league.

In Organized Baseball managers sometimes talk about being a "players' manager", and they will speak about this as if it was something to be proud of. There is no such thing as a players' manager in the Union league. What they mean by a "players' manager" is that he covers up for the players' failings. The manager in the United Democratic Association doesn't do this, and wouldn't be expected to do this. It wouldn't be tolerated by the fans, to whom the manager must answer, and also, the manager, through his press contacts, is shaping the roster of the team for the following season. If he pretends a player is hustling when he isn't, he is helping to keep that player on the roster the following year. There's no percentage in that. If he pretends that a player is a defensive star when he isn't, he may help that player get re-elected to the team, and then he has to live with him another year. Ultimately, it will cost him his job.

The behavior of players across the board in the Union league is just better. If a player gets a reputation for being out on the town at all hours of the night, the reputation may cost him his job before the effects show up on his batting average. The players know this, so behavior that in Organized Baseball is tolerated if not encouraged by the community of players is frowned upon by the players in the Union. Community service by the players is much, much more important—in fact, virtually every player, within weeks of joining a new team, will be active in a handful of community efforts.

The level of effort—hustle—in the Union league is controlled not only by the teams, but also by the league. In Organized Baseball, a young player can behave pretty much however he wants to behave if he has enough talent, because the team, in their constant effort to maximize their talent, cannot afford to sever ties with talented players over anything less than major behavioral issues. Lesser talents, of course, have less rope, but Organized Baseball teams cannot be seen as using one set of rules for the stars, another set for the ordinary players, so the effect is that the team has very little ability to enforce standards of behavior.

But in the Union Democratic Association, if the league doesn't like a particular young player or doesn't approve of his behavior when he is in the developmental process, they can simply release him; they're not under much pressure to keep the very best players in all cases, since the league doesn't care who wins. If a player doesn't hustle in the developmental leagues, he's gone—regardless of how much talent he might have. A player who is elected to Full Team status is safe—he's answerable to the fans, not the league—but only 120 of the league's 464 have that protection. The rest of them, if they don't behave in an appropriate fashion, are simply not offered contracts for the following season.

To an extent, this does reduce the talent level of the players in the Union Democratic Association. There's still a lot of competitive pressure to improve, but it isn't as

What happens when you give people responsibility is what happens to fathers when their children are born: They become more responsible.

constant or unrelenting as the pressure on the front offices of the teams in the AL or NL.

In Organized Baseball you have "revolving door" managers and "revolving door" general managers. This rarely happens in the Union. Because the teams have longer histories with a more limited set of players, they tend to hire new managers from among their former players. General Managers fired by one set of fans in the Union are rarely able to get themselves elected somewhere else.

Because front offices in the Union are constantly open to being taken over by outsiders, they are much, much more open to new ideas than are the American and National League front offices. Sabermetrics was generally embraced by the Union teams by 1990. At the same time, as front offices in the Union are more open they are less professional. Teams are taken over sometimes by "outside agitator" GMs who really have no idea what they are doing once they take over. On the other hand, the GMs in the Union have much less power than in Organized Baseball. GMs in the Union don't negotiate salaries (the salary structure being set by the league in negotiations with the players' union), can't make trades, can't fire the manager, and can't release more than half the roster. They can't sign amateur free agents. Their job is still important, but they do play a more limited role.

There was a fear early on that the fans of Union teams would be irresponsible and would perhaps fire the manager every year, but that hasn't happened. What happens when you give people responsibility is what happens to fathers when their children are born: They become more responsible. The responsible elements in the fan community step forward; the irresponsible ones are generally pushed to the side.

I don't want to make it appear that the Union Democratic Association is a sort of Baseball Utopia, where everyone behaves better and no problems are allowed to develop. The league has politics, lots and lots of politics, and politics is not the most attractive of human activities. The campaigns for the General Managers' positions, which go on virtually the year around, are often annoying and sometimes extremely unpleasant. The quality of play sometimes suffers because the fans protect a popular washed-up veteran, and there is no way to get him off the roster until the next election. Worse yet, the battles for Full Team positions sometimes turn ugly. You may have, for example, a talented young player who is not well liked by the veterans, competing for a Full Team berth with a fading veteran who has been on the team for years. The veterans, at times, will say things to the media about the young player that are not conducive to good relations in the clubhouse, things that they would never say in Organized Baseball. Those players call the Union players the "Phonies Association," because the players do try to curry favor with the fans. Organized Baseball players sort of see themselves as a special class of people, entitled by wealth and talent to make up their own rules, but required to cover for one another within those rules—sort of like the Kennedys. In the Union league the players are more inclined to see themselves as answerable to the fans, and to hell with the other players.

On balance, the Union Democratic Association has been a very interesting experiment.

I don't want to make it appear that the Union Democratic Association is a sort of Baseball Utopia, where everyone behaves better and no problems are allowed to develop.

Toronto Blue Jays

Toronto Blue Jays – 2008
Team Overview

Description		Ranking
Won-Lost Record	86-76	
Place		4th of 5 in American League East
Runs Scored	714	20th in the majors
Runs Allowed	610	1st in the majors
Home Runs	126	21st in the majors
Home Runs Allowed	134	2nd in the majors
Batting Average	.264	15th in the majors
Batting Average Allowed	.244	2nd in the majors
Walks Drawn	521	21st in the majors
Walks Given	467	6th in the majors
OPS For	.731	22nd in the majors
OPS Against	.689	1st in the majors
Stolen Bases	80	17th in the majors
Stolen Bases Allowed	86	11th in the majors

Key Players

Pos	Player	G	AB	R	H	2B	3B	HR	RBI	SB	CS	BB	SO	Avg	OBP	Slg	OPS	WS
C	Rod Barajas	104	349	44	87	23	0	11	49	0	0	17	61	.249	.294	.410	.704	10
1B	Lyle Overbay	158	544	74	147	32	2	15	69	1	2	74	116	.270	.358	.419	.777	14
2B	Joe Inglett	109	344	45	102	15	7	3	39	9	2	28	43	.297	.355	.407	.762	12
3B	Scott Rolen	115	408	58	107	30	3	11	50	5	0	46	71	.262	.349	.431	.780	11
SS	Marco Scutaro	145	517	76	138	23	1	7	60	7	2	57	65	.267	.341	.356	.697	15
LF	Adam Lind	88	326	48	92	16	4	9	40	2	0	16	59	.282	.316	.439	.755	7
CF	Vernon Wells	108	427	63	128	22	1	20	78	4	2	29	46	.300	.343	.496	.840	15
RF	Alex Rios	155	635	91	185	47	8	15	79	32	8	44	112	.291	.337	.461	.798	20
DH	Matt Stairs	105	320	42	80	11	1	11	44	1	1	41	87	.250	.342	.394	.736	5

Key Pitchers

Pos	Player	G	GS	W	L	Sv	IP	H	R	ER	SO	BB	BR/9	ERA	WS
SP	A.J. Burnett	35	34	18	10	0	221.1	211	109	100	231	86	12.44	4.07	14
SP	Roy Halladay	34	33	20	11	0	246.0	220	88	76	206	39	9.91	2.78	23
SP	Jesse Litsch	29	28	13	9	0	176.0	178	79	70	99	39	11.51	3.58	12
SP	Shaun Marcum	25	25	9	7	0	151.1	126	60	57	123	50	10.94	3.39	12
SP	Dustin McGowan	19	19	6	7	0	111.1	115	60	54	85	38	12.77	4.37	5
CL	B.J. Ryan	60	0	2	4	32	58.0	46	21	19	58	28	12.10	2.95	10
RP	Jesse Carlson	69	0	7	2	2	60.0	41	16	15	55	21	9.75	2.25	9
RP	Scott Downs	66	0	0	3	5	70.2	54	15	14	57	27	10.83	1.78	11

Fifteen major league teams in 2008 got more runs scored out of their leadoff men than any other slot. Six teams got the most runs out of the second spot, three teams got the most out of the three spot, and three teams got the most out of the cleanup position. Two teams had ties.

And then there is Toronto. Mostly because of severely disappointing performance from the one and two spots in the batting order, the Blue Jays actually were led in runs scored by their fifth place hitters—Stairs, Lind and Barajas.

1st – 15.5 teams
(1st and 4th slots tied in Cincinnati)

2nd – 6 teams

3rd – 3.5 teams
(3rd and 4th slots tied in Houston)

4th – 4

5th – 1 — Toronto with 94 runs — Primarily filled by Stairs, Lind, and Barajas

Just Imagine
If He Had a Normal-Sized
Strike Zone...

57.3% of the pitches thrown to David Eckstein were in the strike zone, by far the highest percentage in the majors among hitters who batted 300 times. Joey Gathright was next at 55.7%.

83% of the pitches swung at by Marco Scutaro were in the strike zone—the highest percentage of any major league regular.

Marco Scutaro – 2008
Pitch Analysis

Swung At by Pitch Location		
In Strike Zone	734	83%
High	40	5%
Low	37	4%
Inside	39	4%
Outside	31	4%

Dave Eckstein – 2007
Pitch Analysis

Overall		
Pitches Seen	1397	
Taken	785	56%
Swung At	612	44%
Pitches Taken		
Taken for a Strike	337	43%
Called a Ball	448	57%
Pitches Taken by Pitch Location		
In Strike Zone	337	43%
High	113	15%
Low	122	16%
Inside	95	12%
Outside	111	14%
Swung At		
Missed	46	8%
Fouled Off	262	43%
Put in Play	304	50%
Swung At by Pitch Location		
In Strike Zone	463	77%
High	10	2%
Low	50	8%
Inside	15	2%
Outside	65	11%

B.J. Ryan was a one-inning-and-a-shower pitcher last year. He never pitched more than one inning in a game. He never entered a game in the middle of an inning. But he sometimes supplied his own drama. He needed 20 or more pitches to finish 25 of his 58 innings. That's 43% of his innings; the major league average was 23%.

B.J. Ryan – 2008
Inning Analysis

Innings Pitched	58
Runs Allowed	21
Innings Started	58
Runs in Those Innings	21
Shutout Innings	45
One-Run Innings	8
Two-Run Innings	2
Three-Run Innings	3
Got First Man Out	39
Runs Scored in Those Innings	12
Runs/9 Innings	2.77
First Man Reached	19
Runs Scored in Those Innings	9
Runs/9 Innings	4.26
1-2-3 Innings	20
10-pitch Innings (or less)	6
Long Innings (20 or more pitches)	25
Failed to Finish Inning	4

Over the last five years, Vernon Wells has slipped gradually from being one of the best baserunners in baseball to being a below-average baserunner.

Vernon Wells – 2002-2008
Baserunning Analysis

Year	1st to 3rd Adv	Opp	2nd to Home Adv	Opp	1st to Home Adv	Opp	DP Opp	GIDP	Bases Taken	BR Outs	BR Gain	SB Gain	Net Gain
2002	8	23	14	22	2	4	136	15	13	2	2	1	3
2003	9	17	14	19	3	5	175	21	21	4	5	2	7
2004	9	14	14	18	5	6	131	17	21	1	22	5	27
2005	9	25	5	12	2	4	146	13	14	2	9	2	11
2006	3	12	14	19	3	5	150	13	10	4	1	9	10
2007	6	19	11	16	8	9	100	9	14	5	4	2	6
2008	6	15	10	18	2	4	84	16	13	4	-6	0	-6
Totals	50	125	82	124	25	37	922	104	106	22	37	21	58
		40%		66%		68%		11%					

Toronto's bullpen in 2008 had a 2.94 ERA, the best in the majors, and was charged with only 12 blown saves, second-fewest in the majors (the Yankees had only 9). But Toronto relievers were credited with only 15 wins, 23 losses—one of the worst winning percentages of any major league bullpen.

Toronto starting pitchers:
    1) Had the highest average fastball speed of any major league team (92.1 Miles Per Hour), yet
    2) Threw fewer fastballs than any other team.
    Only 48% of pitches thrown by Toronto starters were fastballs. Everybody else was over 50.

Starter	Fast Ball %	Speed
Dustin McGowan	60%	94.8
A.J. Burnett	64%	94.3
Roy Halladay	40%	92.7
David Purcey	70%	91.1
Scott Richmond	53%	90.3
Jesse Litsch	23%	89.9
John Parrish	52%	88.3
Shaun Marcum	39%	86.8

Roy Halladay had a 4.07 ERA in his losses, the lowest figure of any major league pitcher with at least ten losses. The Blue Jays scored 2.1 runs a game in his losses.

Roy Halladay – 2008
Decision Analysis

Group	G	IP	W	L	Pct	H	R	SO	BB	ERA
Wins	20	152.2	20	0	1.000	120	40	124	15	2.12
Losses	11	77.1	0	11	.000	84	43	66	18	4.07
Holds	1	2.1	0	0	—	1	0	2	0	0.00
No Decisions	2	13.2	0	0	—	15	5	14	6	3.29
Quality Starts: 17 in Wins, 5 in Losses, 1 in no-decisions										

Roy Halladay in 2008 became the 10th pitcher in history to finish the season with 20 or more wins, 200 or more strikeouts, and less than 40 walks. The others were: Cy Young (1904), Walter Johnson (1913), Juan Marichal (1966), Ferguson Jenkins (1971), Pedro Martinez (1999), Curt Schilling (2001, 2002 and 2004), and Halladay himself (2003).

Who is more likely to score a run: a batter who reaches base on a walk, or a batter who reaches base on a single?

In a table game, it should be the same. There is an old wives tale…why should we blame wives for this? There is an old bartender's tale that the percentage is dramatically higher after a walk than it is after a single. In reality, it's about the same most of the time—but I will note that, for both of the Blue Jays' 2008 aces, Halladay and Burnett, the percentage is actually consistently lower after a walk than after a single. Since 2002, the percentage against Burnett is 28% after a single (179 for 639), but 23% after a walk (94 for 416). Against Halladay, the percentage is 25% after a single (250 for 1014), but 22% after a walk (60 for 272). Both Burnett and Halladay have had lower percentages after a walk than a single almost every every year since 2002.

Why? Probably because a pitcher can, to an extent, choose when he walks a hitter. If you're 2-0 to a leadoff hitter, you can say to yourself, "If he gets a hit, OK, but I'm not walking the leadoff hitter." If it's later in the inning, you may be more willing to risk the walk, rather than groove a pitch and risk the bomb.

Both Halladay and Burnett are veteran pitchers who know what they are doing. You might get different data for Nuke LaLoosh.

Roy Halladay – 2008
Runs Allowed Analysis

Reached by Single:	162	Scored: 37	23%
Reached by Double:	34	Scored: 13	38%
Reached by Triple:	6	Scored: 4	67%
Reached by Homer:	18		
Reached by Walk:	39	Scored: 8	21%
Reached by HBP:	12	Scored: 2	17%
Reached by Error:	7	Scored: 4	57%
Reached by FC - All Safe:	2	Scored: 1	50%
Reached by FC - Out:	25	Scored: 1	4%
Total On Base	305	Scored: 88	29%
Stolen Bases Allowed:	15	Scored: 3	20%
Caught Stealing:	5	Scored: 0	0%
Steal Attempts:	20	Scored: 3	15%
Intentional Walks:	3	Scored: 0	0%

A.J. Burnett – 2008
Runs Allowed Analysis

Reached by Single:	134	Scored: 37	28%
Reached by Double:	55	Scored: 22	40%
Reached by Triple:	3	Scored: 2	67%
Reached by Homer:	19		
Reached by Walk:	86	Scored: 20	23%
Reached by HBP:	9	Scored: 1	11%
Reached by Error:	9	Scored: 2	22%
Reached by FC - All Safe:	6	Scored: 1	17%
Reached by FC - Out:	18	Scored: 4	22%
Reached by Other:	2	Scored: 1	50%
Total On Base	341	Scored: 109	32%
Stolen Bases Allowed:	22	Scored: 6	27%
Caught Stealing:	9	Scored: 0	0%
Steal Attempts:	31	Scored: 6	19%
Intentional Walks:	2	Scored: 0	0%

Washington Nationals

Washington Nationals – 2008
Team Overview

Description		Ranking
Won-Lost Record	59-102	
Place		5th of 5 in National League East
Runs Scored	641	27th in the majors
Runs Allowed	825	25th in the majors
Home Runs	117	25th in the majors
Home Runs Allowed	190	20th in the majors
Batting Average	.251	26th in the majors
Batting Average Allowed	.270	20th in the majors
Walks Drawn	534	18th in the majors
Walks Given	588	21st in the majors
OPS For	.696	29th in the majors
OPS Against	.778	23rd in the majors
Stolen Bases	81	16th in the majors
Stolen Bases Allowed	118	22nd in the majors

Key Players

Pos	Player	G	AB	R	H	2B	3B	HR	RBI	SB	CS	BB	SO	Avg	OBP	Slg	OPS	WS
C	Jesus Flores	90	301	23	77	18	1	8	59	0	1	15	78	.256	.296	.402	.698	9
1B	Aaron Boone	104	232	23	56	13	1	6	28	0	1	18	52	.241	.299	.384	.683	2
2B	Felipe Lopez	100	325	34	76	20	0	2	25	4	5	32	54	.234	.305	.314	.619	2
3B	Ryan Zimmerman	106	428	51	121	24	1	14	51	1	1	31	71	.283	.333	.442	.774	9
SS	Cristian Guzman	138	579	77	183	35	5	9	55	6	5	23	57	.316	.345	.440	.786	20
LF	Willie Harris	140	367	58	92	14	4	13	43	13	3	50	66	.251	.344	.417	.761	10
CF	Lastings Milledge	138	523	65	140	24	2	14	61	24	9	38	96	.268	.330	.402	.731	11
RF	Austin Kearns	86	313	40	68	10	0	7	32	2	2	35	63	.217	.311	.316	.627	3

Key Pitchers

Pos	Player	G	GS	W	L	Sv	IP	H	R	ER	SO	BB	BR/9	ERA	WS
SP	Tim Redding	33	33	10	11	0	182.0	195	110	100	120	65	13.20	4.95	6
SP	Odalis Perez	30	30	7	12	0	159.2	182	87	77	119	55	13.81	4.34	6
SP	John Lannan	31	31	9	15	0	182.0	172	89	79	117	72	12.41	3.91	9
SP	Jason Bergmann	30	22	2	11	0	139.2	153	94	79	96	47	12.95	5.09	2
SP	Collin Balester	15	15	3	7	0	80.0	92	53	49	50	28	14.18	5.51	1
CL	Jon Rauch	48	0	4	2	17	48.1	42	18	16	44	7	9.12	2.98	9
RP	Joel Hanrahan	69	0	6	3	9	84.1	73	40	37	93	42	12.38	3.95	7
RP	Saul Rivera	76	0	5	6	0	84.0	90	41	37	65	35	13.61	3.96	6

In the major leagues as a whole in 2008, the winning percentage of teams with a Game Score of 50 or above by the starting pitcher was .683—an 111-win pace. The Nationals winning percentage in those games was .513—an 83-win pace.

Washington Nationals – 2008
Performance by Quality of Start

Game Score	#	ERA	W - L
70 to 79	8	1.17	6 - 2
60 to 69	27	2.84	12 - 15
50 to 59	43	3.34	22 - 21
40 to 49	31	5.23	9 - 22
30 to 39	22	5.54	7 - 15
20 to 29	17	7.36	3 - 14
Below 20	13	9.08	0 - 13

Here's one of the great fluke stats of the year: The Nationals were 20-13 in Tim Redding's starts. That's amazingly good, considering that the team went 59-102 overall, but what really makes it incredible is that he clearly wasn't anywhere close to being their best starter. Their real ace, John Lannan, had an ERA more than a full run lower than Redding's, and threw 50% more quality starts. All things being equal, that should have translated into more wins for the team in Lannan's starts than in Redding's, but things were far from equal. Redding got a ton of run support, while Lannan's was among the weakest in the league. The club was unusually lucky in the close games that Redding started, and unusually unlucky in those Lannan started: When the final margin of victory was between 1-3 runs, they were 16-8 in Redding's starts and 2-14 in Lannan's. Given the number of runs the club scored and allowed in their starts, the team should have gone about 18-15 in Redding's starts and 12-19 in Lannan's.

Washington Nationals – 2008
Performance by Starting Pitcher

Games Started By	GS	RS	RA	Won	Lost
Redding, Tim	33	162	149	20	13
Lannan, John	31	117	147	9	22
Perez, Odalis	30	120	140	13	17
Bergmann, Jason	22	71	128	5	17
Balester, Collin	15	64	82	5	10
Hill, Shawn	12	45	67	3	9
Chico, Matt	8	31	53	2	6
Martis, Shairon	4	17	17	1	3
Mock, Garrett	3	7	26	0	3
Clippard, Tyler	2	7	5	1	1
O'Connor, Mike	1	0	11	0	1
Team Totals	161	641	825	59	102

Jason Bergmann of the Nats was the worst-supported starting pitcher in the majors in 2008, with 2.84 runs per nine innings pitched. Bergmann finished 2-11. His teammate, Tim Redding, got 5.5 runs per nine innings pitched to work with, and finished 10-11 with almost the same ERA.

Pitcher	Run Support
Jason Bergmann	2.84
Greg Smith	2.88
Matt Cain	3.14
Aaron Harang	3.22
Jeff Francis	3.51

Washington Nationals

261

Disorder

The Nationals' clean-up hitters contributed a major league-low 73 RBI: only four more than their leadoff men.

Washington Nationals – 2008
Runs and RBI by Batting Order

Pos	Players	Runs	RBI
1	Lopez (42 G), Guzman (40 G), Harris (34 G)	87	69
2	Guzman (82 G), Dukes (23 G), Milledge (17 G)	91	76
3	Zimmerman (104 G), Milledge (31 G)	87	82
4	Kearns (35 G), Milledge (35 G), Young (34 G)	81	73
5	Milledge (41 G), Kearns (25 G), Belliard (24 G)	63	92
6	Flores (34 G), Belliard (23 G), Kearns (17 G)	51	53
7	Pena (28 G), Lopez (19 G), Belliard (17 G)	63	67
8	Nieves (35 G), Harris (25 G)	69	49
9	Redding (32 G), Perez (29 G), Lannan (29 G)	49	47
	Total	641	608

Joel Hanrahan is a classic case of a starting pitcher moving to the bullpen after being unsuccessful using three pitches but doing well throwing just two pitches. He cut his ERA from 6.00 to 3.95.

Joel Hanrahan – 2007
Pitch Type Analysis

Overall		
Total Pitches	1026	
Fastball	684	67%
Changeup	117	11%
Slider	213	21%

Joel Hanrahan – 2008
Pitch Type Analysis

Overall		
Total Pitches	1484	
Fastball	996	65%
Changeup	27	2%
Slider	441	30%

Average speed of Hanrahan fastball:

2007	91.7
2008	95.2

A Whole New Hitter?

Prior to missing the entire 2006 season due to injury, Cristian Guzman was a career .260 hitter (in 3,733 at-bats). He made a statement in his 2007 comeback year hitting .328 in 174 at-bats. He punctuated that statement with a big exclamation point in 2008 with a .316 batting average over the entire season (579 at-bats).

Cristian Guzman

	Prior to Injury	2007-2008
At Bats	3,733	753
Batting Average	.260	.319

Saul Rivera's batting opponents have decent batting averages and they get on base, but they sure don't hit for power. If Rivera's opponents were a batter, they'd be Craig Counsell.

Saul Rivera – 2006-2008
Record of Opposing Batters

Season	AB	R	H	2B	3B	HR	RBI	BB	SO	SB	CS	GIDP	Avg	OBP	Slg	OPS
2006	236	28	59	8	1	4	32	32	41	4	0	3	.250	.348	.343	.691
2007	345	39	88	25	1	1	32	42	64	2	2	12	.255	.336	.342	.678
2008	325	41	90	12	0	3	41	35	65	13	0	9	.277	.345	.342	.687

Last year Aaron Boone went 4-for-52 against pitchers with an ERA of 3.50 or lower. He has struggled against such pitchers every year since coming back from knee surgery in 2005:

Aaron Boone – 2005-2008
Batting Vs. Pitchers with < 3.50 ERA

	AB	H	HR	RBI	Avg	OPS
2005	126	26	2	9	.206	.510
2006	56	11	0	8	.196	.500
2007	43	7	1	5	.163	.536
2008	52	4	0	2	.077	.251
Total	277	48	3	24	.173	.464

Playing just 562 innings in left field in 2008—less than 40% of the schedule—Willie Harris was +22 in left, meaning that he made 22 plays that a left fielder would not ordinarily make. Carl Crawford led the majors among left fielders, with +23. Harris' 2007 data was almost the same—+18 in 620 innings.

Of course, this method implicitly compares the fleet-footed Harris to an average left fielder. Among major league left fielders last year were Adam Dunn, Pat Burrell, Carlos Lee, Raul Ibanez, Luke Scott, Garret Anderson, Manny Ramirez and Jason Bay. Getting to balls that those guys wouldn't get to does not exactly make you Usain Bolt, but it's nice to have the extra outs.

Willie Harris – 2008
Leaderboard, Left Field

Player	+/-
Carl Crawford	+23
Willie Harris	+20
Conor Jackson	+11
Luke Scott	+10
Brandon Boggs	+10
Endy Chavez	+10
Matt Holliday	+9
Josh Willingham	+8
David DeJesus	+8
Skip Schumaker	+8
Ryan Braun	+7

Willie Harris
Left Field Plus/Minus Data

			THROWING					PLAYS		PLUS/MINUS		
Year	Team	Inn	Opps To Advance	Extra Bases	Kills	Pct	Rank	Expected Outs	Outs Made	Total	Enhanced	Rank
2006	Bos	33.0	3	1	1	.333		13	10	-3	-5	
2007	Atl	620.1	71	27	4	.380	22	128	138	+10	+18	3
2008	Was	562.0	63	21	2	.333	13	133	145	+12	+20	2

The Nats have a deep stable of young outfielders with loads of potential, but only Elijah Dukes stepped to the front of that particular line last year. His blend of plate discipline, power and fielding allowed him to rank as one of the top right fielders in the game.

Elijah Dukes – 2008
Skills Assessment

Plate Discipline:	95th percentile	93rd percentile among right fielders
Fielding:		76th percentile among right fielders
Hitting for Power:	72nd percentile	64th percentile among right fielders
Running:	33rd percentile	24th percentile among right fielders
Hitting for Average:	20th percentile	17th percentile among right fielders

Hey Bill

by Bill James and Members of Bill James Online

In the Bill James Online (BJOL) there is a section called "Hey Bill" in which I answer e-mails from readers. In the last year I have answered many hundreds of e-mails, many times with one word ("OK" or "Thanks"), and readers often write in to help out with previous questions. I enjoy the dialogue very much and profit from it, in that readers often suggest lines of research that I hadn't considered. We have selected a few of the letters (below) for inclusion in the book, along with my answers.

Bill, I was wondering if in your adult life you've ever booed anyone at the ballpark. Once in Texas I booed Juan Gonzalez when he loafed to first on an easy out. I heard G. Brett once say that he'd hustle to first on everything if for nothing else, just to see how close he could make it. I love that. Aside from an occasional one at an ump's call, that remains my only boo. Had I been in the park when Reggie Sanders charged Pedro after he hit him in the 7th inning of a perfect game, I might have booed.

Asked by: Chuck
Answered: March 2, 2008

I have booed players, not very often and not recently, but I have. And, again referencing George Brett as if he might be a saint, I remember a game at which Brett made two or three serious mistakes and the crowd booed him. The radio guy was talking about how terrible it was, the Kansas City fans booing George Brett, but Brett said "They ought to boo me, making plays like that."

Bill, I am convinced that the Cubs have been playing at a disadvantage due to a low amount of night games, relative to the rest of MLB. The transition of a new Cub to the cycle of uneven day/night games (as compared to their previous teams) takes some type of acclimatizing period. What are your thoughts and do you believe that the Cubs 60+ year World Series drought coincides with the advent of night baseball?

Asked by: bluedemondave
Answered: March 28, 2008

No. My opinion would be that the law of competitive balance would wipe out the effects of an advantage of that nature. Some teams such as Seattle and Arizona, for example, might feel that the travel schedule places a hardship on them. Nature overcomes those barriers. The Cubs stopped winning in the mid-1940s because they didn't develop a farm system when the other teams did. They were eight or ten years late developing a farm system, which put them behind the curve and crippled them in the 1950s.

In the late 1950s their farm system started to produce (Billy Williams, 1959, Santo, 1960, Ken Hubbs, 1962) and, combined with a few players stolen from other teams (Glenn Beckett and Ferguson Jenkins), they had a team put together by the late 1960s.

I do think that in the late 1960s and the 1970s that franchise did not handle the challenge of playing so many day games very well, and that this did contribute to their frustrations. Since about 1980, however, the Cubs have been a competitive franchise with numerous teams that could have gone to the World Series. They just haven't hit it exactly right.

Has there ever to your knowledge been a better 1B, 2B, SS combo for one season in baseball history than Howard, Utley, Rollins last year?

Asked by: Anthony Z
Answered: April 12, 2008

The 2007 Phillies had 82 Win Shares from Howard (26), Utley (28) and Rollins (28), which obviously is a very impressive total. It is, however, not one of the fifteen top totals of all time. The 1934 Tigers had 92 Win Shares from those three positions from Hank Greenberg (31), Charlie Gehringer (37) and Billy Rogell (24). They also had 88 Win Shares from the same three players in 1935.

(It occurred to me after posting this answer that there was another way to interpret the question, which is "Has there ever been a team on which ALL THREE of those players were that good?" The answer to THAT question would be "No". There has never been any other team on which all three of the players playing those three positions were as good as Howard, Utley and Rollins in 2007.)

Would it have been reasonable to infer from Miguel Tejada's steadily declining Range Factors the last four seasons (4.99, 4.72, 4.56, 4.27) that his age had been measured in Dominican years? Should this become an expression like "Our bullpen has been as reliable as a Dominican birth certificate?"

Asked by: Trailbzr
Answered: April 19, 2008

Well, after all, American baseball players have been lying about their age for a hundred years. And I doubt that a progression of range factors like that would be significantly more common at ages 29-33 than at ages 27-31. I could be wrong about that.

Watching the Mariners game last night I realized that Ichiro is certainly the strangest player I've ever seen—strange swing, strange approach, strange stats, even the way he catches the ball in the outfield is strange. When I say strange, I don't mean unique talent like Ryan or contrived showmanship like the Bird. I mean, he does the fundamental things a baseball player needs to do substantially differently than any of the other thousands of players I've seen. Who is the strangest player you've ever seen?

Asked by: Michael
Answered: April 20, 2008

Tony Batista. You ever watch him? He was like a walking clinic on how not to play baseball. Odd batting stance. Odd approach. Odd fielder. Odd baserunner. Extremely odd habits. I remember one time at a spring training game he was on first base, and the batter behind him hit a double. Batista slid into third, popped up and started screaming at his teammate on second base in Spanish, appeared to be just furious about something. I remember thinking, "You know, if that was anybody else, I'd be thinking this was a little bit strange."

Is there any evidence that the type of pitch thrown (i.e. slider, fastball, curve, etc.) affects where the ball will be hit? It seems to me that this is one element of conventional wisdom that can be tested due to the advent of pitchfx.

Asked by: Chris S. Washington, DC
Answered: April 28, 2008

One would think that it could be. But it could be that the effects of this would be complex enough that they would be difficult to codify.

Why are players who do mostly everything competently or will routinely get overlooked by players who do one or two things spectacularly but don't ultimately contribute as much to the team as the former? I was thinking this recently in regard to David West, and I also think this happens a lot with players such as Tim Raines and Barry Larkin and Alan Trammell.

Asked by: Aaron B.
Answered: May 6, 2008

It is rooted in the nature of perception. Our mind, when we pull in any observation about the world, immediately begins looking for a place to stow the observation. We simplify our perceptions in order to organize our minds. When a player has a fairly straightforward contribution to the team, like Ichiro or Carlos Lee or Ryan Howard, our mind can take that in and find a place for it. When a player's contribution has a complex and irregular shape, our mind tends to break the edges off of it so that it can stack it somewhere.

I first noticed this, not at this level of complexity of course, when I was thirteen years old. The 1960 MVPs were Roger Maris and Dick Groat, but I noticed that if you took half a season of Roger Maris and half a season of Dick Groat, you would get a combination that probably nobody would vote for as the MVP. In 1962 the MVPs were Maury Wills and Mickey Mantle, but if you made up a season that was half Mantle and half Wills, the resulting combination would not be an MVP candidate. I started wondering why that was true, and realized that simple combinations outrank in our minds complex combinations of the same value.

American baseball players have been lying about their age for a hundred years.

Manny asserts that no other Red Sox has defended left field like him because of his familiarity with the intricacies of playing so many games in front of The Wall. I presume most players are devoid of any sense of history at all. Is this your impression as well? Which player(s) can we listen to and appreciate his viewpoint?

Asked by: Tangotiger
Answered: May 12, 2008

Well, yes, it is true that many players have no historical perspective and most have almost no knowledge about the history of the game, but then, why pick on baseball players? If you go to an elementary school near you, and you ask the teachers there who were the best teachers there 30 years ago or 60 years ago, do you think they would know?

Ten years ago I had a discussion with a friend, an African-American sportswriter, who was upset with players today because they don't know who Jackie Robinson was (this was before major league baseball started setting aside two or three weeks every April to talk incessantly about Jackie Robinson). But then I asked him: could you name the pioneering black sportswriters of the 1940s? He couldn't come up with a name.

I am reluctant to place onto baseball players a burden that we do not place on ourselves. And yes, baseball players sometimes say stupid shit because they don't realize the world didn't start the day they were born, but then, so do I, I suspect. I think everybody does.

Why isn't Barry Bonds playing on a major league team?

Asked by: David J. Fleming
Answered: May 22, 2008

He has one-dimensional skills and a poor reputation as a teammate.

Bill, is that one dimension "hitting"? Because Bonds had the best OPS+ in the National League last year. But I suppose he is not as much of a gentleman as Julio Lugo.

Asked by: Blackadder
Answered: May 22, 2008

Well, don't shoot the messenger. Somebody asked me why he wasn't in the majors, and I gave an honest answer. It is not my fault the man can't run, field, throw or get along with people.

I want to apologize for my tone in the last question, which was snarky and unfriendly. But you don't think there are plenty of guys out there who, by all available metrics, are worse fielders and baserunners than Bonds and have no trouble getting major league jobs? And that there aren't plenty of guys out there who seem like just as much of a jerk and have no trouble getting a job? Again, I apologize for my previous tone, but that explanation just doesn't smell right to me. Thanks.

Asked by: Blackadder
Answered: May 22, 2008

Everybody, to have a job, has to fit into a slot somewhere. Bonds, because of the unusual outline of his entire profile, has an awful lot of slots that he doesn't fit. Let's say that there are 400 "slots" available. At least 300 of those, Bonds doesn't fit because of his defensive limitations. He may be a better hitter than most of the other 100, but if I were to look at Bonds from the position of the Pittsburgh Pirates or the Kansas City Royals…well, no; what we're looking at is getting better. We don't want somebody using up at bats now to obstruct the development of young players.

Hi Bill. The other day, a co-worker of mine commented that Milwaukee Brewers starter Manny Parra "throws hard for a lefty." ...This prompted a recurring question: If righties historically do throw harder than lefties, why is that? Is there something physiologically "inherent" in a right-handed pitcher vs. a left-handed pitcher that would cause this characteristic? Is this a nature vs. nurture argument? Regards, Tom

Asked by: Tom R.
Answered: May 25, 2008

Right-handers do throw much harder than left-handers, as major league pitchers. The reason is that, in a counter-clockwise game, being left-handed is an advantage. As such, it acts as a selection mechanism in the long sorting-out process that guards access to the majors. A pitcher must have a certain number of "benefits" or "advantages" to make the majors—a certain level of velocity, command, an understanding of how to throw some different number of pitches. When a group of players has one advantage, they need fewer advantages in other areas in order to get past the sorting hat.

Out of the sacrifice bunt, ninth-inning closer, and intentional walk, what do you think is the worst commonly used managerial strategy?

Asked by: Anonymous
Answered: May 27, 2008

The Intentional Walk, by far. The Sac Bunt is not something I advocate, but the arguments against it in some cases are unconvincing. The Intentional Walk is just a bad play, 99 times in 100.

Hey Bill, This maple bat shattering controversy has become important enough that Bud Selig is now looking for ways to remedy the situation and close a real liability for the MLB. This seems like the perfect time to implement a minimum bat width that is larger than now. This would have the added benefit of promoting contact hitting rather than home run hitting, a change that I am for and I believe you advocated for in the Historical Baseball Abstract. What's your take on this?

Asked by: Henry F.
Answered: June 1, 2008

I did advocate this somewhere, and I still believe in it. The union has the right to sign off on rules changes, but I would predict that the union would OK the rules if the current players were grandfathered in and allowed to use the current bats. This would eliminate 90% of the problem within five or six years, and also contribute powerfully to restoring batting stats to historic norms.

Do you think Ozzie Guillen is this generation's Billy Martin? And by that I mean, is he a) that rare manager who can bring about an immediate, positive change for a team, and b) the kind of manager who, over the long run, eventually loses the trust of players and management. I guess we won't know until the White Sox fire him and another team hires him, but he shares a lot of characteristics with Billy Martin. And Martin, for all his problems, was a damn fine manager.

Asked by: David J. Fleming
Answered: June 5, 2008

Well, I wouldn't want to push the parallels. Ozzie's problem is that he tells the truth about things that managers are expected to be polite about. Martin's problem was that he often chose to get drunk and punch people. These are very different problems.

In his latest "Stat of the Week" John Dewan writes, "For hitters, for years and years, it was batting average that was thought to be the best single statistic to look at to evaluate a hitter. In the last couple of decades, the weaknesses of batting average have been exposed and the value of getting on base and hitting for power have become better recognized." I guess my question is...is this true? I realize that when I was growing up we used to make a much bigger deal about batting

average than we do today, but I look at players of yore like Eddie Joost, Max Bishop, Eddie Yost, Eddie Stanky and others whose primary value was in their ability to draw a walk and get on base (despite relatively poor batting averages) and I can't help but think that clearly there was a time when getting on base was considered a worthwhile skill. Is the discovery in the value of getting on base simply a re-discovery? Was there a time when the value of drawing a walk generally accepted?

Asked by: freejju
Answered: June 6, 2008

If you remember that era then you are certainly more of an expert on that era than I am or John is, since I don't remember it and John is much younger than I am. But let me point out something. In his best season, 1949, Eddie Joost was, by my calculation, the second most-valuable player in the American League, behind Ted Williams. In the MVP voting he finished 13th. In 1951 Ed Yost was the fourth-best player in the American League, behind Williams, Berra and Larry Doby. He finished 32nd in the MVP voting. In 1959 Yost was again one of the five most-Valuable Players in the American League, behind Fox, Mantle, Minoso and Colavito, about even with Francona and Kaline. That year he wasn't mentioned *at all* in the MVP voting.

Yost's teammate that second season was Harvey Kuenn, who won the batting title. Teammates. Yost scored 115 runs, drove in 61 runs, made 391 outs and played third base. Kuenn scored 99 runs, drove in 71 runs, made 378 outs and played right field. Pretty comparable, right? Same team, similar runs scored, RBI, outs made, both played corner positions as opposed to up-the-middle defensive positions. I credit Kuenn with 26 Win Shares, Yost with 27. Kuenn finished 8th in the MVP voting. Yost wasn't mentioned.

In 1945 Eddie Stanky was about the sixth most valuable player in the National League. He finished 34th in the MVP voting.

If you remember that era, I'm not questioning your right to remember it however you remember it. But what I would ask is, what evidence can you point to in support of this position? Joe Cunningham, for example. To those of us who prize on-base percentage, he seems like a treasure, with on-base percentages of .439 in 1957, .449 in 1958, and .453 in 1959. He would hit .300 *and* have strikeout/walk ratios of 1-3. The problem was that, despite his extraordinary ability to get on base, he kept losing his job. In retrospect, it looks like there was just no respect for his skill.

In 1941 Roy Cullenbine had a great season for the Browns, hitting .317 with 121 walks, 98 RBI. He was traded early in the season in 1942. His manager said years later, in one of the Honig books, that he got rid of

Cullenbine because he was a lazy player, trying to get on base by drawing walks.

You say that you were aware of players who drew walks, but how were you aware of them? The main sources for information about players in that era were the batting summaries in the Sunday newspapers, the box scores, the *Sporting News* team batting summaries, and, at year's end, *Who's Who in Baseball*, Topps baseball cards, and *The Sporting News Baseball Register*. None of those sources even listed batter's walks. How could you have been aware of it? You could have been aware of it in a general way, perhaps, in the unusual case. Eddie Yost was called "The Walking Man" because of his walks. But I don't know how you could possibly have been as aware of walks as you were of doubles or triples or batting average, because there simply wasn't any source for it.

The most important offensive statistic is on-base percentage. No source that I am aware of published on-base percentages until 1969. Many minor leagues didn't even COUNT batters walks; there is no record of batters walks for several minor leagues in the fifties. As I say, I'm not trying to tell you how you should remember these things, but I just can't see how I can interpret these facts as consistent with what you say you remember.

Hey Bill! I was wondering, what, in your opinion, needs to happen before fielding can be projected with as much confidence as pitching and batting? Do a certain number of years of play-by-play data need to be gathered?

Asked by: James P
Answered: August 7, 2008

Yes, we need 20/25 years of good data. There have to be methods to translate plays made into runs saved. There have to be multiple methods to do that that converge on a common point by different approaches. There has to be a sustained debate about the utility of one approach as opposed to another, so that we come to understand the limitations of the data looked at in this way or looked at in that way.

We have to learn to factor in park effects, and we have to be much more confident that we're not missing differences in the ability to prevent movement of baserunners. Sometimes, watching the games, one thinks that there are huge differences between outfielders in whether that ball results in a single/first and third or in an RBI double. I'm not confident that we're picking that up.

Hi Bill. I was reading in your 1986 Abstract (in the KC Royals section) that you admire managers who are willing to commit themselves to young players. This prompted a question in my head: **At what point DO you find it reasonable to give up on a young player? As a Brewers fan, I think of a player like Rickie Weeks. What, if any criteria (other than gut instinct and so-called peak age) does one use to make such determinations? Thanks. Tom**

Asked by: Tom R.
Answered: August 21, 2008

Well, in a pennant race, you don't hang on to a player who is failing because of his birth certificate. There can be a million reasons why a young player is struggling, and I think, in individual terms, you have to make the decision with your best understanding of what the problem is. I don't respect a manager who drools over veterans and is afraid to give a young player a chance. But if you give the young player a chance and he doesn't come through and you're in a pennant race, that's a different situation.

There are many theories out there about the best methods to keep pitchers healthy. The rule of 30 says a young pitcher shouldn't increase his workload by 30 innings from year to year. Pitcher abuse points, which I believe you have refuted, states that pitcher's after about 115 pitches might start to get stressed and fatigued and injury risk increases. And then there's Dusty Baker. Obviously there's no perfect solution, but what do you subscribe to?

Asked by: Jeremy
Answered: August 23, 2008

I subscribe to the theory that we shouldn't pretend to understand things we don't. I do think there is good evidence that you need to be careful in stretching a pitcher out to a work level he hasn't seen before. Otherwise, a lot of what we think we know doesn't seem to be terribly well grounded.

Am I misguided to suggest that Bud Selig has been an outstanding baseball commissioner? I think over the years he has been very unfairly maligned, and baseball has blossomed under his leadership. I also think he would be a very tough act to follow. Any comments would be appreciated.

Asked by: Michael Kirlin
Answered: September 6, 2008

I agree that Selig has been a highly successful commissioner. We've gotten past the cycle of self-destructive negotiations with the union…a huge accomplishment. We've basically fixed the umpiring. We have a plethora of new stadiums, which, with all of their faults, are far better than the stadiums of the 70s and 80s. We've taken important strides toward more parity in resources, although the real impact of that won't be felt for a couple of decades. We've had fifteen years of peace and prosperity. He's accomplished a lot.

Mr. James, an analyst on ESPN made a point I have never thought about and he wonders why it doesn't happen and it looked like common sense to me. If you take an organization that really isn't that good and not too deep in the minors, why wouldn't a team in that position trade for impending free agents late in the year, knowing when the players walk in a month or two they can get extra picks for them? Have you ever heard of a team doing this for that reason?

Asked by: robert cola sc
Answered: September 29, 2008

The value of the picks that would be received is factored into the player's value in trade negotiations. But the player you describe has *two* uses to a team in contention— (1) he will bring them draft picks when he leaves, and (2) he can help the team win now. He has only one type of value to a team that is not in contention. Thus, it would be difficult to see how a team that derives only *one* benefit from acquiring a player would be in position to bid more for him than a team that derives both benefits.

What's your take on the impact that the game's great hitters have on the hitter just before them? Or more specifically, do the apparent jumps in success at the plate of those batting in front of Manny Ramirez constitute a verifiable pattern of improved production, or just random hot streaks?

Asked by: Lukey
Answered: October 5, 2008

There is no such effect…absolutely none. It's been studied many times. This just amounts to randomly attributing one player's success to some teammate; that's all. David Ortiz has never hit any better with Manny behind him than without. He's had hundreds of games in Boston with Manny behind him, hundreds without Manny behind him…no effect. Ryan Shealy has a hot streak; is this because Mark Teahen is coming up behind him? It's a specious theory propped up by selective observation.

How would YOU do as a General Manager of a Major League Baseball team?

Asked by: Your Poll Question
Answered: October 23, 2008

In all candor I may not have the social skills of a good General Manager. The good general managers that I have known are people of natural grace. People tend to take offense at things that I say or do, and I avoid people because it is the only way I know to avoid offending people. It doesn't work; people get offended then that I'm avoiding them. I've never been able to figure out how to avoid offending people, and I'm not sure how well this would work as a GM.

Hey Bill! Ryan Ludwick just had a heck of a breakout season at age 30. Is there any kind of real precedent for a guy doing what he did at age 30 and parlaying into a 5- to 10-year run of similar excellence? Bernie Miklasz of the Post-Dispatch suggested Jim Lemon, but Lemon was two years younger, so I don't know how comparable that is. What do you expect of Ludwick for the next decade?

Asked by: mike
Answered: November 10, 2008

I would think Hank Sauer was certainly comparable. Sauer didn't get to play (really) until he was 31, then hit 35 homers a year regularly for seven or eight years, being one of the top home run hitters of all time post-30. Mike Easler didn't get much major league time until he was 29, had a decent career. Ken Williams (St. Louis Browns superstar in the early 1920s) didn't get to play until he was about 30. Dale Long was late getting his shot (29), and Lefty O'Doul, and Ken Phelps. But it's a short list that could match Ludwick.

Hey Bill, in the article about Lincecum winning the Cy Young I realized that Juan Marichal never won a Cy Young. Who do you think is the greatest pitcher since the award was created never to win one? Thanks.

Asked by: Doug
Answered: November 11, 2008

I don't think Nolan Ryan won one, did he? I'd say 1) Marichal, 2) Schilling, 3) Blyleven, 4) Ryan, 5) Don Sutton, maybe.

I'm not trying to tell you how you should remember these things, but I just can't see how I can interpret these facts as consistent with what you say you remember.

Do you follow the independent league teams much, and if so how much more room for growth do you think they have?

Asked by: J. McCann
Answered: November 20, 2008

My opinion is that the Independent Leagues will continue to grow until they draw as many fans as the established major leagues and become, in effect, rival majors. It will take 60 to 80 years to accomplish that, but I would predict that it will happen.

Who would you rather have as your closer: Soria, Rivera, K-Rod, or Joe Nathan? 2nd choice? 3rd choice?

Asked by: Anonymous
Answered: November 23, 2008

Well…Soria would be first in that group and K-Rod fourth, certainly. Rivera is the greatest ever and still in outstanding shape, and we don't really know how long his arm might last pitching 60 innings a year.

I am reluctant to place onto baseball players a burden that we do not place on ourselves.